VBScript 2 & ActiveX Programming

Scott Palmer

an International Thomson Publishing company I(T)P®

Albany, NY • Belmont, CA • Bonn • Boston • Cincinnati • Detroit • Johannesburg • London
Madrid • Melbourne • Mexico City • New York • Paris • Singapore • Tokyo • Toronto • Washington

PUBLISHER	KEITH WEISKAMP
PROJECT EDITOR	PAULA KMETZ
PRODUCTION PROJECT COORDINATOR	NOMI SCHALIT
COVER ARTIST	GARY SMITH
COVER DESIGN	ANTHONY STOCK
INTERIOR DESIGN	NICOLE COLÓN
COMPOSITOR	ROB MAUHAR
COPYEDITOR	JEFF KELLUM
PROOFREADER	BONNIE TRENGA
INDEXER	JANET PERLMAN
CD-ROM DEVELOPMENT	ROBERT CLARFIELD

Visual Developer VBScript 2 and ActiveX Programming
ISBN: 1-57610-161-4
Copyright © 1997 by The Coriolis Group, Inc.

All rights reserved. This book may not be duplicated in any way without the express written consent of the publisher, except in the form of brief excerpts or quotations for the purposes of review. The information contained herein is for the personal use of the reader and may not be incorporated in any commercial programs, other books, databases, or any kind of software without written consent of the publisher. Making copies of this book or any portion for any purpose other than your own is a violation of United States copyright laws.

Limits of Liability and Disclaimer of Warranty

The author and publisher of this book have used their best efforts in preparing the book and the programs contained in it. These efforts include the development, research, and testing of the theories and programs to determine their effectiveness. The author and publisher make no warranty of any kind, expressed or implied, with regard to these programs or the documentation contained in this book.

The author and publisher shall not be liable in the event of incidental or consequential damages in connection with, or arising out of, the furnishing, performance, or use of the programs, associated instructions, and/or claims of productivity gains.

Trademarks

Trademarked names appear throughout this book. Rather than list the names and entities that own the trademarks or insert a trademark symbol with each mention of the trademarked name, the publisher states that it is using the names for editorial purposes only and to the benefit of the trademark owner, with no intention of infringing upon that trademark.

The Coriolis Group, Inc.
An International Thomson Publishing Company
14455 N. Hayden Road, Suite 220
Scottsdale, Arizona 85260

602/483-0192
FAX 602/483-0193
http://www.coriolis.com

Printed in the United States of America
10 9 8 7 6 5 4 3 2 1

Dedicated to Eve, Darrin, Aaron, and Rachel

CONTENTS

INTRODUCTION   XV

CHAPTER 1   WHAT IS VISUAL BASIC SCRIPT?   1

What VBScript Is—And Isn't   2
Using HTML With VBScript   3
HTML And VBScript: A Simple Example   5
HTML And VBScript: A More Interesting Example   8
HTML And VBScript: The Bottom Line   11

VBScript And ActiveX Controls   12
Where To From Here?   13

CHAPTER 2   YOUR FIRST VBSCRIPT PROGRAM   15

The "Hello" Program   15
The <script> Tag   18
The Comment Delimiters   18
Program Comments In VBScript   19
A Sub Procedure   19
The **MsgBox** Statement   20

Adding A Variable To The "Hello" Program — 22
Adding A Text Box   23
Declaring A Variable   24
Assigning A Value To The Variable   25
Using The Variable With The Message Box   26

Using ActiveX Controls: A Preview — 26
What Happens Inside The ActiveX Example   29
Adding A Function To The ActiveX Example   31

Chapter 3   Data, Variables, And Constants — 35

Data In Visual Basic Script — 36

Data Types — 37
Inside The Data Types Program   40
VBScript "Data Subtypes"   45

Declaring Variables — 45
Using **option explicit**   46
Declaring Constants   47
Naming Variables And Other Program Elements   48
Scope Of Variables And Constants   48

Declaring And Using Arrays — 49
Assigning Values To Array Slots   51
A Simple Array Demonstration   52
Inside The Array Code   54

Chapter 4   Operators And Expressions — 57

What Are Operators? — 58
Expressions Have Values   59

Arithmetic Operators — 59
Addition, Subtraction, And Multiplication   60
Division   66
Modulus   70

Logical Operators — 74
Logical Negation 75
Logical Disjunction 75
Logical Conjunction 79
XOr, Equivalence, And Implication 82

Comparison (Relational) Operators — 84

Chapter 5 Making Your Program Make Decisions — 87

Types Of Control Structures — 88

Using if Statements — 89
Single-Line **if** Statements 89
Multiple-Line **if** Statements 89
if...else Statements 91

A More Sophisticated Example — 91
Setup Tasks In The Trivia, Forsooth Code 98
Getting A Question 99
Giving An Answer 101

Looping Statements — 102
for Loops 102
A Simple **for** Loop Example 103
do Loops 107

Using select case Statements — 108
A Simple **select case** Example 109
A More Sophisticated **select case** Example 113

Chapter 6 Using Subs And Functions — 121

Subs Vs. Functions: Vive La Différence — 121
The **MsgBox** Sub Vs. The **MsgBox** Function 122

Creating Your Own Subs — 130
Inside The Sub Code 134
And, Of Course, The **InputBox** Function 135

Creating Your Own Functions — 136
Inside The Function Demo Code   140

Using VBScript's Built-In Subs And Functions — 141
Inside The String-Parsing Code   145

Chapter 7 Using ActiveX Controls With VBScript — 147

Objects, Properties, And Events — 147
Important Properties Of ActiveX Controls   149

Important ActiveX Controls — 150
The Label And Text Box Controls   150
The Command Button Control   151
The Option Button Control   151
The Checkbox Control   153
The Spin Button Control   153

You're Not Limited To ActiveX Controls — 154

Chapter 8 Using The ActiveX Control Pad — 157

Parts Of The ActiveX Control Pad — 158

Creating An HTML Layout — 159
Drawing A Control   159
Using The Properties Window   164

Adding Code With The Script Wizard — 168

Inserting A Layout In An HTML Document — 170

ActiveX Control Pad Tips And Techniques — 171
Adding Controls To The Toolbox   171
Deleting Controls From The Toolbox   173
Automatic Coding With The Script Wizard's List View   174

Chapter 9 — The Scripting Object Model — 177

Objects, Properties, And Events — 178
The Object Hierarchy   178
Attaching Scripts To Objects   180
Referring To Objects   184

The Objects Themselves — 184
The **window** Object   185
The **document** Object   187
The **form** Object   192

Chapter 10 — Client-Side Data Validation — 193

Client-Side Vs. Server-Side Data Validation — 194

Client-Side Validation With VBScript And HTML — 195
Stepping Through The Example Code   197
Creating A Data-Checking Function   200

Client-Side Data Validation With An ActiveX Layout — 203
Stepping Through The Example Code   212

Sending Data From An ActiveX Layout To The Web Server — 214
The Secret Trick: Use The Scripting Object Model   224
Inside The Example Code   233

Chapter 11 — An ActiveX Miscellany — 237

The List Box Control — 238
Writing VBScript Code For The List Box Control   241

The Combo Box Control — 242
Writing VBScript Code For The Combo Box Control   246

The Option Button Control — 246
Writing VBScript Code For Option Button Controls   251

The Toggle Button Control — 252
Writing VBScript Code For The Toggle Button Control 256
The Scrollbar Control — 256
Writing VBScript Code For The Scrollbar Control 259

CHAPTER 12 IMAGES, VIDEO, AND SOUND — 261
Using ActiveX Image Controls — 261
Using Images In HTML — 264
Playing Video With HTML — 267
Playing Video With ActiveX — 269
Playing Sound On Your Web Page — 271

CHAPTER 13 A VBSCRIPT AND ACTIVEX FAQ — 275

CHAPTER 14 A MULTIMEDIA WEB GAME, PART 1 — 279
Designing The Game — 279
Laying Out A Game Map 280
Doing A Walkthrough — 280
Beginning The Game 281
Entering The Mall 285
Avoiding The Pit 287
More Deadly Traps To Avoid 289
Winning The Game 293
Designing The Game Pages — 297

CHAPTER 15 CODING THE HAUNTED MALL — 299
Setting Up The Game Pages — 300
Creating The Intro With The Timer And **Window.Location** 300
Creating The Main Game Page 302
Creating The End-Sequence Page 304

Creating The Program Framework — 304
Declaring Variables And Constants 314
Setting Up To Play 317
Action, Inventory, And Room Object Buttons 318
Moving From Room To Room 318

Coding The Game — 320
Using The **OnLoad** Event For Game Setup Tasks 321
Moving From Room To Room 327
Performing Game Actions 346
Setting The Traps 350
Adding Music To The Game 352
Bringing It All Together 352

CHAPTER 16 WRITING CGI PROGRAMS WITH VISUAL BASIC 5 — 353

Web Servers And CGI: The Basics — 354
From The Web Browser To The Web Server 355
From The CGI Program To The Web Server 357

Setting Up To Test Your CGI Programs — 357
Testing The Form-CGI Connection 358

Writing A Simple CGI Program In Visual Basic — 361
Creating The CGI Program Itself 363
Inside The Orderbk1.bas Code Module 368
Sending A Report Back To The Customer's Web Browser 370

Adding Server-Side Data Validation — 372
Changing The **CGI_Main**() Procedure 379
Checking The Order Data 379
Redisplaying The Order Form 380

CHAPTER 17 USING COOKIES WITH VBSCRIPT — 383

Creating Cookies In Your Code — 384

Inside The Cookie Code — 387

Chapter 18 Web Database Publishing Made Easy — 391

How Web Database Publishing Ought To Work — 392

The Easy Way To Publish Data — 394
Exporting Table Data From Access 97 394
Creating The Database Frameset Document 396

Appendix A What's New In VBScript 2? — 399

Declaring Identifiers — 400

Control Structures — 401

Array Handling — 401

Dates And Times — 401
The **DateAdd** Function 401
The **DateDiff** Function 402
The **DatePart** Function 403
The **Weekday** Function 403

String Formatting — 403
The **FormatCurrency** Function 404
The **FormatDateTime** Function 405
The **FormatNumber** Function 406
The **FormatPercent** Function 406

General String Handling — 406

System I/O And Object Handling — 409

Data Types — 411

Miscellaneous Functions — 412

APPENDIX B   VBSCRIPT 2 FOR VISUAL BASIC USERS   413

Handling Forms   413
Handling Data Types   414
Handling Record Data   415
Using Separate Modules (Not) And Option Explicit   417
Controls You Can Use—And Some You Can't   417
Visual Basic Features Left Out Of VBScript 2   418

INDEX   421

INTRODUCTION

The Web has come a long way from its humble beginnings. Once the preserve of glitzy, well-funded corporate sites and caffeine-addled techno-nerds, Web pages can now be created by almost anyone with an Internet connection.

But creating Web pages is easy. Creating *great* Web pages is what *Visual Developer VBScript 2 & ActiveX Programming* is all about. By combining HTML tricks with the latest ActiveX technology and VBScript 2, you can design dazzling Web pages that go far beyond the passive display of information. You can position elements exactly where you want them on a Web page, embed ActiveX miniprograms in a page, even make a Web page respond intelligently to user input.

All it takes is a little effort and the knowledge you'll find in this book. If you already know Visual Basic, you're way ahead of the game, because VBScript 2 is a stripped-down version of Visual Basic. If you don't know Visual Basic yet, you'll find VBScript so simple and easy to learn that you'll be creating VBScript Web-page scripts in no time.

This book is your guide to using VBScript 2 and ActiveX. It doesn't assume that you know HTML, though it helps if you do. In these pages, you'll learn how to do things that even a year ago would have been difficult or impossible for most people:

- Write Web page scripts with VBScript 2
- Create ActiveX Web page layouts with the ActiveX Control Pad
- Make VBScript 2 work with CGI programs on a Web server
- Create Web server CGI programs in Visual Basic
- Use "cookies" to create a Web shopping cart system
- Publish databases on the Web—the fast and easy way
- Create hot multimedia Web games with VBScript 2 and ActiveX

How To Use This Book

This book is organized so that you can use it in two ways. If you want a complete, systematic tutorial on VBScript 2 and ActiveX, you can simply work through the book from front to back.

However, you can also dip into the book a chapter at a time, looking up topics and techniques as you need them. Each chapter is independent of the others, so you can plow through any chapter without worrying about the content of previous chapters.

The best way to *learn* programming is to *do* programming, so work through the examples in the book. Write the VBScript 2 code yourself, and create your ActiveX layouts using the ActiveX Control Pad. If you don't have the ActiveX Control Pad, you can download it from www.microsoft.com.

The most important thing is: *Have fun!* Good luck in your VBScript and Web page adventures.

How This Book Is Structured

This book is structured so that you can use it either as a front-to-back tutorial or as a ready reference.

- Chapters 1-6 cover all the basics of VBScript 2: variables, control structures, operators, subs, and functions. If you're already familiar with Visual Basic and programming concepts, you can simply glance through this section and then look at Appendix B, which details the main differences between Visual Basic and VBScript 2.

- Chapters 7-9 cover more advanced VBScript topics, including how to use VBScript 2 with ActiveX controls and with the Internet Explorer Scripting Object Model. Even if you already know Visual Basic, you should read this section, because it contains important information for using VBScript.

- Chapters 10-18 show you how to perform specific tasks with VBScript 2 and ActiveX, including data validation, Web order systems, and game programming. You can dip into these chapters *ad libitum* whenever you need help in a particular area.

What You Need To Use This Book

To use this book, you need to have Microsoft Internet Explorer 3.0 or a later version, VBScript 2, and the ActiveX Control Pad. All can be downloaded free from Microsoft's Web site, www.microsoft.com. To do the CGI programs in Chapter 16, you need Visual Basic 5.

This book doesn't assume that you have any prior programming knowledge or experience, although it certainly helps if you do. All you need is a desire to learn and to have fun with VBScript and ActiveX.

Technical Support

If you have trouble with the book or the CD-ROM, or if you find errors in the book, you can send email to techsupport@coriolis.com.

Acknowledgments

This book benefitted greatly from the work of Paula Kmetz at Coriolis, who's one of the finest project editors in the business. Jeff Kellum also lent his sharp eyes and keen editorial sense to shaping up the text.

I would also like to thank Nomi Schalit, Rob Mauhar, and Bonnie Trenga for the quality they each added to the book.

What Is Visual Basic Script?

Visual Basic Script isn't exactly Visual Basic, but it's pretty close. And once you know how it differs, you can use it to make your Web pages jump!

If you've only been following the news casually—glancing at *InfoWorld* while shaving your cat, or catching Microsoft sound bites during the hockey playoffs—you might think that Visual Basic Script (VBScript, for short) is a visual development environment much like Visual Basic itself. In that environment, you'd develop your Web pages by the following process:

1. Draw the Web page on your PC's screen, using visual tools provided with the VBScript product.

2. Using the mouse, position controls from a toolbox on the Web page. The toolbox would be just like the one provided with Visual Basic, except that the controls would be designed for Web pages instead of regular PC programs.

3. Write Visual Basic "engine code" that interacts with the controls, getting data from the user, doing calculations, and returning results—whether as more data or as multimedia events such as graphics, animation, and sound.

That's a pretty reasonable guess, and as Meatloaf once said, "Two out of three ain't bad." But it's a little off the mark. You do use controls, and you do write code. After that, the similarity to Visual Basic gets a little tricky.

What VBScript Is—And Isn't

The process of developing a Web page with VBScript is significantly different from that of developing a program with Visual Basic. To develop a program with Visual Basic, you need know only Visual Basic itself. That's because you do everything inside the Visual Basic development environment.

VBScript, however, isn't a user product like Visual Basic. Instead, it's an interpreter that can be incorporated into a Web browser. A Web browser equipped with the interpreter can run VBScript mini-programs that are embedded in Web pages. Microsoft's Internet Explorer 3.02 (as well as Internet Explorer 4.0, which was in beta testing as this book was being written) includes a VBScript interpreter, and Microsoft is making it easy for other Web browsers to use VBScript, too.

If VBScript isn't a development environment, then what is it? That's already implied: It's a language for writing mini-programs that you embed in your Web pages. It's a lot like a stripped-down version of regular Visual Basic. Variables are declared in the same way, the same control structures are used (**if...endif**, **select case**, and so on), and you write subs and functions in pretty much the same way. If you already know Visual Basic, then writing VBScript code will be instantly familiar. The two things that won't be familiar from Visual Basic are:

- The way you create Web pages

- The way you insert controls such as buttons and text boxes into those pages

Because VBScript is just a scripting language, it won't by itself suffice to create any Web pages. You need two other elements: HTML and ActiveX controls. It also helps if you use the ActiveX Control Pad, a separate product that helps you create control layouts and VBScript code: It's as close to a "VBScript visual development tool" as you're likely to get. Even with the ActiveX Control Pad, you still have to create the Web pages pretty much on your own.

Where To Learn More About Visual Basic
This book teaches you about VBScript, not about Visual Basic proper. If you need a quick, fun introduction to Visual Basic programming, check out *Visual Basic 5 Programming EXplorer* (Coriolis, 1997). For more advanced Visual Basic techniques—including some that are similar to tricks we'll do in this book—check out *Visual Basic 5 Object-Oriented Programming* and *Developing ActiveX Controls with Visual Basic 5* (Coriolis, 1997).

Using HTML With VBScript

Love it or hate it, HTML is the language you'll use to create your Web pages. When you need to put explanatory text in one location, radio buttons in another, a list box, image file, and command buttons elsewhere on your Web page, you'll use HTML. Unlike Visual Basic, VBScript doesn't do any of that for you.

At the same time, you should realize that in laying out your Web pages with HTML, you aren't doing anything all that different from what you'd do in Visual Basic. It's just more trouble because there's no visual draw-the-interface tool to help you along. If you've ever loaded a Visual Basic form file into a text editor, you saw the same kind of fiddly stuff that you write in HTML—just in Visual Basic. Figure 1.1 shows an example of a Visual Basic form, while Listing 1.1

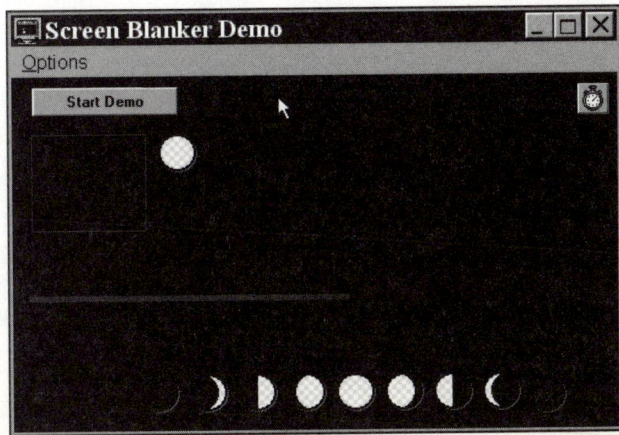

Figure 1.1
A form in Visual Basic.

shows you a bit of the code that Visual Basic generates behind the scenes to create that form.

Listing 1.1 PART OF THE CODE THAT CREATES THE FORM IN FIGURE 1.1.

```
Begin VB.Form DemoForm
    BackColor       =   &H00000000&
    Caption         =   "Screen Blanker Demo"
    ClientHeight    =   4425
    ClientLeft      =   960
    ClientTop       =   1965
    ClientWidth     =   7470
    BeginProperty Font
        name            =   "MS Sans Serif"
        charset         =   1
        weight          =   700
        size            =   8.25
        underline       =   0   'False
        italic          =   0   'False
        strikethrough   =   0   'False
    EndProperty
    ForeColor       =   &H00000000&
    Height          =   5115
    Icon            =   "BLANKER.frx":0000
    Left            =   900
    LinkMode        =   1   'Source
    LinkTopic       =   "Form1"
    ScaleHeight     =   4425
    ScaleWidth      =   7470
    Top             =   1335
    Width           =   7590

    Begin VB.Timer Timer1
        Interval    =   1
        Left        =   6960
        Top         =   120
    End

    Begin VB.CommandButton cmdStartStop
        BackColor   =   &H00000000&
        Caption     =   "Start Demo"
        Default     =   -1  'True
        Height      =   390
        Left        =   240
```

```
        TabIndex         =    0
        Top              =    120
        Width            =    1830
     End

     Begin VB.PictureBox picBall
        AutoSize         =    -1  'True
        BackColor        =    &H00000000&
        BorderStyle      =    0   'None
        ForeColor        =    &H00FFFFFF&
        Height           =    480
        Left             =    1800
        Picture          =    "BLANKER.frx":030A
        ScaleHeight      =    480
        ScaleWidth       =    480
        TabIndex         =    1
        Top              =    720
        Visible          =    0   'False
        Width            =    480
     End
```

Just as in an HTML file, the code in Listing 1.1 first sets up the form (page) itself, including the title. Then, it sets about defining various controls and where they will be placed on the form.

HTML And VBScript: A Simple Example

To see the continuity between Visual Basic proper and VBScript with HTML, let's look at a couple of examples. At this point, don't worry too much about the details of the code. We'll go into all that later on in the book. Here, just start to get a feeling for how VBScript fits into HTML code.

The first example we'll look at is a generic "Hello, world" script. Yes, I know: snooze city. I've spiced it up a little, if you want to call it that, by using a little dialect from the wonderful novel *Christy*, by Catherine Marshall. Instead of saying "Hello," this script will "Swap Howdys" with the user of the Web page. The HTML document that includes the script is shown in Listing 1.2. The Web page it generates (in Microsoft's Internet Explorer 3.02) is shown in Figure 1.2, and the message box the script displays is shown in Figure 1.3.

Listing 1.2 A SIMPLE HTML DOCUMENT WITH A VBSCRIPT SCRIPT.

```
<html>
<head>
<title>How VBScript Fits Into an HTML Document</title>
</head>

<body>
<font size=5>

<center>
<h1>Using VBScript in an HTML document</h1>
</center>
<p>
<p>In HTML, you define the Web page, including any controls
that the page should contain. Then, in VBScript, you can
define how those controls should respond to various events.</p>
<p>In this case, you use HTML to define a button. Then, you
use VBScript to tell Internet Explorer how it should react
when the user clicks the button: It should display a message
box saying "Hello, VBScript wizard-to-be!"</p>
<br><br>
<center>
<input type=button value="Swap Howdys" name="Btn_HelloWorld">
</center>

<script language="vbscript">
<!--
'
' Notice that comments inside the script
' use Visual Basic comment notation instead
' of HTML comment notation.
'
    Sub Btn_HelloWorld_OnClick
        MsgBox "Hello, VBScript wizard-to-be!",0,"VBScript Example"
    End Sub
-->
</script>
</body>
</html>
```

Listing 1.2 and the Web page it generates are still pretty simple stuff. As I said before, we'll get into the details of how to write VBScript code in the chapters that follow. But for now, just look at how the VBScript code fits into the HTML

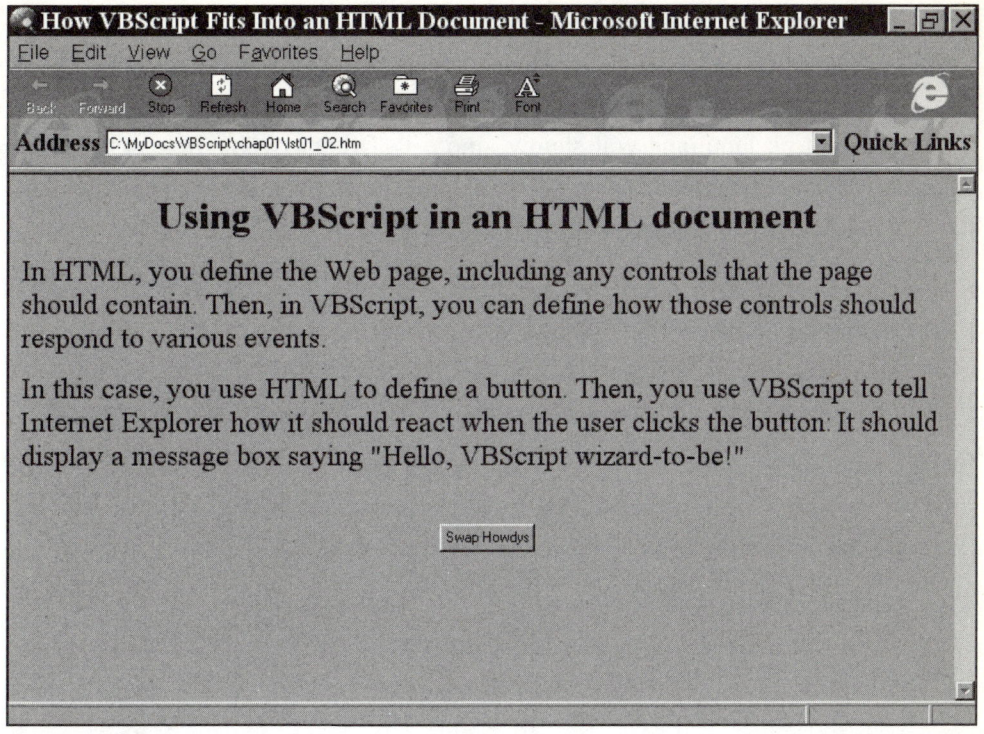

Figure 1.2
The Web page created by the HTML code in Listing 1.2.

document. First, we've got all the usual HTML tags—beginning the document, doing a little formatting, and displaying a button. (Note: If Listing 1.2 doesn't work in your Web browser, add a line above **<input type=button...>** with the tag **<FORM>**, then add a line below **<input type=button...>** with the tag **</FORM>**.)

Once that's out of the way, we see our first bit of VBScript. We use the HTML script tag to indicate the beginning of the script and the language it will use. Then, inside HTML comment tags, we insert the script code itself.

Figure 1.3
The message box displayed by the VBScript code in Listing 1.2.

Always Put Your Script Inside HTML Comment Tags

It bears repeating: Always put your VBScript code inside HTML comment tags. That way, browsers that do not support VBScript as a scripting language will simply ignore it. Otherwise, such a non-VBScript browser will most likely display the code on the Web page, as some non-JavaScript browsers do even now.

Inside the HTML comment tags, we're in the VBScript world, so regular Visual Basic comment syntax applies: When you start a line with an apostrophe or the word **rem**, the line is ignored by the VBScript interpreter. And because it's already inside the HTML comment tags, it's also ignored by the Web browser.

In this particular script, all we've done is define an event procedure for the input button specified in the HTML code. When the user clicks on the button, the code inside the event procedure will be executed.

The event procedure is the only thing in this particular script, so after that, we close the script with a closing HTML comment tag followed by the script-ending tag **</script>**. Presto! We're done.

HTML And VBScript: A More Interesting Example

Perhaps we can at least make the Web page do something a little more interesting. Instead of simply saying a generic "Howdy," let's make it prompt the user for his or her name, then incorporate that name into the "Howdy" greeting. That sounds a little more like a real program. Listing 1.3 shows the HTML document with embedded VBScript code to do just that. Figure 1.4 shows the Web page created by the code in Listing 1.3.

Listing 1.3   PROMPTING THE USER FOR HIS/HER NAME.

```
<html>
<head>
<title>How VBScript Fits Into an HTML Document</title>
</head>

<body>
<font size=5>
```

```
<center>
<h1>A Little More You Can Do with VBScript</h1>
</center>
<p>
<p>This shows a little more of what you can do with VBScript.
In Listing 1.2, clicking the button just gave a generic Hello
message. In this listing, the user enters his/her name, then
the VBScript mini-program assigns the name text to a variable
and uses the name in the Hello message!</p>
<p>Sure, it's not rocket science--yet--but it gives you a
taste of what's to come: Web pages that interact with the user
in ways previously undreamt of!</p>
<p>
<p>
<p>
<center>
<br><br>
<p>Enter your first name:</p>
<input type=text value="" align=left name="TB_UserName">
<p>
<input type=button value="Swap Howdys" name="Btn_HelloWorld">
</center>

<script language="VBScript">
<!--
'
' Notice that comments inside the script
' use Visual Basic comment notation instead
' of HTML comment notation.
'
     dim UserName ' declare variable to hold user's name

     Sub Btn_HelloWorld_OnClick
         UserName = TB_UserName.value
         MsgBox "Howdy, " & Username & "!",0,"VBScript Example"
     End Sub
-->
</script>
</body>
</html>
```

This Web page is a little more fun than the generic "Howdy" page. It contains a text box in which the user can enter his or her name. Once the name is entered, clicking on the command button activates the **HelloWorld_OnClick** event procedure.

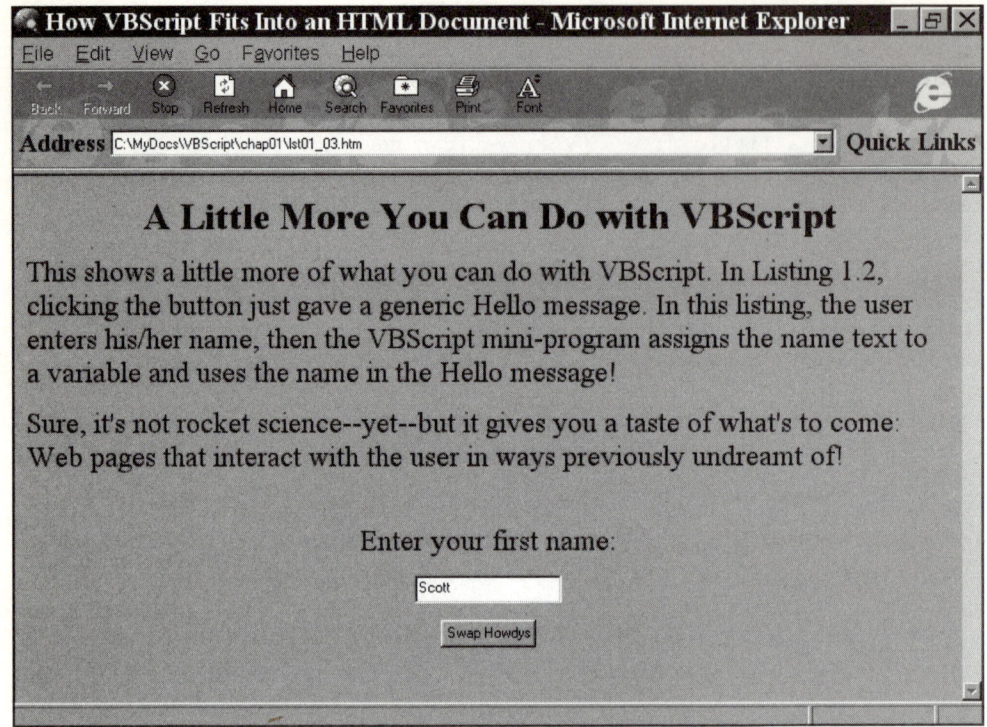

Figure 1.4
The Web page created by the HTML code in Listing 1.3.

If you look at the VBScript code, you'll see that just above the event procedure, we declared (**dim**ensioned) a variable to hold the name from the text box created by the HTML code. The idea of using a **dim** statement to declare a variable is familiar to all Visual Basic programmers. What's less familiar is that, unlike Visual Basic, VBScript has only one data type: the all-purpose **variant** data type that can handle anything you throw at it. That's why the **dim** statement doesn't declare the variable *as* any particular data type.

Once the variable is declared, the rest is easy. When the user clicks on the button control, its **OnClick** event fires, causing the event procedure to execute. Inside the event procedure, VBScript assigns the text control's **value** property to the **UserName** variable. Then, it uses the VBScript **MsgBox** statement to display the "Howdy" message and glom it together with the **UserName** variable. The result is shown in Figure 1.5.

Figure 1.5
The message box displayed by the VBScript code in Listing 1.3, assuming your name is "Scott."

The rest of the listing proceeds exactly as before. The end-of-comment mark terminates the comment containing the VBScript code, the **</script>** tag formally ends the script, and the **</body>** and **</html>** tags terminate the document body and the HTML document, respectively.

HTML And VBScript: The Bottom Line

The bottom line is this: *You must know HTML if you're going to use Visual Basic Script.* In order to work, your VBScript mini-programs will need to be in an HTML document that includes appropriate ActiveX controls or other kinds of applets. If you don't have HTML, you don't have a Web page. If you don't have a Web page, VBScript can't do a thing.

> *Note: If you're new to Web page development, you might be confused by the word* script. *Very often, you'll hear people talk about* CGI scripts. *These are programs on a Web server that can create new Web pages in response to user input. CGI scripts can be written in a variety of languages, including Visual Basic, as we'll see later in this book. However, CGI scripts are a completely different kind of script from those you'll be creating with VBScript. Don't confuse the two.*

If you need to get up to speed on HTML, there are several excellent books on the subject. One of the best is *Netscape and HTML EXplorer* (Coriolis, 1995). Another is *Serving the Web* (Coriolis, 1995), which also contains a superb explanation of CGI scripts.

Although Microsoft stays pretty close to the HTML standard, Microsoft's Internet Explorer has its own set of HTML extensions. You can find out about Explorer's HTML extensions at Microsoft's Web site, http://www.microsoft.com.

If You Really, Really Don't Want To Mess With HTML . . .

If you really, really don't want to mess with HTML, there is an alternative. Microsoft's FrontPage Web design package allows you to visually lay out your Web pages, much as you would lay out a form in Visual Basic. It's fast, easy, and powerful. It's also pretty expensive—at this writing, $140—but well worth the money. If you're a little less HTML-phobic, an excellent and much cheaper alternative (around $50) is Allaire Corps' HomeSite, deservedly one of the most popular Web page editors around.

Apart from the fact that FrontPage includes a standalone Web server so that you can test entire networks of Web pages, the main difference between FrontPage and HotDog is that FrontPage insulates you almost completely from the HTML code: Everything is visual. HomeSite, on the other hand, sports toolbar buttons that insert HTML tags for you, making it unnecessary for you to type them or remember their exact syntax. Neither can do anything for you that you can't do on your own, but they both make your life as a Web author much easier.

VBScript And ActiveX Controls

If VBScript is just a language, and includes neither a development environment nor controls like those in Visual Basic, then where do you get the controls to use with your VBScript mini-programs?

The answer is that you use ActiveX controls. *ActiveX* is just Microsoft's new name for Internet-ready OCX controls. Some controls are included with Internet Explorer itself, as follows:

- **Intrinsic.** These are controls such as command buttons, list boxes, radio buttons, checkboxes, and text boxes.
- **Chart.** This is a versatile control that lets you create line graphs, bar charts, area charts, and many other types of charts.
- **Label.** This is a clickable text label that can display text at any angle.

- **New item.** This is a time-sensitive label that marks a particular line of your Web page as "New!" and then, obligingly, disappears on a date you specify.
- **Preloader.** This downloads the contents of a Web address and lets you speed up certain types of page and image displays.
- **Timer.** This is very much like the Timer control used in Visual Basic. It fires an event at intervals you specify, causing an event procedure to execute.
- **ActiveVRML.** This can be used to display interactive 3D animations.

Other ActiveX controls are available from Microsoft and third-party vendors. You insert an ActiveX control by using the HTML **<object>** tag (which the ActiveX Control Pad does for you), then call it in your VBScript code in much the same way as you saw in Listings 1.2 and 1.3. You'll see many examples of how to use ActiveX controls as you progress through this book.

You'll also sometimes use HTML "intrinsic" controls. These are controls—such as input buttons and text boxes—defined by the HTML language itself. However, ActiveX controls are generally better for anything but the simplest Web pages.

Where To From Here?

In the chapters that follow, you'll learn all about VBScript and what you can do with it—from the basic stuff to the truly wizardly! So if you need to review HTML or Visual Basic, go to the restroom, or get a snack, do it now: It's going to be a fast ride.

2 Your First VBScript Program

Ready to get down and dirty? More fun than a Jello jump, safer than dissing your mother-in-law, VBScript lets you power up Web pages with surprising ease. In this chapter, you'll create programs that show you all the basics.

In the previous chapter, we looked at the Big Picture. I included a couple of short VBScript programs, but they weren't explained in any detail. Now, I'll walk you through those programs to show you how they were put together so you can start creating your own VBScript programs.

Of course, even if we're in the beginning stages of working with VBScript, there's a lot more to Web pages than simple "Hello" scripts. So later in the chapter, you'll learn how to incorporate ActiveX controls into your Web pages and use them in your VBScript code. You'll be amazed at how easy it is.

The "Hello" Program

In Chapter 1, we started off with a version of the "Hello, world" program that has been in almost every programming book ever written. There's a reason, other than lack of imagination, why this example is so popular: It illustrates all the essential jobs a program has to do, but has no extraneous features to complicate

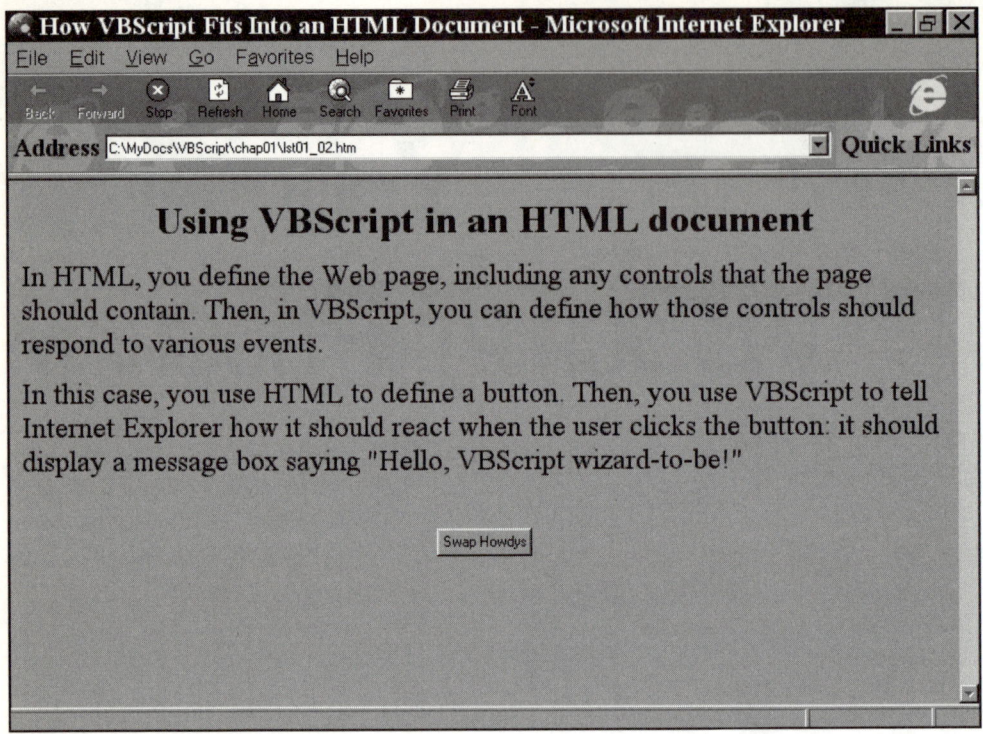

Figure 2.1
The Web page created by the HTML code in Listing 2.1.

things. For your convenience, it's reproduced in Listing 2.1. The resulting Web page is shown in Figure 2.1.

 Did Someone Say "Active Scripting"?

In this book, I talk a lot about writing scripts (scripting) with VBScript. Sometimes, however, you'll encounter books and articles that refer to "active" scripting. Don't get frazzled: active scripting is the same thing as scripting. "Active" is Microsoft's primary marketing buzzword for its Web products, so Gates groupies try to work it into the conversation whenever they can: "active" scripting, "active" content, "active" server pages, doing things "actively" (i.e., with a script), and so on.

When in doubt, just remember *Cooper's Law:* If you don't understand a technical buzzword, ignore it. The sentence will make perfect sense without it. There's also *Bogovich's Corollary:* If a statement makes no sense without a buzzword, then it makes no sense *with* the buzzword either.

Listing 2.1 A SIMPLE HTML DOCUMENT WITH VBSCRIPT.

```
<html>
<head>
<title>How VBScript Fits Into an HTML Document</title>
</head>

<body>
<font size=5>

<center>
<h1>Using VBScript in an HTML document</h1>
</center>
<p>
<p>In HTML, you define the Web page, including any controls
that the page should contain. Then, in VBScript, you can
define how those controls should respond to various events.</p>
<p>In this case, you use HTML to define a button. Then, you
use VBScript to tell Internet Explorer how it should react
when the user clicks the button: it should display a message
box saying "Hello, VBScript wizard-to-be!"</p>
<br><br>
<center>
<form>
<input type=button value="Swap Howdys" name="Btn_HelloWorld">
</form>
</center>

<script language="vbscript">
<!--
'
' Notice that comments inside the script
' use Visual Basic comment notation instead
' of HTML comment notation.
'
    Sub Btn_HelloWorld_OnClick
        MsgBox "Hello, VBScript wizard-to-be!",0,"VBScript Example"
    End Sub
-->
</script>
</body>
</html>
```

In this case, of course, it's a little more complicated than most "Hello" examples because it has all that HTML code in it, too. But it's still an excellent way to see the main features of a VBScript program. Let's examine the listing one feature at a time. We won't rehearse the intricacies of the HTML code except where they're relevant to VBScript.

The <script> Tag

The first thing to notice is that the whole section of VBScript code is surrounded by the HTML tags that mark the beginning and end of a script. **<script>** marks the beginning, and (as you might expect) **</script>** marks the end.

Don't Forget The </script> Tag!
If you can load your HTML document into your Web browser, but nothing much seems to happen—not even an error message—then make sure that you've remembered to end the script with a **</script>** tag. Failure to do so will lead to unpredictable consequences, but one possible result is that you'll see a blank Web page with absolutely *nothing* going on.

The Comment Delimiters

Inside the **<script>...</script>** tags, you can also see that the entire script is enclosed inside HTML comment marks, as shown in the following code snippet:

```
<!--
    Sub Btn_HelloWorld_OnClick
        MsgBox "Hello, VBScript wizard-to-be!",0,"VBScript Example"
    End Sub
-->
```

The reason for enclosing the script inside comment marks is that some Web browsers don't yet support Visual Basic Script. When someone uses one of those browsers to load your Web page, the comment marks will keep the VBScript code from displaying on the page as normal text.

A Few Browsers Don't Recognize Multiline Comments
The HTML comment marks themselves have been around for a while, but until the development of the HTML 3.x standard, they could only be used for single-line comments—*not* for multiline comments like a section of VBScript code. As a result, a few older browsers might not support multiline comments, and there's just no way to keep these browsers from displaying your VBScript code as regular text.

Program Comments In VBScript

Inside the script, you're no longer in HTML: You're in VBScript country now, pardner. As a result, you can use regular Visual Basic comment marks. There are two comment marks in Visual Basic, and both apply to single lines: Unlike C, C++, Pascal, and HTML (!), Visual Basic and VBScript don't yet support multiline comments.

Both comment marks are placed to the left of the comment. Another way of looking at the situation is that the VBScript interpreter will ignore anything on a line that is to the *right* of a comment mark. Acceptable VBScript comment marks are the apostrophe (') and the word **rem**, for "remark."

THE APOSTROPHE

You can place this at the beginning of a line, as in Listing 2.1, or in the middle of a line, to the right of some code. Often, you might use an apostrophe "in the middle" to explain a particular code line. Here's an example of each:

```
' The apostrophe at the beginning of the line.
MsgBox "Blah blah blah."  ' This starts in the middle.
```

THE WORD **rem**

Like the apostrophe, you can place this anywhere on a line. There's just one difference: If you put the **rem** comment mark in the middle of a line, it must be preceded by a colon. That tells the compiler that a **rem** comment is coming. Here's an example of each:

```
rem The remark at the beginning of the line.
MsgBox "Blah blah blah."  : rem This starts in the middle.
```

Note that Visual Basic and VBScript are generally not case sensitive, so they treat **rem**, **REM**, **rEm**, and other upper- or lowercase variations as the same word.

A Sub Procedure

The word *sub* in VBScript refers to "subroutine," and is synonymous with "procedure." A sub (or procedure) is a named block of code that does something: It might display some text in a text box, perform arithmetic, or play music. If you're not sure what a "named block of code" is, well, it's a bunch of code lines that you refer to by a single name, such as **Btn_HelloWorld_OnClick**. In Listing 2.1, you used a very simple sub:

```
Sub Btn_HelloWorld_OnClick
    MsgBox "Hello, VBScript wizard-to-be!",0,"VBScript Example"
End Sub
```

This is a block of code (three lines of VBScript) with a name (**Btn_HelloWorld_OnClick**) that does something (displays a message box on the user's PC screen). In this case, the name of the sub also tells you when it's activated: whenever the user clicks on the button with the name **Btn_HelloWorld**.

OnClick Vs. Click

File this in your memory for later reference: When you click on a command button that was created with the HTML **<input>** tag, you generate an **OnClick** event—hence, the name of the sub procedure in this section. However, clicking on an ActiveX command button generates an event named **Click** rather than **OnClick**. An ActiveX command button's click sub procedure, accordingly, has to be named **(ButtonName).Click**.

Note that there are two kinds of subs: ones that you write yourself and ones that come built into VBScript (or Visual Basic). **Btn_HelloWorld_OnClick** is the kind of sub that you write yourself. But **MsgBox** is also a sub: It's one that is predefined in VBScript. Predefined subs are often called *statements*.

The MsgBox Statement

The **MsgBox** statement, as its name implies, simply displays a message box on the user's screen, as shown in Figure 2.2. Its code line, however, is just a little cluttered:

```
MsgBox "Hello, VBScript wizard-to-be!",0,"VBScript Example"
```

To display a message box, you first use the VBScript keyword **MsgBox**. (Capitalization generally doesn't matter in VBScript, so **MsgBox** works just the same as **msgbox** or **MSGBOX**.) Then, you can include several *parameters*—i.e., values that you pass to the sub:

Figure 2.2
The message box displayed by the "Hello" program in Listing 2.1.

- A text string for the prompt to be displayed in the message box. Here, it's "Hello, VBScript wizard-to-be!"

- A number (or expression) indicating which buttons should be displayed in the message box, such as OK, Yes, No, and Cancel. If you don't specify a number, you need to include two commas to indicate that this parameter is left blank. In that case, VBScript assumes that the number is zero. However, each different kind of button (OK, Yes, Cancel, etc.) returns a different integer value to tell the program which button the user clicked. With the program in Listing 2.1, we haven't set up any way to catch the value, so there's not much point in fiddling with different buttons. We'll see how to do that later in the book.

- A text string for the title of the message box. In this case, it's "VBScript Example."

There are a couple of other optional parameters (helpfile and context), but they're less commonly used, so don't worry about them right now.

The parameters *must* be separated by commas. If you don't want to include a parameter, there are two possible cases:

- If you're omitting a parameter that would be the last one in the parameter list—i.e., you aren't including any more parameters to the right of it—then you can just omit the parameter and that's all you have to do.

- If you're omitting a parameter that *isn't* the last parameter in the list—i.e., you're including parameters that come after it—then you should put two commas to mark where you *would have* put the parameter you're omitting. This tells VBScript that you're leaving out that parameter. If we had wanted to omit the button parameter in the message box code line (which we could have done, since it defaults to zero anyway), it would have looked like the following code line:

```
MsgBox "Hello, VBScript wizard-to-be!",,"VBScript Example"
```

Different Kinds Of Message Boxes

To avoid confusion, you should be aware (at least in the back of your mind) that there are two versions of **MsgBox**: the *sub* version, which you've just seen in action, and the *function* version, which you haven't seen yet. We'll explain functions a little later in the chapter. But if you see a **MsgBox** statement that looks a little odd, chances are it's the **MsgBox** function instead of the sub. Oddly, though Microsoft's own VBScript examples use the **MsgBox** sub all over the place, only the **MsgBox** function is mentioned in its official VBScript documentation.

Adding A Variable To The "Hello" Program

And now for something that's not *completely* different (but different enough to have a point). In the second version of our "Hello" program, we prompted the user for his/her name and then displayed the name in the message box. That required a couple of new tricks that you'll use again and again in your VBScript programming. For your convenience, Listing 2.2 reproduces the code for the Web page with the modified "Hello" program.

Listing 2.2   Prompting the user for his/her name.

```
<html>
<head>
<title>How VBScript Fits Into an HTML Document</title>
</head>

<body>
<font size=5>

<center>
<h1>A Little More You Can Do with VBScript</h1>
</center>
<p>
<p>This shows a little more of what you can do with VBScript.
In Listing 2.1, clicking the button just gave a generic "Hello"
message. In this listing, the user enters his/her name, then
the VBScript mini-program assigns the name text to a variable
and uses the name in the "Hello" message!</p>
<p>Sure, it's not rocket science--yet--but it gives you a
taste of what's to come: Web pages that interact with the user
in ways previously undreamt of!</p>
<p>
<p>
<p>
<center>
<br><br>
```

```
<p>Enter your first name:</p><form name="HowdyForm">
<input type=text value="" align=left name="TB_UserName"><p>
<input type=button value="Swap Howdys" name="Btn_HelloWorld">
</form>
</center>

<script language="VBScript">
<!--
'
' Notice that comments inside the script
' use Visual Basic comment notation instead
' of HTML comment notation.
'
    dim UserName ' declare variable to hold user's name

    Sub Btn_HelloWorld_OnClick
        UserName = Document.HowdyForm.TB_UserName.value
        MsgBox "Howdy, " & Username & "!",0,"VBScript Example"
    End Sub
-->
</script>
</body>
</html>
```

The differences between this and Listing 2.1 are small but significant. First, in the HTML code, we provide a text box where the user can type his/her name, along with naming the HTML form so that our VBScript code can pluck the user's name from the text box. Second, in the VBScript code, we define and use a variable to hold the name. Third, we use the ampersand (&) to string together the user's name and some other text in the message box. Let's look at each of these changes in turn.

Adding A Text Box

We won't spend too much time on this, inasmuch as it's HTML rather than VBScript per se. The relevant HTML code is shown in the following code snippet:

```
<center>
<br><br>
<p>Enter your first name:</p>
<form name="HowdyForm">
<input type=text value="" align=left name="TB_UserName">
<p>
<input type=button value="Swap Howdys" name="Btn_HelloWorld">
```

```
</form>
</center>
```

After inserting a couple of line breaks to separate the text box from what's above it, we first put in a text prompt that tells the user what the text box is for: "Enter your first name." Then, we use the HTML **<input>** tag to insert the text box, setting the type to **text** (hence, it's a text box), the initial value to "" (blank), and the name to **TB_UserName** (for text box—user name). That's pretty much it.

Declaring A Variable

If you've done programming before, the concept of a variable will be familiar. What do you do when somebody hands you a rock, but you need to keep your hands free so you can do other things? Very simple: You find someplace to put the rock, such as a pocket or a little box. A variable is just like a little box where you can store things until you need them. In a computer program, those things are *values*—text strings, numbers, and so on.

With most programming languages—including "regular" Visual Basic—you need to use a different type of variable for each type of value. If you create two text variables and store numbers in them, you can't then do arithmetic with the numbers. To do that, you need to create number-type variables and store the numbers in *them,* not in text-type variables.

In VBScript, however, you don't have to worry about that. You'll still deal with numbers, text, and other types of values, but to VBScript, they'll all be treated as a single type: the *variant* type. This is an all-purpose data type that VBScript inherits from Visual Basic: You can stick any kind of value in it and, on demand, convert it into the type you need. For practical purposes, you might even think of VBScript as considering all your variables to be text until and unless you tell it otherwise.

In Listing 2.2, we declared a variable by using the VBScript **dim** (for "dimension") statement:

```
dim UserName ' declare variable to hold user's name
```

To declare a variable, you simply use a **dim** statement, then the name of the variable. From that point on, whenever you need to refer to a value that's stored in the variable, you'll use the variable's name. Here, it's **UserName**. Remember, by the way, that VBScript generally doesn't pay any attention to capitalization: **UserName**, **USERNAME**, and **userNaMe** would all be treated as the same word.

A ONE-LINE COMMENT EXAMPLE

The code line at the bottom of page 24 also shows a typical use of a VBScript comment. After the **dim** statement, there's an apostrophe (comment mark) and a short explanation of what the code line does. This comment was included as an example. Normally, if the purpose of a code line is blindingly obvious, you don't need to write a comment explaining it.

Assigning A Value To The Variable

Once you've declared the variable in Listing 2.2, the next step is to give it a value. Assume that the user of your Web page has now typed his/her name into the text box, and clicked on the button. This fires the button's **OnClick** event, which in turn activates the **Btn_HelloWorld_OnClick** sub, shown in the following code snippet:

```
Sub Btn_HelloWorld_OnClick
    UserName = Document.HowdyForm.TB_UserName.value
    MsgBox "Howdy, " & Username & "!",0,"VBScript Example"
End Sub
```

Assigning a value to a variable is pretty simple stuff. You just construct a statement using the VBScript *assignment operator*, which is the equal sign (=). On the left side of the assignment operator, you put the name of the variable to which you'd like to assign a value. On the right side of the assignment operator, you put the value you'd like to assign. The only thing that makes this example a little complicated is the long, involved name we use for the value in the text box. That's dictated by the scripting object model, which will be covered in Chapter 9. In this example, at any rate, we're assigning the value property of a text box, but we could just as easily assign other things:

```
UserName = "Jim"                    ' assigns a text value
UserName = "Winona" & "Ryder"       ' joins text values and assigns them
UserName = (5 + 3) - (87.75)        ' does arithmetic and assigns result
UserName = SomeVariableName         ' assigns the value in another variable
```

Remember that **UserName** is a **variant** type variable, so it can hold different types of values, even if some of them would be absurd or pointless, as in this case.

Using The Variable With The Message Box

The final step is to use the variable's value as part of the text in the message box. To do this, you use the ampersand to "concatenate" (glom together) the variable with the other text that will display in the message box, as shown in the following code line:

```
MsgBox "Howdy, " & Username & "!",0,"VBScript Example"
```

Remember that the first parameter after **MsgBox** is a text string for the text that will display in the message box. This doesn't need to be a "single" text string: You can use the ampersand to glom together several pieces of text into one big text string. That's what we've done in this line of code. The result is shown in Figure 2.3.

Using ActiveX Controls: A Preview

In much the same manner as in Chapter 1, where we simply looked at an example to get a feel for it, but deferred a full explanation for later in the book, let's close this chapter with a look at how you'll use ActiveX controls in your VBScript programs.

You've probably heard the term "ActiveX" but aren't sure what it means. Well, join the club: Most of the world, including the techno-billionaires at Microsoft, is still trying to pin down exactly what it means. The short version, however, is this: An ActiveX control is a mini-mini-program that you can insert into a Web page and use in VBScript. If you're a tekkie, it's the latest incarnation of what used to be called OCX controls, and before that, VBX controls. It's like the command buttons, radio buttons, and list boxes you use in all your regular programs—in fact, those are some ActiveX controls you can use with VBScript!

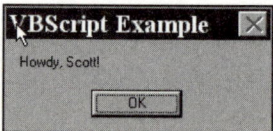

Figure 2.3
The message box shows the glommed-together text.

In this example, we'll insert two ActiveX controls in an HTML document and use them in a VBScript program. The code is shown in Listing 2.3. The result is shown in Figure 2.4.

Listing 2.3 USING VBSCRIPT SUBS WITH ACTIVEX CONTROLS.

```
<HTML>
<HEAD>
<TITLE> A Slightly Hotter VBScript Example</TITLE>
</HEAD>
<BODY leftmargin=10 topmargin=30 bgcolor="white">

<OBJECT
    classid="clsid:99B42120-6EC7-11CF-A6C7-00AA00A47DD2"
        CODEBASE="c:\windows\system\ielabel.ocx"
    id=label1
    width=300
    height=100
    align=left
>
<param name="alignment" value="4" >
<param name="caption" value="0">
<param name="FontName" value="Arial">
<param name="FontSize" value="36">
</OBJECT>

<OBJECT
    ID=timer1
    CLASSID="CLSID:59CCB4A0-727D-11CF-AC36-00AA00A47DD2"
    codebase="c:\windows\system\ietimer.ocx"
    WIDTH=80
    HEIGHT=30 >
    <param name="Interval" value="1000">
    <param name="Enabled" value="False">
</OBJECT>

<br><br><br><br><br>
<FORM>
<input type=button value="Toggle the timer"
    align=middle name="Btn_Timer">
</FORM>

<script language="VBS">
<!--
    dim ClickNum
```

Chapter 2

```
    sub timer1_timer
        ClickNum = ClickNum + 1
        label1.caption = ClickNum
    end sub

    sub Btn_Timer_OnClick
        ClickNum = 0
        label1.caption = ClickNum
        timer1.enabled = not timer1.enabled
    end sub
-->
</script>

</BODY>
</HTML>
```

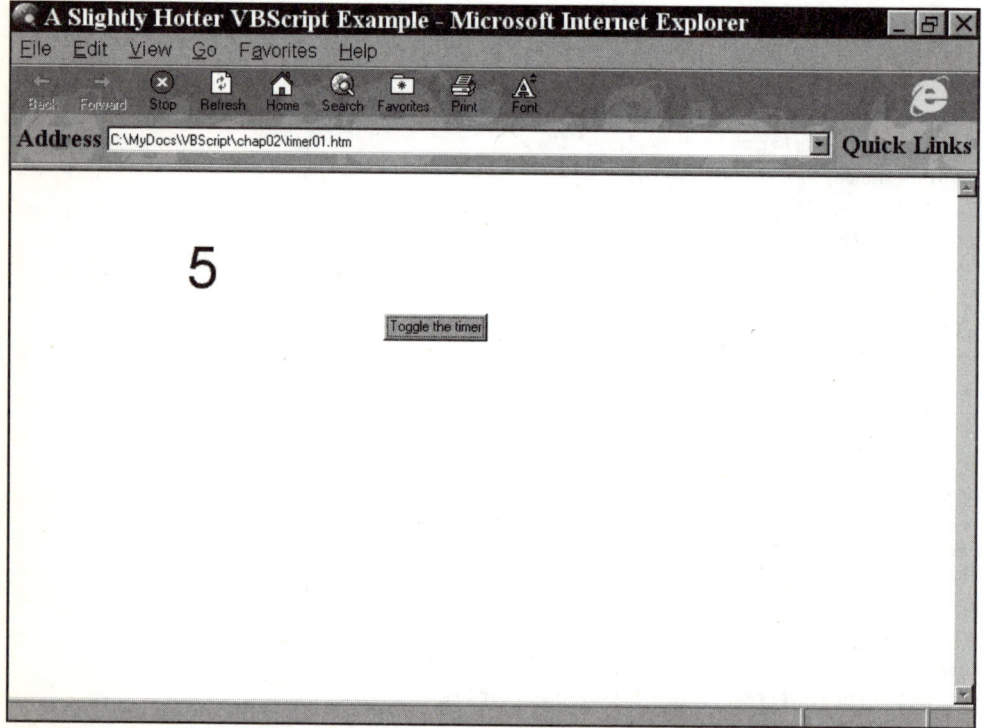

Figure 2.4
VBScript causes the ActiveX timer to update the text label.

What Happens Inside The ActiveX Example

We'll go into the full details of using ActiveX controls in Chapter 7. For now, however, let's take a look at the main features of Listing 2.3. It has two ActiveX controls: a label control and a timer control.

The label control is inserted by using the HTML **<object>** tag, as shown in the following code snippet:

```
<OBJECT
    classid="clsid:99B42120-6EC7-11CF-A6C7-00AA00A47DD2"
        CODEBASE="c:\windows\system\ielabel.ocx"
    id=label1
    width=300
    height=100
    align=left
>
<param name="alignment" value="4" >
<param name="caption" value="0">
<param name="FontName" value="Arial">
<param name="FontSize" value="36">
</OBJECT>
```

Don't worry about the details, but notice a few things. First, when it's needed, the **codebase** line tells the Web browser the name of the ActiveX control and where to find it. Here, that's in the \Windows\System directory of my PC, but in a "live" Web site, it might be a URL address. Second, the **id** line specifies the name by which we'll refer to this control. Third, the **width**, **height**, and **align** lines specify the size and alignment of the label control on the Web page. Finally, four parameter lines specify various starting values for the control, such as the number it displays (0) when the user first loads the Web page.

The ActiveX timer control is inserted in the HTML document in exactly the same way, as shown in the following code snippet:

```
<OBJECT
    ID=timer1
    CLASSID="CLSID:59CCB4A0-727D-11CF-AC36-00AA00A47DD2"
    codebase="c:\windows\system\ietimer.ocx"
    WIDTH=80
    HEIGHT=30 >
    <param name="Interval" value="1000">
    <param name="Enabled" value="False">
</OBJECT>
```

Pay attention, however, to the different parameters. For a timer, the "interval" specifies the number of milliseconds (thousandths of a second) between clicks of the timer. Each time the timer clicks, a timer event fires and VBScript executes the **sub** procedure for the timer. And the "enabled" value specifies whether the timer is turned on or off. When it's off, it doesn't click. To get it to click, you must reset the enabled value to **true**.

Look at the **sub** procedure for the timer, shown in the following code snippet:

```
sub timer1_timer
    ClickNum = ClickNum + 1
    label1.caption = ClickNum
end sub
```

On each click of the timer—that's every second, since the interval was specified as 1,000 milliseconds—the timer sub will add 1 to the current value of the **ClickNum** variable. Then, it will assign that value to the **caption** property of the label control. This means that as long as the timer is enabled, the label control will display numbers in sequence, one after another: 1, 2, 3, 4, and so on. Each time the timer clicks, the sub adds 1 to the **ClickNum** variable and updates the caption of the label control.

Now, look at the code for the button control, shown in the following code snippet:

```
sub Btn_Timer_OnClick
    ClickNum = 0
    label1.caption = ClickNum
    timer1.enabled = not timer1.enabled
end sub
```

Each time the user clicks on the button, it does three things. First, it sets the value of **ClickNum** back to zero. Second, it updates the label control's caption, causing it to display the number zero. Finally, it either turns the timer on (if it's off) or turns it off (if it's on). This is a fairly typical way to work with a timer control.

Watch Out For endif

If you've already done some programming in "regular" Visual Basic, you might have acquired the habit of terminating a multiline **if** statement with the single word **endif**. However, you might not have paid attention to the fact that the Visual Basic development environment automatically parses that into **end if**. If you're writing a

VBScript in a text editor or HTML editor and you type **endif** at the end of a multiline **if** statement, it won't be changed to **end if**, and the VBScript interpreter will flag it as an error.

Adding A Function To The ActiveX Example

The previous example introduced you to ActiveX controls and gave you yet another chance to see VBScript sub procedures in action. But there's another kind of VBScript routine that's just as useful as the sub, but significantly different: the *function*. Functions are like subs in that:

- They're named blocks of code.
- They can accept values and variables as parameters.
- They can have local variables declared inside them.
- They do processing and then pass control back to wherever they got it from in the first place.
- Some of them are already built into VBScript, but you can create your own for specialized jobs.

The main difference between functions and subs is their purpose: In a nutshell, subs *do program tasks* and functions *return values*. If you only use subs and ignore functions, you've lost much of the power of VBScript.

Let's modify the example in Listing 2.3 so that it uses a function in addition to the two subs. The function we'll create, admittedly, has no real purpose other than to show how functions work: It will check to see if the "click number" of the timer is greater than 9.

If the click number is greater than 9, then the sub for the timer event will start adding 5 instead of 1 to the **ClickNum** variable. As a result, the Web page label showing the click number will first increase by 1 per click: 1, 2, 3, 4, and so on, until it gets to 10. Then, it will start increasing by 5 on each click: 15, 20, 25, and so on, until the user turns off the timer. The code is shown in Listing 2.4.

Listing 2.4 ADDING A FUNCTION TO THE ACTIVEX EXAMPLE.

```
<HTML>
<HEAD>
<TITLE> A VBScript Example Using Both Subs and Functions</TITLE>
```

```
</HEAD>
<BODY leftmargin=10 topmargin=30 bgcolor="white">

<OBJECT
    classid="clsid:99B42120-6EC7-11CF-A6C7-00AA00A47DD2"
        CODEBASE="c:\windows\system\ielabel.ocx"
    id=label1
    width=300
    height=100
    align=left
>
<param name="alignment" value="4" >
<param name="caption" value="0">
<param name="FontName" value="Arial">
<param name="FontSize" value="36">
</OBJECT>

<OBJECT
    ID=timer1
    CLASSID="CLSID:59CCB4A0-727D-11CF-AC36-00AA00A47DD2"
    codebase="c:\windows\system\ietimer.ocx"
    WIDTH=80
    HEIGHT=30 >
    <param name="Interval" value="1000">
    <param name="Enabled" value="False">
</OBJECT>

<br><br><br><br><br>
<FORM>
<input type=button value="Toggle the timer"
        align=middle name="Btn_Timer">
</FORM>

<script language="VBS">
<!--
    dim ClickNum

    function IsMoreThan9(TheNum)
        if TheNum > 9 then
            IsMoreThan9 = true
        else
            IsMoreThan9 = false
        end if
    end function

    sub timer1_timer
        if IsMoreThan9(ClickNum) then
            ClickNum = ClickNum + 5
```

```
        else
            ClickNum = ClickNum + 1
        end if
        label1.caption = ClickNum
    end sub

    sub Btn_Timer_OnClick
        ClickNum = 0
        label1.caption = ClickNum
        timer1.enabled = not timer1.enabled
    end sub

-->
</script>
</BODY>
</HTML>
```

This listing differs from the previous listing in two ways: First, we've added a function called **IsMoreThan9**(). Second, we've incorporated that function into the body of the timer event sub. Let's see how each of these changes works. The new function is shown in the following code snippet:

```
function IsMoreThan9(TheNum)
    if TheNum > 9 then
        IsMoreThan9 = true
    else
        IsMoreThan9 = false
    end if
end function
```

If you have any programming experience, this is pretty simple stuff. The function takes a single parameter, **TheNum**: The parameter is how we get the **ClickNum** variable inside the function. It's kind of a specialized doorway. Inside the function, an **if…else** statement checks to see if **TheNum** (the *nom de voyage* under which **ClickNum** is known inside the sub) is greater than 9. If it is, the **if** statement assigns the value **true** to the function. If any part of the program looks at the function, it will now see only the value **true** where the function is supposed to be.

On the other hand, if **TheNum** is less than or equal to 9, the **else** clause kicks in and sets the function to a value of **false**. And if any part of the program looks at the function, it will see only the value **false**.

Now, let's see how the function is incorporated into the event sub for the timer. The code is shown in the following snippet:

```
sub timer1_timer
    if IsMoreThan9(ClickNum) then
        ClickNum = ClickNum + 5
    else
        ClickNum = ClickNum + 1
    end if
    label1.caption = ClickNum
end sub
```

Notice that although there were several lines of code *inside* the **IsMoreThan9()** function, the actual *use* of the function is baby simple. In the timer event code, the **if** clause passes a value to the **IsMoreThan9()** function—i.e., the **ClickNum** variable. The function, using its internal code, looks at this value and determines if it's more than 9. If it's more than 9, the function tells the timer sub, "Yes, this value sure is more than 9"—in other words, it returns a value of **true** in the **if** clause.

We'll cover **if** clauses in more detail later in the book, but it should be obvious what's going on here. If **ClickNum**'s current value is more than 9—that is, if **IsMoreThan9()** returns a value of **true**—then the timer event adds 5 to the **ClickNum** variable. If **ClickNum** isn't over 9, and **IsMoreThan9()** returns a value of **false**, then we drop down to the **else** clause, and the timer event adds only 1 to the **ClickNum** variable.

Finally, as before, the timer event sub assigns the current value of **ClickNum** to the label control's **caption** property. This causes the current value of **ClickNum** to display on the Web page, making it look as if the page is counting 1-2-3... then 10-15-20... and so on.

Well, that's your introduction to ActiveX, subs, and functions. Try experimenting with these listings yourself. Change the interval property of the timer control and other initial values. Try creating a function that tests **ClickNum** in a different way.

Once you've played with them a little, you'll have a head start on understanding and using not only ActiveX controls, but VBScript subs and functions.

Data, Variables, and Constants

In this chapter, you'll learn about some building blocks of a VBScript program: data, variables, and constants. Armed with that knowledge, you can start creating your own VBScript programs right away!

Now that you've seen a few simple examples of how VBScript works in practice, it's time to buckle down and learn at least the basics of the language.

Yes, it's true: Writing real programs is a lot more fun, just as chatting up French actress Charlotte Gainsbourg ("*Bonsoir, mademoiselle, vous êtes très belle*") is a lot more fun than memorizing the forms of French words. In both cases, however, a little preliminary study is essential. Without it, you might write a VBScript program that doesn't work, or tell Ms. Gainsbourg that she's *beau* instead of *belle* and get your face slapped for using the masculine form of the adjective.

In this chapter, we'll start with a simple concept—*data*—and see where it leads us.

Data In Visual Basic Script

Data is, well, simply information. Your name is an item of data (a "datum"); so are your phone number, your street address, your age, and your weight—although those last two items might be considered *private* data.

One of the main occupations of any computer program in any language is to get data from someplace, massage it, and then hand it back to someone. Visual Basic Script programs are no exception. Let's go back to the version of the "Howdy" program that, in Chapter 2, got the user's name and then displayed it in a message box. For your convenience, the program code is reproduced in Listing 3.1. You've already seen the HTML code that surrounds the VBScript code, so I won't bore you with it again.

Listing 3.1 AN EXAMPLE OF USING DATA IN VBSCRIPT.

```
<script language="VBScript">
<!--
    dim UserName ' declare variable to hold user's name

    Sub Btn_HelloWorld_OnClick
        UserName = TB_UserName.value
        MsgBox "Howdy, " & Username & "!",0,"VBScript Example"
    End Sub
-->
</script>
```

The Web page containing this VBScript code displayed a text box, named **TB_UserName**, in which the user could type his/her name. The name, of course, is data. But once we've got the name from the user, we need someplace to put it so that our VBScript program can refer to it as needed.

That "place" is provided by a *variable,* which is essentially just a little box where VBScript can store data until it's needed by the program. Once you've "declared" the variable by using the **dim** statement—more about that in a moment—you can put things in it. Normally, a variable can only hold one thing at a time, but there are exceptions. If the program needs to look at the data, it just uses the variable's name, which is also the name of the data it contains.

In concept, that's really all there is to it. As usual, however, there's more of the story waiting to be told.

Data Types

Items of data represent aspects of the real world, and just like the real world, data comes in different types. In the real world, there are animals, vegetables, and minerals; uptunes and ballads; PCs and Macintoshes; Democrats and Republicans. In the computer world, there are whole numbers, decimal numbers, text strings, true/false values, and lots of other types of data.

The reason for having different types of things—whether in the real world or in a computer program—is for efficiency. Once we know what type of thing we're dealing with, we have a fair idea of how to deal with it. If someone hands us a rock, we know that we don't have to experiment to find out if it's good to eat; if someone hands us a cupcake, we know immediately that it *is* good to eat (even if it's not good *for* us). Similarly, if a computer program knows that something is a text string, it won't bother trying to add it as if it were a number.

When you declare a variable (or constant) in a computer program, you normally have to specify what data type it's supposed to be. For example, you might declare different types of variables as shown in the following code lines:

```
dim UserName as String
dim Weight as Integer
dim Price as Currency
dim NumberOfStars as Long
```

Visual Basic Script (and Visual Basic itself) simplify the situation considerably by having an all-purpose data type called the *variant* type. A variant-type variable can hold any type of data. That's why, in Listing 3.1, it wasn't necessary to specify a data type for the **UserName** variable. All we had to do was declare it:

```
dim UserName
```

Now, Visual Basic proper has the variant data type *in addition to* several other official data types. VBScript, however, has *only* the variant type as an official data type. If the data in a variable looks like it's a number, VBScript treats it as a number; if it looks like text, VBScript treats it as text. Listing 3.2 shows a simple example of using different kinds of data and putting them in variant-type variables. Figure 3.1 shows the Web page created by the HTML code in Listing 3.2.

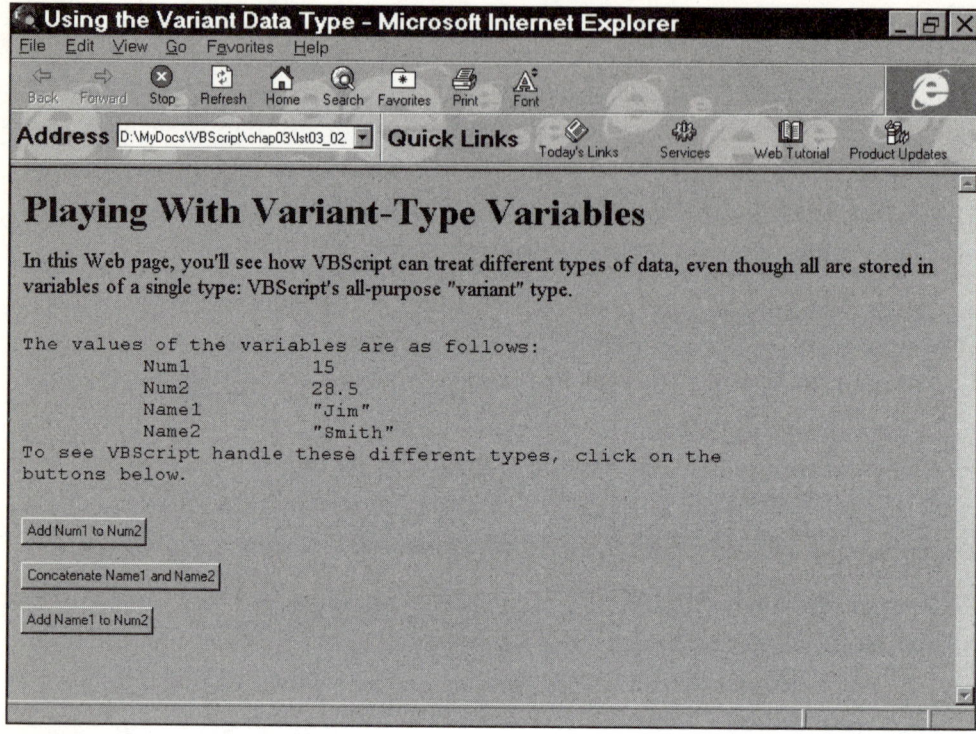

Figure 3.1
The Web page created by Listing 3.2.

Listing 3.2 THE VARIANT TYPE AUTOMATICALLY HANDLES DIFFERENT KINDS OF DATA.

```
<HTML>
<HEAD>
<TITLE>Using the Variant Data Type</TITLE>
</HEAD>
<BODY>
<H1>Playing With Variant-Type Variables</H1>
<font size=4>
<p>In this Web page, you'll see how VBScript can treat
different types of data, even though all are stored in
variables of a single type: VBScript's all-purpose
"variant" type.</p>
<pre>
The values of the variables are as follows:
        Num1            15
        Num2            28.5
        Name1           "Jim"
        Name2           "Smith"
```

Data, Variables, And Constants

To see how VBScript handles these different types, click on the buttons below.

```
</pre>
<br>
<FORM>
<INPUT TYPE="button" name="Btn_AddNums"
        value="Add Num1 to Num2"><br><br>
<INPUT TYPE="button" name="Btn_ConcatNames"
        value="Concatenate Name1 and Name2"><br><br>
<INPUT TYPE="button" name="Btn_AddNameNum"
        value="Add Name1 to Num2">
</FORM>

<script language="vbs">

<!--
' declare variables to hold numbers
dim Num1, Num2

' declare variables to hold text
dim Name1, Name2

'assign values to the variables
Num1 = 15
Num2 = 28.5

Name1 = "Jim"
Name2 = "Smith"

sub Btn_AddNums_OnClick()
    dim total
    total = Num1 + Num2
    MsgBox "The total is " _
        & total & ".",,"Numbers added!"
end sub

sub Btn_ConcatNames_OnClick()
    dim fullname
    fullname = Name1 & " " & Name2
    MsgBox "The person's full name is " _
        & fullname & ".",,"Name assembled!"
end sub

sub Btn_AddNameNum_OnClick()
    dim NameNum
    NameNum = Name1 + Num2
    MsgBox "The sum is " _
        & NameNum & ".",,"What happened?"
```

```
end sub
-->
</script>

</BODY>
</HTML>
```

Inside The Data Types Program

The program in Listing 3.2 performs some fairly simple—but revealing—tasks. As you can see, the HTML code sets up three command buttons. When each one is clicked, it tells VBScript to carry out the corresponding **OnClick** sub, as defined in the script code.

The script code itself uses **dim** statements to declare four variables, *all* of the variant data type. The two variables meant to hold numbers are named **Num1** and **Num2**, while the two variables meant to hold text strings are named **Name1** and **Name2**. Naturally, VBScript attaches no significance to those variable names: We could quite easily use **Num1** to hold a text value or **Name2** to hold a number.

Declaring Multiple Variables In One Statement

Notice that Listing 3.2 declares the **Num1** and **Num2** variables with a single **dim** statement, and uses another single **dim** statement to declare the **Name1** and **Name2** variables. This is a trick from Visual Basic: If several variables are of the same type, you can declare them all in one **dim** statement, as long as you separate the variable names by inserting commas between them.

In this case, of course, *all* the variables are of the same type—variant—so it really wasn't necessary to declare the **Num** and **Name** variables in separate **dim** statements. There are only two good reasons to do so. First, it makes the code easier to understand, because variables meant to hold different types of values are declared separately. Second, it just feels more comfortable for an old Visual Basic programmer who's used to doing things that way.

Once the variables are declared ("**dim**ensioned"), the script loads values into them. One of the variables gets a whole number, another gets a decimal number, and two get text strings, as shown in the following code snippet:

```
Num1 = 15
Num2 = 28.5

Name1 = "Jim"
Name2 = "Smith"
```

Now, part of our purpose here is to prove that VBScript *really does* automatically decide what type of data a variable contains. If VBScript knows that **Num1** and **Num2** contain numbers, while **Name1** and **Name2** contain text, then we should be able to do arithmetic with one and string concatenation (or "glomming," to use the technical term) with the other. Let's see if it works.

The **OnClick** event code for the first button attempts to add **Num1** to **Num2**, as shown in the following code snippet:

```
sub Btn_AddNums_OnClick()
    dim total
    total = Num1 + Num2
    MsgBox "The total is " _
        & total & ".",,"Numbers added!"
end sub
```

First, inside the **sub**, we declare the "local" variable **total** to hold the total of the two numbers. As a local variable, it can only be seen and used by code inside the **sub** where it's declared. Then, we add the values of **Num1** and **Num2**: This is the part that will only work if VBScript knows that the values are numbers. Finally, we assign the sum to the **total** variable and use **total** in a message box statement to display the result. The process succeeds, as shown in Figure 3.2.

Likewise, the **OnClick** event code for the second button attempts to concatenate the two text values "Jim" and "Smith," which have been assigned to the **Name1** and **Name2** variables. It uses the same method as the previous **sub**, as shown in the following code snippet:

Figure 3.2
VBScript adds two variables containing numbers.

```
sub Btn_ConcatNames_OnClick()
    dim fullname
    fullname = Name1 & " " & Name2
    MsgBox "The person's full name is " _
        & fullname & ".",,"Name assembled!"
end sub
```

As before, the process works like a charm. The result is shown in Figure 3.3.

Finally, the event code for the third button tries to do something that should be impossible (that is, if VBScript really *does* keep track of the data types stored in variant-type variables). It tries to add the text stored in **Name1** to the number stored in **Num2**, as shown in the following code snippet:

```
sub Btn_AddNameNum_OnClick()
    dim NameNum
    NameNum = Name1 + Num2
    MsgBox "The sum is " _
        & NameNum & ".",,"What happened?"
end sub
```

Will it succeed? Not on your life. The result is shown in Figure 3.4. VBScript really does keep track of the data type of values stored in variant-type variables.

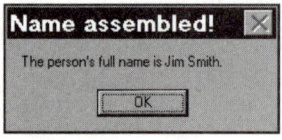

Figure 3.3
VBScript concatenates two text strings.

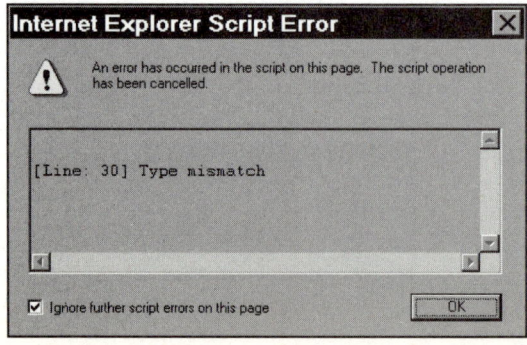

Figure 3.4
VBScript flags an error when the code tries to add text to a number.

One point should be mentioned before we move on. In this example, we've assigned values to variables by using what are called "literal" values—e.g., numbers and text strings, as shown in the following code snippet:

```
Num1 = 15
Num2 = 28.5

Name1 = "Jim"
Name2 = "Smith"
```

That's only one way to assign values to variables. The other, very common way to assign values to variables is to assign the value of one variable to another variable, as shown in the following code snippet:

```
Num1 = Num2
Num2 = Name1

Name1 = Name2
Name2 = Num1
```

Here, the first statement takes whatever value is in **Num2** and copies it into **Num1**. The value in **Num2** is left undisturbed by this process. Likewise, the second statement copies the current value of **Name1** into **Num2**, and so on. If we had started out with the values assigned in the previous code snippet, here's how the variables would have ended up:

- Num1 now has the value 28.5.
- Num2 now has the value "Jim".
- Name1 now has the value "Smith".
- Name2 now has the value 28.5 (because we changed the value of Num1 in the first line of code).

Making The Code More Efficient

For now, at least, nobody is going to accuse VBScript of being a speed demon. However, there's one thing we can do to make the program in Listing 3.2 run just a bit faster. Notice that in each **OnClick** sub, Listing 3.2 declares a separate variable to hold the result of the addition or concatenation, as shown in the following code snippet:

```
sub Btn_ConcatNames_OnClick()
    dim fullname
    fullname = Name1 & " " & Name2
    MsgBox "The person's full name is " _
        & fullname & ".",,"Name assembled!"
end sub
```

Now, this has the advantage of being a simple and straightforward way to handle the situation. You need to display the full name, so you create a variable to hold it. However, declaring the **fullname** variable and loading it with a value takes two lines of VBScript code that we really don't need. And each of those lines requires a small but finite amount of time to execute. The routine will run a little faster if we can get rid of them.

Fortunately, it's pretty easy, and if you're already a veteran programmer, you guessed the answer as soon as we asked the question. It's shown in the following code snippet:

```
sub Btn_ConcatNames_OnClick()
    MsgBox "The person's full name is " _
        & Name1 & " " & Name2 _
        & ".",,"Name assembled!"
end sub
```

All we had to do was drop the extra variable and concatenate the first and last names in the **MsgBox** statement itself—thus saving two steps and a couple of milliseconds.

You might be tempted to try the same thing with the routine that adds two numbers, shown in the following code snippet:

```
sub Btn_AddNums_OnClick()
    MsgBox "The total is " _
        Num1 + Num2 & total & _
        ".",,"Numbers added!"
end sub
```

Unfortunately, that requires more than just concatenating two text strings. It requires doing arithmetic, and the **MsgBox** statement isn't quite that smart. For dealing with numbers, you'll still need the extra two program statements.

VBScript "Data Subtypes"

Even though Visual Basic Script has only the variant type as an official data type, other types are "snuck in" as *subtypes* of the variant type. It's these subtypes that VBScript uses when it automatically determines the data type of the value in a variable. The data subtypes are shown in Table 3.1.

Declaring Variables

Declaring variables in VBScript is a fairly simple affair, but there are a few things you need to know.

TABLE 3.1

Data subtypes in VBScript.

Subtype	Explanation
Empty	No value has been put in the variable. If you're treating the variable as a number type, then the empty value is 0 (zero). For a text type variable, it's an empty string ("").
Null	A value has been assigned to the variable, but it's an empty value. The variable contains no data.
Boolean	A true or false value.
Byte	An integer in the range 0 to 255.
Integer	An integer in the range -32,768 to +32,767.
Long	An integer in the range -2,147,483,648 to +2,147,483,647.
Single	A single-precision floating point (decimal) number in a range so vast that it's almost meaningless.
Double	A double-precision floating point (decimal) number in a range even vaster than the single subtype.
Date	A number that represents a date between January 1, 100 and December 31, 9999.
String	A text string of up to two billion characters in length, limited only by your hardware.
Object	An OLE automation object for running other programs inside VBScript.
Error	An error number for catching program malfunctions.

First, in VBScript (and Visual Basic), there are two ways to declare a variable: *explicitly* and *implicitly*. You declare a variable explicitly when you name it in a **dim** statement, as we've seen many times already:

```
dim TheNum
```

But you can also declare a variable implicitly, simply by using a new variable name in your VBScript code. The following code lines give a couple of examples:

```
EinNummer = 15
MeinName = "Scott"
```

Those two code lines implicitly declare the variables **EinNummer** and **MeinName**, even if they're not set up with **dim** statements anywhere else in the code.

Using **option explicit**

There's a way to make VBScript reject any implicit variable declarations and require that all variables be "officially" declared through **dim** statements. That way is to put the code **option explicit** as the very first line in your Visual Basic script, as shown in the following code snippet:

```
<script language="vbs">
<!--
option explicit
```

When you include this line at the top of your code, VBScript won't allow any implicit variable declarations. If you have a VBScript program of more than half a page, it's a very good idea to include **option explicit** as a safeguard.

option explicit Only Applies To The Current Script
When you put **option explicit** at the top of a script, it only applies within that script—i.e., only within that pair of **<script>...</script>** tags: Other scripts in your HTML document are unaffected. To get the full benefit of **option explicit**, you must either put all your VBScript code into one script or put **option explicit** at the top of every script in your HTML document.

Now, you might be a little puzzled. If you don't want any implicit variable declarations, why not just refrain from making any? The answer is that if you make an implicit variable declaration *on purpose,* it's not very likely to cause problems—although it might.

You don't need **option explicit** to keep yourself from deliberately making implicit variable declarations. You do, however, need it to keep yourself from *accidentally* making implicit declarations. That's where problems usually arise. Suppose that your finger slips on the keyboard and you type a variable name incorrectly in an assignment statement. Presto! You've just created a new variable, assigned a value to it, and *failed* to assign a value to the variable to which you *thought* you were assigning a value. Your program will malfunction because it expects to get the original variable with a certain value. When you look at the code, 9 times out of 10 you'll miss the typo in the variable name.

The bottom line is that accidental implicit declarations can cause program bugs that are maddeningly hard to identify. **Option explicit** protects you from those bugs.

Declaring Constants

Program constants are useful because they give you easy-to-remember words that stand for particular values. For instance, you might use the constant **max_balance** to stand for the maximum allowable account balance for your Web customers.

Besides being easy to remember, constants give you a way to make "global" changes in your program without having to comb through your code. Suppose that you used a literal value for the maximum balance, such as 1000. If you wanted to increase the maximum balance to 1500, you would have to look through your code, find every occurrence of 1000, and change all of them to 1500—unless, of course, a particular occurrence of 1000 stood for something else, such as a particular customer's *actual* account balance.

If you used a constant, however, you need only change the value of the constant. Then, every place in your code where the constant is used, the value changes automatically.

The original version of VBScript, as a stripped-down version of Visual Basic, didn't have any built-in support for creating constants. VBScript 2, however, has a **const** keyword that works the same as in "regular" Visual Basic, so you can declare real-live constants in your programs:

```
const Max_Balance = 1000
const pi = 3.14159
```

Naming Variables And Other Program Elements

When you name variables, you must follow the same rules that apply to naming anything else in your VBScript program. Upper- and lowercase are not significant, so the variable names **SlotNum**, **SLOTNUM**, and **SloTnuM** are all treated as the same. In VBScript, a variable name:

- Must begin with a letter
- Can't contain a period
- Can't exceed 255 characters in length
- Must be unique within its scope

All those requirements should be pretty clear, except for the last one: "Must be unique within its scope." Scope is explained in the next section.

Table 3.2 shows a few examples of legal and illegal variable names.

Scope Of Variables And Constants

In the discussion of Listing 3.2, one issue came up that shouldn't be passed over: *scope*. In a computer program, all identifiers—that is, names for things in the program—have a particular scope. The scope of an identifier is the part of the program in which it can be seen and used. If it can't be seen and used in a particular part of the program, an identifier is said to be "out of scope."

A variable declared *inside* a sub or function can't be seen or used by any code outside the sub or function. When we declared a **total** variable inside the **OnClick** sub for one of the buttons, it could not be seen anywhere outside the sub.

Table 3.2
Some examples of legal and illegal variable names.

Variable Name	Legal?	Explanation
MyNum	Yes	Starts with a letter, contains no periods, not too long
2LiveCrew	No	Doesn't start with a letter; no talent
Doo.Be.Doo.Be	No	Contains periods and gratuitous Sinatra reference
Eeee_yaaaah	Yes	Underscore character is legal; accidentally dropped a Chevy on my foot

That means we could use the same variable name anywhere outside the sub, and VBScript would have no chance of getting confused. Inside the sub, it would know that **total** always refers to the local variable declared inside the sub; outside the sub, **total** would refer to whichever variable named **total** had been declared in that part of the program.

A discussion of scope can get messy, so let's boil it down to a few rules of thumb:

- A variable (or constant) declared inside a sub or function can only be seen inside that sub or function.

- A variable (or constant) declared outside of any sub or function can be seen by any code anywhere in the program, as long as the code comes *after* the declaration in the program listing. In other words, you can't use a variable or constant before it's been declared.

- If a variable (or constant) will only be used inside one sub or function, then it should be declared as a local variable inside that sub or function. Otherwise—if it must be used by more than one part of the program—a variable (or constant) should be declared at the top of your Visual Basic script as a "global" program element.

Declaring And Using Arrays

In addition to the simple data types already discussed, VBScript lets you define and use complex data types called *arrays*. The best way to think of an array is as a sort of "rack" having a predetermined number of slots that can hold data items, as shown in Figure 3.5.

In the figure, you can see how arrays differ from normal variables. A normal variable holds just one value, such as "Kelly" or 3.14159. An array can hold multiple values of the same type, such as "Jim," "Cindy," "Brandon," and "Brenda," which are all Walshes, I mean, text strings.

In an array, each slot has a number, and the first slot gets the number 0 (zero). To refer to a particular slot in the array, you just use the name of the array, then the slot number in parentheses.

Chapter 3

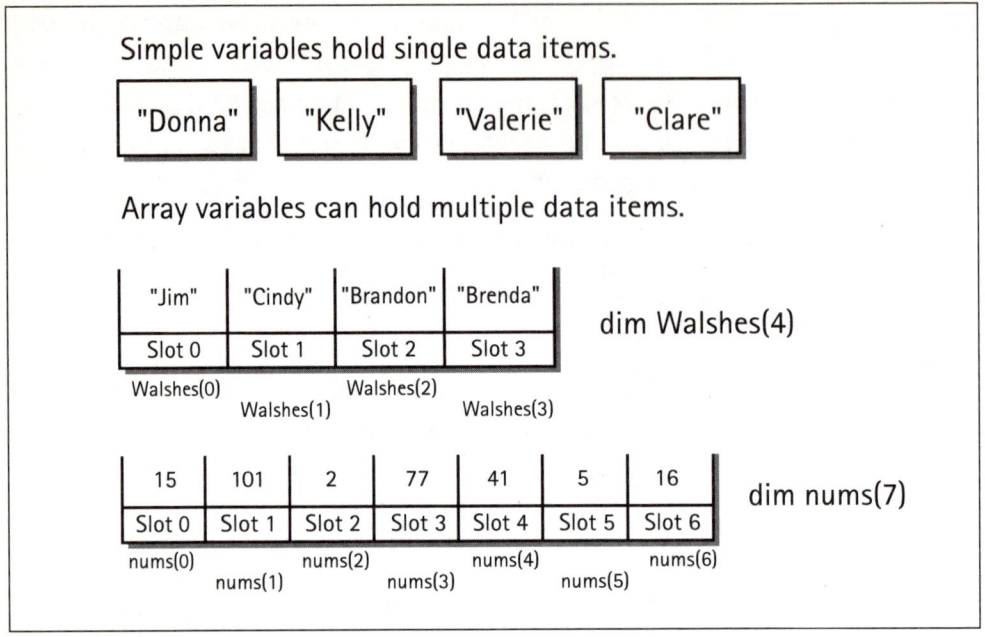

Figure 3.5
An array variable is like a rack with slots to hold values.

 Don't Forget That The First Slot Is Numbered Zero

Don't forget that the first slot in a VBScript array is numbered zero—not 1. That means if you want to go from the beginning to the end of a 10-slot array (called "traversing" the array), you start at slot 0. Regular Visual Basic lets you number the first slot 1 instead of 0, but VBScript doesn't.

If you're an experienced programmer, there's one more "gotcha." In most languages, if you create a 10-element array and the slots start at 0, then the slots go from 0 to 9. In VBScript, if you declare a 10-element array, the slots go from 0 to 10—i.e., there are actually 11 elements. It doesn't actually hurt if you do it "the normal way" and assume that a 10-slot array has slots numbered 0 to 9: All it means is that you have that extra array slot on the end, unemployed.

To declare an array variable, you simply use a normal **dim** statement. After the variable name, however, you add a left parenthesis, the number of slots you want in the array, and a right parenthesis, as shown in the following code line:

```
dim NumArray(10)
```

The parentheses and number mark the variable as being an array. Once you've declared the array, you can refer to individual array slots just as if they were "standalone" variables. To refer to an array slot—or to the value it contains—you simply use the name of the array with the desired slot number in parentheses. In Figure 3.5, for instance, **Walshes(2)** is the third slot in the first array and has a value of "Brandon," while **nums(6)** is the seventh slot in the second array and has a value of 16.

Assigning Values To Array Slots

You assign values to slots in an array just as if they were individual variables, by using the VBScript assignment operator. The following code line, for example, assigns the value "Andrea" to slot 3 of the **Walshes** array:

```
Walshes(3) = "Andrea"
```

One advantage of arrays is that if you want to assign values that bear some relation to each other, you can often use a VBScript **for...next** loop (covered in Chapter 4) to do so. This is shown in the following code snippet:

```
for loopcounter = 0 to 6
     nums(loopcounter) = 0
next
```

Such loops are usually used to initialize (set initial values for) arrays, particularly when the initial values are null, such as 0 (for arrays of numbers) or "" (for arrays of text strings).

Once an array's slots are loaded with values, you can use any one of those values simply by using the name of the array with the appropriate slot number. For example, the following code line shows how you might use the value in slot 0 of Figure 3.5's **Walshes** array:

```
MsgBox "The father of Brandon & Brenda is " & Walshes(0) & "."
```

Last but not least, you can *change* the value in an array slot in exactly the same way as you'd change the value of any other variable. Just use the array slot on the left side of an assignment statement. If the current value of **Walshes(0)** is "Jim," you could change it as shown in the following code line:

```
Walshes(0) = "Larry Mollin"
```

52   Chapter 3

No "Record" Type In VBScript
If you're a Visual Basic programmer who likes to use the **type...end type** construct to declare data types that correspond to Pascal **record**s and C **struct**s, you're in for a mild disappointment. Visual Basic Script doesn't have the **type...end type** construct, and you cannot create those data types in VBScript. This limitation of the original VBScript is still there in VBScript 2.

A Simple Array Demonstration

Let's conclude this chapter with a look at how you might load and use a simple array in VBScript. Listing 3.3 shows how you would declare an array, set its initial values, and then access those values to display them in a message box. Figure 3.6 shows the Web page created by the code in Listing 3.3.

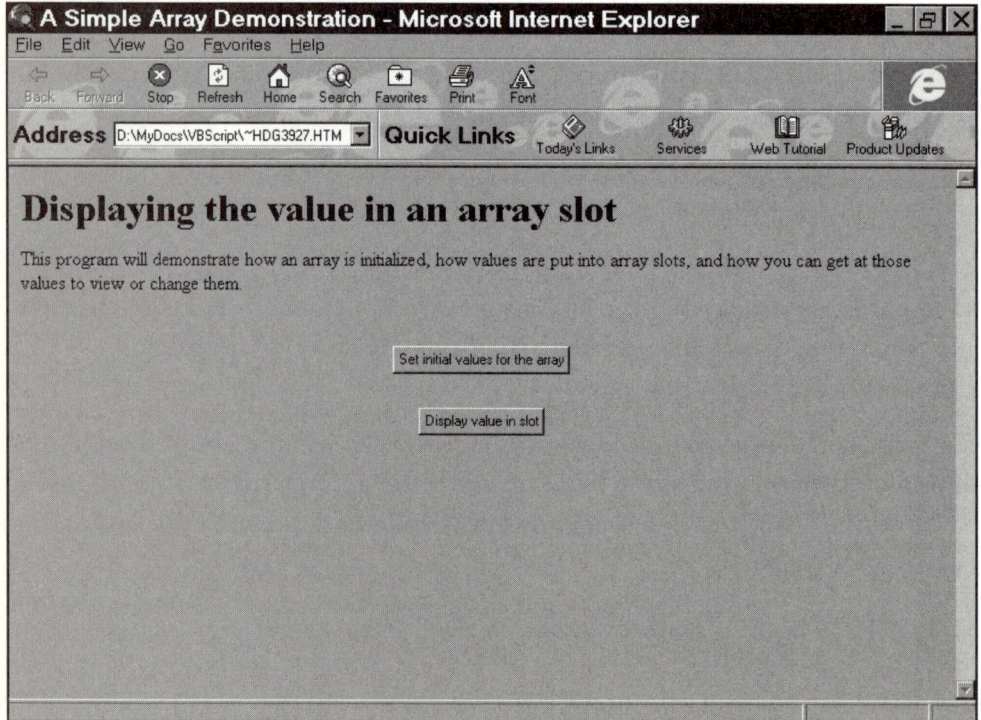

Figure 3.6
The Web page created by Listing 3.3.

Listing 3.3 A SIMPLE ARRAY DEMONSTRATION.

```
<HTML>
<HEAD>
<TITLE>A Simple Array Demonstration</TITLE>
</HEAD>
<BODY>
<H1>Displaying the value in an array slot</H1>
<P>This program will demonstrate how an array is
initialized, how values are put into array slots, and
how you can get at those values to view or change
them.</p>
<center>
<FORM>
<br><br>
<INPUT NAME="Btn_SetupArray"
    TYPE="BUTTON"
    value="Set initial values for the array">
    <br><br><br>

<INPUT NAME="Btn_DisplayVal"
    TYPE="BUTTON"
    value="Display value in slot">
</center>
</FORM>

<script language="VBS">
<!--
option explicit
dim AnArray(10)
dim SlotNum

sub Btn_SetupArray_OnClick()
    dim loopcounter

    for loopcounter = 0 to 9
        AnArray(loopcounter) = _
            (loopcounter * 2)
    next
    slotnum = 0
end sub

sub Btn_DisplayVal_OnClick()
    MsgBox "The value in slot number " _
        & SlotNum & " is " & AnArray(SlotNum) _
        & ".",,"Array Demo"
```

```
        if slotnum < 9 then
                slotnum = slotnum + 1
        else
                slotnum = 0
        end if
end sub

-->
</script>

</BODY>
</HTML>
```

Inside The Array Code

Let's see how the code in Listing 3.3 uses the array techniques we've discussed. By now, the HTML techniques should be familiar: We set up two buttons on the Web page; one initializes the array and the other displays the value in a given array slot.

At the top of the script, we put **option explicit** as a safeguard (though it's not really needed in a program this size). Then, as shown in the following code snippet, we declare two global variables, which have to be global because they're used by more than one sub:

```
<script language="VBS">
<!--
option explicit
dim AnArray(10)
dim SlotNum
```

One of the global variables, of course, is our array. It has 10 slots, numbered from 0 to 9. The second global variable, **SlotNum**, will help us keep track of which array slot we're using at the moment.

The first sub is the **OnClick** event procedure for the button that initializes the array, shown in the following code snippet:

```
sub Btn_SetupArray_OnClick()
        dim loopcounter

        for loopcounter = 0 to 9
            AnArray(loopcounter) = _
                (loopcounter * 2)
```

```
        next
    slotnum = 0
end sub
```

It first declares a local **loopcounter** variable to use with the **for...next** loop that will actually insert values into the array slots. The **loopcounter** variable is declared locally inside this sub, instead of as a global variable, because it's used *only* inside this sub.

The loop to load values into the array slots is a standard **for...next** loop. On the first pass through the loop, the value of **loopcounter** is 0, so **AnArray(loopcounter)** refers to the first slot in the array. As you can see, the assignment statement—here, split with the VBScript line continuation character (_) to stay within the book's page margins—assigns the value **loopcounter * 2** (the value of **loopcounter** times 2) to the current array slot. At the **next** line, the value of **loopcounter** gets increased by 1, and we go back to the top of the **for...next** loop to run through it again.

The whole process continues until the value of **loopcounter** gets to 9. At that point, we run through the loop a final time, assigning the value 18 to the array slot **AnArray(9)**. Then we drop out of the loop and move to the code line below the **next** statement. The value of the **SlotNum** variable is set to zero, and we're ready to display values in the array slots.

To display the values in the array slots, we move on to the **OnClick** event procedure for the Btn_DisplayValue button. This is shown in the following code snippet:

```
sub Btn_DisplayVal_OnClick()
    MsgBox "The value in slot number " _
        & SlotNum & " is " & AnArray(SlotNum) _
        & ".",,"Array Demo"
    if slotnum < 9 then
        slotnum = slotnum + 1
    else
        slotnum = 0
    end if
end sub
```

Once again, VBScript line continuation characters have been used here to keep the code lines within the page margins of the book: You don't need to use them in your own code.

The first part of the sub is a simple **MsgBox** statement. It displays the text "The value in slot number" and concatenates that text with:

- The **SlotNum** variable, meaning that the current value of **SlotNum** will be displayed in the message box
- The **AnArray(SlotNum)** array slot, meaning that whatever value is in that array slot will be displayed in the message box

After the **MsgBox** statement, we get to an interesting little construct called an **if...else** statement, which will be explained fully in Chapter 4. Here, however, what it does is pretty simple:

- If the current value of **SlotNum** is less than 9, the first part of the **if** statement adds 1 to the value of **SlotNum**. This means that the next time the user clicks the button, the message box will display the value of the *next* array slot.
- If the current value of **SlotNum** is not less than 9, the second part of the **if** statement (the **else** clause) sets the value of **SlotNum** back to 0. This means that the next time the user clicks the button, the message box will again display the value in the first array slot, and the cycle can start over again.

And that's pretty much it! Experiment with your own data, variables, and constants so that you get a feel for how they work. In Chapter 4, we'll take an in-depth look at the different kinds of statements you can use in VBScript, as well as the operators and expressions that make those statements work.

4

Operators And Expressions

Data and variables are the building blocks of a VBScript program: Operators and expressions are the glue that holds them together. In this chapter, you'll learn how to use VBScript operators to create expressions that use your data and variables.

Depending on your personal proclivities, the word "operator" might suggest different things to you. If you're a *Saturday Night Live* fan, it might call up an image of Lily Tomlin doing her character as the prissy telephone operator. If you're a political animal, it might make you think of Hillary Clinton.

But if you're a programmer, operators mean something else entirely. If data and variables are the bricks of a VBScript program, operators are the mortar that binds them together into expressions—and expressions are the control switches that the program uses to decide what it should do or how it should display information. With operators and expressions, you're on your way to performing truly amazing tricks with VBScript and ActiveX technology.

What Are Operators?

Operators aren't anything exotic: You use them every day. If you say, "I'll go to the store or shave the cat," you've just used **or**, which is a VBScript logical operator. If you add up your grocery bill, calculate the sales tax, and then add up the total, you've used two more VBScript operators: addition (+) and real-number division (/), which are—you guessed it—arithmetic operators. And if you say something really strange, like, "If my purse matches my shoes, then I have a color-coordinated outfit," you've used two more VBScript operators: equality (=), which is a relational operator, and implication (**imp**), which is another logical operator.

Operators apply to *terms,* which are sometimes also called *arguments*. For example, consider this use of the addition operator:

```
a + b
```

In this example, the operator is + (addition), while the terms are *a* and *b*. The whole thing, operator plus terms, is an *expression*. And terms don't have to be simple: A term can be an expression itself, as in the following example:

```
((a + b) / c) + d
```

Here, the first term is the expression *((a + b) / c)*—that is, the sum of *a* and *b*, divided by *c*. The second term is *d*. And the operator, again, is +. As before, the whole thing forms an expression. The situation is illustrated in Figure 4.1.

Most operators are *binary,* which means that they take two terms. The negation operator, however, only takes one term. It's called a *monadic* operator, and it reverses the value of the term to which it's applied. The negation operator is explained later in this chapter.

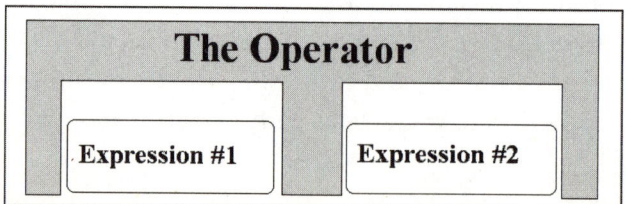

Figure 4.1
How an operator works with terms.

Expressions Have Values

Just like individual variables, constants, and literal values, expressions have values. If you took algebra, it's easy for you to see that if you plug in certain values for *a, b, c,* and *d,* then *((a + b) / c) + d* will have a specific value that depends on them. That example, of course, is familiar, but non-arithmetic expressions have values, too. Consider the following logical expression:

```
It is raining imp The streets are wet
```

This uses the implication operator **imp** to make what amounts to a causal statement: *If* it's raining, *then* the streets are wet. And this whole statement is an expression with a value, just as much as *a + b* is an expression with a value. The only difference is that *a + b* is an arithmetic expression using an arithmetic operator, and it will have an arithmetic value.

The expression *It is raining* **imp** *The streets are wet* is a logical expression and will have a logical value of **true** (which in VBScript is -1) or **false** (which in VBScript is 0). And just as you determine the value of *a + b* by looking at the values of its terms, so you look at the truth-values of *It is raining* and *The streets are wet* to determine if the whole expression is true or false. In the particular case of logical implication—don't worry, we'll come back to it later in the chapter—the whole expression is true unless the antecedent (*It is raining*) is true while the consequent (*The streets are wet*) is false.

But that's all abstract discussion. Let's talk about the specific operators and how they're used to create expressions. As you work through several examples, you'll get a better understanding of both individual operators and the concept of operators in general.

Arithmetic Operators

Arithmetic operators, unsurprisingly, are those used with arithmetical and algebraic expressions in VBScript. The arithmetic operators are summarized in Table 4.1.

Let's see how the more important arithmetic operators are applied in VBScript programs.

TABLE 4.1
ARITHMETIC OPERATORS IN VBSCRIPT.

Operator	Meaning	Example
+	Addition	a + b
-	Subtraction	a - b
*	Multiplication	a * b
/	Division	a / b
\	Integer Division	a \ b (always yields an integer result, discarding any decimal part)
mod	Modulus	a mod b gives the integer remainder from dividing a by b
-	Arithmetical Negation	–a reverses the sign of a
^	Exponentiation	a^b is a raised to the power of b
&	Concatenation	"The " & "Cat" equals "The Cat". Not really an arithmetic operator, but shoved into that category because it doesn't fit anywhere else.

Addition, Subtraction, And Multiplication

Our first example is a simple one: Just add some numbers. As usual, it's a little more complicated to do it in a Web page than it is just to use your fingers. Listing 4.1 shows how the VBScript code is set up in the HTML document. Figure 4.2 shows the Web page created by the code. For the checkboxes, we used the Microsoft Forms 2.0 Checkbox ActiveX control.

Listing 4.1 USING THE ADDITION OPERATOR IN VBSCRIPT.

```
<HTML>
<HEAD>
<TITLE>Some Simple Operator Demonstrations</TITLE>
</HEAD>
<BODY>
<H1>Using Simple Arithmetic Operators</H1>
<pre>
    <OBJECT ID="Label1"
     CLASSID="CLSID:978C9E23-D4B0-11CE-BF2D-00AA003F40D0"
     STYLE="TOP:17pt;LEFT:116pt;WIDTH:239pt;
     HEIGHT:41pt;ZINDEX:0;">
        <PARAM NAME="Caption" VALUE="Ordering Some Books">
```

```
            <PARAM NAME="Size" VALUE="8431;1446">
            <PARAM NAME="FontName" VALUE="Times New Roman">
            <PARAM NAME="FontHeight" VALUE="320">
            <PARAM NAME="FontCharSet" VALUE="0">
            <PARAM NAME="FontPitchAndFamily" VALUE="2">
            <PARAM NAME="FontWeight" VALUE="0">
    </OBJECT>

<OBJECT ID="CB_VBS" WIDTH=425 HEIGHT=24
 CLASSID="CLSID:8BD21D40-EC42-11CE-9E0D-00AA006002F3">
        <PARAM NAME="BackColor" VALUE="2147483663">
        <PARAM NAME="ForeColor" VALUE="2147483666">
        <PARAM NAME="DisplayStyle" VALUE="4">
        <PARAM NAME="Size" VALUE="11245;635">
        <PARAM NAME="Value" VALUE="0">
        <PARAM NAME="Caption" VALUE=
            "Visual Developer VBScript &amp; ActiveX Programming, $39.99">
        <PARAM NAME="FontEffects" VALUE="1073741825">
        <PARAM NAME="FontHeight" VALUE="200">
        <PARAM NAME="FontCharSet" VALUE="0">
        <PARAM NAME="FontPitchAndFamily" VALUE="2">
        <PARAM NAME="FontWeight" VALUE="700">
</OBJECT>

<OBJECT ID="CB_VB5OOP" WIDTH=385 HEIGHT=24
 CLASSID="CLSID:8BD21D40-EC42-11CE-9E0D-00AA006002F3">
        <PARAM NAME="BackColor" VALUE="2147483663">
        <PARAM NAME="ForeColor" VALUE="2147483666">
        <PARAM NAME="DisplayStyle" VALUE="4">
        <PARAM NAME="Size" VALUE="10186;635">
        <PARAM NAME="Value" VALUE="0">
        <PARAM NAME="Caption" VALUE=
            "Visual Basic 5 Object-Oriented Programming, $49.99">
        <PARAM NAME="FontEffects" VALUE="1073741825">
        <PARAM NAME="FontHeight" VALUE="200">
        <PARAM NAME="FontCharSet" VALUE="0">
        <PARAM NAME="FontPitchAndFamily" VALUE="2">
        <PARAM NAME="FontWeight" VALUE="700">
</OBJECT>

<OBJECT ID="CB_VB5EXP" WIDTH=339 HEIGHT=24
 CLASSID="CLSID:8BD21D40-EC42-11CE-9E0D-00AA006002F3">
        <PARAM NAME="BackColor" VALUE="2147483663">
        <PARAM NAME="ForeColor" VALUE="2147483666">
        <PARAM NAME="DisplayStyle" VALUE="4">
        <PARAM NAME="Size" VALUE="8943;635">
        <PARAM NAME="Value" VALUE="0">
```

```
        <PARAM NAME="Caption" VALUE=
            "Visual Basic 5 Programming EXplorer, $49.99">
        <PARAM NAME="FontEffects" VALUE="1073741825">
        <PARAM NAME="FontHeight" VALUE="200">
        <PARAM NAME="FontCharSet" VALUE="0">
        <PARAM NAME="FontPitchAndFamily" VALUE="2">
        <PARAM NAME="FontWeight" VALUE="700">
</OBJECT>

<OBJECT ID="Cmd_Subtotal"
CLASSID="CLSID:D7053240-CE69-11CD-A777-00DD01143C57"
STYLE="TOP:182pt;LEFT:140pt;WIDTH:173pt;
    HEIGHT:41pt;TABINDEX:4;ZINDEX:4;">
        <PARAM NAME="Caption" VALUE="Display Subtotal">
        <PARAM NAME="Size" VALUE="6103;1446">
        <PARAM NAME="FontCharSet" VALUE="0">
        <PARAM NAME="FontPitchAndFamily" VALUE="2">
        <PARAM NAME="ParagraphAlign" VALUE="3">
        <PARAM NAME="FontWeight" VALUE="0">
</OBJECT>

</pre>

<script language="VBS">
<!--

dim subtotal

sub Cmd_Subtotal_Click
    subtotal = 0.0
    if CB_VBS then subtotal = subtotal + 39.99
    if CB_VB500P then subtotal = subtotal + 49.99
    if CB_VB5EXP then subtotal = subtotal + 49.99

    MsgBox "The subtotal is currently $" & subtotal & ".",, _
        "Subtotal calculated."

end sub

-->
</script>
</BODY>
</HTML>
```

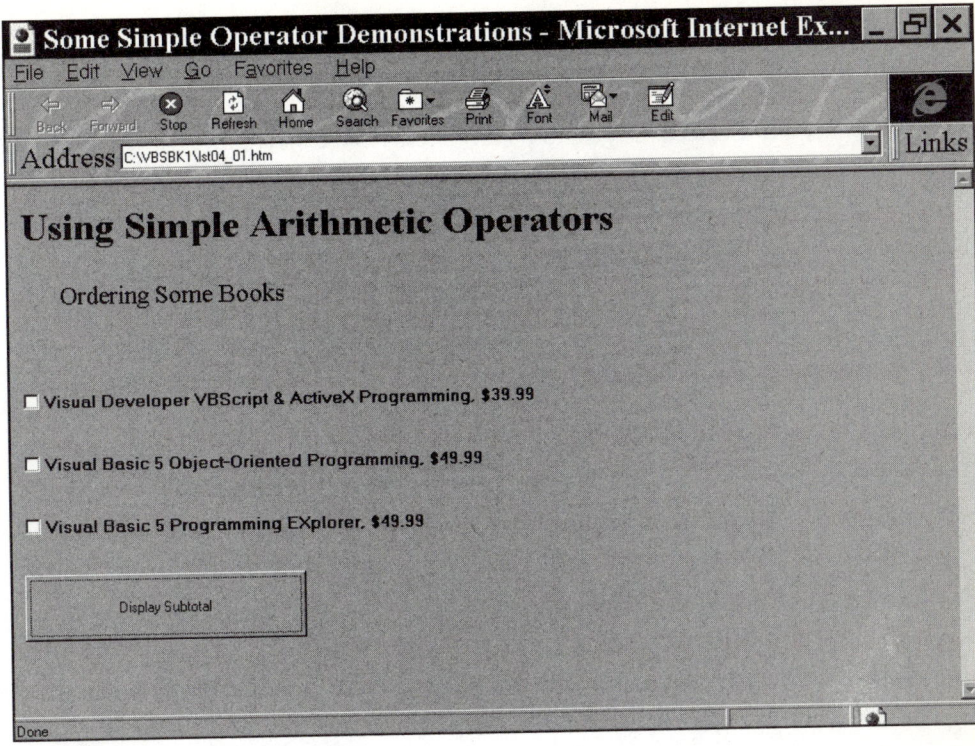

Figure 4.2
The Web page created by the code in Listing 4.1.

Don't Type ActiveX Object Tags

When you're inserting object tags for ActiveX controls in an HTML document, it's both easier and safer to use either the ActiveX Control Pad (discussed in Chapter 8) or the ActiveX Control Lister (AClist). These programs, both available free at http://www.microsoft.com, insert the object tag for you. By using one of these programs, you avoid the risk of typos in your object tags—mistakes that could eat up both your time and that of your users.

As you progress toward greater proficiency with VBScript, we're getting a little fancier in the code listings. In previous chapters, we've generally used HTML form controls to get input from the user. Here, we switch to an all-ActiveX lineup. In an HTML "layout"—a super-advanced, brand-new HTML feature—you can position ActiveX controls any way you like on a Web document. Later in the book, we'll cover HTML layouts, as well as Microsoft's HTML Layout control and the ActiveX

Control Pad. But for the moment, let's see how simple arithmetic operators are used here. We'll also get just a taste of how some ActiveX controls are used with VBScript.

How To Create Layouts With ActiveX Controls

If you want to start creating layouts with ActiveX controls right away, the best thing you can do is go to http://www.microsoft.com and download the latest version of the ActiveX Control Pad. It lets you visually lay out a Web page with ActiveX controls, and automatically generates the correct **<object>** tags for the controls, just like the ones in Listing 4.1.

As you can see in Figure 4.2, Listing 4.1 sets up a Web page with three checkboxes and a command button—all ActiveX controls. Each checkbox corresponds to a particular book that someone might order from The Coriolis Group. When the user clicks the command button, the VBScript code determines which checkboxes are checked. For each checked checkbox, the script adds the appropriate amount of money to the subtotal, using the addition operator. When the user clicks the command button, the click event code fires, displaying the message box shown in Figure 4.3.

HOW ACTIVEX CONTROLS ARE USED IN LISTING 4.1

There are a couple of interesting things to notice about this code. First, observe that when you're creating a click event sub for an ActiveX command button instead of an HTML form button, you name the sub **Click** instead of **OnClick**, as in the following code line:

```
sub Cmd_Subtotal_Click
```

Each kind of ActiveX control, just like a regular Visual Basic control, has certain associated properties and events. The name of the click event for an ActiveX command button is, well, **Click**.

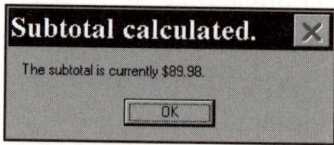

Figure 4.3
The message box displayed by Listing 4.1.

Second, Listing 4.1 uses the properties of the checkbox controls to determine when to add to the subtotal variable. Observe how the values of the checkboxes are used in the sub, as shown in the following code snippet:

```
if CB_VBS then subtotal = subtotal + 39.99
if CB_VB500P then subtotal = subtotal + 49.99
if CB_VB5EXP then subtotal = subtotal + 49.99
```

If a checkbox is checked, then its **value** property is set to **true**. If its value is **true**, then when you put the control's name in the antecedent of an **if** statement, it causes the **if** statement to fire off, executing whatever instruction is in the **then** clause. If the checkbox isn't checked, then its **value** property is set to **false**, so the **if** statement doesn't fire.

There are two other ways we might have written those lines, but the way we did it is the most economical. The most obvious alternative is shown in the following code snippet:

```
if CB_VBS.value then subtotal = subtotal + 39.99
if CB_VB500P.value then subtotal = subtotal + 49.99
if CB_VB5EXP.value then subtotal = subtotal + 49.99
```

This approach uses basically the same logic, but it uses more words to accomplish the same result. It wastes words because it ignores one of the most useful features of ActiveX controls: Each type of ActiveX control has a *default* property. If you don't specify a property, and simply give the name of the control, then VBScript assumes you are talking about the control's default property. In the case of a checkbox control, the default property is—you guessed it—the "checked" status of the checkbox. Thus, in Listing 4.1, it was unnecessary to refer to the value property of each checkbox control: Leave out any mention of a property, and VBScript automatically uses the value property.

An even less economical way of writing the code is to write things like **if CB_VBS.value = true**, but that should be pretty clear from the foregoing discussion.

Subtraction works just like addition, except that it's, well, subtraction. If that's not crystal clear, you have a bright future calculating the government's budget deficit. Multiplication, which uses the asterisk character (*), also works the same as in first-grade arithmetic.

Division

Division gets its own section because VBScript gives it a couple of interesting wrinkles. To be more specific, there are two kinds of division in VBScript: regular division and *integer* division. These two kinds of division are illustrated in Listing 4.2. The Web page created by Listing 4.2 is shown in Figure 4.4.

Listing 4.2 USING VBSCRIPT'S TWO KINDS OF DIVISION.

```
<HTML>
<HEAD>
<TITLE>Some Simple Operator Demonstrations</TITLE>
</HEAD>
<BODY>
<H1>Regular Division vs. Integer Division</H1>
<pre>
    <OBJECT ID="Label2"
     CLASSID="CLSID:978C9E23-D4B0-11CE-BF2D-00AA003F40D0"
     STYLE="TOP:66pt;LEFT:116pt;WIDTH:91pt;
     HEIGHT:17pt;ZINDEX:1;">
        <PARAM NAME="Caption" VALUE="Enter a decimal number:">
        <PARAM NAME="Size" VALUE="3201;582">
        <PARAM NAME="FontCharSet" VALUE="0">
        <PARAM NAME="FontPitchAndFamily" VALUE="2">
        <PARAM NAME="FontWeight" VALUE="0">
    </OBJECT>

    <OBJECT ID="TB_Num1"
     CLASSID="CLSID:8BD21D10-EC42-11CE-9E0D-00AA006002F3"
     STYLE="TOP:83pt;LEFT:116pt;WIDTH:66pt;
     HEIGHT:25pt;TABINDEX:3;ZINDEX:3;">
        <PARAM NAME="VariousPropertyBits" VALUE="746604571">
        <PARAM NAME="Size" VALUE="2328;873">
        <PARAM NAME="FontCharSet" VALUE="0">
        <PARAM NAME="FontPitchAndFamily" VALUE="2">
        <PARAM NAME="FontWeight" VALUE="0">
    </OBJECT>

    <OBJECT ID="Label3"
     CLASSID="CLSID:978C9E23-D4B0-11CE-BF2D-00AA003F40D0"
     STYLE="TOP:124pt;LEFT:116pt;WIDTH:116pt;HEIGHT:17pt;ZINDEX:2;">
        <PARAM NAME="Caption" VALUE="Enter another decimal number:">
        <PARAM NAME="Size" VALUE="4074;583">
        <PARAM NAME="FontCharSet" VALUE="0">
        <PARAM NAME="FontPitchAndFamily" VALUE="2">
        <PARAM NAME="FontWeight" VALUE="0">
    </OBJECT>
```

```
        <OBJECT ID="TB_Num2"
         CLASSID="CLSID:8BD21D10-EC42-11CE-9E0D-00AA006002F3"
         STYLE="TOP:149pt;LEFT:116pt;WIDTH:66pt;
         HEIGHT:25pt;TABINDEX:4;ZINDEX:4;">
            <PARAM NAME="VariousPropertyBits" VALUE="746604571">
            <PARAM NAME="Size" VALUE="2328;873">
            <PARAM NAME="FontCharSet" VALUE="0">
            <PARAM NAME="FontPitchAndFamily" VALUE="2">
            <PARAM NAME="FontWeight" VALUE="0">
        </OBJECT><br>

        <OBJECT ID="Cmd_RegularDiv"
         CLASSID="CLSID:D7053240-CE69-11CD-A777-00DD01143C57"
         STYLE="TOP:190pt;LEFT:116pt;WIDTH:107pt;
         HEIGHT:24pt;TABINDEX:5;ZINDEX:5;">
            <PARAM NAME="Caption" VALUE="Do Regular Division">
            <PARAM NAME="Size" VALUE="3783;846">
            <PARAM NAME="FontCharSet" VALUE="0">
            <PARAM NAME="FontPitchAndFamily" VALUE="2">
            <PARAM NAME="ParagraphAlign" VALUE="3">
            <PARAM NAME="FontWeight" VALUE="0">
        </OBJECT><br>

        <OBJECT ID="Cmd_IntegerDiv"
         CLASSID="CLSID:D7053240-CE69-11CD-A777-00DD01143C57"
         STYLE="TOP:231pt;LEFT:116pt;WIDTH:107pt;
         HEIGHT:24pt;TABINDEX:6;ZINDEX:6;">
            <PARAM NAME="Caption" VALUE="Do Integer Division">
            <PARAM NAME="Size" VALUE="3783;846">
            <PARAM NAME="FontCharSet" VALUE="0">
            <PARAM NAME="FontPitchAndFamily" VALUE="2">
            <PARAM NAME="ParagraphAlign" VALUE="3">
            <PARAM NAME="FontWeight" VALUE="0">
        </OBJECT>
</pre>

<script language="VBS">
<!--

dim num1, num2, result

sub Cmd_RegularDiv_Click
    num1 = TB_Num1.text
    num2 = TB_Num2.text

    result = num1 / num2
    MsgBox "With regular division, the result of " & _
        "dividing the first number by the second is " _
```

Chapter 4

```
            & result & ".",,"Regular Division"
end sub

sub Cmd_IntegerDiv_Click

    num1 = TB_Num1.text
    num2 = TB_Num2.text

    result = num1 \ num2
    MsgBox "With integer division, the result of " & _
        "dividing the first number by the second is " _
        & result & ".",,"Integer Division"

end sub

-->
</script>
</BODY>
</HTML>
```

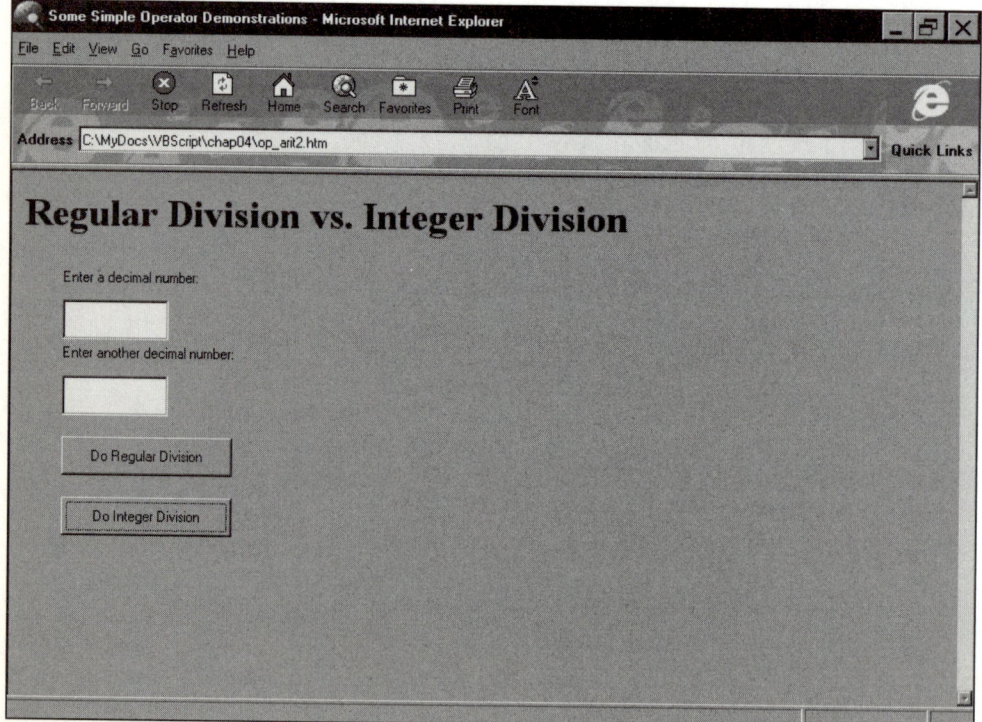

Figure 4.4
The Web page created by Listing 4.2.

As before, this is pretty simple stuff in principle, but it helps to see an example. It sets up a Web page with two text boxes where you can enter two decimal numbers—that is, numbers with a nonzero part to the right of the decimal point. When the user clicks either of the command buttons, the first number is divided by the second.

There is, however, a big difference between the results of clicking the different buttons. If the user clicks the first button, the **Click** event sub uses regular division (/), as shown in the following code snippet:

```
num1 = TB_Num1.text
num2 = TB_Num2.text

result = num1 / num2
```

If the user entered 5.7 for the first number and 2.1 for the second number, the program would display the message box shown in Figure 4.5.

You can see that the result is 2.7 followed by a long string of decimal digits. This is quite different from the result you get with integer division. If the user clicks that button instead—with the same numbers entered in the text boxes—he/she gets the result shown in Figure 4.6.

As you can see, integer division rounds off the result to the nearest whole number, which in this case is 3.

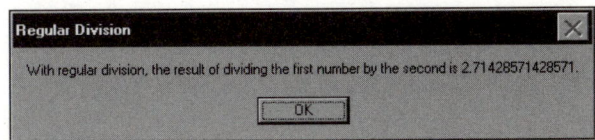

Figure 4.5
The message box displayed by the "regular division" button.

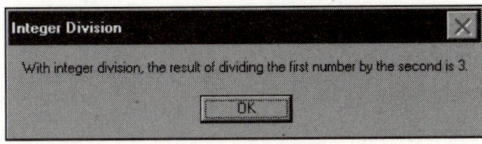

Figure 4.6
The message box displayed by the "integer division" button.

Modulus

The modulus (**mod**) operator gives the remainder from an integer division. For example, if you divide 5 by 14, don't do any rounding (unlike VBScript's integer division), and insist on an integer result, then the answer is 0—because 14 doesn't go evenly into 5 at all. The remainder is 5, so *5 mod 14* is 5.

Unless you've used the **mod** operator at some point in your own programming, the most obvious question is, "What the heck is it good for?" Odd as it might seem, the **mod** operator is very useful in controlling processes that cycle over and over. Consider *X mod 12*: Some of its possible values are shown in Table 4.2.

TABLE 4.2
SOME POSSIBLE VALUES OF X MOD 12.

Value of X	Number of times 12 evenly divides X	Remainder (Value of X mod 12)
1	0	1
2	0	2
3	0	3
4	0	4
5	0	5
6	0	6
7	0	7
8	0	8
9	0	9
10	0	10
11	0	11
12	1	0
13	1	1
14	1	2
15	1	3
16	1	4
17	1	5
18	1	6

(continued)

TABLE 4.2
Some possible values of X mod 12 (continued).

Value of X	Number of times 12 evenly divides X	Remainder (Value of X mod 12)
19	1	7
20	1	8
21	1	9
22	1	10
23	1	11
24	2	0

If that series of numbers reminds you of anything, it should: Our system of clock time in North America is **mod** 12. The table also illustrates that when you set up a **mod** cycle, you often need to treat even multiples of the **mod** number as a special case. In our system of clock time, the twelfth and twenty-fourth hours are twelve o'clock, not zero o'clock.

At any rate, the **mod** operator is particularly useful when you want certain events to recur at specified intervals. Because the numbers in a **mod** cycle begin at zero, cycle to one less than the **mod** number, then start at zero again. It's a very predictable way to make events repeat. Listing 4.3 shows a simplified example of using the **mod** operator: not industrial strength, but adequate to show you how it's used. Figure 4.7 shows the Web page created by the code in Listing 4.3.

Listing 4.3 VBScript code using the mod operator.

```
<HTML>
<HEAD>
<TITLE>Some Simple Operator Demonstrations</TITLE>
</HEAD>
<BODY>
<H1>Using The Modulus Operator</H1>
<pre>
    <OBJECT ID="Label2"
      CLASSID="CLSID:978C9E23-D4B0-11CE-BF2D-00AA003F40D0"
      STYLE="TOP:66pt;LEFT:116pt;WIDTH:300pt;
      HEIGHT:17pt;ZINDEX:1;">
        <PARAM NAME="Caption" VALUE="Enter an integer:">
        <PARAM NAME="Size" VALUE="3201;582">
        <PARAM NAME="FontCharSet" VALUE="0">
```

```
            <PARAM NAME="FontPitchAndFamily" VALUE="2">
            <PARAM NAME="FontWeight" VALUE="0">
       </OBJECT>

       <OBJECT ID="TB_Num1"
        CLASSID="CLSID:8BD21D10-EC42-11CE-9E0D-00AA006002F3"
        STYLE="TOP:83pt;LEFT:116pt;WIDTH:66pt;
        HEIGHT:25pt;TABINDEX:3;ZINDEX:3;">
            <PARAM NAME="VariousPropertyBits" VALUE="746604571">
            <PARAM NAME="Size" VALUE="2328;873">
            <PARAM NAME="FontCharSet" VALUE="0">
            <PARAM NAME="FontPitchAndFamily" VALUE="2">
            <PARAM NAME="FontWeight" VALUE="0">
       </OBJECT><br>

       <OBJECT ID="Label3"
        CLASSID="CLSID:978C9E23-D4B0-11CE-BF2D-00AA003F40D0"
        STYLE="TOP:124pt;LEFT:116pt;WIDTH:300pt;HEIGHT:17pt;ZINDEX:2;">
            <PARAM NAME="Caption" VALUE="Enter another integer:">
            <PARAM NAME="Size" VALUE="4074;583">
            <PARAM NAME="FontCharSet" VALUE="0">
            <PARAM NAME="FontPitchAndFamily" VALUE="2">
            <PARAM NAME="FontWeight" VALUE="0">
       </OBJECT>

       <OBJECT ID="TB_Num2"
        CLASSID="CLSID:8BD21D10-EC42-11CE-9E0D-00AA006002F3"
        STYLE="TOP:149pt;LEFT:116pt;WIDTH:66pt;
        HEIGHT:25pt;TABINDEX:4;ZINDEX:4;">
            <PARAM NAME="VariousPropertyBits" VALUE="746604571">
            <PARAM NAME="Size" VALUE="2328;873">
            <PARAM NAME="FontCharSet" VALUE="0">
            <PARAM NAME="FontPitchAndFamily" VALUE="2">
            <PARAM NAME="FontWeight" VALUE="0">
       </OBJECT><br>

       <OBJECT ID="Cmd_ShowMod"
        CLASSID="CLSID:D7053240-CE69-11CD-A777-00DD01143C57"
        STYLE="TOP:190pt;LEFT:116pt;WIDTH:107pt;
        HEIGHT:24pt;TABINDEX:5;ZINDEX:5;">
            <PARAM NAME="Caption" VALUE="Show The Mod Value">
            <PARAM NAME="Size" VALUE="3783;846">
            <PARAM NAME="FontCharSet" VALUE="0">
            <PARAM NAME="FontPitchAndFamily" VALUE="2">
            <PARAM NAME="ParagraphAlign" VALUE="3">
            <PARAM NAME="FontWeight" VALUE="0">
       </OBJECT><br>
</pre>
```

```
<script language="VBS">
<!--

dim num1, num2, result

sub Cmd_ShowMod_Click
    num1 = TB_Num1.text
    num2 = TB_Num2.text

    result = num1 mod num2
    MsgBox "The first number mod the second number is " & _
        result & ".",,"The Modulus Operator"
end sub

-->
</script>
</BODY>
</HTML>
```

The operation of the program is fairly simple. The user of the Web page enters a whole number in each text box. When he/she clicks on the command button,

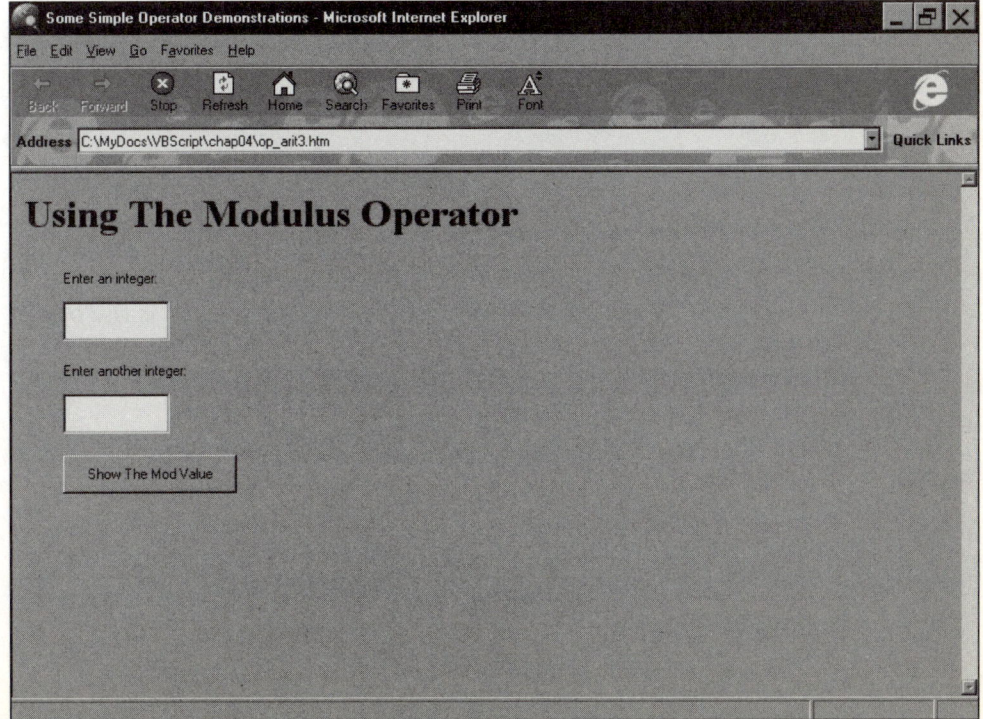

Figure 4.7
A Web page to demonstrate the **mod** operator.

the **Click** event code assigns the number in each text box to a corresponding variable in the VBScript program. (Remember that VBScript looks at data and automatically decides what type it's likely to be. In this case, it looks at the "text" in the text boxes and decides that it's probably numeric.)

The sub then uses the **mod** operator with the two numbers, assigning the result to the variable **result**. A message box displays the result. That's all there is to it.

As for the other arithmetic operators—negation, exponentiation, and concatenation—their application is obvious, so we won't waste time on them here.

Logical Operators

Logical operators are the next group we'll look at. Logical operators work with terms that are true (–1) or false (0). They are summarized in Table 4.3.

In the following examples, we'll look at the logical operators one at a time. However, you should keep in mind that you can *combine* expressions with logical operators any way you like, as long as you follow the syntactical rules of VBScript. The following code snippet shows a few examples:

```
(a and b) or c
not a and not b and c
a or (not b and c)
not a or b and a imp b
```

That last line, by the way, is what's known as a *tautology*: an expression that will always be true. The reason is that *not a or b* is logically equivalent to *a imp b*: Whenever one is true, so is the other, and whenever one is false, so is the other.

TABLE 4.3
LOGICAL OPERATORS IN VBSCRIPT.

Operator	Meaning	Example
not	Logical Negation	not(a = b)
or	Logical Disjunction	(a = b) or (c < d)
and	Logical Conjunction	(a = b) and (c < d)
xor	Logical Exclusion (a.k.a. "exclusive **or**")	(a = b) xor (c < d)
eqv	Logical Equivalence	(a = b) eqv (c < d)
imp	Logical Implication	(a = b) imp (c < d)

Logical Negation

Logical negation is the simplest logical operator. Unlike most operators, it takes only one term. And like much political rhetoric, it reverses the truth-value of terms to which it's applied, turning false values into true and true into false. The "truth table" for negation is shown in Table 4.4.

Truth tables are easy to read. Row one of Table 4.4 says that if an expression *p* is true, then *not p* is false, while row two says that if an expression *p* is false, then *not p* is true. Row three says that if *p* has no truth value (i.e., it has a null value), then applying the negation operator has no effect.

Logical Disjunction

Disjunction is just a big word that means "or." A disjunction expression is true if at least one of its terms is true. Although disjunctions will usually have only two terms, they can have more than that: *a or b or c or d...* and so on. The truth table for disjunction is shown in Table 4.5.

What you can tell from this truth table is that there's only one case in which the expression *p or q* is false: when *p* and *q* are *both* false. In all other cases where both *p* and *q* have values, the disjunctive expression is true. If *p* or *q* has a null

TABLE 4.4

THE TRUTH TABLE FOR LOGICAL NEGATION.

p	not p
true	false
false	true
null	null

TABLE 4.5

THE TRUTH TABLE FOR LOGICAL DISJUNCTION.

p	q	p or q
true	true	true
true	false	true
false	true	true
false	false	false

value, it gets a little messy, but the big rule still applies: If at least one of its terms is true, then a disjunctive expression is true. If none of its terms is true, but one of its terms is null, then the expression as a whole takes a value of null.

Listing 4.4 shows VBScript code that puts the disjunction operator to work. Figure 4.8 shows the Web page created by the code.

Listing 4.4 AN EXAMPLE OF LOGICAL DISJUNCTION IN VBSCRIPT.

```
<HTML>
<HEAD>
<TITLE>Some Simple Operator Demonstrations</TITLE>
</HEAD>
<BODY>
<H1>Using The OR Operator</H1>
<pre>
<DIV STYLE="LAYOUT:FIXED;WIDTH:488pt;HEIGHT:260pt;">
    <OBJECT ID="Label1"
      CLASSID="CLSID:978C9E23-D4B0-11CE-BF2D-00AA003F40D0"
      STYLE="TOP:17pt;LEFT:116pt;WIDTH:239pt;
      HEIGHT:41pt;ZINDEX:0;">
        <PARAM NAME="Caption"
            VALUE="People Who Might Have Paper Clips">
        <PARAM NAME="Size" VALUE="8440;1455">
        <PARAM NAME="FontName" VALUE="Times New Roman">
        <PARAM NAME="FontHeight" VALUE="320">
        <PARAM NAME="FontCharSet" VALUE="0">
        <PARAM NAME="FontPitchAndFamily" VALUE="2">
        <PARAM NAME="FontWeight" VALUE="0">
    </OBJECT>

    <OBJECT ID="CB_Joe"
      CLASSID="CLSID:8BD21D40-EC42-11CE-9E0D-00AA006002F3"
      STYLE="TOP:74pt;LEFT:116pt;WIDTH:124pt;
      HEIGHT:17pt;TABINDEX:1;ZINDEX:1;">
        <PARAM NAME="BackColor" VALUE="-2147483633">
        <PARAM NAME="ForeColor" VALUE="-2147483630">
        <PARAM NAME="DisplayStyle" VALUE="4">
        <PARAM NAME="Size" VALUE="4365;582">
        <PARAM NAME="Value" VALUE="False">
        <PARAM NAME="Caption" VALUE="Joe">
        <PARAM NAME="FontCharSet" VALUE="0">
        <PARAM NAME="FontPitchAndFamily" VALUE="2">
        <PARAM NAME="FontWeight" VALUE="0">
    </OBJECT>
```

```
    <OBJECT ID="CB_Jane"
     CLASSID="CLSID:8BD21D40-EC42-11CE-9E0D-00AA006002F3"
     STYLE="TOP:107pt;LEFT:116pt;WIDTH:132pt;
     HEIGHT:17pt;TABINDEX:2;ZINDEX:2;">
        <PARAM NAME="BackColor" VALUE="-2147483633">
        <PARAM NAME="ForeColor" VALUE="-2147483630">
        <PARAM NAME="DisplayStyle" VALUE="4">
        <PARAM NAME="Size" VALUE="4656;582">
        <PARAM NAME="Value" VALUE="False">
        <PARAM NAME="Caption" VALUE="Jane">
        <PARAM NAME="FontCharSet" VALUE="0">
        <PARAM NAME="FontPitchAndFamily" VALUE="2">
        <PARAM NAME="FontWeight" VALUE="0">
    </OBJECT>

    <OBJECT ID="CB_Sally"
     CLASSID="CLSID:8BD21D40-EC42-11CE-9E0D-00AA006002F3"
     STYLE="TOP:140pt;LEFT:116pt;WIDTH:140pt;
     HEIGHT:21pt;TABINDEX:3;ZINDEX:3;">
        <PARAM NAME="BackColor" VALUE="-2147483633">
        <PARAM NAME="ForeColor" VALUE="-2147483630">
        <PARAM NAME="DisplayStyle" VALUE="4">
        <PARAM NAME="Size" VALUE="4947;741">
        <PARAM NAME="Value" VALUE="False">
        <PARAM NAME="Caption" VALUE="Sally">
        <PARAM NAME="FontCharSet" VALUE="0">
        <PARAM NAME="FontPitchAndFamily" VALUE="2">
        <PARAM NAME="FontWeight" VALUE="0">
    </OBJECT>

    <OBJECT ID="Cmd_Borr"
     CLASSID="CLSID:D7053240-CE69-11CD-A777-00DD01143C57"
     STYLE="TOP:182pt;LEFT:140pt;WIDTH:173pt;
     HEIGHT:41pt;TABINDEX:4;ZINDEX:4;">
        <PARAM NAME="Caption"
            VALUE="Can I borrow a paper clip?">
        <PARAM NAME="Size" VALUE="6112;1455">
        <PARAM NAME="FontCharSet" VALUE="0">
        <PARAM NAME="FontPitchAndFamily" VALUE="2">
        <PARAM NAME="ParagraphAlign" VALUE="3">
        <PARAM NAME="FontWeight" VALUE="0">
    </OBJECT>
</DIV>
</pre>

<script language="VBS">
<!--
```

78   Chapter 4

```
sub Cmd_Borr_Click

    if CB_Joe or CB_Jane or CB_Sally then
        MsgBox "Yes, someone is sure to have one." _
            ,,"OR Demonstration"
    else
        MsgBox "No, nobody has any paper clips. Sorry." _
            ,,"OR Demonstration"
    end if
end sub

-->
</script>
</BODY>
</HTML>
```

The code in Listing 4.4 poses the musical question, "Can I borrow a paper clip?" It sets up a Web page with three checkboxes, each corresponding to a person in your office who might have some paper clips. If any one of those

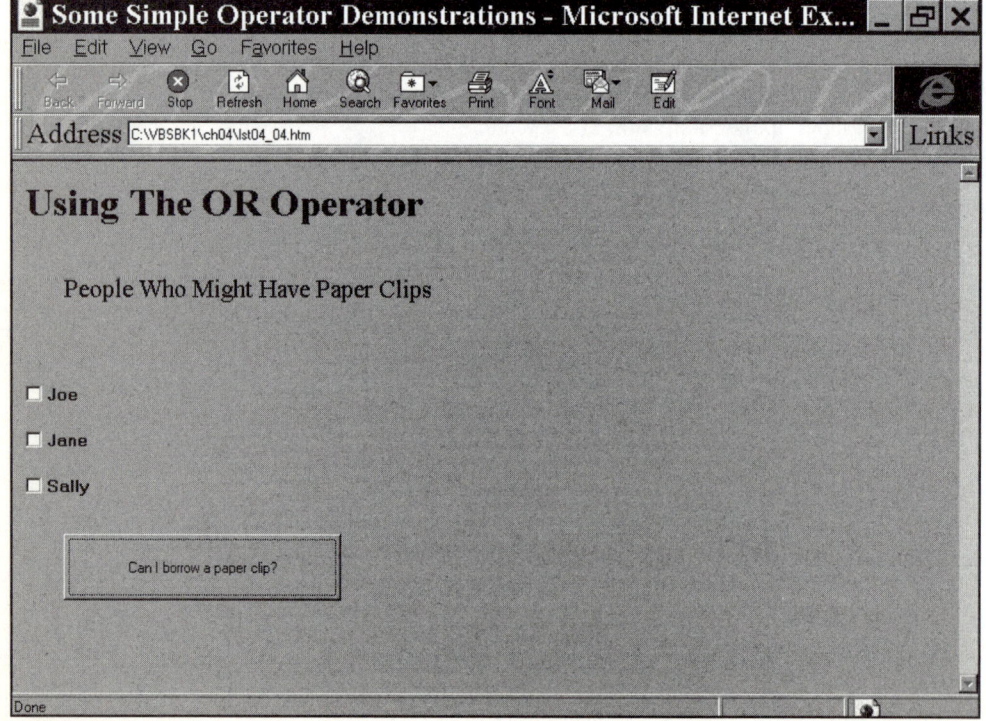

Figure 4.8
A Web page that uses disjunction.

people has some paper clips, then you can borrow one. The only case in which you can't borrow a paper clip is if no one else in your office has any, either. This is the situation embodied in the central code line of the **Click** event sub for the command button, as follows:

```
if CB_Joe or CB_Jane or CB_Sally then
```

The expression *CB_Joe or CB_Jane or CB_Sally* is true if at least one of its terms is true: that is, if the user checked at least one of the checkboxes. Of course, there's nothing special about three terms: you could have only two, or you could have fifteen. The results of clicking the command button are shown in Figures 4.9 and 4.10.

Logical Conjunction

Logical conjunction is the flip side of logical disjunction. A disjunctive expression is false only if all of its terms are false, while a *conjunctive* expression is *true* only if both of its terms are *true*. That means if even one term in a conjunctive expression is false, then the whole thing is false. The truth table for conjunction is shown in Table 4.6.

As with disjunction, the inclusion of null values makes things a little messy, but the big rule stays the same: The only way for a conjunctive expression to be true is for all of its terms to be true. Otherwise, if all of its terms have truth values, then a conjunctive expression is false. If all of its terms aren't true, and some of its terms are null, then the expression as a whole takes a null value.

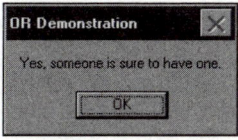

Figure 4.9
The disjunctive expression is true.

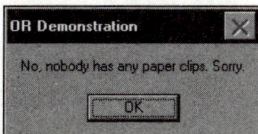

Figure 4.10
The disjunctive expression is false.

TABLE 4.6
THE TRUTH TABLE FOR CONJUNCTION.

p	q	p and q
true	true	true
true	false	false
false	true	false
false	false	false

Listing 4.5 shows an example of VBScript code that puts the conjunction operator to work. In this case, the user is trying to assemble a meeting that must include Joe, Jane, and Sally. Figure 4.11 shows the Web page created by the code.

Listing 4.5 USING THE CONJUNCTION OPERATOR IN VBSCRIPT.

```
<HTML>
<HEAD>
<TITLE>Some Simple Operator Demonstrations</TITLE>
</HEAD>
<BODY>
<H1>Using The AND Operator</H1>
<pre>
<DIV STYLE="LAYOUT:FIXED;WIDTH:488pt;HEIGHT:260pt;">
    <OBJECT ID="Label1"
     CLASSID="CLSID:978C9E23-D4B0-11CE-BF2D-00AA003F40D0"
     STYLE="TOP:17pt;LEFT:116pt;WIDTH:239pt;HEIGHT:41pt;ZINDEX:0;">
        <PARAM NAME="Caption"
            VALUE="People Who Must Be At The Meeting">
        <PARAM NAME="Size" VALUE="8440;1455">
        <PARAM NAME="FontName" VALUE="Times New Roman">
        <PARAM NAME="FontHeight" VALUE="320">
        <PARAM NAME="FontCharSet" VALUE="0">
        <PARAM NAME="FontPitchAndFamily" VALUE="2">
        <PARAM NAME="FontWeight" VALUE="0">
    </OBJECT>

    <OBJECT ID="CB_Joe"
     CLASSID="CLSID:8BD21D40-EC42-11CE-9E0D-00AA006002F3"
     STYLE="TOP:74pt;LEFT:116pt;WIDTH:124pt;
     HEIGHT:17pt;TABINDEX:1;ZINDEX:1;">
        <PARAM NAME="BackColor" VALUE="-2147483633">
        <PARAM NAME="ForeColor" VALUE="-2147483630">
        <PARAM NAME="DisplayStyle" VALUE="4">
```

```
    <PARAM NAME="Size" VALUE="4365;582">
    <PARAM NAME="Value" VALUE="False">
    <PARAM NAME="Caption" VALUE="Joe">
    <PARAM NAME="FontCharSet" VALUE="0">
    <PARAM NAME="FontPitchAndFamily" VALUE="2">
    <PARAM NAME="FontWeight" VALUE="0">
</OBJECT>

<OBJECT ID="CB_Jane"
 CLASSID="CLSID:8BD21D40-EC42-11CE-9E0D-00AA006002F3"
 STYLE="TOP:107pt;LEFT:116pt;WIDTH:132pt;
 HEIGHT:17pt;TABINDEX:2;ZINDEX:2;">
    <PARAM NAME="BackColor" VALUE="-2147483633">
    <PARAM NAME="ForeColor" VALUE="-2147483630">
    <PARAM NAME="DisplayStyle" VALUE="4">
    <PARAM NAME="Size" VALUE="4656;582">
    <PARAM NAME="Value" VALUE="False">
    <PARAM NAME="Caption" VALUE="Jane">
    <PARAM NAME="FontCharSet" VALUE="0">
    <PARAM NAME="FontPitchAndFamily" VALUE="2">
    <PARAM NAME="FontWeight" VALUE="0">
</OBJECT>

<OBJECT ID="CB_Sally"
 CLASSID="CLSID:8BD21D40-EC42-11CE-9E0D-00AA006002F3"
 STYLE="TOP:140pt;LEFT:116pt;WIDTH:140pt;
 HEIGHT:21pt;TABINDEX:3;ZINDEX:3;">
    <PARAM NAME="BackColor" VALUE="-2147483633">
    <PARAM NAME="ForeColor" VALUE="-2147483630">
    <PARAM NAME="DisplayStyle" VALUE="4">
    <PARAM NAME="Size" VALUE="4947;741">
    <PARAM NAME="Value" VALUE="False">
    <PARAM NAME="Caption" VALUE="Sally">
    <PARAM NAME="FontCharSet" VALUE="0">
    <PARAM NAME="FontPitchAndFamily" VALUE="2">
    <PARAM NAME="FontWeight" VALUE="0">
</OBJECT>

<OBJECT ID="Cmd_Borr"
 CLASSID="CLSID:D7053240-CE69-11CD-A777-00DD01143C57"
 STYLE="TOP:182pt;LEFT:140pt;WIDTH:173pt;
 HEIGHT:41pt;TABINDEX:4;ZINDEX:4;">
    <PARAM NAME="Caption"
        VALUE="Can everyone attend a meeting at 9am?">
    <PARAM NAME="Size" VALUE="6112;1455">
    <PARAM NAME="FontCharSet" VALUE="0">
    <PARAM NAME="FontPitchAndFamily" VALUE="2">
```

```
            <PARAM NAME="ParagraphAlign" VALUE="3">
            <PARAM NAME="FontWeight" VALUE="0">
        </OBJECT>
    </DIV>
</pre>

<script language="VBS">
<!--

sub Cmd_Borr_Click

    if CB_Joe and CB_Jane and CB_Sally then
      MsgBox "Yes, everyone is available for the meeting." _
             ,,"AND Demonstration"
    else
      MsgBox "No, some people can't make the meeting." & _
             " Pick another time." _
             ,,"AND Demonstration"
    end if
end sub

-->
</script>
</BODY>
</HTML>
```

If you've already perused the previous example (disjunction), then the concept here should be familiar. The central line of code appears in the event sub for the command button, as shown in the following code line:

```
if CB_Joe and CB_Jane and CB_Sally then
```

If any of the checkboxes is *not* checked, then the whole expression takes a value of false, meaning that at least one person can't attend the meeting, and it must be rescheduled. The results of the program are shown in Figures 4.12 and 4.13.

XOr, Equivalence, And Implication

Logical exclusion (exclusive "or"), logical equivalence, and logical implication are operators you'll use less often, but they do have their applications. An exclusive-or expression is true if only *one* of its terms is true: In all other cases, it's false. An equivalence expression is true only if its terms have the *same* truth value: In all other cases, it's false. And a logical implication expression is false

Operators And Expressions   83

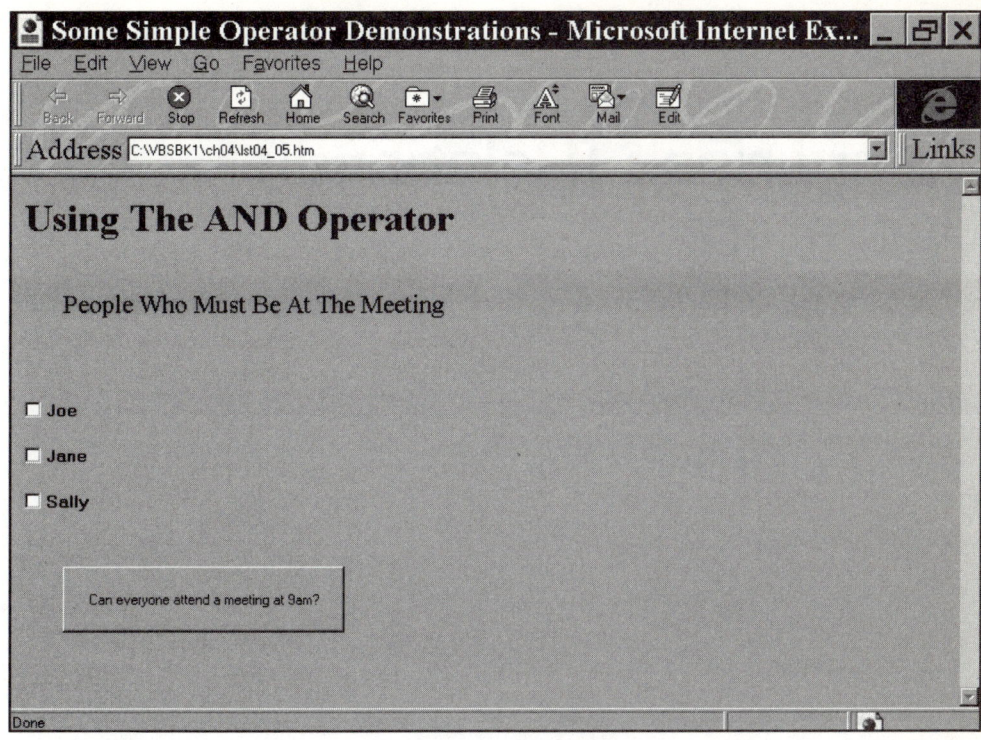

Figure 4.11
The Web page created by Listing 4.5.

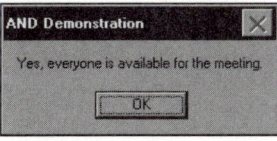

Figure 4.12
All the boxes are checked, so the expression is true.

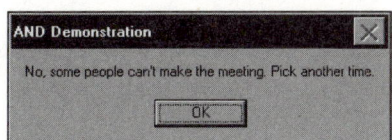

Figure 4.13
Not all of the boxes are checked, so the expression is false.

only if its first term is true and its second term is false: In all other cases, it's true. The truth tables for these operators are shown in Tables 4.7, 4.8, and 4.9.

Comparison (Relational) Operators

Comparison operators, often called "relational" operators, compare the values of two or more expressions. These operators are all so familiar to anyone who

TABLE 4.7
THE TRUTH TABLE FOR LOGICAL EXCLUSION (EXCLUSIVE "OR").

p	q	p xor q
true	true	false
true	false	true
false	true	true
false	false	false

TABLE 4.8
THE TRUTH TABLE FOR EQUIVALENCE.

p	q	p eqv q
true	true	true
true	false	false
false	true	false
false	false	true

TABLE 4.9
THE TRUTH TABLE FOR IMPLICATION.

p	q	p imp q
true	true	true
true	false	false
false	true	true
false	false	true

made it past sixth grade that we won't rehearse them here in any great detail. Their meaning and use are the same in VBScript as everywhere else. An expression with a comparison operator takes a value of true, false, or null. The operators are summarized in Table 4.10.

Equal (=) Doesn't Always Mean "Equal"

It might have occurred to you that VBScript uses the same character (=) for both the equality operator and the assignment operator. But if you're inclined to worry about the situation, don't. VBScript automatically looks at the context and determines if a particular instance of = should be interpreted as the equality operator or the assignment operator.

The only comparison operator that's at all unfamiliar is the object equivalence operator. It's used to determine whether two expressions refer to the same object. We'll discuss object equivalence in detail later in the book.

TABLE 4.10

COMPARISON (RELATIONAL) OPERATORS IN VBSCRIPT.

Operator	Meaning	Example
=	Equality	a = b, true if a and b are equal
<>	Inequality	a <> b, true if a and b are not equal
<	Less than	a < b, true if a is less than b
>	Greater than	a > b, true if a is greater than b
<=	Less than or equal to	a <= b, true if a is less than or equal to b
>=	Greater than or equal to	a >= b, true if a is greater than or equal to b
Is	Object equivalence	a Is b, true if a and b refer to the same object

5
MAKING YOUR PROGRAM MAKE DECISIONS

Are you just a teensy bit indecisive? At least you can get away with it:
Your VBScript program can't. Here's how your program decides
how to respond to things that happen while it's running.

In Chapters 3 and 4, we looked at the various kinds of data, variables, and expressions you can use in VBScript. But we didn't really talk much about what you use them for. In this chapter, we'll look at how all these program elements work with special kinds of VBScript statements, called *control structures*.

Control structures allow your program to respond in different ways to different events. In fact, you've seen one control structure—the **if...then** statement—several times already. If the value of a variable is one thing, the **if** statement makes your program take action X; if the value is something else, your program takes action Y. Almost all uses of control structures are variations on that theme.

Types Of Control Structures

Control structures fall into two general categories: branching statements and looping statements. Branching statements make the program take one path or another based on the value of a variable or expression—just like the **if** statements you've already seen. Looping statements, on the other hand, make the program repeat a sequence of actions until a certain condition is reached.

In VBScript, branching statements are variations on **if...then**, as follows:

- **if**—This simply tells your program that if a certain condition is true (such as **Name = "Scott"** or a number being greater than 10), then it should carry out a certain statement or sequence of statements.

- **if...else**—Just like a plain **if** statement, this tells your program that if a certain condition is true, it should carry out a certain statement or sequence of statements. But it adds another instruction: **if** the condition is *not* true, then the program should do some other statement or sequence of statements. That's the **else** clause.

- **if...elseif**—With a simple **if** statement, your program decides its next move based on a single condition: the **if** clause. With an **if...else** statement, there are two conditions: the **if** clause and the **else** clause. With an **if...elseif** statement, there are multiple conditions: **if** A is true, then do B, **else if** C is true, then do D, **else if** E is true, then do F, and so on. Frankly, **if...elseif** statements are confusing and error-prone: They can usually be replaced by a sequence of simpler **if...else** statements, which is a good idea when possible.

- **select case**—This is a very sleek and economical replacement for a series of **if...else** statements when you have to deal with multiple alternatives. It's a special kind of branching statement that we'll cover at the end of the chapter.

Those are the branching statements. What about the looping statements? There are several of them, as follows:

- **for...next**—This allows you to set up a loop that will execute a specified number of times. Each time the loop executes, any statements in it are carried out. This type of loop is most useful when you know in advance how many times the loop should execute. The **for** loop is often used to initialize or traverse arrays.

- **for each...next**—This allows you to traverse an array (visit all the slots in a multislot variable) without setting up a regular **for** loop. It also requires slightly less code than a plain **for** loop, albeit at the cost of making your code a bit trickier. Microsoft's VBScript documentation says that **for each...next** also applies to collections, but VBScript doesn't support collections. Because **for each...next** loops are generally no more useful than **for** loops while being much more error-prone, we won't discuss them any further in this book.
- **do...loop**—This repeats a statement or sequence of statements until a certain condition becomes true or false, depending on how you set up the loop.
- **while...wend**—Like a **do** loop, this repeats a statement or sequence of statements as long as a certain condition is true. It's not used very often, because anything you can do with **while...wend**, you can do with a **do** loop. It's included mainly because old-time Basic programmers still like it.

Using if Statements

You've seen **if** statements often enough by now that the concept should be familiar. There are just a few wrinkles you need to know. In particular, there are variations on the **if** statement. The important ones are the single-line **if** statement, the multiple-line **if** statement, and the **if...else** statement.

Single-Line if Statements

Single-line **if** statements, as their name implies, require only a single line of code. More significant is that when their **if** clause is true, they only carry out a single statement in their **then** clause. Here are a couple of examples:

```
if a = 10 then MsgBox "The value is 10."
if (temp > 212 and substance = "water") then CoffeeIsReady = true
```

The key factor is that there's only a single statement in the **then** clause. The syntax of a single-line **if** statement is *if X then Y*.

Multiple-Line if Statements

Multiple-line **if** statements contain more than one statement in their **then** clause. As a result, they need an **end if** at the end to tell VBScript that the **then** clause is over and that the next line of code is not subject to the **if** clause.

That's a little abstract, so let's look at a specific code example. Suppose that we wanted to write some VBScript-like code to tell us things to do on Sunday afternoon. Consider how it might look with **if...then...endif**:

```
if Temperature > 100 then
    Say "The temperature is over 100."
    AdjustThermostat
end if
VacuumRug
GoShopping
WalkTheDog
```

It's fairly easy to see what's going on. If the temperature is over 100, announce the fact, then adjust the thermostat. After that, in completely unrelated business, vacuum the rug, go shopping, and walk the dog.

But suppose that we forgot to include the **end if** part of the **if** statement. The pseudocode would then look like this:

```
if Temperature > 100 then
    Say "The temperature is over 100."
    AdjustThermostat
VacuumRug
GoShopping
WalkTheDog
```

As a person, you can make a guess that vacuuming the rug, going shopping, and walking the dog have nothing to do with the temperature being over 100. But VBScript (and PCs generally) aren't that smart. All VBScript knows is that it saw an **if** statement and is busily carrying out the statements following the **then**. If the temperature were not over 100, then none of the non-temperature-related items would get done—because VBScript would think they were part of the **then** clause. That's why **end if** is needed in multiple-line **if** statements. The syntax of a multiple-line **if** statement is:

```
if X then
    Y
    Z
    (etc.)
end if
```

if...else Statements

The final type of **if** statement is the **if...then...else** statement. This is usually a multiple-line **if** statement, though it doesn't have to be: You can combine **if**, **then**, and **else** in a single-line **if** statement. The big difference is that after the **then** clause, there's an **else** clause that tells VBScript what to do if the **if** condition isn't true. The syntax of an **if...then...else** statement is:

```
if A then B else C
```

For a multiple-line **if...then...else** statement, you make the obvious changes, as shown in the following:

```
if A then
    B
    C
else
    D
    E
end if
```

A More Sophisticated Example

You've seen enough examples of simple **if** statements that you'd probably be bored by another one. So let's look at a more sophisticated example. This will not only show you a few neat tricks, but it will also prove how much VBScript power you already have at your disposal. With **if** statements and a few other simple things you've learned, we're going to create a Trivial Pursuit-style game for a Web page. We'll call it *Trivia, Forsooth*, because we don't want to get sued by the makers of Trivial Pursuit. The Web page from which a user can play Trivia, Forsooth is shown in Figure 5.1.

Playing the game is easy. The user first clicks on the Set Up A New Game button. That loads the questions and answers. Then, to get a question, the user clicks on the Get A Question button. A question appears in the text area at the left. At the right, the captions of the three option buttons change to the possible answers to the question. The user clicks in the option button he/she thinks gives the correct answer, then clicks on the Give Your Answer button. If the answer is correct, a congratulatory message box appears. If it's incorrect, a "wrong answer" message box appears, as shown in Figure 5.2.

92   Chapter 5

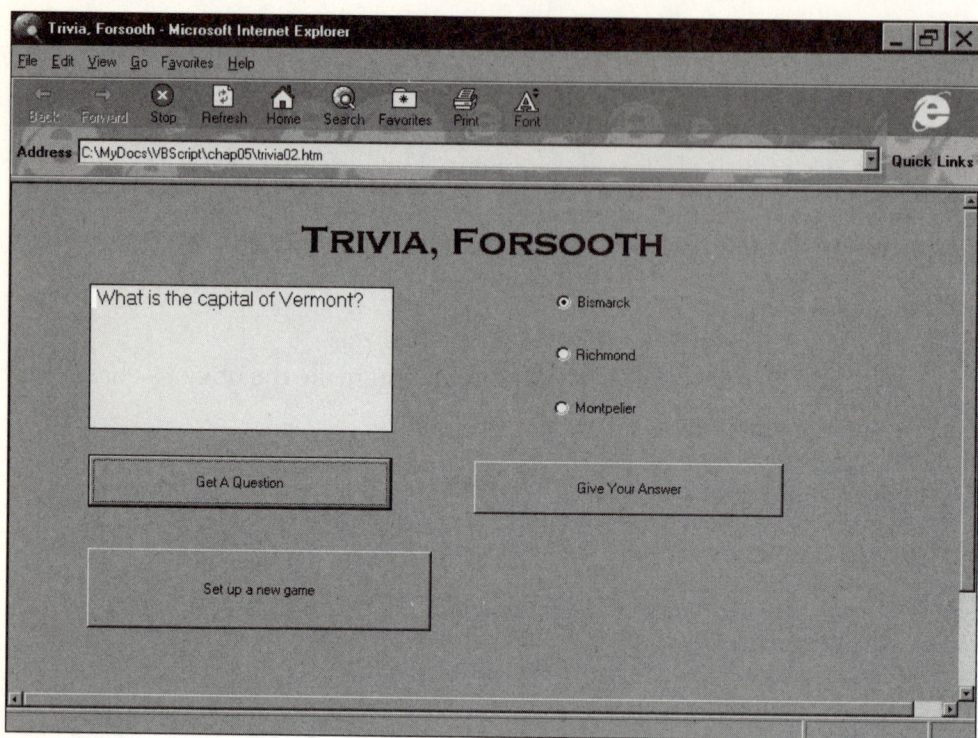

Figure 5.1
The Trivia, Forsooth game page.

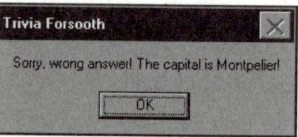

Figure 5.2
A message box tells the player if he/she answered the question correctly.

Okay, so it's not Doom. It's still a pretty snazzy game created with some fairly simple VBScript programming techniques. I created the page layout with Microsoft's ActiveX Control Pad, which is explained in Chapter 8. The code that sets up the Web page is shown in Listing 5.1: It uses the HTML layout control to position the various ActiveX controls on the page. The layout code itself, including the VBScript code that actually runs the game, is shown in Listing 5.2.

Don't worry too much about the ActiveX and layout issues right now: We'll cover those fully in the chapter on the ActiveX Control Pad.

Listing 5.1 CODE TO CREATE THE WEB PAGE FOR THE GAME.

```
<HTML>
<HEAD>
<TITLE>Trivia, Forsooth</TITLE>
</HEAD>
<BODY>

<OBJECT CLASSID="CLSID:812AE312-8B8E-11CF-93C8-00AA00C08FDF"
ID="trivia2" STYLE="LEFT:0;TOP:0">
<PARAM NAME="ALXPATH" REF VALUE="trivia2.alx">
</OBJECT>

</BODY>
</HTML>
```

Listing 5.2 THE VBSCRIPT CODE AND ACTIVEX CONTROL LAYOUT.

```
<SCRIPT LANGUAGE="VBScript">
<!--
dim Questions(5)
dim Choices(5,3)
dim QuestionNum
dim GameSetUp

Sub Cmd_Setup_Click()
    GameSetUp = True

    QuestionNum = 0

    Questions(0) = "What is the capital of Vermont?"
    Questions(1) = "What is the best movie ever made?"
    Questions(2) = "What is the best scripting language?"
    Questions(3) = "Who played ""Blossom Russo"" on TV?"
    Questions(4) = "Who was the Lone Ranger's sidekick?"

    Choices(0,0) = "Bismarck"
    Choices(0,1) = "Richmond"
    Choices(0,2) = "Montpelier"

    Choices(1,0) = "Casablanca"
    Choices(1,1) = "The Never Ending Story"
    Choices(1,2) = "Waterworld"
```

```
      Choices(2,0) = "VBScript"
      Choices(2,1) = "JavaScript"
      Choices(2,2) = "Eszterhas"

      Choices(3,0) = "Kellie Martin"
      Choices(3,1) = "Jodie Foster"
      Choices(3,2) = "Mayim Bialik"

      Choices(4,0) = "Kato"
      Choices(4,1) = "Tonto"
      Choices(4,2) = "Snoop Doggy Dogg"

      QuestionNum = -1
   end sub

   Sub Cmd_Question_Click()
      if not GameSetUp then
         msgbox "You must click the Setup button first."
         exit sub
      else
         QuestionNum = (QuestionNum + 1) mod 5
         Lbl_Question.caption = Questions(QuestionNum)
         OB_Answer1.value = true
         OB_Answer1.caption = Choices(QuestionNum, 0)
         OB_Answer2.caption = Choices(QuestionNum, 1)
         OB_Answer3.caption = Choices(QuestionNum, 2)
      end if
   end sub

   Sub Cmd_Answer_Click()
      if QuestionNum = 0 then
         if OB_Answer3.value = true then
            msgbox "That's right! It's Montpelier!",, _
               "Trivia, Forsooth"
         else
            msgbox "Sorry, wrong answer! The capital is Montpelier!",, _
               "Trivia, Forsooth"
         end if
      end if

      if QuestionNum = 1 then
         if OB_Answer2.value = true then
            msgbox "That's right! It's ""The Never Ending Story!""",, _
               "Trivia, Forsooth"
         else
            msgbox "Sorry, wrong answer! " & _
               "It's ""The Never Ending Story!""",,"Trivia, Forsooth"
```

```
            end if
        end if

        if QuestionNum = 2 then
            if OB_Answer1.value = true then
                msgbox "That's right! It's VBScript!",,"Trivia, Forsooth"
            else
                msgbox "Sorry, wrong answer! It's VBScript!",, _
                    "Trivia, Forsooth"
            end if
        end if

        if QuestionNum = 3 then
            if OB_Answer3.value = true then
                msgbox "That's right! It's Mayim Bialik!",,"Trivia, Forsooth"
            else
                msgbox "Sorry, wrong answer! It's Mayim Bialik!",, _
                    "Trivia, Forsooth"
            end if
        end if

        if QuestionNum = 4 then
            if OB_Answer2.value = true then
                msgbox "That's right! It was Tonto!",,"Trivia, Forsooth"
            else
                msgbox "Sorry, wrong answer! It was Tonto!",, _
                    "Trivia, Forsooth"
            end if
        end if

end sub

-->
</SCRIPT>

<DIV STYLE="LAYOUT:FIXED;WIDTH:597pt;HEIGHT:370pt;">
    <OBJECT ID="Label1"
      CLASSID="CLSID:978C9E23-D4B0-11CE-BF2D-00AA003F40D0"
      STYLE="TOP:8pt;LEFT:173pt;WIDTH:231pt;HEIGHT:33pt;ZINDEX:0;">
        <PARAM NAME="Caption" VALUE="Trivia, Forsooth">
        <PARAM NAME="Size" VALUE="8149;1164">
        <PARAM NAME="FontName" VALUE="Copperplate Gothic Bold">
        <PARAM NAME="FontEffects" VALUE="1073741825">
        <PARAM NAME="FontHeight" VALUE="480">
        <PARAM NAME="FontCharSet" VALUE="0">
        <PARAM NAME="FontPitchAndFamily" VALUE="2">
        <PARAM NAME="FontWeight" VALUE="700">
    </OBJECT>
```

```
<OBJECT ID="Lbl_Question"
 CLASSID="CLSID:978C9E23-D4B0-11CE-BF2D-00AA003F40D0"
 STYLE="TOP:50pt;LEFT:41pt;WIDTH:190pt;HEIGHT:91pt;ZINDEX:1;">
    <PARAM NAME="BackColor" VALUE="16777215">
    <PARAM NAME="Size" VALUE="6703;3210">
    <PARAM NAME="BorderStyle" VALUE="1">
    <PARAM NAME="FontHeight" VALUE="240">
    <PARAM NAME="FontCharSet" VALUE="0">
    <PARAM NAME="FontPitchAndFamily" VALUE="2">
    <PARAM NAME="FontWeight" VALUE="0">
</OBJECT>

<OBJECT ID="Cmd_Question"
 CLASSID="CLSID:D7053240-CE69-11CD-A777-00DD01143C57"
 STYLE="TOP:157pt;LEFT:41pt;WIDTH:190pt;
        HEIGHT:33pt;TABINDEX:2;ZINDEX:2;">
    <PARAM NAME="Caption" VALUE="Get A Question">
    <PARAM NAME="Size" VALUE="6703;1164">
    <PARAM NAME="FontCharSet" VALUE="0">
    <PARAM NAME="FontPitchAndFamily" VALUE="2">
    <PARAM NAME="ParagraphAlign" VALUE="3">
    <PARAM NAME="FontWeight" VALUE="0">
</OBJECT>

<OBJECT ID="OB_Answer1"
 CLASSID="CLSID:8BD21D50-EC42-11CE-9E0D-00AA006002F3"
 STYLE="TOP:50pt;LEFT:330pt;WIDTH:139pt;HEIGHT:17pt;
        TABINDEX:3;ZINDEX:3;">
    <PARAM NAME="BackColor" VALUE="-2147483633">
    <PARAM NAME="ForeColor" VALUE="-2147483630">
    <PARAM NAME="DisplayStyle" VALUE="5">
    <PARAM NAME="Size" VALUE="4904;600">
    <PARAM NAME="Value" VALUE="True">
    <PARAM NAME="Caption" VALUE="Answer #1">
    <PARAM NAME="FontCharSet" VALUE="0">
    <PARAM NAME="FontPitchAndFamily" VALUE="2">
    <PARAM NAME="FontWeight" VALUE="0">
</OBJECT>

<OBJECT ID="OB_Answer2"
 CLASSID="CLSID:8BD21D50-EC42-11CE-9E0D-00AA006002F3"
 STYLE="TOP:83pt;LEFT:329pt;WIDTH:132pt;HEIGHT:16pt;
        TABINDEX:4;ZINDEX:4;">
    <PARAM NAME="BackColor" VALUE="-2147483633">
    <PARAM NAME="ForeColor" VALUE="-2147483630">
    <PARAM NAME="DisplayStyle" VALUE="5">
    <PARAM NAME="Size" VALUE="4657;564">
```

```html
      <PARAM NAME="Value" VALUE="False">
      <PARAM NAME="Caption" VALUE="Answer #2">
      <PARAM NAME="FontCharSet" VALUE="0">
      <PARAM NAME="FontPitchAndFamily" VALUE="2">
      <PARAM NAME="FontWeight" VALUE="0">
    </OBJECT>

    <OBJECT ID="OB_Answer3"
     CLASSID="CLSID:8BD21D50-EC42-11CE-9E0D-00AA006002F3"
     STYLE="TOP:116pt;LEFT:329pt;WIDTH:132pt;HEIGHT:17pt;
         TABINDEX:5;ZINDEX:5;">
      <PARAM NAME="BackColor" VALUE="-2147483633">
      <PARAM NAME="ForeColor" VALUE="-2147483630">
      <PARAM NAME="DisplayStyle" VALUE="5">
      <PARAM NAME="Size" VALUE="4657;600">
      <PARAM NAME="Value" VALUE="False">
      <PARAM NAME="Caption" VALUE="Answer #3">
      <PARAM NAME="FontCharSet" VALUE="0">
      <PARAM NAME="FontPitchAndFamily" VALUE="2">
      <PARAM NAME="FontWeight" VALUE="0">
    </OBJECT>

    <OBJECT ID="Cmd_Answer"
     CLASSID="CLSID:D7053240-CE69-11CD-A777-00DD01143C57"
     STYLE="TOP:158pt;LEFT:281pt;WIDTH:190pt;HEIGHT:33pt;
         TABINDEX:6;ZINDEX:6;">
      <PARAM NAME="Caption" VALUE="Give Your Answer">
      <PARAM NAME="Size" VALUE="6703;1164">
      <PARAM NAME="FontCharSet" VALUE="0">
      <PARAM NAME="FontPitchAndFamily" VALUE="2">
      <PARAM NAME="ParagraphAlign" VALUE="3">
      <PARAM NAME="FontWeight" VALUE="0">
    </OBJECT>

    <OBJECT ID="Cmd_Setup"
     CLASSID="CLSID:D7053240-CE69-11CD-A777-00DD01143C57"
     STYLE="TOP:215pt;LEFT:41pt;WIDTH:215pt;HEIGHT:50pt;
         TABINDEX:7;ZINDEX:7;">
      <PARAM NAME="Caption" VALUE="Set up a new game">
      <PARAM NAME="Size" VALUE="7585;1764">
      <PARAM NAME="FontCharSet" VALUE="0">
      <PARAM NAME="FontPitchAndFamily" VALUE="2">
      <PARAM NAME="ParagraphAlign" VALUE="3">
      <PARAM NAME="FontWeight" VALUE="0">
    </OBJECT>

  </DIV>
```

Setup Tasks In The Trivia, Forsooth Code

This program example uses **if...then...else** statements, as well as many of the concepts you learned in Chapters 3 and 4. The first thing the code does is declare some global variables. Normally, variables should be hidden inside subs or functions, but these variables need to be used by several different subs: That's why they have to be global. The variables are declared as follows:

```
dim Questions(5)
dim Choices(5,3)
dim QuestionNum
dim GameSetUp
```

The variables **Questions** and **Choices** are all arrays—that is, variables that have slots to hold multiple variables. Arrays are covered in Chapter 3. The variables do the following jobs:

- **Questions** holds the text of questions to be displayed on the Web page in the question box.

- **Choices** holds the possible answers to the questions. The only thing that's a little odd is that the **Choices** array is followed by two numbers in parentheses: This means that it's a two-dimensional array. The first number indicates the question number. For each question, we want to display three possible answers as captions for the three option buttons on the Web page. Therefore, for each value in the question-number slot of the array, there are three corresponding values in the answer slots of the array.

- **QuestionNum** keeps track of the current question number.

- **GameSetUp** is a true-false variable that keeps track of whether or not the user has clicked the Setup button.

Once the variables are declared, the next step required to play the game is for the user to click on the **Cmd_Setup** button. The **Click** event for the button loads the questions and answers into the **Questions** and **Choices** arrays, as well as sets values for **GameSetUp** and **QuestionNum**. From the code, you can see that you access array slots by using the name of the array and the number of the slot: Other than that, you can treat them just as you would any other variable.

At the end of the **Cmd_Setup_Click** sub, the code sets the **QuestionNum** variable to −1. That's so that when the user clicks on the Get A Question button, the value can always be increased by 1 and display the correct question.

Getting A Question

The next step for the user is to click on the Get A Question button. The code for this button's **Click** event is shown in the following code snippet:

```
Sub Cmd_Question_Click()
    if not GameSetUp then
        msgbox "You must click the Setup button first."
        exit sub
    else
        QuestionNum = (QuestionNum + 1) mod 5
        Lbl_Question.caption = Questions(QuestionNum)
        OB_Answer1.value = true
        OB_Answer1.caption = Choices(QuestionNum, 0)
        OB_Answer2.caption = Choices(QuestionNum, 1)
        OB_Answer3.caption = Choices(QuestionNum, 2)
    end if
end sub
```

The first thing that the sub does is check to see if the game has been set up properly—in particular, if the user has already clicked on the **Cmd_Setup** button. If the user hasn't done so, then the sub displays a message telling the user about the problem. It then uses the statement **exit sub** to exit from the sub. That way, if the game hasn't been set up, VBScript won't waste its time carrying out the rest of the code lines in the sub. Notice that the code in the **Cmd_Question_Click** sub is a classic example of a multiple-line **if...then...else** statement, complete with an **end if** at the end.

The **else** clause is where the action begins. First, the code adds 1 to the **QuestionNum** variable. We've allowed room in the **Questions** array for five questions. That leaves us with the problem of what to do when the user clicks on the Get A Question button but has already reached the last question. In this case, we've decided to send the user back to the first question. Remember in Chapter 4 when we looked at the **mod** operator? Any number mod will give you a repeating sequence of values, as shown on the next page:

```
0
1
2
3
4
0
1
2
3
4
(and so on)
```

As it happens, 0, 1, 2, 3, 4 are the numbers of the slots in the **Questions** array. After the last question has been played, the **mod** operator makes the game cycle back to the first question.

The next line of code displays the current question in the label control at the left side of the Web page:

```
Lbl_Question.caption = Questions(QuestionNum)
```

Notice that we assigned text from the current **Questions** array slot to the **caption** property of the label control.

At the right side of the Web page, of course, we have three option buttons (radio buttons) where the player can select an answer to the question. The next lines of code set up these buttons:

```
OB_Answer1.value = true
OB_Answer1.caption = Choices(QuestionNum, 0)
OB_Answer2.caption = Choices(QuestionNum, 1)
OB_Answer3.caption = Choices(QuestionNum, 2)
```

The **value** property of an option button indicates whether or not it appears checked—that is, whether or not there's a black dot in the center of the button. When a question is first loaded, we always want the first option button to be selected. Therefore, we assign true to its **value** property.

Next, we load possible answers into the **caption** properties of the option buttons. For each question, there are three possible answers. Thus, for each value in the **QuestionNum** slot of the array, we cycle through all the slots containing answers—0, 1, 2. Each slot contains text (assigned when the user clicked on the

Cmd_SetUp button) with a possible answer to the current question. Each possible answer is now displayed next to an option button.

Remember How Array Slots Are Numbered
Remember that array slot numbering in VBScript always begins at 0. That's why our three possible answers to each Trivia, Forsooth question are in slots numbered 0, 1, and 2.

After that, an **end if** statement ends the **if** statement. That's all there is in the sub for getting a question.

Giving An Answer

When the user clicks on the Give Your Answer button, the event code for that button is carried out. It's a long sub, but it's really quite simple because it repeats the same code pattern for each different question. The code for the first question is shown in the following code snippet:

```
if QuestionNum = 0 then
    if OB_Answer3.value = true then
        msgbox "That's right! It's Montpelier!",, _
            "Trivia, Forsooth"
    else
        msgbox "Sorry, wrong answer! The capital is Montpelier!",, _
            "Trivia, Forsooth"
    end if
end if
```

Essentially, this is just another **if...then...else** statement. The **if** clause checks the value of the option button that holds the correct answer for the current question number. If the player has checked that option button, then its value will be true. The sub displays a message box congratulating the player on giving the right answer.

If the correct option button is not checked, then the **else** clause kicks in. VBScript displays a message box telling the player that his/her answer was incorrect and giving the correct answer.

There's only one other thing about this code pattern that's kind of interesting. Notice that we've embedded one **if..then..else** statement inside a multiple-line **if** statement. First, the "big" **if** statement checks the current question number.

If the question number doesn't match—in the code snippet, if it's not 0 and we're not on the first question—then VBScript skips everything else in that particular **if** statement and goes on to the next big **if** statement. The next big **if** statement asks if **QuestionNum = 1**, meaning, Are we on the second question in the game?, and so on.

Embedding one **if** statement inside another is something you'll do very often. All you need to remember is that an **if** statement is a statement. When you're embedding it inside another **if** statement, you follow the same rules as you would if you were embedding any other statement, such as a **MsgBox** statement.

And that's it for Trivia, Forsooth! I hope that this example has not only given you a better understanding of how **if** statements work, but has also shown you the immense VBScript power that you already have in your hands.

Looping Statements

A different kind of control structure is the *looping statement*. A looping statement causes a statement or sequence of statements to repeat. The most common kinds of looping statement are the **for** loop and the **do** loop. (VBScript 2 also supports a **for each...next** loop, but you're likely to use that less often and I won't cover it here.)

for Loops

A **for** loop usually counts from one number to another number, and on each count, carries out the statements inside the loop. That's why it's ideal when you know in advance how many times the loop should repeat. Here's a typical example of a **for** loop:

```
for i = 0 to 9
    AnArray(i) = ""
next
```

This **for** loop initializes an array by inserting a blank value in each array slot. The syntax of the **for** loop is as follows:

```
for x=1 to y
    A
    B
    C
next
```

Here, **x** is a loop counter variable that you have to declare separately from the loop itself. On each pass through the loop, the loop statements (A, B, and C) are carried out. Then, **next** sends VBScript back to the top of the loop, the value of the loop counter variable is increased by 1, and the loop statements execute again. This process continues until the loop counter variable's value exceeds the value of **y**. At that point, the program drops out of the loop and goes on with the next statement (if any).

There's also an optional **step** part of the loop statement. With **step**, you can control how much the loop counter variable increases on each pass through the loop. The following code snippet gives an example:

```
for x = 0 to 25 step 5
    MsgBox "The current loop number is " & x & "."
next
```

Without the **step** option, this loop would display the following sequence of messages:

```
The current loop number is 0.
The current loop number is 1.
The current loop number is 2.
The current loop number is 3.
The current loop number is 4.
The current loop number is 5.
(and so on)
```

However, with the **step** option set to 5, the following messages would be displayed:

```
The current loop number is 0.
The current loop number is 5.
The current loop number is 10.
The current loop number is 15.
The current loop number is 20.
The current loop number is 25.
```

A Simple for Loop Example

That's all abstract, so let's look at a specific example. Listing 5.3 gives the HTML code for a page that demonstrates a simple **for** loop, while Listing 5.4 gives the ActiveX layout and the VBScript code. The resulting Web page is shown in Figure 5.3.

Listing 5.3 HTML CODE FOR THE WEB PAGE IN FIGURE 5.3.

```
<HTML>
<HEAD>
<TITLE>For Loop Demonstration</TITLE>
</HEAD>
<BODY>

<OBJECT CLASSID="CLSID:812AE312-8B8E-11CF-93C8-00AA00C08FDF"
ID="forloop1" STYLE="LEFT:0;TOP:0">
<PARAM NAME="ALXPATH" REF VALUE="file:C:\MyDocs\VBScript\
    chap05\forloop1.alx">
</OBJECT>

</BODY>
</HTML>
```

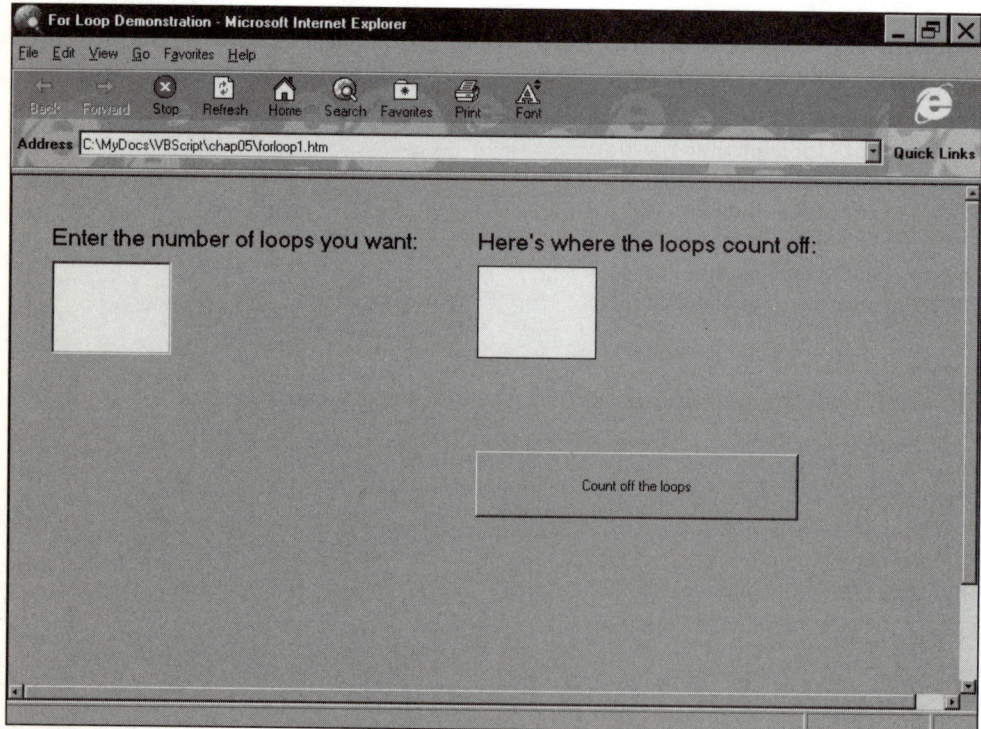

Figure 5.3
Demonstrating a very fast for loop.

Listing 5.4 VBSCRIPT CODE AND ACTIVEX LAYOUT FOR THE WEB PAGE.

```
<SCRIPT LANGUAGE="VBScript">
<!--
Sub Cmd_DoLoops_Click()
dim LoopCounter, NumLoops
if TB_NumberOfLoops.text = "" then
   msgbox "You must enter the number of loops first.",, _
      "For Loop Demonstration"
else
   NumLoops = TB_NumberOfLoops.text
   for LoopCounter = 1 to NumLoops
      Lbl_LoopDisplay.caption = LoopCounter
   next
end if

end sub
-->
</SCRIPT>
<DIV STYLE="LAYOUT:FIXED;WIDTH:597pt;HEIGHT:370pt;">
    <OBJECT ID="Lbl_LoopDisplay"
     CLASSID="CLSID:978C9E23-D4B0-11CE-BF2D-00AA003F40D0"
     STYLE="TOP:41pt;LEFT:281pt;WIDTH:74pt;HEIGHT:58pt;ZINDEX:0;">
        <PARAM NAME="BackColor" VALUE="16777215">
        <PARAM NAME="Size" VALUE="2611;2046">
        <PARAM NAME="BorderStyle" VALUE="1">
        <PARAM NAME="FontName" VALUE="Times New Roman">
        <PARAM NAME="FontHeight" VALUE="480">
        <PARAM NAME="FontCharSet" VALUE="0">
        <PARAM NAME="FontPitchAndFamily" VALUE="2">
        <PARAM NAME="FontWeight" VALUE="0">
    </OBJECT>

    <OBJECT ID="TB_NumberOfLoops"
     CLASSID="CLSID:8BD21D10-EC42-11CE-9E0D-00AA006002F3"
     STYLE="TOP:41pt;LEFT:17pt;WIDTH:74pt;HEIGHT:58pt;
        TABINDEX:1;ZINDEX:1;">
        <PARAM NAME="VariousPropertyBits" VALUE="746604571">
        <PARAM NAME="Size" VALUE="2611;2046">
        <PARAM NAME="FontName" VALUE="Times New Roman">
        <PARAM NAME="FontHeight" VALUE="480">
        <PARAM NAME="FontCharSet" VALUE="0">
        <PARAM NAME="FontPitchAndFamily" VALUE="2">
        <PARAM NAME="FontWeight" VALUE="0">
    </OBJECT>
```

```
        <OBJECT ID="Label2"
         CLASSID="CLSID:978C9E23-D4B0-11CE-BF2D-00AA003F40D0"
         STYLE="TOP:17pt;LEFT:17pt;WIDTH:248pt;
                HEIGHT:17pt;ZINDEX:2;">
            <PARAM NAME="Caption"
                VALUE="Enter the number of loops you want:">
            <PARAM NAME="Size" VALUE="8749;600">
            <PARAM NAME="FontHeight" VALUE="280">
            <PARAM NAME="FontCharSet" VALUE="0">
            <PARAM NAME="FontPitchAndFamily" VALUE="2">
            <PARAM NAME="FontWeight" VALUE="0">
        </OBJECT>

        <OBJECT ID="Label3"
         CLASSID="CLSID:978C9E23-D4B0-11CE-BF2D-00AA003F40D0"
         STYLE="TOP:17pt;LEFT:281pt;WIDTH:239pt;HEIGHT:17pt;ZINDEX:3;">
            <PARAM NAME="Caption" VALUE="Here's where the loops
                count off:">
            <PARAM NAME="Size" VALUE="8431;600">
            <PARAM NAME="FontHeight" VALUE="280">
            <PARAM NAME="FontCharSet" VALUE="0">
            <PARAM NAME="FontPitchAndFamily" VALUE="2">
            <PARAM NAME="FontWeight" VALUE="0">
        </OBJECT>

        <OBJECT ID="Cmd_DoLoops"
         CLASSID="CLSID:D7053240-CE69-11CD-A777-00DD01143C57"
         STYLE="TOP:157pt;LEFT:281pt;WIDTH:198pt;
                HEIGHT:41pt;TABINDEX:4;ZINDEX:4;">
            <PARAM NAME="Caption" VALUE="Count off the loops">
            <PARAM NAME="Size" VALUE="6985;1446">
            <PARAM NAME="FontCharSet" VALUE="0">
            <PARAM NAME="FontPitchAndFamily" VALUE="2">
            <PARAM NAME="ParagraphAlign" VALUE="3">
            <PARAM NAME="FontWeight" VALUE="0">
        </OBJECT>
</DIV>
```

This program uses a fairly simple—if somewhat atypical—**for** loop. The user enters a number in the text box on the left side of the Web page. Then, when he/she clicks the command button, the **for** loop executes. On each pass through the loop, it displays the current loop number in the label on the right side of the Web page.

Now, if you run this program, all you're likely to see displayed is the last number in the sequence—i.e., the same number the user entered in the text box.

That's because the loop runs so blindingly fast that the other numbers whiz by too quickly for you to see. It's not a big worry, because **for** loops are used most often to initialize arrays and for other tasks that don't need to be slowed down for human eyes.

do Loops

The other major kind of loop in VBScript (apart from **while...wend**, which we won't cover here) is the **do** loop. This type of loop is normally used when you do not know in advance how many times the loops should execute: All you know is that it should execute either (a) *as long as* a certain condition is true, in which case, you'd add a **while** clause; or (b) *until* a certain condition becomes true, in which case, you'd add an **until** clause.

Whether you use **while** or **until**, there are two varieties of **do** loops. When you're setting up a **do** loop, you need to ask if the loop should always execute at least once, no matter what. For example, suppose that you set up a loop to execute while **x** is less than 10 and the program gets to the **do** loop and **x** already equals 15. Do you still need the loop statements to be carried out at least once?

Your answer to that question will determine which kind of **do** statement you use. If you don't want the loop statements to execute at all if the loop condition is false when the program gets to the loop, you put **while** or **until** at the top of the loop, as shown in the following code snippet:

```
do while x < 10
    A
    B
    C
loop
```

When the program reaches this loop, it first checks to see if **x** is less than 10. If it is, then the program carries out statements **A**, **B**, **C**, and **x = x + 1**. The **loop** keyword then sends the program back to the first line of the loop, and the **x** check is repeated. This process continues as long as **x** is less than 10. The value of **x** might be set by a user clicking a button: Make absolutely sure that you always include a way for your loop to terminate. Otherwise, your program will go into an endless loop, and you'll miss dinner.

If you want the loop to execute at least once, whether or not the loop condition is true when the program gets to the loop, you put **while** or **until** at the bottom of the loop. This is shown in the following code snippet:

```
do
    A
    B
    C
loop while x < 10
```

In this case, when the program gets to the loop, it does not first check to see if the loop condition is true. That means it will always execute the statements in the loop at least once. After executing the loop statements, the program gets to the **loop while** clause and checks to see if the loop condition is true. If it is, then it goes back to the top of the loop and repeats the process. Otherwise, it goes on to the next statement following the loop.

Using **select case** Statements

VBScript's **if** statements are fine, but you saw how involved and repetitive they could get with only five alternatives—the five questions in Trivia, Forsooth. If you wanted to increase the number of questions to 15 or 20, your VBScript code would get terribly cluttered with all those **if...else** statements.

Fortunately, there's an alternative: **select case**. This type of branching statement, often called simply a "case" statement for short, gives you a neat and economical way to handle multiple alternatives. The basic syntax of a **select case** statement is as follows:

```
select case ControlVariable
    case X
        ' Some VBScript statements
    case Y
        ' Some VBScript statements
    case Z
        ' Some VBScript statements
    case else
        ' Some VBScript statements
end select
```

The **select case** statement tests the value of the control variable—here, rather unimaginatively called **ControlVariable**. Each case has a list of one or more constants, which can be numbers, strings, or any valid VBScript data type. When the value of the control variable matches a particular case, VBScript does all the statements for that case. If the control variable doesn't match a value in any of the cases, then VBScript does the statements that go with **case else**. Finally, the program drops out of the **select case** statement and moves on to the next statement after **end select**.

Each case, by the way, can include more than one value. You can have a list of values, or a range, or even an inequality, as shown in the following code lines:

```
case 10, 20, 25, 31
case 10 to 20
case 21 to 30, 75 to 80
case is < 15      ' When specifying a range, use the word IS.
```

Obviously, you wouldn't see all of those cases in a single **select case** statement, inasmuch as there's quite a bit of overlap. But they show what you can do in setting up cases for a **select case** statement.

A Simple **select case** Example

Let's look at a simple example of a **select case** statement in action. Listing 5.5 shows the VBScript code and ActiveX layout for a Web page that gets the user's first name, then makes a comment about it. Listing 5.6 shows the HTML code that uses the layout. Figure 5.4 shows the Web page set up by the code.

Listing 5.5 A SIMPLE **select case** EXAMPLE.

```
<SCRIPT LANGUAGE="VBScript">
<!--
Sub Cmd_Ask_Click()
   dim UserName

   UserName = TB_UserName.text

   select case UserName
   case "Scott"
      msgbox "Are you the author of this book?",,"Select Case _
         Statements"
   case "Ludwig"
      msgbox "Are you of Germanic ancestry?",,"Select Case _
         Statements"
```

```
      case "Fabio"
        msgbox "Are you a total and utter geek?",,"Select Case _
           Statements"
      case else
        msgbox "That's a very nice name!",,"Select Case Statements"
      end select

end sub
-->

</SCRIPT>

<DIV STYLE="LAYOUT:FIXED;WIDTH:597pt;HEIGHT:370pt;">
    <OBJECT ID="Label1"
     CLASSID="CLSID:978C9E23-D4B0-11CE-BF2D-00AA003F40D0"
     STYLE="TOP:99pt;LEFT:116pt;WIDTH:140pt;HEIGHT:25pt;ZINDEX:0;">
        <PARAM NAME="Caption" VALUE="Enter your first name:">
        <PARAM NAME="Size" VALUE="4948;873">
        <PARAM NAME="FontName" VALUE="Times New Roman">
        <PARAM NAME="FontHeight" VALUE="320">
        <PARAM NAME="FontCharSet" VALUE="0">
        <PARAM NAME="FontPitchAndFamily" VALUE="2">
        <PARAM NAME="FontWeight" VALUE="0">
    </OBJECT>

    <OBJECT ID="TB_UserName"
     CLASSID="CLSID:8BD21D10-EC42-11CE-9E0D-00AA006002F3"
     STYLE="TOP:99pt;LEFT:272pt;WIDTH:140pt;
            HEIGHT:25pt;TABINDEX:1;ZINDEX:1;">
        <PARAM NAME="VariousPropertyBits" VALUE="746604571">
        <PARAM NAME="Size" VALUE="4948;873">
        <PARAM NAME="FontHeight" VALUE="360">
        <PARAM NAME="FontCharSet" VALUE="0">
        <PARAM NAME="FontPitchAndFamily" VALUE="2">
        <PARAM NAME="FontWeight" VALUE="0">
    </OBJECT>

    <OBJECT ID="Cmd_Ask"
     CLASSID="CLSID:D7053240-CE69-11CD-A777-00DD01143C57"
     STYLE="TOP:157pt;LEFT:182pt;WIDTH:182pt;
            HEIGHT:33pt;TABINDEX:2;ZINDEX:2;">
        <PARAM NAME="Caption" VALUE="Ask VBScript about your name">
        <PARAM NAME="Size" VALUE="6403;1164">
        <PARAM NAME="FontCharSet" VALUE="0">
        <PARAM NAME="FontPitchAndFamily" VALUE="2">
        <PARAM NAME="ParagraphAlign" VALUE="3">
        <PARAM NAME="FontWeight" VALUE="0">
    </OBJECT>
```

```
        <OBJECT ID="Label2"
         CLASSID="CLSID:978C9E23-D4B0-11CE-BF2D-00AA003F40D0"
         STYLE="TOP:33pt;LEFT:83pt;WIDTH:380pt;HEIGHT:41pt;ZINDEX:3;">
            <PARAM NAME="Caption"
                VALUE="A Demonstration of Select Case Statements">
            <PARAM NAME="Size" VALUE="13388;1455">
            <PARAM NAME="FontName" VALUE="Times New Roman">
            <PARAM NAME="FontEffects" VALUE="1073741825">
            <PARAM NAME="FontHeight" VALUE="400">
            <PARAM NAME="FontCharSet" VALUE="0">
            <PARAM NAME="FontPitchAndFamily" VALUE="2">
            <PARAM NAME="FontWeight" VALUE="700">
        </OBJECT>
</DIV>
```

Listing 5.6 HTML CODE FOR THE LAYOUT IN LISTING 5.5.

```
<HTML>
<HEAD>
<TITLE>Select Case Statements</TITLE>
</HEAD>
<BODY>

<OBJECT CLASSID="CLSID:812AE312-8B8E-11CF-93C8-00AA00C08FDF"
ID="select1" STYLE="LEFT:0;TOP:0">
<PARAM NAME="ALXPATH" REF VALUE=
     "file:C:\MyDocs\VBScript\chap05\select1.alx">
</OBJECT>

</BODY>
</HTML>
```

Let's take a look at how **select case** works in this program. The command button's click event sub begins with two code lines, as follows:

```
dim UserName
UserName = TB_UserName.text
```

The first line declares a local variable to hold the name that the user enters in the text box. The second line assigns the text box's text property to the variable. We'll then use the variable to control the action of the **select case** statement, as follows:

```
select case UserName
   case "Scott"
      msgbox "Are you the author of this book?",, _
          "Select Case Statements"
```

112   Chapter 5

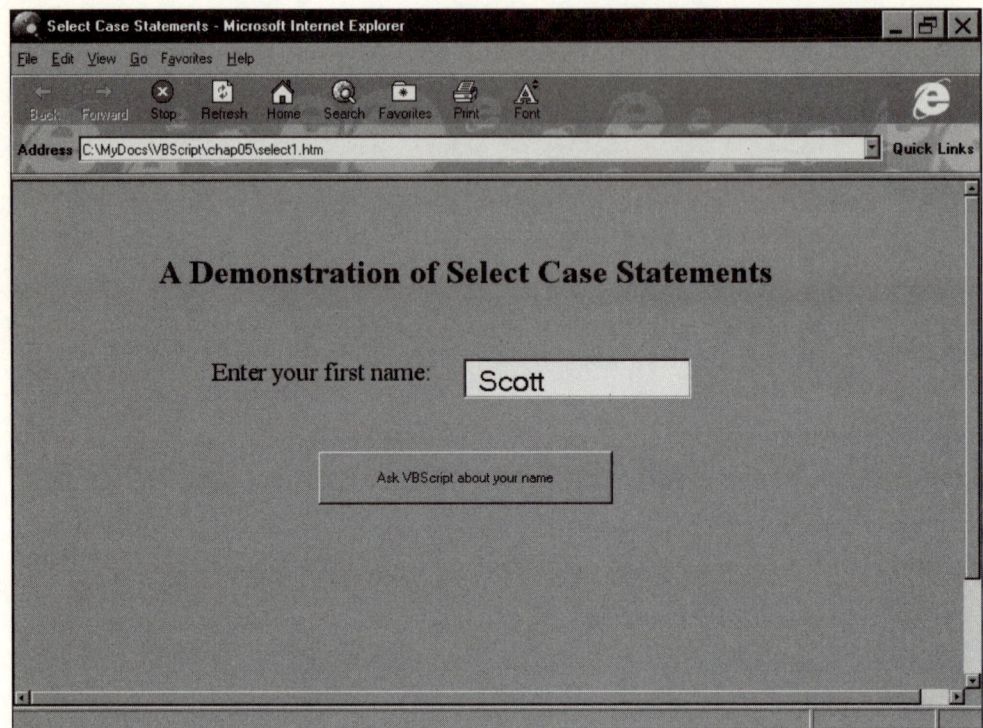

Figure 5.4
The Web page set up by Listings 5.5 and 5.6.

This pattern is repeated for each case, until we get to the optional **case else** clause. That clause is simply a way to catch any cases that we haven't anticipated. At the end of all the cases, we use an **end select** statement to tell VBScript that no more cases are coming.

When the user enters his or her name and clicks on the command button, a message box is displayed like the one shown in Figure 5.5.

Figure 5.5
The program displays a message box.

What, No Break?
If you're coming to VBScript from C or C++, you might wonder why the statements for each case don't end with something like **break**, and why the whole **select case** statement seems devoid of the punctuation (colons, semicolons, etc.) that you use to parse case (i.e., **switch**) statements in C and C++.

The answer is that because of the way VBScript processes **select case** statements, a **break** statement is unnecessary. Moreover, unlike most other languages, such as C, C++, and Pascal, VBScript is a line-oriented language. As a result, no extra punctuation is necessary to distinguish one line from another, whether in a **select case** statement or elsewhere.

A More Sophisticated select case Example

Let's apply the **select case** technique to Trivia, Forsooth to see how it might smooth out our code if we increased the number of questions to 15. Listing 5.7 shows how our VBScript code would change for a game with 15 questions if we used a **select case** statement instead of a series of **if...else** statements. (The HTML code that appears in Listing 5.1 doesn't change, so we won't reproduce it here.) The game works exactly the same as before, but you can imagine how long and cluttered the code would be with three times as many **if...else** statements as appeared earlier in Listing 5.2!

Listing 5.7 Using select case in the Trivia, Forsooth code.

```
<SCRIPT LANGUAGE="VBScript">
<!--
dim Questions(15)
dim Choices(15,3)
dim QuestionNum
dim GameSetUp

Sub Cmd_Setup_Click()

    GameSetUp = True
    MsgBox "The game is ready to play! Click " & _
        ""Get A Question"" to begin.",,"Trivia, Forsooth"
```

```
Questions(0) = "What is the capital of Vermont?"
Questions(1) = "What is the best movie ever made?"
Questions(2) = "What is the best scripting language?"
Questions(3) = "Who played ""Blossom Russo"" on TV?"
Questions(4) = "Who was the Lone Ranger's sidekick?"

Questions(5) = "How many biblical commandments are " & _
    "recognized by Orthodox Judaism?"
Questions(6) = "What is Pee-Wee Herman's real name?"
Questions(7) = "Which Constitutional amendment reserves " & _
    "powers to the states or the people?"
Questions(8) = "How many pounds are in a kilogram?"
Questions(9) = "In what year did Jodie Foster act in the " & _
    " TV series ""Paper Moon""?"

Questions(10) = "In what year did the Germans bomb Pearl Harbor?"
Questions(11) = "Selenium is ..."
Questions(12) = "What is the sixth planet in the solar system?"
Questions(13) = "In Norse mythology, where did the gods live?"
Questions(14) = "Who invented the Pascal programming language?"


Choices(0,0) = "Bismarck"
Choices(0,1) = "Richmond"
Choices(0,2) = "Montpelier"

Choices(1,0) = "Casablanca"
Choices(1,1) = "The Never Ending Story"
Choices(1,2) = "Waterworld"

Choices(2,0) = "VBScript"
Choices(2,1) = "JavaScript"
Choices(2,2) = "Eszterhas"

Choices(3,0) = "Kellie Martin"
Choices(3,1) = "Jodie Foster"
Choices(3,2) = "Mayim Bialik"

Choices(4,0) = "Kato"
Choices(4,1) = "Tonto"
Choices(4,2) = "Snoop Doggy Dogg"

Choices(5,0) = "10"
Choices(5,1) = "613"
Choices(5,2) = "5,280"
```

```
    Choices(6,0) = "Marion Mercer"
    Choices(6,1) = "Paul Rubenfeld"
    Choices(6,2) = "Archibald Leach"

    Choices(7,0) = "The 5th"
    Choices(7,1) = "The 2nd"
    Choices(7,2) = "The 10th"

    Choices(8,0) = "2.2"
    Choices(8,1) = "1.77"
    Choices(8,2) = "5"

    Choices(9,0) = "1980"
    Choices(9,1) = "1961"
    Choices(9,2) = "1974"

    Choices(10,0) = "1945"
    Choices(10,1) = "1941"
    Choices(10,2) = "1918"

    Choices(11,0) = "A planet"
    Choices(11,1) = "A chemical element"
    Choices(11,2) = "The capital of Moldavia"

    Choices(12,0) = "Saturn"
    Choices(12,1) = "Neptune"
    Choices(12,2) = "Mars"

    Choices(13,0) = "Mt. Olympus"
    Choices(13,1) = "Valhalla"
    Choices(13,2) = "Asgard"

    Choices(14,0) = "Antony Hoare"
    Choices(14,1) = "Niklaus Wirth"
    Choices(14,2) = "Mary Worth"

    QuestionNum = -1
end sub

Sub Cmd_Question_Click()
    if not GameSetUp then
        msgbox "You must click the Setup button first.",, _
            "Trivia, Forsooth"
        exit sub
    else
        QuestionNum = (QuestionNum + 1) mod 15
        Lbl_Question.caption = Questions(QuestionNum)
        OB_Answer1.value = true
```

```
            OB_Answer1.caption = Choices(QuestionNum, 0)
            OB_Answer2.caption = Choices(QuestionNum, 1)
            OB_Answer3.caption = Choices(QuestionNum, 2)
        end if
end sub

Sub Cmd_Answer_Click()

    Select Case QuestionNum
    case 2, 8, 12
        if OB_Answer1.value = true then
            MsgBox "That's right! The answer is " & _
                Choices(QuestionNum, 0) & "!",,"Trivia, Forsooth"
        else
            MsgBox "Sorry, wrong! The answer is " & _
                Choices(QuestionNum, 0) & "!",,"Trivia, Forsooth"
        end if
    case 1, 4, 5, 6, 11, 14
        if OB_Answer2.value = true then
            MsgBox "That's right! The answer is " & _
                Choices(QuestionNum, 1) & "!",,"Trivia, Forsooth"
        else
            MsgBox "Sorry, wrong! The answer is " & _
                Choices(QuestionNum, 1) & "!",,"Trivia, Forsooth"
        end if
    case 0, 3, 7, 9, 13
        if OB_Answer3.value = true then
            MsgBox "That's right! The answer is " & _
                Choices(QuestionNum, 2) & "!",,"Trivia, Forsooth"
        else
            MsgBox "Sorry, wrong! The answer is " & _
                Choices(QuestionNum, 2) & "!",,"Trivia, Forsooth"
        end if
    case 10
        MsgBox "SUCKER! It was the Japanese who bombed " & _
            "Pearl Harbor, not the Germans!",,"Trivia, Forsooth"
    case else
        MsgBox "Warning! Program error! Run for your lives!",, _
            "Trivia, Forsooth"
    end select

    Cmd_Question_Click

end sub

-->
```

```
</SCRIPT>
<DIV STYLE="LAYOUT:FIXED;WIDTH:597pt;HEIGHT:370pt;">
    <OBJECT ID="Label1"
     CLASSID="CLSID:978C9E23-D4B0-11CE-BF2D-00AA003F40D0"
     STYLE="TOP:8pt;LEFT:173pt;WIDTH:231pt;HEIGHT:33pt;ZINDEX:0;">
        <PARAM NAME="Caption" VALUE="Trivia, Forsooth">
        <PARAM NAME="Size" VALUE="8149;1164">
        <PARAM NAME="FontName" VALUE="Copperplate Gothic Bold">
        <PARAM NAME="FontEffects" VALUE="1073741825">
        <PARAM NAME="FontHeight" VALUE="480">
        <PARAM NAME="FontCharSet" VALUE="0">
        <PARAM NAME="FontPitchAndFamily" VALUE="2">
        <PARAM NAME="FontWeight" VALUE="700">
    </OBJECT>

    <OBJECT ID="Lbl_Question"
     CLASSID="CLSID:978C9E23-D4B0-11CE-BF2D-00AA003F40D0"
     STYLE="TOP:50pt;LEFT:41pt;WIDTH:190pt;HEIGHT:91pt;ZINDEX:1;">
        <PARAM NAME="BackColor" VALUE="16777215">
        <PARAM NAME="Size" VALUE="6703;3210">
        <PARAM NAME="BorderStyle" VALUE="1">
        <PARAM NAME="FontHeight" VALUE="240">
        <PARAM NAME="FontCharSet" VALUE="0">
        <PARAM NAME="FontPitchAndFamily" VALUE="2">
        <PARAM NAME="FontWeight" VALUE="0">
    </OBJECT>

    <OBJECT ID="Cmd_Question"
     CLASSID="CLSID:D7053240-CE69-11CD-A777-00DD01143C57"
     STYLE="TOP:157pt;LEFT:41pt;WIDTH:190pt;
            HEIGHT:33pt;TABINDEX:2;ZINDEX:2;">
        <PARAM NAME="Caption" VALUE="Get A Question">
        <PARAM NAME="Size" VALUE="6703;1164">
        <PARAM NAME="FontCharSet" VALUE="0">
        <PARAM NAME="FontPitchAndFamily" VALUE="2">
        <PARAM NAME="ParagraphAlign" VALUE="3">
        <PARAM NAME="FontWeight" VALUE="0">
    </OBJECT>

    <OBJECT ID="OB_Answer1"
     CLASSID="CLSID:8BD21D50-EC42-11CE-9E0D-00AA006002F3"
     STYLE="TOP:50pt;LEFT:330pt;WIDTH:139pt;
            HEIGHT:17pt;TABINDEX:3;ZINDEX:3;">
        <PARAM NAME="BackColor" VALUE="-2147483633">
        <PARAM NAME="ForeColor" VALUE="-2147483630">
        <PARAM NAME="DisplayStyle" VALUE="5">
        <PARAM NAME="Size" VALUE="4904;600">
        <PARAM NAME="Value" VALUE="True">
```

```
        <PARAM NAME="Caption" VALUE="Answer #1">
        <PARAM NAME="FontCharSet" VALUE="0">
        <PARAM NAME="FontPitchAndFamily" VALUE="2">
        <PARAM NAME="FontWeight" VALUE="0">
</OBJECT>

<OBJECT ID="OB_Answer2"
 CLASSID="CLSID:8BD21D50-EC42-11CE-9E0D-00AA006002F3"
 STYLE="TOP:83pt;LEFT:329pt;WIDTH:132pt;
        HEIGHT:16pt;TABINDEX:4;ZINDEX:4;">
        <PARAM NAME="BackColor" VALUE="-2147483633">
        <PARAM NAME="ForeColor" VALUE="-2147483630">
        <PARAM NAME="DisplayStyle" VALUE="5">
        <PARAM NAME="Size" VALUE="4657;564">
        <PARAM NAME="Value" VALUE="False">
        <PARAM NAME="Caption" VALUE="Answer #2">
        <PARAM NAME="FontCharSet" VALUE="0">
        <PARAM NAME="FontPitchAndFamily" VALUE="2">
        <PARAM NAME="FontWeight" VALUE="0">
</OBJECT>

<OBJECT ID="OB_Answer3"
 CLASSID="CLSID:8BD21D50-EC42-11CE-9E0D-00AA006002F3"
 STYLE="TOP:116pt;LEFT:329pt;WIDTH:132pt;
        HEIGHT:17pt;TABINDEX:5;ZINDEX:5;">
        <PARAM NAME="BackColor" VALUE="-2147483633">
        <PARAM NAME="ForeColor" VALUE="-2147483630">
        <PARAM NAME="DisplayStyle" VALUE="5">
        <PARAM NAME="Size" VALUE="4657;600">
        <PARAM NAME="Value" VALUE="False">
        <PARAM NAME="Caption" VALUE="Answer #3">
        <PARAM NAME="FontCharSet" VALUE="0">
        <PARAM NAME="FontPitchAndFamily" VALUE="2">
        <PARAM NAME="FontWeight" VALUE="0">
</OBJECT>

<OBJECT ID="Cmd_Answer"
 CLASSID="CLSID:D7053240-CE69-11CD-A777-00DD01143C57"
 STYLE="TOP:158pt;LEFT:281pt;WIDTH:190pt;
        HEIGHT:33pt;TABINDEX:6;ZINDEX:6;">
        <PARAM NAME="Caption" VALUE="Give Your Answer">
        <PARAM NAME="Size" VALUE="6703;1164">
        <PARAM NAME="FontCharSet" VALUE="0">
        <PARAM NAME="FontPitchAndFamily" VALUE="2">
        <PARAM NAME="ParagraphAlign" VALUE="3">
        <PARAM NAME="FontWeight" VALUE="0">
</OBJECT>
```

```
      <OBJECT ID="Cmd_Setup"
       CLASSID="CLSID:D7053240-CE69-11CD-A777-00DD01143C57"
       STYLE="TOP:215pt;LEFT:41pt;WIDTH:215pt;
              HEIGHT:50pt;TABINDEX:7;ZINDEX:7;">
         <PARAM NAME="Caption" VALUE="Set up a new game">
         <PARAM NAME="Size" VALUE="7585;1764">
         <PARAM NAME="FontCharSet" VALUE="0">
         <PARAM NAME="FontPitchAndFamily" VALUE="2">
         <PARAM NAME="ParagraphAlign" VALUE="3">
         <PARAM NAME="FontWeight" VALUE="0">
      </OBJECT>
</DIV>
```

Other than the **select case** statement, the code works the same as before, so let's focus on the **select case** statement. As in our simpler **select case** example, it begins by specifying the control variable:

```
Select Case QuestionNum
```

Each case corresponds to one of the possible answers to a question—answer 1, answer 2, or answer 3. For example, if you scan through the answers, you'll see that the user gives a correct answer to questions 2, 8, and 12 by clicking on the first option button—that is, by picking the first possible answer. Therefore, the first case in the **select case** statement is as follows:

```
case 2, 8, 12
      if OB_Answer1.value = true then
         MsgBox "That's right! The answer is " & _
            Choices(QuestionNum, 0) & "!",,"Trivia, Forsooth"
      else
         MsgBox "Sorry, wrong! The answer is " & _
            Choices(QuestionNum, 0) & "!",,"Trivia, Forsooth"
      end if
```

The statements in this case, of course, will only be executed if the value of **QuestionNum** is 2, 8, or 12. VBScript then checks to see if the user selected the first option button. If so, then the user gave the correct answer and gets a congratulatory message box. Otherwise—as in the **else** clause—the user gave an incorrect answer and gets a message box about the error.

Notice that we've made one other enhancement in the code. In the original version, the message boxes were hard-coded with the specific answer to an individual question, as in the following:

```
msgbox "That's right! It's VBScript!",,"Trivia, Forsooth"
```

When we're grouping together several questions in each case, that kind of hard-coding isn't possible. Fortunately, it isn't necessary, either. All we needed to do was remember that the correct answer for each question is stored in a particular slot of the **Choices** array. Then, for each case, we simply pull the answer out of that slot and plug it into the message boxes we show to the user, as follows:

```
MsgBox "That's right! The answer is " & _
            Choices(QuestionNum, 0) & "!",,"Trivia, Forsooth"
```

That's it for control structures! In the next chapter, we'll take our first look at the ActiveX Control Pad and how you can use it to create snazzy Web page layouts like the one used in the Trivia, Forsooth game.

6

Using Subs And Functions

By now, you've seen lots of subs and functions. This chapter will give you all the details on how, when, and why to create them.

We've been using subs and functions all through the previous five chapters, but we've never really paused to examine what they are or how they work. Both subs and functions are named blocks of code. However, they differ in an important way. In a nutshell:

- Subs (procedures) *perform program tasks.*
- Functions *return values.*

VBScript comes with a large number of predefined subs and functions. You can also create your own for program-specific tasks.

Subs Vs. Functions: Vive La Différence

Subs do things like responding to events and directing the program to go in one direction or another. Every time the user clicks a command button, that button's **Click** sub fires, executing the statements it contains and performing a specific program action.

Functions, on the other hand, simply take values, massage them, and return new values based on the ones they received. For example, you might need to know the square root of a number. You could hand the number to VBScript's **sqr()** function, and the function would immediately hand back the square root.

A good way to visualize the contrast between subs and functions is to think of subs as complete sentences and functions as individual words. Consider **MsgBox**, which comes in both a sub version (the **MsgBox** statement) and a function version (the **MsgBox** function). A **MsgBox** statement (or sub) stands by itself on a code line, as follows:

```
MsgBox "This is the message box caption." _
    ,,"This is the message box title."
```

The **MsgBox** function, on the other hand, is part of a program statement, just as an English word is part of a spoken or written statement. This is illustrated in the following code line:

```
UserChoice = MsgBox("This is the message box caption.",3, _
    "This is the message box title.")
```

There are a couple of other differences, but the main point should be clear: A sub is like a complete sentence, whereas a function is like a word.

The **MsgBox** Sub Vs. The **MsgBox** Function

Let's look at an example that illustrates this contrast. In previous chapters, we've used the **MsgBox** statement several times to display message boxes on the user's screen. These message boxes really didn't do anything but display a message. Often, that's plenty.

But suppose you want to display a message box that gets a value from the user. By using the **MsgBox** function instead of the **MsgBox** statement, you can display a message box that has multiple buttons and immediately hands back a value indicating which button the user clicked. Listing 6.1 shows the VBScript code and ActiveX layout for a program that uses both the **MsgBox** statement and the

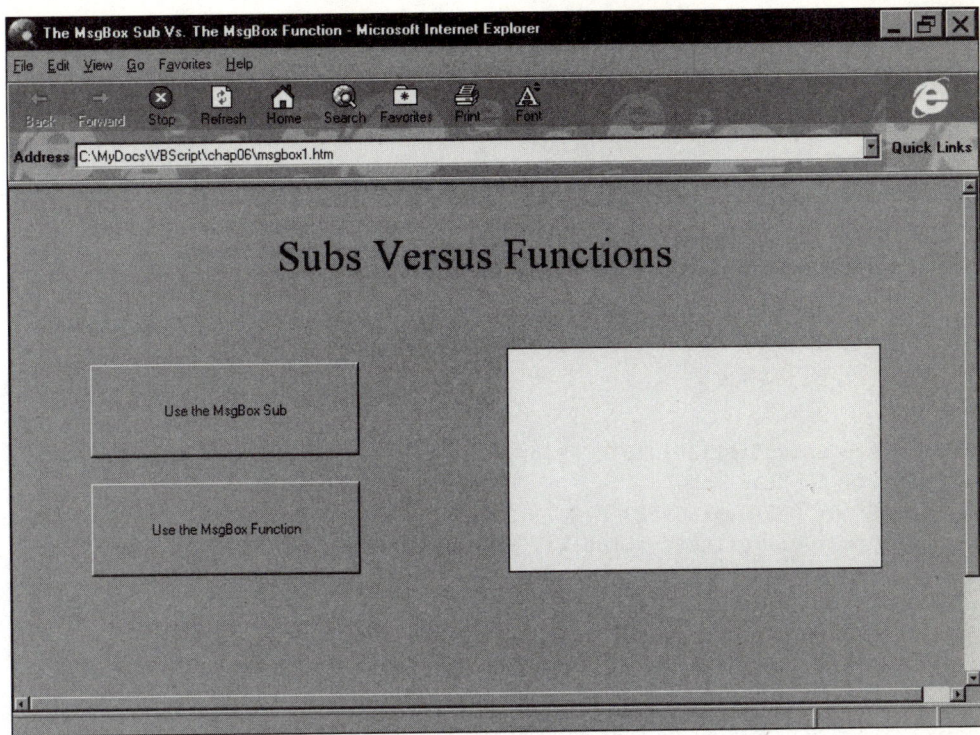

Figure 6.1
A Web page that uses both the **MsgBox** statement and the **MsgBox** function.

MsgBox function; Listing 6.2 shows the HTML code that sets up the containing Web page. Figure 6.1 shows the Web page created by Listings 6.1 and 6.2.

Listing 6.1 VBSCRIPT CODE AND ACTIVEX LAYOUT FOR A **MsgBox** DEMONSTRATION.

```
<SCRIPT LANGUAGE="VBScript">
<!--
Sub Cmd_Function_Click()
dim UserChoice

UserChoice = MsgBox("This is displayed by the MsgBox function. " & _
    "It gets a value from the user. Do you want to display your " & _
    "answer in the label control at the right?",3,"Subs vs. Functions")

    select case UserChoice
        case 6
            Lbl_Answer.caption = "Yes!"
        case 7
            lbl_Answer.caption = "No!"
```

```
        case 2
            lbl_Answer.caption = ""
    end select

end sub

Sub Cmd_Sub_Click()
MsgBox "This is displayed by the MsgBox sub. It simply " & _
    "displays information: It doesn't get a value back from " & _
    "the user.",,"Subs vs. Functions"
end sub
-->
</SCRIPT>

<DIV STYLE="LAYOUT:FIXED;WIDTH:597pt;HEIGHT:370pt;">
    <OBJECT ID="Label1"
     CLASSID="CLSID:978C9E23-D4B0-11CE-BF2D-00AA003F40D0"
     STYLE="TOP:17pt;LEFT:157pt;WIDTH:256pt;HEIGHT:33pt;ZINDEX:0;">
        <PARAM NAME="Caption" VALUE="Subs Versus Functions">
        <PARAM NAME="Size" VALUE="9031;1164">
        <PARAM NAME="FontName" VALUE="Times New Roman">
        <PARAM NAME="FontHeight" VALUE="520">
        <PARAM NAME="FontCharSet" VALUE="0">
        <PARAM NAME="FontPitchAndFamily" VALUE="2">
        <PARAM NAME="FontWeight" VALUE="0">
    </OBJECT>

    <OBJECT ID="Cmd_Sub"
     CLASSID="CLSID:D7053240-CE69-11CD-A777-00DD01143C57"
     STYLE="TOP:99pt;LEFT:41pt;WIDTH:165pt;HEIGHT:58pt;
            TABINDEX:1;ZINDEX:1;">
        <PARAM NAME="Caption" VALUE="Use the MsgBox Sub">
        <PARAM NAME="Size" VALUE="5821;2046">
        <PARAM NAME="FontCharSet" VALUE="0">
        <PARAM NAME="FontPitchAndFamily" VALUE="2">
        <PARAM NAME="ParagraphAlign" VALUE="3">
        <PARAM NAME="FontWeight" VALUE="0">
    </OBJECT>

    <OBJECT ID="Cmd_Function"
     CLASSID="CLSID:D7053240-CE69-11CD-A777-00DD01143C57"
     STYLE="TOP:173pt;LEFT:41pt;WIDTH:165pt;HEIGHT:58pt;
            TABINDEX:2;ZINDEX:2;">
        <PARAM NAME="Caption" VALUE="Use the MsgBox Function">
        <PARAM NAME="Size" VALUE="5821;2046">
        <PARAM NAME="FontCharSet" VALUE="0">
        <PARAM NAME="FontPitchAndFamily" VALUE="2">
```

```
            <PARAM NAME="ParagraphAlign" VALUE="3">
            <PARAM NAME="FontWeight" VALUE="0">
    </OBJECT>

    <OBJECT ID="Lbl_Answer"
      CLASSID="CLSID:978C9E23-D4B0-11CE-BF2D-00AA003F40D0"
      STYLE="TOP:91pt;LEFT:297pt;WIDTH:231pt;
           HEIGHT:140pt;ZINDEX:3;">
            <PARAM NAME="BackColor" VALUE="16777215">
            <PARAM NAME="Size" VALUE="8149;4939">
            <PARAM NAME="BorderStyle" VALUE="1">
            <PARAM NAME="FontName" VALUE="Times New Roman">
            <PARAM NAME="FontHeight" VALUE="720">
            <PARAM NAME="FontCharSet" VALUE="0">
            <PARAM NAME="FontPitchAndFamily" VALUE="2">
            <PARAM NAME="FontWeight" VALUE="0">
    </OBJECT>
</DIV>
```

Listing 6.2 HTML code for the Web page that uses Listing 6.1.

```
<HTML>
<HEAD>
<TITLE>The MsgBox Sub Vs. The MsgBox Function</TITLE>
</HEAD>
<BODY>

<OBJECT CLASSID="CLSID:812AE312-8B8E-11CF-93C8-00AA00C08FDF"
ID="msgbox1" STYLE="LEFT:0;TOP:0">
<PARAM NAME="ALXPATH" REF
     VALUE="file:C:\MyDocs\VBScript\chap06\msgbox1.alx">
</OBJECT>

</BODY>
</HTML>
```

The most immediate difference between the two is visual. When the user clicks on the button labeled Use The MsgBox Sub, a simple message box appears, as shown in Figure 6.2. It has only an OK button. Clicking on the OK button simply closes the message box.

But when the user clicks on the button labeled Use The MsgBox Function, a different result appears. This time, the message box has three buttons: Yes, No, and Cancel, as shown in Figure 6.3. Clicking on the Yes button causes the user's choice to be displayed in the label control at the right, as shown in Figure 6.4.

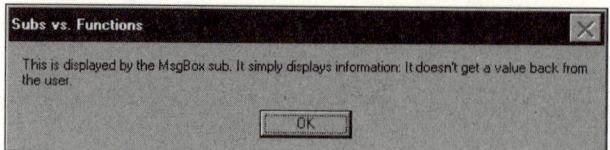

Figure 6.2
The message box displayed by the **MsgBox** sub.

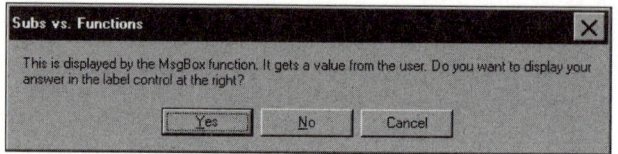

Figure 6.3
The message box displayed by the **MsgBox** function.

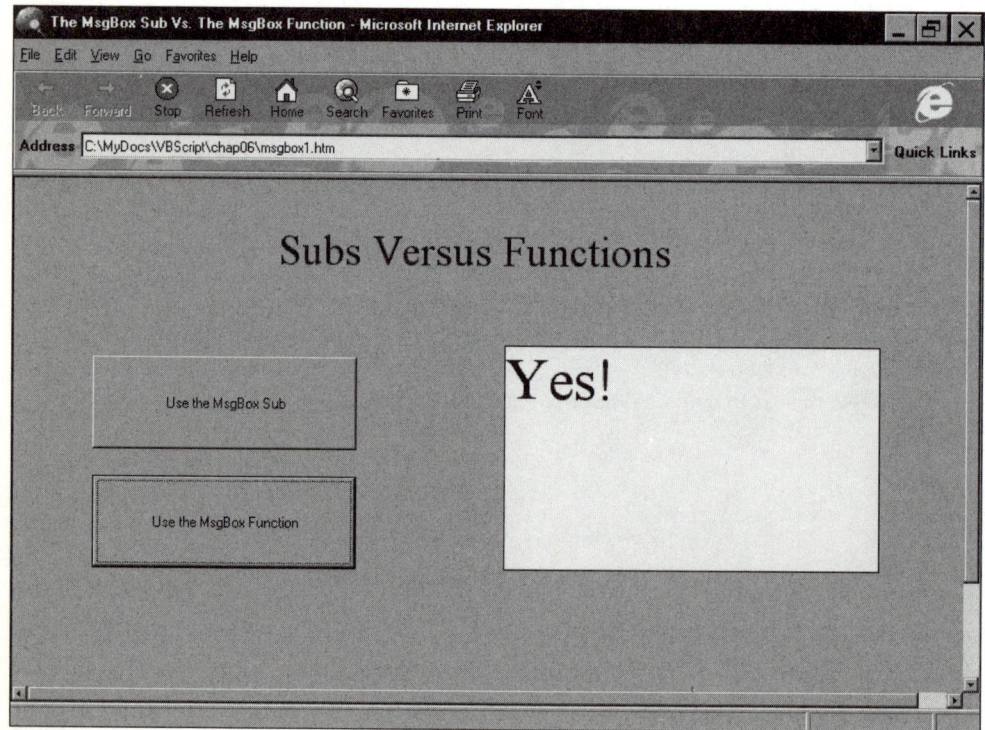

Figure 6.4
The label control displays the user's choice.

DIFFERENCES IN THE CODE

Let's see how the code differs when we compare the sub versus function versions of **MsgBox**. In Listing 6.1, the **Click** event sub for the first command button goes like this:

```
Sub Cmd_Sub_Click()
MsgBox "This is displayed by the MsgBox sub. It simply " & _
    "displays information: It doesn't get a value back from " & _
    "the user.",,"Subs vs. Functions"
end sub
```

This is the same pattern we've seen over and over in previous chapters. First, there's the word **MsgBox**, then the message text, then two commas indicating that a parameter has been omitted, and finally the title of the message box itself. Nothing really new there. But look at the **Click** event sub for the second command button, which uses the **MsgBox** function instead of the sub version:

```
Sub Cmd_Function_Click()
dim UserChoice

UserChoice = MsgBox("This is displayed by the MsgBox function. " & _
    "It gets a value from the user. Do you want to display your " & _
    "answer in the label control at the right?",3,"Subs vs. Functions")

    select case UserChoice
        case 6
            Lbl_Answer.caption = "Yes!"
        case 7
            lbl_Answer.caption = "No!"
        case 2
            lbl_Answer.caption = ""
    end select

end sub
```

This code not only gets the user's choice, but it stores that choice in a variable and then displays the choice in a label control on the Web page. Let's take it from the top.

The first thing that the sub has to do is declare a variable to catch the value returned by the **MsgBox** function—something you don't need to do with the sub version, because it doesn't return a value. **UserChoice** is the variable that will catch the value.

Next, we actually use the **MsgBox** function. Unlike the sub version, however, it doesn't stand on its own in the program statement. Instead, the whole **MsgBox** expression is the right side of an assignment statement. There are two other important differences in the use of the **MsgBox** function itself:

- With the **MsgBox** function, you must put parentheses around the parameter list. You don't have to do that with the **MsgBox** sub.

- With the **MsgBox** function, you should include a parameter for the buttons to be displayed in the message box. That's the parameter after the message text. We usually omit it from calls to the **MsgBox** sub, indicating the omission with two commas (,,). You don't have to include this parameter, but inasmuch as the whole point of using the **MsgBox** function is to get a response from the user, it makes little sense to leave it out.

Finally, we set up a **select case** statement to process the value returned by the message box. If the user clicks on the Yes button, the message box returns a value of 6; if the user clicks on the No button, it returns a value of 7; and if the user clicks on the Cancel button, it returns a value of 2. Depending on which value is returned, the **select case** statement takes an appropriate action.

VALUES THAT DISPLAY BUTTONS OR ICONS IN A MESSAGE BOX

If you're using the **MsgBox** function, you need to know which values will display which buttons. The values are shown in Table 6.1, along with the buttons displayed by each. Some of the values also display icons, such as exclamation marks, in the message box.

But wait! There's more to the story. You aren't limited to the specific entries in the table: You can add them together to display multiple table entries. For example, suppose you wanted to display a message box with Yes, No, and Cancel buttons, along with a Critical Message icon. The value to display Yes, No, and Cancel buttons is 3; the value to display a Critical Message icon is 16. Therefore, as the second parameter in the **MsgBox** function call, you'd put 3 + 16, or 19.

In VBScript 2, it's even easier. Now that there are real program constants, you no longer have to remember the numeric values in the table. Instead, you can use the mnemonic constant names, such as **vbYesNoCancel**. To display the same message box as before, with Yes, No, and Cancel buttons as well as a

Table 6.1

Values that display buttons in message boxes.

Constant	Value	Explanation
vbOKOnly	0	Display OK button.
vbOKCancel	1	Display OK and Cancel buttons.
vbAbortRetryIgnore	2	Display Abort, Retry, and Ignore buttons.
vbYesNoCancel	3	Display Yes, No, and Cancel buttons.
vbYesNo	4	Display Yes and No buttons.
vbRetryCancel	5	Display Retry and Cancel buttons.
vbCritical	16	Display Critical Message icon.
vbQuestion	32	Display Warning Query icon.
vbExclamation	48	Display Warning Message icon.
vbInformation	64	Display Information Message icon.

Critical Message icon, you'd simply write **vbYesNoCancel + vbCritical** instead of the number 19.

In addition to the values that display various things in a message box, there are other values that control how the message box operates. For example, suppose the user simply presses Enter instead of clicking on a button. Which button should that select? The value that sets a "default" button, along with several other values, is shown in Table 6.2.

By adding the desired values from Table 6.1 to the desired values (if any) from Table 6.2, you can make your message box work a few different ways.

Table 6.2

Values that control the operation of message boxes.

Constant	Value	Explanation
vbDefaultButton1	0	First button is the default.
vbDefaultButton2	256	Second button is the default.
vbDefaultButton3	512	Third button is the default.
vbDefaultButton4	768	Fourth button is the default.

TABLE 6.3
VALUES RETURNED BY CLICKING ON MESSAGE BOX BUTTONS.

Constant	Value	Explanation
vbOK	1	OK button was pressed.
vbCancel	2	Cancel button was pressed.
vbAbort	3	Abort button was pressed.
vbRetry	4	Retry button was pressed.
vbIgnore	5	Ignore button was pressed.
vbYes	6	Yes button was pressed.
vbNo	7	No button was pressed.

Finally, it's not enough to put buttons in a message box: When a user clicks on a button, you need to know how to interpret the value it returns. Table 6.3 shows the values returned when the user clicks on the various message box buttons.

Subs, Functions, And Information Hiding
Here's a trick question: How does the **MsgBox** function work? You don't know? Fine. You don't *need* to know. And that spotlights a very important feature of properly designed subs and functions. Other parts of the program should be able to use a sub or function without needing to know anything about its internal workings. All that should be necessary to use a sub or function is its name and parameter list.

Creating Your Own Subs

Most of the subs we've discussed so far have been event handlers for specific controls—in particular, for the click events of various command buttons. That's a very important kind of sub, but it's not the only kind. You can create your own subs that aren't associated with any particular ActiveX controls. These subs can perform tasks that are needed by several controls or other parts of your program. When you create and use your own sub, there are two parts in the process:

- First, you *declare* the sub, in much the same way as you'd declare a variable.
- Second, you *call* the sub, just as you'd call any of VBScript's built-in subs (statements).

To declare a sub, you use the following syntax:

```
Sub ThisIsTheSubName(ParameterName1, ParameterName2, ...)
    ' The code that performs the sub's tasks.
End sub
```

To call the sub, you use its name as a statement in VBScript, adding the desired values as parameters, as follows:

```
ThisIsTheSubName "Joe", 15
```

Inside the sub, the values **Joe** and **15** will be known by their parameter names—**ParameterName1** and **ParameterName2**. Listing 6.3 shows the VBScript code and ActiveX layout for a program demonstrating such a sub. Listing 6.4 shows the HTML code that sets up the Web page. Figure 6.5 shows the Web page created by the listings.

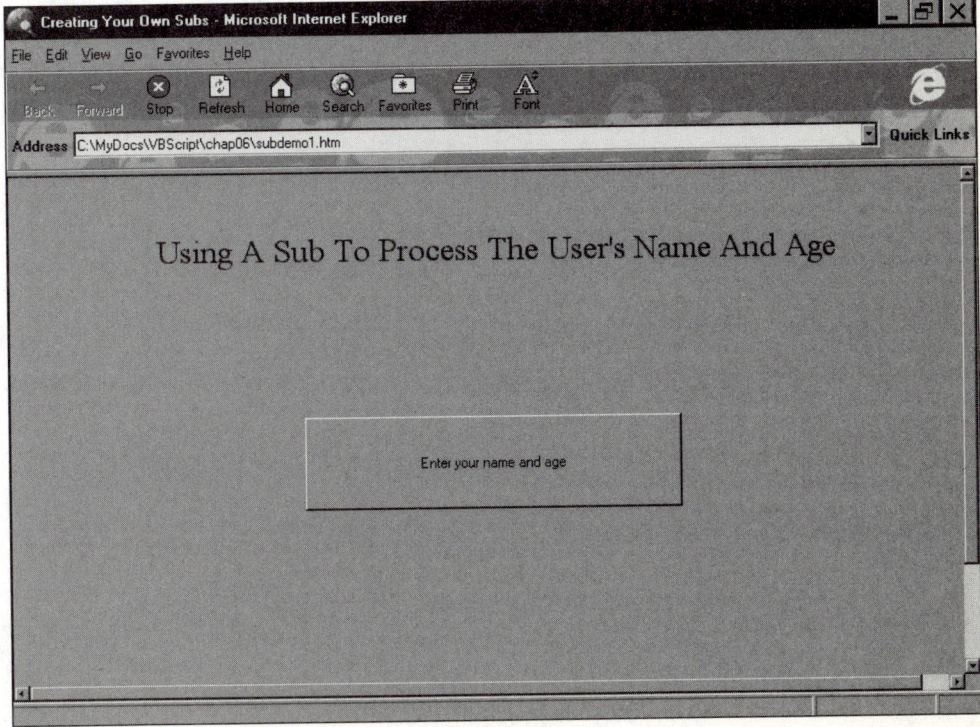

Figure 6.5
The Web page created by Listings 6.3 and 6.4.

Listing 6.3 VBScript code with a sub to get a user's name and age.

```
<SCRIPT LANGUAGE="VBScript">
<!--
dim UserName, UserAge

Sub ProcessNameAndAge(Name, Age)

    If Name = "Larry" then msgbox "Are you Larry Laffer?",, _
        "Sub Demonstration"

    if Age < 16 then
        msgbox "Sorry, " & Name & ", you must be at least 16.",, _
            "Sub Demonstration"
    end if

    if Age > 15 and age < 31 then
        msgbox "Have fun, " & Name & "!",,"Sub Demonstration"
    end if

    if Age > 30 then
        msgbox Name & ", it's good to see older people using PCs.",, _
            "Sub Demonstration"
    end if

end sub

Sub CommandButton1_Click()

    UserName = InputBox("Enter your name","Sub Demonstration","")
    UserAge = InputBox("Enter your age","Sub Demonstration","")
    ProcessNameAndAge UserName, UserAge

end sub
-->
</SCRIPT>
<DIV STYLE="LAYOUT:FIXED;WIDTH:597pt;HEIGHT:370pt;">
    <OBJECT ID="CommandButton1"
      CLASSID="CLSID:D7053240-CE69-11CD-A777-00DD01143C57"\
      STYLE="TOP:140pt;LEFT:173pt;WIDTH:231pt;HEIGHT:58pt;
      TABINDEX:0;ZINDEX:0;">
        <PARAM NAME="Caption" VALUE="Enter your name and age">
        <PARAM NAME="Size" VALUE="8149;2037">
        <PARAM NAME="FontCharSet" VALUE="0">
        <PARAM NAME="FontPitchAndFamily" VALUE="2">
        <PARAM NAME="ParagraphAlign" VALUE="3">
```

Using Subs And Functions   133

```
            <PARAM NAME="FontWeight" VALUE="0">
       </OBJECT>

       <OBJECT ID="Label1"
        CLASSID="CLSID:978C9E23-D4B0-11CE-BF2D-00AA003F40D0"
        STYLE="TOP:25pt;LEFT:83pt;WIDTH:421pt;HEIGHT:33pt;ZINDEX:1;">
            <PARAM NAME="Caption"
                VALUE="Using A Sub To Process The User's Name And Age">
            <PARAM NAME="Size" VALUE="14843;1164">
            <PARAM NAME="FontName" VALUE="Times New Roman">
            <PARAM NAME="FontHeight" VALUE="400">
            <PARAM NAME="FontCharSet" VALUE="0">
            <PARAM NAME="FontPitchAndFamily" VALUE="2">
            <PARAM NAME="FontWeight" VALUE="0">
       </OBJECT>
</DIV>
```

Listing 6.4 HTML code that sets up the Web page.

```
<HTML>
<HEAD>
<TITLE>Creating Your Own Subs</TITLE>
</HEAD>
<BODY>

<OBJECT CLASSID="CLSID:812AE312-8B8E-11CF-93C8-00AA00C08FDF"
ID="subdemo1" STYLE="LEFT:0;TOP:0">
<PARAM NAME="ALXPATH" REF
     VALUE="file:C:\MyDocs\VBScript\chap06\subdemo1.alx">
</OBJECT>

</BODY>
</HTML>
```

When the user clicks on the command button, he/she is first confronted with an input box asking for his/her name, as shown in Figure 6.6. Then, another

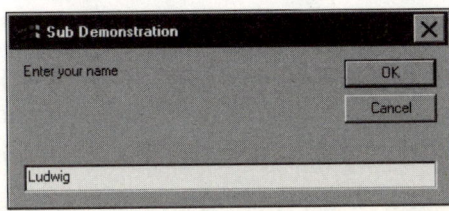

Figure 6.6
Asking for the user's name.

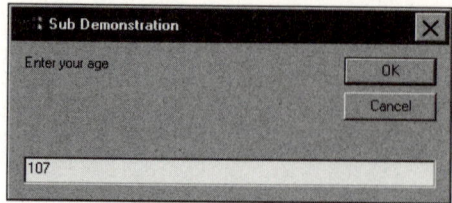

Figure 6.7
Asking for the user's age.

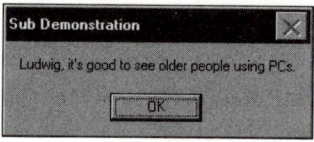

Figure 6.8
Responding to the user's name and age.

input box asks for the user's age, as shown in Figure 6.7. Finally, a message box responds to the information, as shown in Figure 6.8.

All Subs Can Be Called, Even Event Subs

In our examples so far, the **Click** event subs for command buttons have been activated only when the user clicks on the command buttons. But any sub can be called from another sub, so you can artificially "click" a command button simply by using the name of its **Click** event sub. For example, if a command button were named Cmd_Jump, you could make your code click the button by using the statement **Cmd_Jump_Click**. Then, all the event code inside the sub would execute, just as if the user had actually clicked the button.

Inside The Sub Code

The sub in this case is a very simple one. As parameters, it takes the user's name and age. Then, it looks at the name and age values and gives a response. The code inside the sub is unremarkable, so we won't tarry over it here. But this example makes two very important points that need to be emphasized.

The first point is that a sub is declared, then used. Let's put the header line of the sub declaration next to the line where the sub is called. That should spotlight how they differ:

```
Sub ProcessNameAndAge(Name, Age)
ProcessNameAndAge UserName, UserAge
```

The header line from the **sub** declaration begins, as you'd expect, with the word **sub**. It then gives the name of the sub, and a parameter list. The names of the parameters are how the values passed to the sub will be known *inside* the sub. The parameters are in parentheses.

The line that calls the sub is somewhat different. It doesn't begin with the word **sub** and its parameters aren't in parentheses. Moreover, the parameters aren't the same as the parameter names in the sub declaration: Instead, they're the names of variables that are passed to the sub for processing.

Watch For Needless Parentheses

If you're coming to VBScript from C, C++, or Pascal, you'll have an ingrained habit of putting parameters in parentheses when you call a sub. This isn't wrong in VBScript, but if you include the parentheses when you call a sub, you must begin the statement with the word *call*. If you include the parentheses but don't include the word *call*, it can cause hard-to-diagnose errors in your program.

The easiest solution is simply to remember not to include parentheses when you call a sub.

Inside the sub, the variables passed to the sub are known by their parameter names, as if traveling under an alias in a foreign land:

```
If Name = "Larry" then msgbox "Are you Larry Laffer?",, _
    "Sub Demonstration"

    if Age < 16 then
        msgbox "Sorry, " & Name & ", you must be at least 16.",, _
            "Sub Demonstration"
    end if
```

And, Of Course, The **InputBox** Function

There's one other new wrinkle in Listing 6.3, and we've deferred it until last because it has no particular connection with creating your own subs. That's the **InputBox** function used to get the user's name and age. Usually, we've obtained that kind of information by putting text boxes on the Web page, and I felt it was time for a change.

The **InputBox** function works a lot like the **MsgBox** function, except that it has fewer options. Just like the **MsgBox** function, it gets a value from the user and gives it back to your VBScript program. VBScript will look at the value and automatically decide if it's text, a number, or some other subtype of the basic VBScript *variant* data type. The syntax of the **InputBox** function is as follows:

```
ValueCatcher = InputBox(Prompt, Title, Default Text, Xpos, Ypos)
```

There are two other parameters, but you'll very seldom use them, so they're omitted here. The parameters are mostly self-explanatory. The default text is the text displayed in the input box's blank, where the user enters his/her information.

Creating Your Own Functions

Homemade functions are quite similar to homemade subs, except that they're lower in fat and cholesterol. And there's an even more important difference: At some point in every function—usually the last line—there's a statement that assigns a value to the function *itself.* That's because the function is a "word" in a larger program statement, and when you assign a value to the function itself, you tell VBScript which value to use for that word. To declare a function, you use the following syntax. It's almost exactly like the syntax for declaring a sub, except that you use the word **function**:

```
Function FunctionName(ParameterName1, ParameterName2, ..)
    ' Code that does the processing inside the function
end function
```

Like most abstract explanations, that still sounds a little murky. Let's look at a specific example of a homemade function. Listing 6.5 gives the VBScript code and ActiveX layout for a program that uses a function to multiply two numbers. Listing 6.6 gives the HTML code that sets up the Web page. And Figure 6.9 shows the Web page created by the listings.

Using Subs And Functions 137

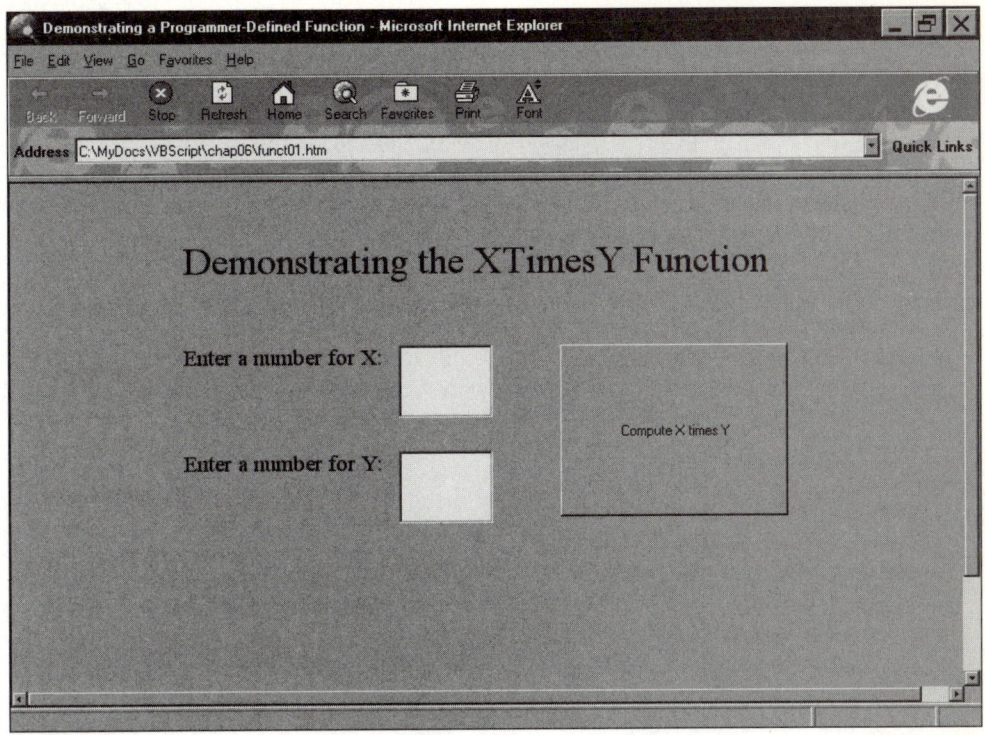

Figure 6.9
The Web page created by Listings 6.5 and 6.6.

Listing 6.5 VBScript code and ActiveX layout to use a homemade function.

```
<SCRIPT LANGUAGE="VBScript">
<!--

Function XTimesY(NumX, NumY)

   XTimesY = NumX * NumY

end function

Sub Cmd_ComputeXTimesY_Click()
   dim TheAnswer

   TheAnswer = XTimesY(TB_X, TB_Y)
   MsgBox "X times Y is " & TheAnswer & ".",,"Function Demonstration"
end sub
```

```
-->
</SCRIPT>
<DIV STYLE="LAYOUT:FIXED;WIDTH:597pt;HEIGHT:370pt;">
    <OBJECT ID="Label1"
     CLASSID="CLSID:978C9E23-D4B0-11CE-BF2D-00AA003F40D0"
     STYLE="TOP:25pt;LEFT:99pt;WIDTH:363pt;HEIGHT:33pt;ZINDEX:0;">
        <PARAM NAME="Caption"
            VALUE="Demonstrating the XTimesY Function">
        <PARAM NAME="Size" VALUE="12806;1164">
        <PARAM NAME="FontName" VALUE="Times New Roman">
        <PARAM NAME="FontHeight" VALUE="480">
        <PARAM NAME="FontCharSet" VALUE="0">
        <PARAM NAME="FontPitchAndFamily" VALUE="2">
        <PARAM NAME="FontWeight" VALUE="0">
    </OBJECT>

    <OBJECT ID="Label2"
     CLASSID="CLSID:978C9E23-D4B0-11CE-BF2D-00AA003F40D0"
     STYLE="TOP:91pt;LEFT:99pt;WIDTH:124pt;HEIGHT:17pt;ZINDEX:1;">
        <PARAM NAME="Caption" VALUE="Enter a number for X:">
        <PARAM NAME="Size" VALUE="4365;583">
        <PARAM NAME="FontName" VALUE="Times New Roman">
        <PARAM NAME="FontHeight" VALUE="280">
        <PARAM NAME="FontCharSet" VALUE="0">
        <PARAM NAME="FontPitchAndFamily" VALUE="2">
        <PARAM NAME="FontWeight" VALUE="0">
    </OBJECT>

    <OBJECT ID="Label3"
     CLASSID="CLSID:978C9E23-D4B0-11CE-BF2D-00AA003F40D0"
     STYLE="TOP:157pt;LEFT:99pt;WIDTH:124pt;HEIGHT:17pt;ZINDEX:2;">
        <PARAM NAME="Caption" VALUE="Enter a number for Y:">
        <PARAM NAME="Size" VALUE="4365;582">
        <PARAM NAME="FontName" VALUE="Times New Roman">
        <PARAM NAME="FontHeight" VALUE="280">
        <PARAM NAME="FontCharSet" VALUE="0">
        <PARAM NAME="FontPitchAndFamily" VALUE="2">
        <PARAM NAME="FontWeight" VALUE="0">
    </OBJECT>

    <OBJECT ID="TB_X"
     CLASSID="CLSID:8BD21D10-EC42-11CE-9E0D-00AA006002F3"
     STYLE="TOP:91pt;LEFT:231pt;WIDTH:58pt;HEIGHT:45pt;
            TABINDEX:3;ZINDEX:3;">
        <PARAM NAME="VariousPropertyBits" VALUE="746604571">
        <PARAM NAME="Size" VALUE="2037;1588">
```

```
            <PARAM NAME="FontHeight" VALUE="480">
            <PARAM NAME="FontCharSet" VALUE="0">
            <PARAM NAME="FontPitchAndFamily" VALUE="2">
            <PARAM NAME="FontWeight" VALUE="0">
        </OBJECT>

        <OBJECT ID="TB_y"
         CLASSID="CLSID:8BD21D10-EC42-11CE-9E0D-00AA006002F3"
         STYLE="TOP:157pt;LEFT:231pt;WIDTH:58pt;HEIGHT:45pt;
                TABINDEX:4;ZINDEX:4;">
            <PARAM NAME="VariousPropertyBits" VALUE="746604571">
            <PARAM NAME="Size" VALUE="2037;1588">
            <PARAM NAME="FontHeight" VALUE="480">
            <PARAM NAME="FontCharSet" VALUE="0">
            <PARAM NAME="FontPitchAndFamily" VALUE="2">
            <PARAM NAME="FontWeight" VALUE="0">
        </OBJECT>

        <OBJECT ID="Cmd_ComputeXTimesY"
         CLASSID="CLSID:D7053240-CE69-11CD-A777-00DD01143C57"
         STYLE="TOP:91pt;LEFT:330pt;WIDTH:140pt;HEIGHT:107pt;
                TABINDEX:5;ZINDEX:5;">
            <PARAM NAME="Caption" VALUE="Compute X times Y">
            <PARAM NAME="Size" VALUE="4947;3784">
            <PARAM NAME="FontCharSet" VALUE="0">
            <PARAM NAME="FontPitchAndFamily" VALUE="2">
            <PARAM NAME="ParagraphAlign" VALUE="3">
            <PARAM NAME="FontWeight" VALUE="0">
        </OBJECT>
</DIV>
```

Listing 6.6 HTML CODE THAT SETS UP THE WEB PAGE.

```
<HTML>
<HEAD>
<TITLE>Demonstrating a Programmer-Defined Function</TITLE>
</HEAD>
<BODY>

<OBJECT CLASSID="CLSID:812AE312-8B8E-11CF-93C8-00AA00C08FDF"
ID="funct01" STYLE="LEFT:0;TOP:0">
<PARAM NAME="ALXPATH" REF
    VALUE="file:C:\MyDocs\VBScript\chap06\funct01.alx">
</OBJECT>

</BODY>
</HTML>
```

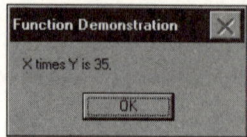

Figure 6.10
The product of X and Y.

When the user enters a number in each of the text boxes on the Web page, then clicks the command button, the VBScript program displays a message box. The message box is shown in Figure 6.10.

Inside The Function Demo Code

This is a very simple example, which makes it a good one for showing the key features of declaring and using a function. Let's start by looking at the function declaration itself:

```
Function XTimesY(NumX, NumY)

    XTimesY = NumX * NumY

end function
```

As expected, the first line of the declaration starts with the word *function*, gives the name of the function, and then gives the parameter list. Inside the function, there's only one statement: It assigns the product of *X* and *Y* as the value of the function itself. Then an **end function** ends the declaration. That's it.

Now, let's see how this fits into the actual call to the function. This occurs in the **Click** event sub for the command button, as follows:

```
Sub Cmd_ComputeXTimesY_Click()
   dim TheAnswer

   TheAnswer = XTimesY(TB_X, TB_Y)
   MsgBox "X times Y is " & TheAnswer & ".",,"Function Demonstration"
end sub
```

First, of course, we declare a local variable to catch the value returned by the function. Then, we embed the function call as a "word" in the statement assigning its value to the **TheAnswer** variable. The assignment statement makes it plain why the last line *inside* the function sets the value of the function itself: What gets assigned to **TheAnswer** is the value of the function itself.

As Rabbi Akiva remarked after summarizing *The Bible* with the statement "Do unto others as you'd want them to do unto you," the rest is commentary. Those are the really important points to remember about creating your own functions. (And about doing unto others.)

Designing A Program With Homemade Subs And Functions

When you're first designing a program with homemade subs and functions, avoid filling in the details of the code inside the subs and functions. Instead, simply put a **MsgBox** statement in each sub or function: The **MsgBox** statement should say that the particular sub has run. That way, you can get your overall program framework up and working without needing to worry about possible errors inside individual subs or functions.

Once you have the framework established, code the subs and functions one at a time, testing the program after you finish each one to make sure that no errors have been introduced. That can dramatically reduce the time you have to spend "bug hunting" later on.

Using VBScript's Built-In Subs And Functions

This book is meant to show the most important VBScript concepts and techniques, not to be an exhaustive reference about the VBScript language. However, we can give you a flavor of the amazing things you can do with some of the subs and functions that come ready-to-use with VBScript.

Let's create with VBScript a simple version of what, in the 1980s, would have been called an "artificial intelligence" (AI) program. Now, the idea of artificial intelligence is a moving target: It seems to mean whatever is currently at the leading edge of computer science. But parsing a natural language has always been an important field of AI research. And that's pretty much what we're going to do here. Once again, we'll create an amazingly simple program that demonstrates some amazingly powerful techniques. These are the same kinds of techniques, on a much smaller scale, as those used in some of the most sophisticated programs for natural language processing (NLP).

To keep it simple, let's get a two-word text string from the user. We'll then parse the string into its constituent words. As you can imagine, this technique, applied on a larger scale, is the first step toward making a computer program understand English. Listing 6.7 shows the VBScript code and ActiveX layout for the program, while Listing 6.8 shows the HTML code that sets up the Web page. And Figure 6.11 shows the Web page created by the code.

Listing 6.7 VBScript code and ActiveX layout to parse a text string.

```
<SCRIPT LANGUAGE="VBScript">
<!--
Sub Cmd_Separate_Click()

    dim SpacePos, FirstName, LastName
    SpacePos = InStr(TB_Names.text, " ")

    FirstName = Mid(TB_Names.text, 1, SpacePos - 1)
    LastName = Mid(TB_Names.text, SpacePos + 1)

    MsgBox "Your first name is " & FirstName & chr(13) & _
        "and your last name is " & LastName & "." _
        ,,"Parsing a Text String"

end sub
-->
</SCRIPT>
<DIV STYLE="LAYOUT:FIXED;WIDTH:597pt;HEIGHT:370pt;">
    <OBJECT ID="Label1"
      CLASSID="CLSID:978C9E23-D4B0-11CE-BF2D-00AA003F40D0"
      STYLE="TOP:17pt;LEFT:83pt;WIDTH:388pt;HEIGHT:25pt;ZINDEX:0;">
        <PARAM NAME="Caption"
            VALUE="Using Functions To Parse A Text String">
        <PARAM NAME="Size" VALUE="13688;882">
        <PARAM NAME="FontName" VALUE="Times New Roman">
        <PARAM NAME="FontHeight" VALUE="480">
        <PARAM NAME="FontCharSet" VALUE="0">
        <PARAM NAME="FontPitchAndFamily" VALUE="2">
        <PARAM NAME="FontWeight" VALUE="0">
    </OBJECT>
```

```
        <OBJECT ID="TB_Names"
         CLASSID="CLSID:8BD21D10-EC42-11CE-9E0D-00AA006002F3"
         STYLE="TOP:74pt;LEFT:132pt;WIDTH:281pt;HEIGHT:41pt;
                TABINDEX:1;ZINDEX:1;">
            <PARAM NAME="VariousPropertyBits" VALUE="746604571">
            <PARAM NAME="Size" VALUE="9913;1446">
            <PARAM NAME="FontHeight" VALUE="480">
            <PARAM NAME="FontCharSet" VALUE="0">
            <PARAM NAME="FontPitchAndFamily" VALUE="2">
            <PARAM NAME="FontWeight" VALUE="0">
        </OBJECT>

        <OBJECT ID="Label2"
         CLASSID="CLSID:978C9E23-D4B0-11CE-BF2D-00AA003F40D0"
         STYLE="TOP:124pt;LEFT:140pt;WIDTH:264pt;HEIGHT:25pt;ZINDEX:2;">
            <PARAM NAME="Caption"
                VALUE="Type your first and last names, separated by
                a space.">
            <PARAM NAME="Size" VALUE="9313;882">
            <PARAM NAME="FontName" VALUE="Times New Roman">
            <PARAM NAME="FontEffects" VALUE="1073741825">
            <PARAM NAME="FontHeight" VALUE="240">
            <PARAM NAME="FontCharSet" VALUE="0">
            <PARAM NAME="FontPitchAndFamily" VALUE="2">
            <PARAM NAME="FontWeight" VALUE="700">
        </OBJECT>

        <OBJECT ID="Cmd_Separate"
         CLASSID="CLSID:D7053240-CE69-11CD-A777-00DD01143C57"
         STYLE="TOP:173pt;LEFT:149pt;WIDTH:248pt;HEIGHT:58pt;
                TABINDEX:3;ZINDEX:3;">
            <PARAM NAME="Caption" VALUE="Separate the names">
            <PARAM NAME="Size" VALUE="8749;2046">
            <PARAM NAME="FontCharSet" VALUE="0">
            <PARAM NAME="FontPitchAndFamily" VALUE="2">
            <PARAM NAME="ParagraphAlign" VALUE="3">
            <PARAM NAME="FontWeight" VALUE="0">
        </OBJECT>
</DIV>
```

Listing 6.8 HTML CODE THAT SETS UP THE WEB PAGE.

```
<HTML>
<HEAD>
<TITLE>Using Functions To Parse A Text String</TITLE>
</HEAD>
<BODY>
```

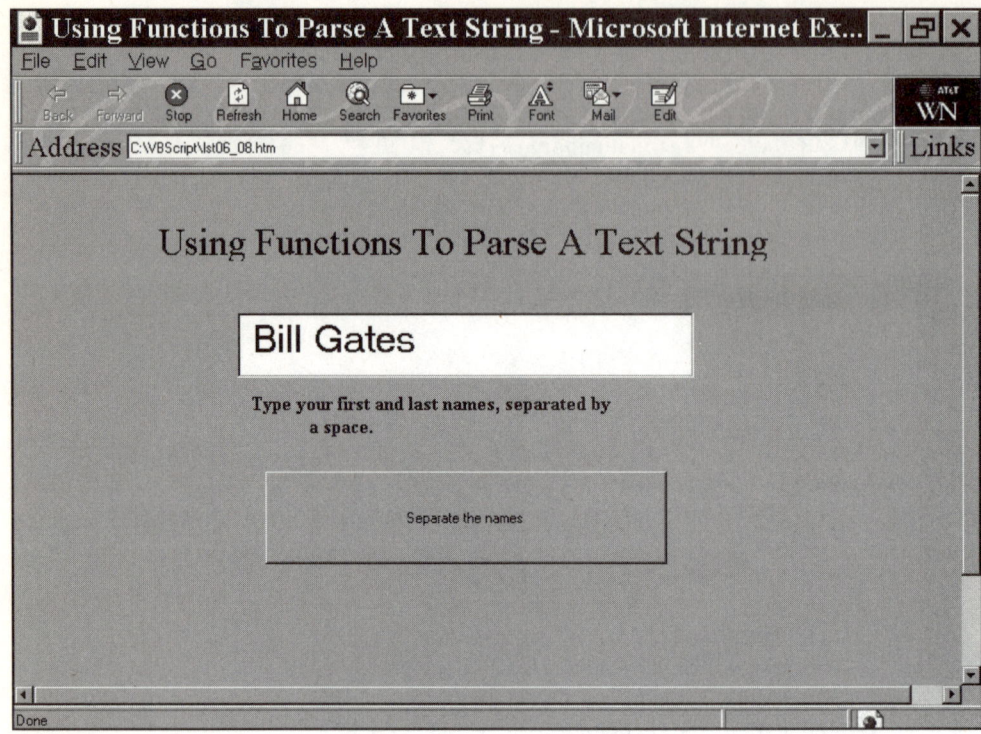

Figure 6.11
A Web page that parses a text string.

```
<OBJECT CLASSID="CLSID:812AE312-8B8E-11CF-93C8-00AA00C08FDF"
ID="parse01" STYLE="LEFT:0;TOP:0">
<PARAM NAME="ALXPATH" REF
    VALUE="file:C:\MyDocs\VBScript\chap06\parse01.alx">
</OBJECT>

</BODY>
</HTML>
```

 ### Inserting A Line Break In Message Box Text

In Listing 6.7's sub for the command button, you might have noticed something new in the middle of the message box text: **chr(13)**. That calls VBScript's **chr** function to insert a line break in the message box text. The ASCII number for a carriage return-line feed is 13, and the **chr** function returns the character associated with the number it gets as a parameter. So when you insert **chr(13)** in the middle of a text string, it starts a new line at that point.

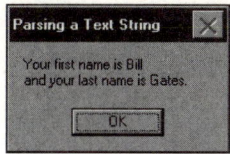

Figure 6.12
The message box shows the user's first and last names.

When the user types his/her name in the text box, then clicks on the command button, the program parses the name, separating the first and last names. Then, it displays the result, as shown in Figure 6.12.

Inside The String-Parsing Code

The code that parses the text string is in the **Click** event sub for the command button. It uses two built-in VBScript functions—**InStr** and **Mid**.

- **InStr** searches a text string for a particular substring. In this case, it's simply the space that separates the user's first and last names.
- **Mid** pulls substrings out of a larger string. To use it, give it the starting position of each substring, along with the number of characters you want it to get.

Let's see how these functions are used in Listing 6.7. First, the sub declares some local variables:

```
dim SpacePos, FirstName, LastName
```

The **FirstName** and **LastName** variables are self-explanatory. The **SpacePos** variable will hold the position of the space character in the text string entered by the user. Now, we make a call to the **InStr** function:

```
SpacePos = InStr(TB_Names.text, " ")
```

This tells VBScript to look in the **text** property of **TB_Names**—that's the text box on the Web page—and find the position of the space character. If the user entered the name "Bill Gates," then the space character would be at position 5, because the first four positions in the string are occupied by the word "Bill".

Once we have the position of the space character, we can use it to break the string. We call the **Mid** function twice—first to get the first name, then to get the last name, as follows:

```
FirstName = Mid(TB_Names.text, 1, SpacePos - 1)
LastName = Mid(TB_Names.text, SpacePos + 1)
```

In both cases, we tell **Mid** to look at the text string that's in the **text** property of **TB_Names**. To get the first name, we tell **Mid** to start at position 1, then pull out *SpacePos – 1* characters from the big text string. To get the last name, we tell **Mid** to start at position *SpacePos + 1*. We don't need to specify how many characters it should get, because we want it to go all the way to the end of the text string.

Once the first and last names are loaded into separate variables, we use a message box to display them on the user's screen.

As simple as this example is, you can see how the same techniques can be extended to parse any number of words from text input. It's a powerful technique that you'll probably use from time to time in your VBScript career.

That's it for subs and functions. In Chapter 7, we'll take a closer look at how ActiveX controls fit into your Web pages and VBScript programs.

7

Using ActiveX Controls With VBScript

We've used ActiveX controls in most of our VBScript sample programs so far. But what are ActiveX controls, anyway? In this chapter, you'll learn the concepts and techniques for using any ActiveX control, whether or not you're already familiar with ActiveX.

Next to the VBScript language itself, ActiveX controls are probably the most important tools for developing programs with VBScript. And though we've used ActiveX controls very often in the previous chapters, we've never really talked about what they are. If you want to get the most out of using ActiveX controls, you will need that knowledge.

Objects, Properties, And Events

ActiveX controls are program *objects*. They are pre-packaged capsules of program functionality that you can simply plug into a Web page or a Visual Basic form and use. You don't have to worry about how they were created—unless you want to create them yourself. And you don't have to worry about how they work "inside": All you need to know is how your VBScript programs can work *with* them.

Just like real-world objects, ActiveX controls have properties and events to which they can respond. Think about that for a moment. A grizzly bear has certain properties: seven feet tall, 400 pounds, big sharp teeth, and a hearty appetite. It also has events to which it can respond. If a hapless VBScript programmer annoys a grizzly bear at dinner time, the bear will eat the programmer. (We can at least hope that he'll get an upset stomach for his trouble.) There are also certain events to which a grizzly bear can't respond. If a sound truck started blasting the latest heavy metal songs into the forest, the bear would be unable to sing along or dance to the music. It would only, as would most of us, run away in abject terror.

ActiveX controls are a lot like grizzly bears. Sure, they lack the teeth, the fur, and the smell, but each ActiveX control has certain properties, as well as a list of events to which it can respond. When you click on a command button and it executes the statements in its **Click** event sub, it's responding to an event. On the other hand, if you started speaking French at the computer screen, the command button would be oblivious and wouldn't respond at all.

Therefore, when you encounter a new ActiveX control, there are a few important questions to ask about it:

- What's it good for? That is, how are you most likely to use it—and *are* you likely to use it?

- What events will it respond to? Of those events, which are going to be the most often used?

- What properties does it have? Of those properties, which are going to be the most often used?

- What is its default property, i.e., the property that is used if you simply give the control name and don't specify a property?

A gallery of some of the most important ActiveX controls is shown in Figure 7.1.

Using ActiveX Controls With VBScript   149

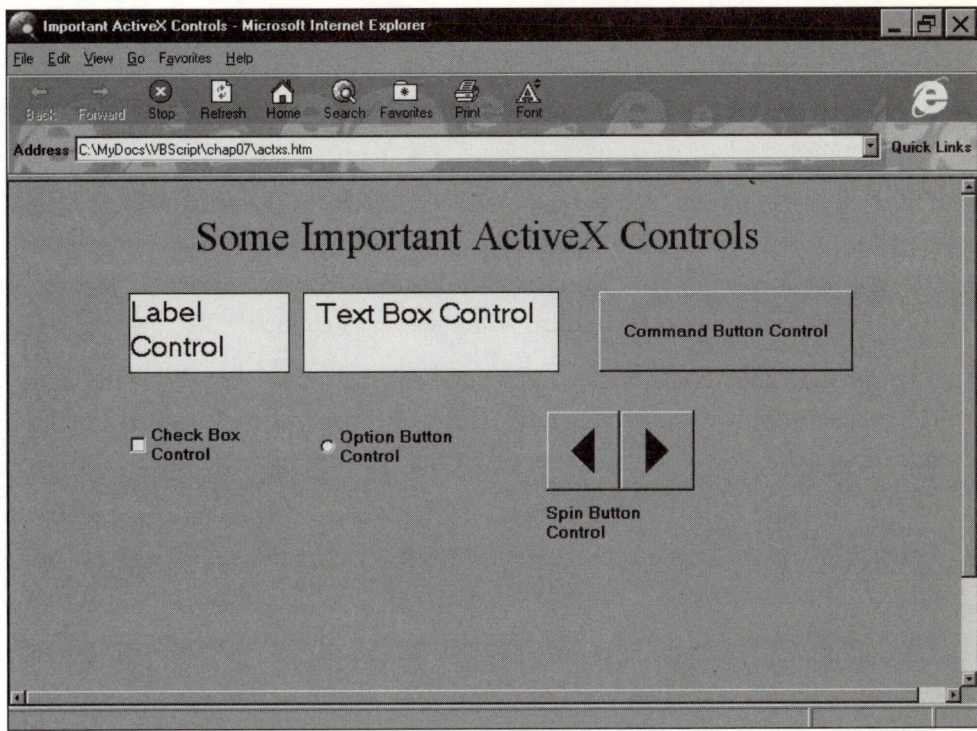

Figure 7.1
Important ActiveX controls.

Important Properties Of ActiveX Controls

There are certain properties of ActiveX controls that you'll use again and again. Knowing these properties in advance can save you programming time later on. In order of importance—not an exact ranking, but good enough for government work—the properties are as follows:

- **ID.** This is a value you should *always* set before you write any code in VBScript. The reason is that your VBScript code will refer to each ActiveX control by its **ID** property. If, later on, you change that property—i.e., change the name of the control—then you'll have to rewrite all your code. The **ID** property should reflect two things: the type of control and the purpose of the control. For example, a command button used to multiply two numbers might be named *Cmd_Multiply*, while a text box intended to get a user's name might be called *TBUserName*. Having a consistent and sensible way to name your controls makes the names easier to remember when you're writing code.

- **Value.** This indicates whether checkboxes and option buttons are selected. If the value is **true** (–1), then the control is selected. If it's **false** (0), the control is not selected.

- **Caption.** This is the text displayed in a label control or command button. For a text box control, the corresponding property is the **text** property: Text box controls do not have a **caption** property. As you've seen in many of the program examples so far, changing the **caption** or **text** property of a control is one way to display information in response to events.

- **Tabindex.** If an HTML layout has several controls, this property determines the order in which a user can "tab" from one control to another. The first **tabindex** value is 0, and each control in the tab order has a **tabindex** value 1 higher than the control before it.

- **Font.** This controls the type face, size, and style of the text displayed in a control. In the ActiveX Control Pad, you can double-click on this property in the Properties window to see a dialog box in which you can select the type face, size, and style you want.

- **Enabled.** This determines whether a control is active or not. If a control's **enabled** property is set to **false**, it won't respond to events. (You've already seen one use of the **enabled** property: In Listing 2.3, we turned a timer control on and off by manipulating its **enabled** property.)

Important ActiveX Controls

With that general introduction, let's look at some of the ActiveX controls you'll use most often, along with their most important properties.

The Label And Text Box Controls

In previous chapters, you saw many examples of label and text box controls. And you might have wondered: If all we're using them for is to display text on a Web page, why do we bother using two kinds of controls instead of just one?

There's a very simple answer: Although both label and text box controls can display text on a Web page, *only* the text box control allows the user to type text directly into the control. Thus, if you want to allow the user to enter text into the control, use a text box control. If, however, you want to display text but not allow the user to change it—at least not directly by typing it into the control—then use a label control.

Table 7.1 shows the most important properties of label controls, while Table 7.2 shows the most important properties of text box controls.

The Command Button Control

The command button control should also be quite familiar by now. Its most often-used event is its **Click** event, and it's used almost exclusively to get input from the user. The most important properties of command button controls are listed in Table 7.3.

The Option Button Control

The option button control is helpful when you want the user to choose one—and only one—from a group of mutually exclusive alternatives. For example, you might want to give the user an option to display a text message as either red, green, or purple—but you want the user to pick only one of those colors. In such a case, a group of option buttons is appropriate.

TABLE 7.1

IMPORTANT PROPERTIES OF LABEL CONTROLS.

Property	Explanation
BackColor	Color of label background.
BorderStyle	Determines if label has a visible border.
Caption	Text displayed in label.
ForeColor	Color of label text.
Font	Type face, size, and style of label text.
ID	Name by which VBScript code refers to label.
Left, Top	Determine the position of the label in the HTML layout. You will usually position the label by dragging it in the ActiveX Control Pad.
Height, Width	Determine the size of the label. You will usually size the label by dragging its borders in the ActiveX Control Pad.
WordWrap	Determines if label can display multiple lines of text.

Table 7.2

Important properties of text box controls.

Property	Explanation
BackColor	Color of text box background.
BorderStyle	Determines if text box has a visible border.
ForeColor	Color of text box text.
Font	Type face, size, and style of text box text.
ID	Name by which VBScript code refers to text box.
Left, Top	Determine the position of the text box in the HTML layout. You will usually position the text box by dragging it in the ActiveX Control Pad.
Height, Width	Determine the size of the text box. You will usually size the text box by dragging its borders in the ActiveX Control Pad.
Text	Text displayed in text box.
WordWrap	Determines if text box can display multiple lines of text.

Table 7.3

Important properties of command button controls.

Property	Explanation
Caption	Text displayed on the command button.
Enabled	Determines if command button will respond to events.
Font	Type face, size, and style of text displayed on the command button.
ID	Name by which VBScript code refers to the command button.
Left, Top	Determine the position of the command button in the HTML layout. You will usually position the command button by dragging it in the ActiveX Control Pad.
Height, Width	Determine the size of the command button. You will usually size the command button by dragging its borders in the ActiveX Control Pad.
WordWrap	Determines if command button can display multiple lines of text.

You've already seen a fairly realistic example of option buttons in the Trivia, Forsooth game developed in Chapter 5. The most important properties of option buttons are shown in Table 7.4.

The Checkbox Control

Checkboxes are similar to option buttons, but with an important difference. In a group of checkboxes, more than one checkbox can be selected at the same time. This makes checkboxes good for allowing the user to select nonexclusive alternatives, such as ordering one or more books from a bookstore. The important properties of checkboxes are shown in Table 7.5.

The Spin Button Control

The spin button control is useful when you want the user to be able to increase or decrease a value by clicking on a button. The spin button control is actually two buttons with arrows pointing in opposite directions. Click one button, and

TABLE 7.4

IMPORTANT PROPERTIES OF OPTION BUTTONS.

Property	Explanation
BackColor	Color of option button background.
Caption	Text displayed next to option button.
ForeColor	Color of option button text.
Font	Type face, size, and style of option button text.
ID	Name by which VBScript code refers to option button.
Left, Top	Determine the position of the option button in the HTML layout. You will usually position the option button by dragging it in the ActiveX Control Pad.
Height, Width	Determine the size of the option button. You will usually size the option button by dragging its borders in the ActiveX Control Pad.
Value	Determines whether or not the option button is selected. In any group of option buttons, only one can have its value property set to true. The others are automatically false.
WordWrap	Determines if option button can display multiple lines of text.

Table 7.5
Important properties of check box controls.

Property	Explanation
BackColor	Color of check box background.
Caption	Text displayed next to check box.
ForeColor	Color of check box text.
Font	Type face, size, and style of check box text.
ID	Name by which VBScript code refers to check box.
Left, Top	Determine the position of the check box in the HTML layout. You will usually position the check box by dragging it in the ActiveX Control Pad.
Height, Width	Determine the size of the check box. You will usually size the check box by dragging its borders in the ActiveX Control Pad.
Value	Determines whether or not the check box is selected. In any group of check boxes, any number can be selected. A checkmark appears in any check box that is selected.
WordWrap	Determines if check box can display multiple lines of text.

the number in the spin control's **value** property increases by a specific amount. Click the other button, and the spin control's **value** property decreases by the same amount. The important properties of the spin button control are shown in Table 7.6.

You're Not Limited To ActiveX Controls

When VBScript and Microsoft's Internet Explorer 3.0 were released, many companies announced new ActiveX versions of older OCX controls. And as the technology advances, more ActiveX controls are announced every week. ActiveX controls are designed to work with Internet Explorer and the Web, as well as with standard PC programs. Older OCX controls are not specifically designed for Internet Explorer or the Web.

Even so, you can often use existing OCX controls with VBScript and Internet Explorer. Figure 7.2 shows an example of a Web page that uses VBScript with two OCX controls: a command button and a spin control.

TABLE 7.6

IMPORTANT PROPERTIES OF THE SPIN BUTTON CONTROL.

Property	Explanation
Enabled	Determines whether or not the control will respond to events.
ID	Name by which VBScript code refers to the spin control.
Left, Top	Determine the position of the spin control in the HTML layout. You will usually position the spin control by dragging it in the ActiveX Control Pad.
Height, Width	Determine the size of the spin control. You will usually size the spin button by dragging its borders in the ActiveX Control Pad.
Min, Max	Determine the top and bottom values that the spin control can have.
SmallChange	Determines how much the value of the spin control changes (up or down) when one of the buttons is clicked.
Value	The current number associated with the spin control. This is increased by clicking one of the buttons and decreased by clicking the other.

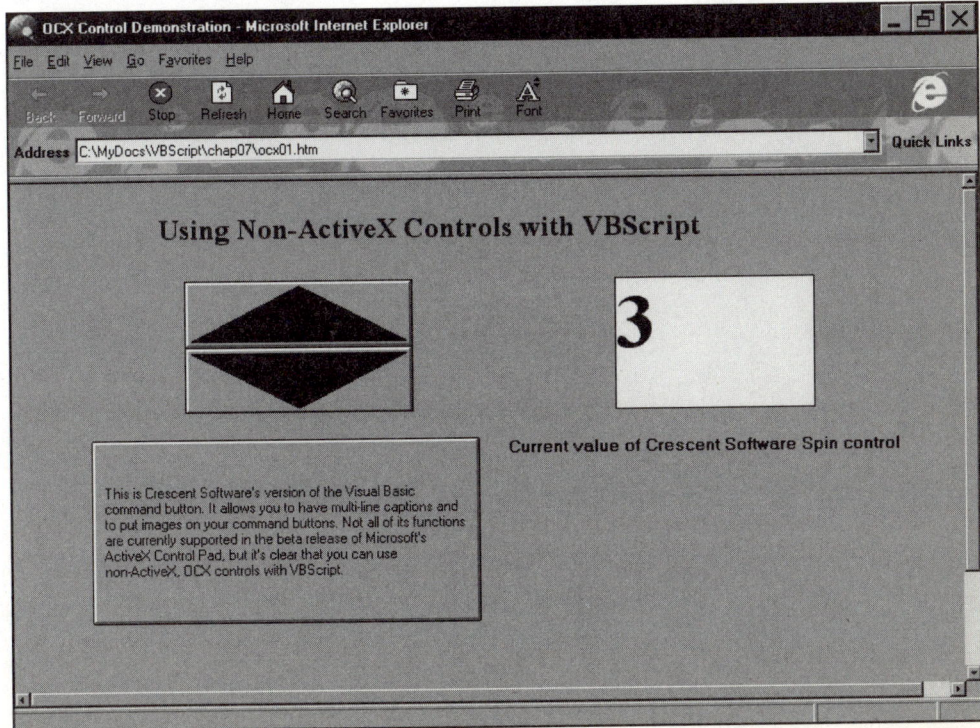

Figure 7.2
Using older OCX controls with VBScript and Internet Explorer.

These controls were designed by Crescent Software for use with Visual Basic 4. (Crescent has since introduced newer, ActiveX versions, but we're using the older controls here to illustrate a point.) The older OCX controls are highly—but not totally—compatible with VBScript and Internet Explorer. You can often use some of their properties but not others. But if you have some OCX controls on hand that do what you need, give it a try—they'll often work just fine.

In Chapter 8, we'll take an in-depth look at using the ActiveX Control Pad to create HTML layouts with ActiveX controls.

Using The ActiveX Control Pad

The ActiveX Control Pad is the first of many tools for visual design of Web pages with ActiveX controls and Visual Basic scripting. Once you learn to use it, you'll be creating amazing Web pages in no time!

So far, our focus has been mainly on VBScript itself. We've examined scripts that work with some hot-looking Web pages, but we've deferred the question of how to create those Web pages—until now. The answer to this question is the ActiveX Control Pad, shown in Figure 8.1.

In this chapter, you'll learn how to create Web page layouts with Microsoft's ActiveX Control Pad: a remarkably powerful and easy-to-understand tool for laying out Web pages with ActiveX controls.

You can download the ActiveX Control Pad from Microsoft's Web site: http://www.microsoft.com. It's free.

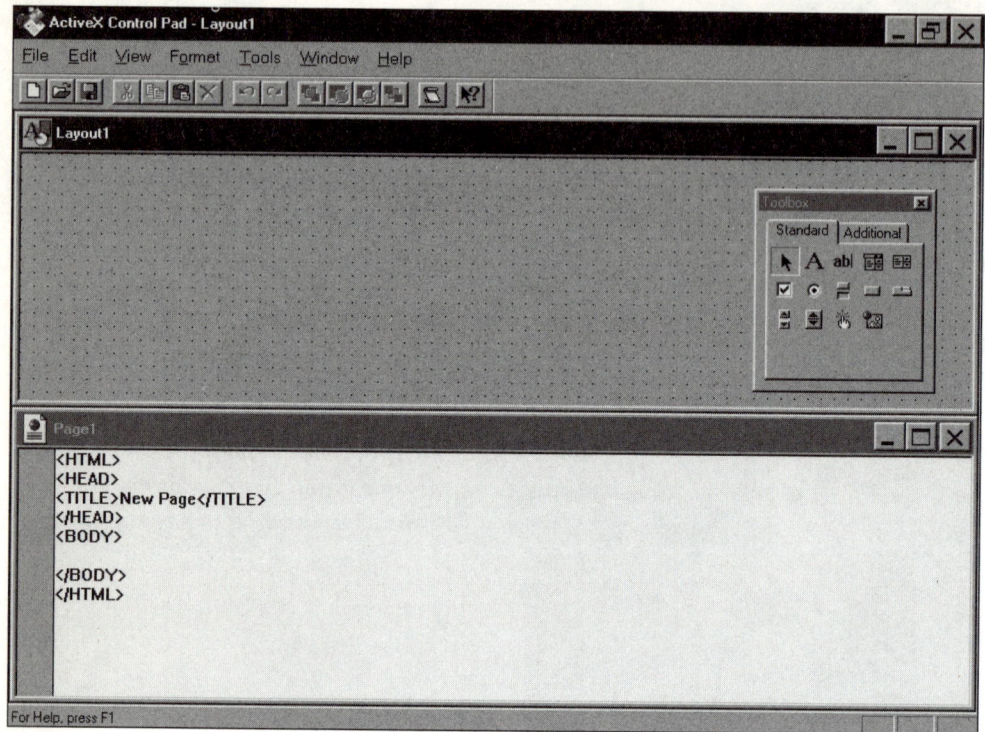

Figure 8.1
The ActiveX Control Pad.

Parts Of The ActiveX Control Pad

Although the most important thing you can do with the ActiveX Control Pad is create HTML layouts for your Web pages, there's a lot more you can do with it. Let's take inventory of all the different features offered by the ActiveX Control Pad. It includes:

- A text editor for creating and editing HTML documents. This is essentially the same as Windows Notepad, with a built-in template for HTML documents.

- An ActiveX insertion tool. This lets you insert the correct **<object>** tags for ActiveX controls into HTML documents. This tool is appropriate when you want to lay out your Web page "manually" with HTML code instead of using an HTML layout with Microsoft's HTML Layout control.

- A Visual Basic-like visual editor that lets you lay out HTML pages by selecting ActiveX controls from a toolbox, then drawing them on the screen. This is the powerhouse of the ActiveX Control Pad: It makes Web page creation incredibly easy.

- A toolbox ("palette") of ActiveX controls that are ready to use in your Web page layouts. As you acquire new ActiveX controls, you can add them to the toolbox.
- A script wizard that makes it easy to add VBScript code to ActiveX controls and to your HTML document.

Creating An HTML Layout

Let's start by creating a simple HTML layout in the ActiveX Control Pad. Before we get down to the specific steps, it's worthwhile to remember what happens when we create a layout and incorporate it into a Web page:

1. Using the ActiveX Control Pad, some other tool, or even a plain text editor, we create an HTML layout and save it in a file with the extension .ALX. The HTML layout consists largely of <object> tags that specify the properties and positions of particular ActiveX controls in the layout.

2. Using the ActiveX Control Pad, some other tool, or even a plain text editor, we insert an <object> tag for the HTML Layout control—an ActiveX control—in the <body> area of the HTML document. This <object> tag names our just-created HTML layout as the file that should be loaded by the HTML Layout control.

When the user loads the HTML document into his/her Web browser, it's the HTML Layout control—not the Web browser—that formats the layout in the Web page. This is a departure from HTML's historic approach, which was to let the Web browser do the work of interpreting the HTML document. The drawback of the old approach was that every Web browser had to support every new HTML coding trick devised.

With the new approach, however, a Web browser only needs to know how to work with ActiveX controls. If it does, then the ActiveX controls *themselves* can provide the special features—such as layouts—for the Web pages.

Drawing A Control

Let's create a simple Web page layout to see how it's done. When you first start the ActiveX Control Pad, you see a blank HTML document, as shown in Figure 8.2.

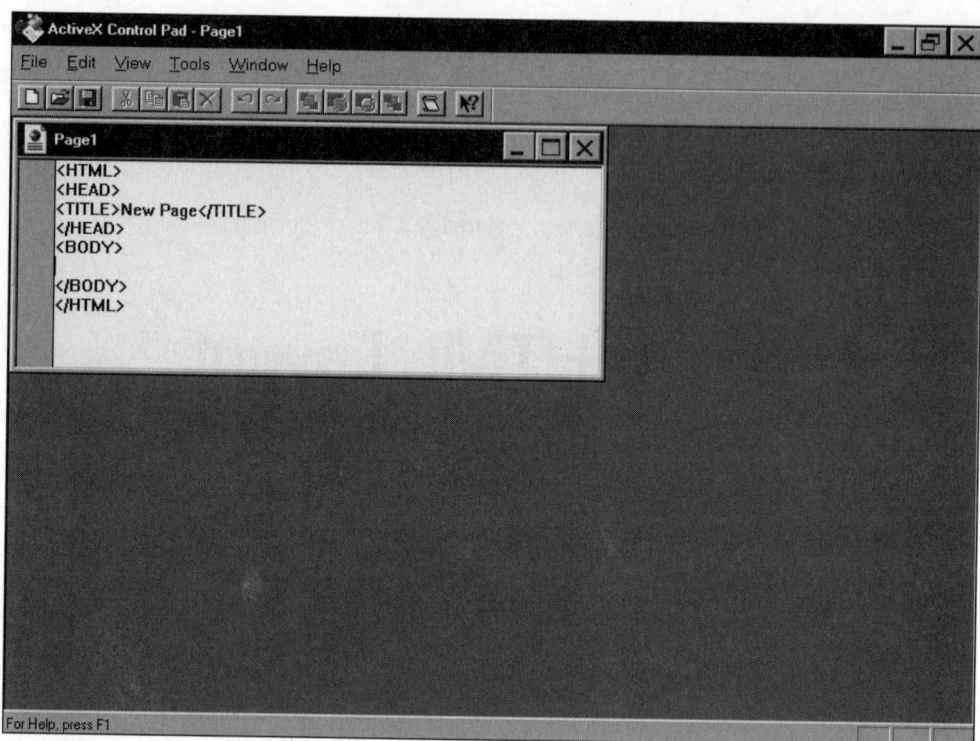

Figure 8.2
The ActiveX Control Pad's initial window.

To create a Web page layout, first close the HTML window. Then, open the File menu and select New HTML Layout. An HTML layout window will appear on your screen. When you maximize the window, it should look something like Figure 8.3.

 How To Find The Control You Want
If you're not sure which Toolbox control is the one you want, just position the mouse pointer over a control and leave it there. A "tip box" will appear over the control, telling you the name of that control.

The first step in drawing a control is to select the control in the Toolbox, shown in Figure 8.4. To keep things simple, let's draw a command button and a label. Follow these steps:

1. In the Toolbox, click on the label control (that's the one with a big "A"). Your mouse pointer will change to an A with a small cross. The cross marks

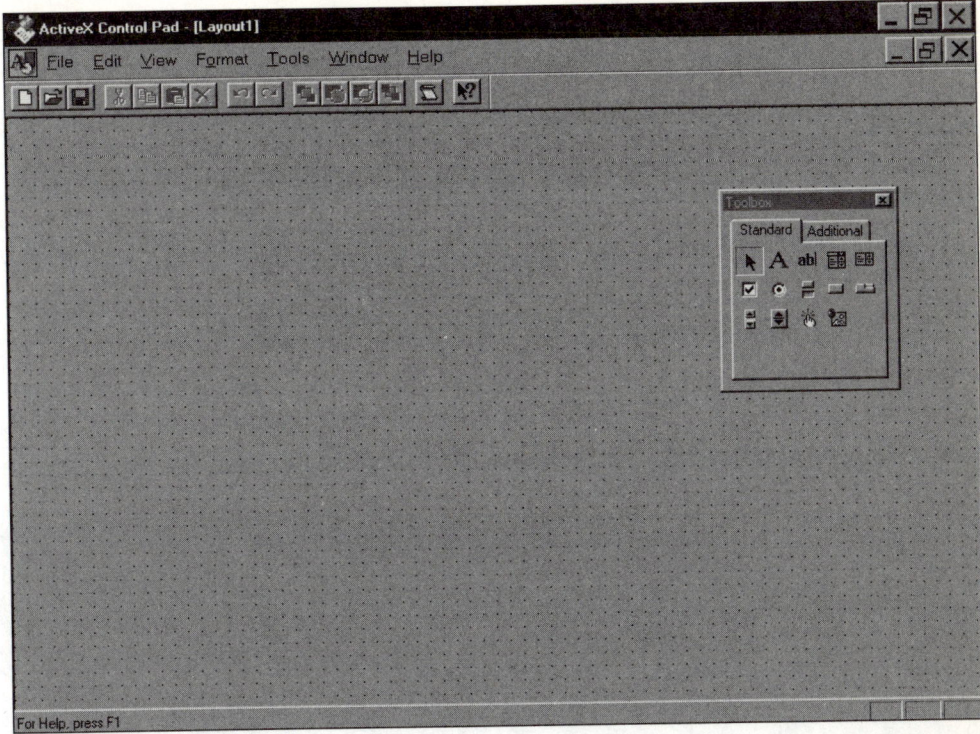

Figure 8.3
The HTML Layout window.

the point in the layout area where the label will be inserted when you click the mouse button.

2. In the top-left quadrant of the layout area, click and hold down the left mouse button. This anchors the top-left corner of the label control.

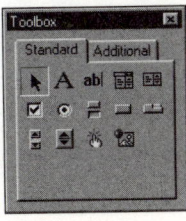

Figure 8.4
The ActiveX Control Pad Toolbox.

3. Still holding down the left mouse button, drag the mouse pointer down and to the right of your screen until the label outline is big enough to hold a sentence of text. This sets the size of the control in the layout.

4. Release the mouse button. The control is now located and sized on the HTML layout.

If it doesn't look too impressive so far, don't worry. It will *be* impressive very shortly. Now, let's add another control. This time, we'll draw a command button underneath the label control. In the Toolbox, select the command button control: It's the one that looks like a plain gray button. Then, follow the same procedure as in Steps 2 through 4 to position the command button. When you're finished, your screen should look similar to Figure 8.5.

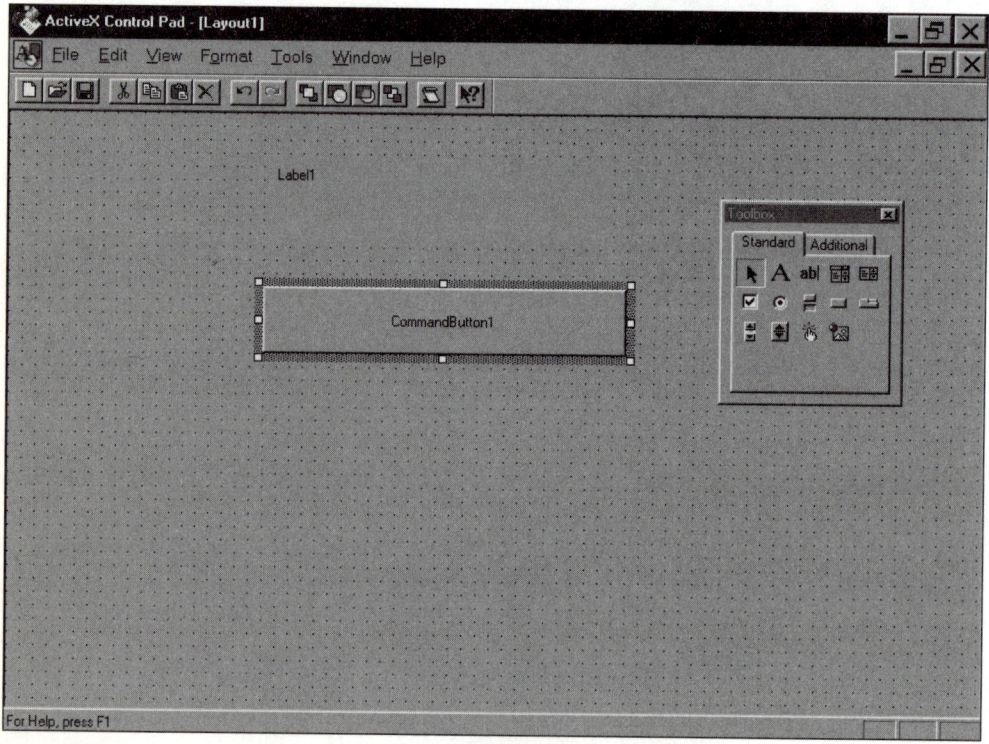

Figure 8.5
An HTML layout with label and command button.

Changing The Mouse Pointer Back To An Arrow
If you select a control in the Toolbox and then draw the control on the layout, the mouse pointer automatically changes back to an arrow. However, if you decide not to draw the control, you can change the mouse pointer back to an arrow by clicking on the Arrow button in the Toolbox.

Changing The Size Or Position Of A Control

If you're not totally satisfied with the size of a control or its location on the HTML layout, it's easy to change. To change the size of a control, follow these steps:

1. Click on the control to select it. A gray border will appear around the control. In the border are small, white squares, as shown in Figure 8.6.

2. Position the mouse pointer over one of the squares. The mouse pointer will change to a double arrow. The arrows indicate the directions in which you can drag the control's border, thereby resizing the control.

3. Click the left mouse button to "grab" the square you want.

4. Holding down the mouse button, drag the square (and thus, the control's border) in the direction you want to resize the control. For example, to make a control wider, you would drag its right border farther to the right; to make it narrower, you would drag its right border to the left.

5. When the control is the size you want it, release the mouse button. The control will appear on the layout with its new size.

Changing the position of a control is even easier. Simply select the control and, with the mouse pointer in the middle of the control, hold down the left mouse button and drag the control to the desired position. Then, release the mouse button. Presto! The control has been moved to its new location in the layout.

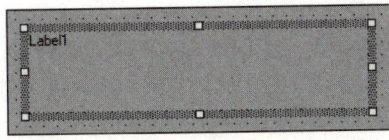

Figure 8.6
You can drag the white squares to resize the control.

With Label And Text Box Controls, There's Just One Thing To Be Aware Of

When you select a label or text box control, sometimes the ActiveX Control Pad will think you want to change the control's **caption** or **text** property. If that happens, you'll see a little text cursor inside the control and you won't be able to drag the control, resize it, or open its Properties window.

The solution is simply to click somewhere else in the layout area—which deselects the control—and then click on the control a second time. This should allow you to select the control so that you can drag it or perform other operations on it.

Using The Properties Window

Yes, the HTML layout we've created so far looks pretty drab. Let's see if we can spruce it up a bit by using the Properties window to set properties of the controls we've drawn. There are three ways to view the Properties window for a control:

- Double-click on the control. The Properties window will appear. This is the easiest method, but it occasionally fails to work because the ActiveX Control Pad thinks you want to change the control's caption or do something else with it.

- Right-click on the control. The shortcut menu for that control will appear, as shown in Figure 8.7. In the menu, select Properties. The Properties window will appear.

- Click on the control to select it. Then, open the View menu and select Properties. The Properties window will appear.

The Properties window always looks about the same, but it contains different properties depending on the type of control you've selected. Let's change the properties of the label control first. Follow these steps:

1. Double-click on the label control in the layout. The label control's Properties window will appear, as shown in Figure 8.8.

2. Double-click on the **caption** property line. The current caption will appear, highlighted, in the blank area at the top of the Properties window, as shown in Figure 8.9. At this point, anything you type will replace the current caption.

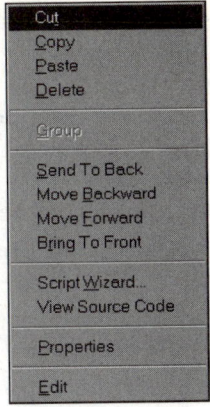

Figure 8.7
The shortcut menu for an ActiveX control.

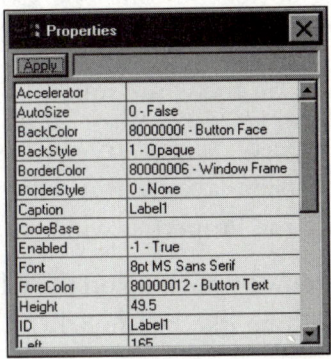

Figure 8.8
The Properties window for the label control.

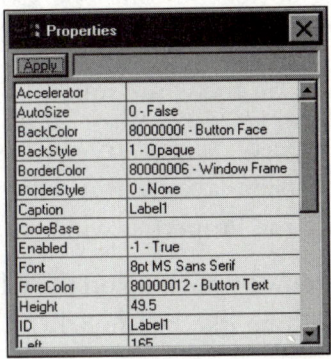

Figure 8.9
Replacing the text in the **caption** property.

3. Press the Delete key to delete the current caption. We want the label control to be blank when the Web page loads.

4. Press the Enter key. The caption text disappears from the **caption** property line, indicating that the **caption** property is now blank.

5. Double-click on the **borderstyle** property line. The **borderstyle** changes from *0 - None* to *1- Single*. A single line will now show the edges of the label control in the layout.

6. Single-click in the **backcolor** property line. The current label background color appears in the blank area at the top of the Properties window. But there's something more important to notice. At the right end of the blank area, a button with three dots appears.

7. Click on the new three-dotted button. The Color Palette will appear, as shown in Figure 8.10.

8. In the Color Palette, click on the white square. Then, click on OK.

   The label's **backcolor** property changes to white, setting it off from the gray background of the Web page layout. You will probably be able to see it peeking out from behind the Properties window.

9. Close the Properties window by clicking on the Close Window button. Your screen should look something like Figure 8.11.

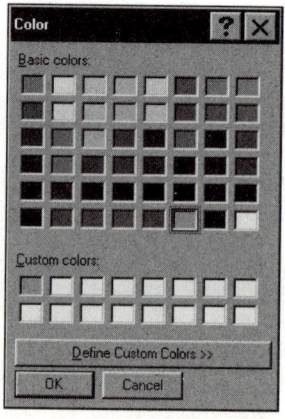

Figure 8.10
The ActiveX Control Pad Color Palette.

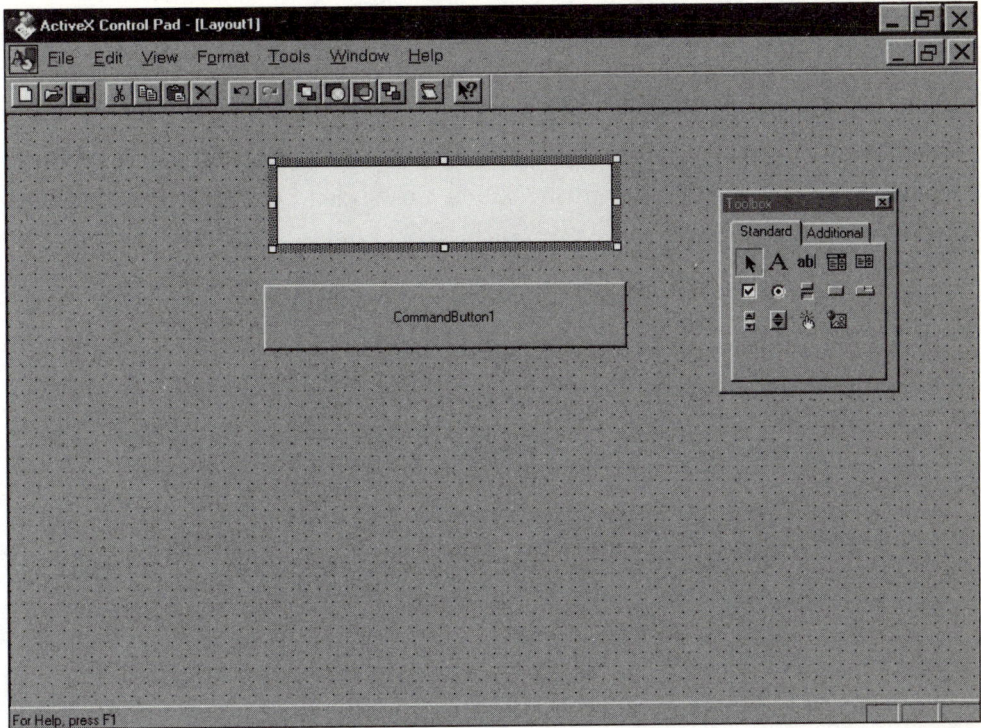

Figure 8.11
The label control's properties have changed.

Now, let's use the Properties window to change the **caption** property of the command button. Using the same methods as in Steps 1 and 2, select the command button control, open its Properties window, and select the **caption** property. This time, change the caption to "Display some text in the label control."

At this point, it would be good to save your work. Open the File menu and select Save. Give the layout a name that indicates its role in your set of Web pages, then put it in the appropriate directory. ActiveX Control Pad will automatically save it with an .ALX file extension.

 Learning About The Properties Window
You've seen a little bit of how to use the Properties window, but the best way to learn about it—and also about the properties of various controls—is simply to experiment. The more you use the Properties window, the more adept you'll become at using ActiveX controls in HTML layouts.

Adding Code With The Script Wizard

So far, our Web page layout looks nice, but it doesn't do much. Let's add some event code to the command button. When a user clicks on the command button, we want it to display some text in the label control. Follow these steps:

1. Click on the command button to select it.

2. Open the Tools menu and select Script Wizard. The Script Wizard window will appear, as shown in Figure 8.12. Notice that on the left, the window lists items to which you can add code: the command button, the label control, and the HTML layout itself. On the right, it shows a list of actions that those items can perform.

3. In the list at the left, double-click on the command button entry. Under the command button entry, a list opens, showing the events to which code can be added.

4. In the event list for the command button, click on the entry for the **Click** event.

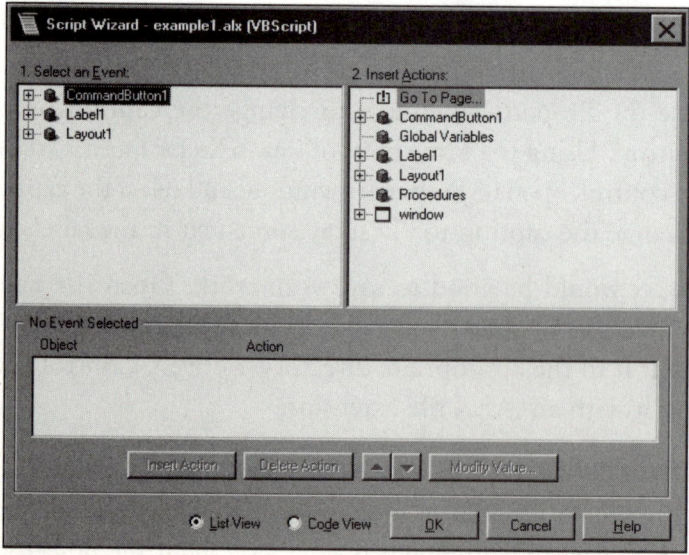

Figure 8.12
The Script Wizard window.

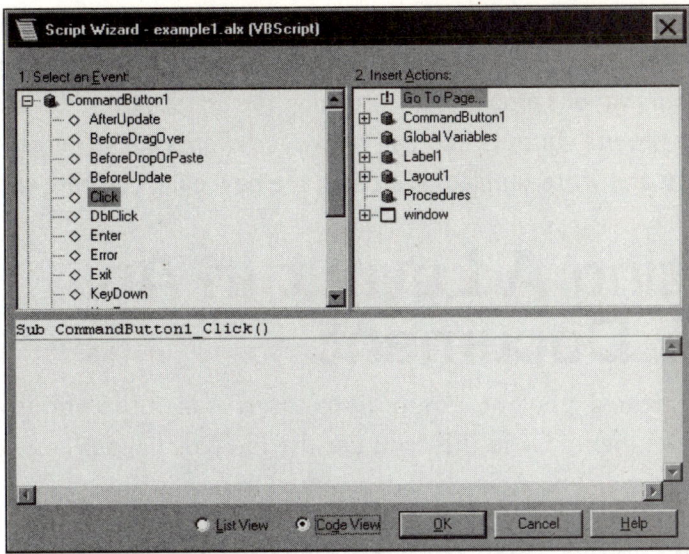

Figure 8.13
The code window for the command button's **Click** sub.

5. At the bottom of the Script Wizard window, select the option button labeled *Code View*. A code window for the command button's **Click** sub will appear, as shown in Figure 8.13.

6. In the code window, under *Sub CommandButton1_Click()*, enter the following code: *label1.caption = "This text is displayed by a sub created in the Script Wizard."*

7. Click on OK. The Script Wizard adds the code to the command button.

8. Save your Web page layout.

9. Close the Layout window. This closes the layout file so you can insert it into an HTML document.

There's one more step in creating a Web page that includes an HTML layout: inserting the layout into the "master" Web document via the HTML Layout control. That's what you'll learn to do in the next section.

Learning More About Properties And Events
Curious about the properties of different ActiveX controls and the events to which they can respond? A great way to learn about both is to browse through the Properties window and Script Wizard with

different kinds of controls. By double-clicking on a particular control, you can open its Properties window to view and experiment with its various properties. By opening the Script Wizard for a page with several controls, you can see which events each control supports, and write simple test subs to see how each control behaves.

Inserting A Layout In An HTML Document

Once you've created a layout, you need to insert it into the **<body>** section of an HTML document. To do this, you use the HTML Layout control, which is an ActiveX control. The ActiveX Control Pad makes it easy.

You Already Have The HTML Layout Control

You don't need to worry about getting a copy of the HTML Layout control. It's included with the ActiveX Control Pad, and it will be included with the official release of Microsoft's Internet Explorer version 3.0. If you have either of those software packages—and if you've been working through this book, you almost certainly have both of them—then you already have the HTML Layout control.

If you don't have an HTML document window open in the ActiveX Control Pad, open the File menu, and select New HTML. An "empty" HTML document window will appear: All it contains is a simple HTML template, including tags for document **<title>** and **<body>**. To insert your layout, follow these steps:

1. Position the text cursor on the line between the **<body>** and **</body>** HTML tags.

2. Open the Edit menu and select Insert HTML Layout, as shown in Figure 8.14. A File Open dialog box will appear.

3. In the dialog box, select the layout file you want to insert. Then click on OK. The ActiveX Control Pad inserts an **<object>** tag for the HTML Layout control at the cursor location in your HTML document window. If you look at the **<object>** tag, you'll see that it gives the directory path and file name of your HTML layout.

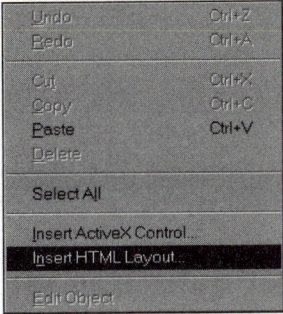

Figure 8.14
Inserting an HTML layout.

4. Add title text between the <title> and </title> tags. In this case, title the Web page *HTML Layout Demonstration* or something equally soporific.

5. Save the HTML document file and close the ActiveX Control Pad.

Your final step is to view the result of your hard work. Start up Internet Explorer and load the HTML document file. Your screen should look something like Figure 8.15.

When you click on the command button, it fires the sub you created in the Script Wizard. The result is shown in Figure 8.16.

ActiveX Control Pad Tips And Techniques

There are three other tricks you can use to make the ActiveX Control Pad even more effective:

- You can add new ActiveX (or OCX) controls to the Toolbox.
- You can delete controls from the Toolbox.
- You can make the Script Wizard write event code for you by switching to List View.

Adding Controls To The Toolbox

As you get new ActiveX controls, you'll want to add them to the ActiveX Control Pad Toolbox. It's quite easy to do. In the ActiveX Control Pad, simply display an HTML layout window. Then, follow these steps:

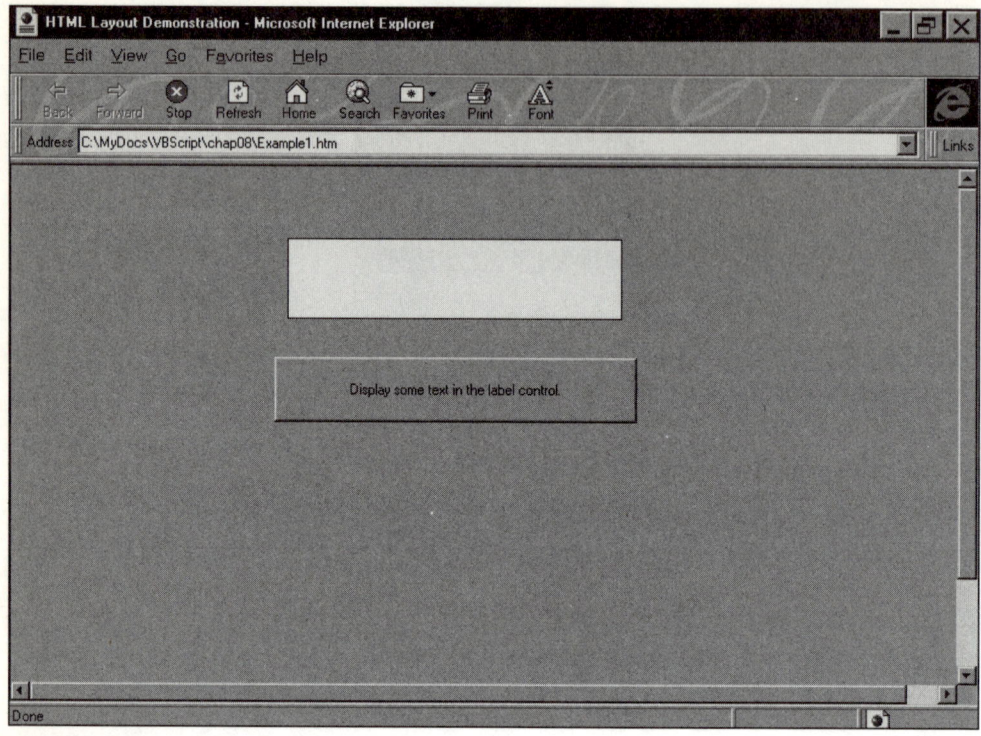

Figure 8.15.
The Web page created by our HTML layout.

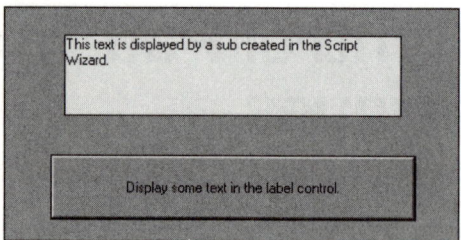

Figure 8.16
The command button's **Click** event sub displays text in the label control.

1. Right-click on the Toolbox, but in a spot that's outside any of the pages with controls on them. A shortcut menu will appear, as shown in Figure 8.17.

2. In the menu, select New Page. A new, blank control page will appear in the Toolbox.

3. Right-click on the new page. A shortcut menu will appear.

Using The ActiveX Control Pad   173

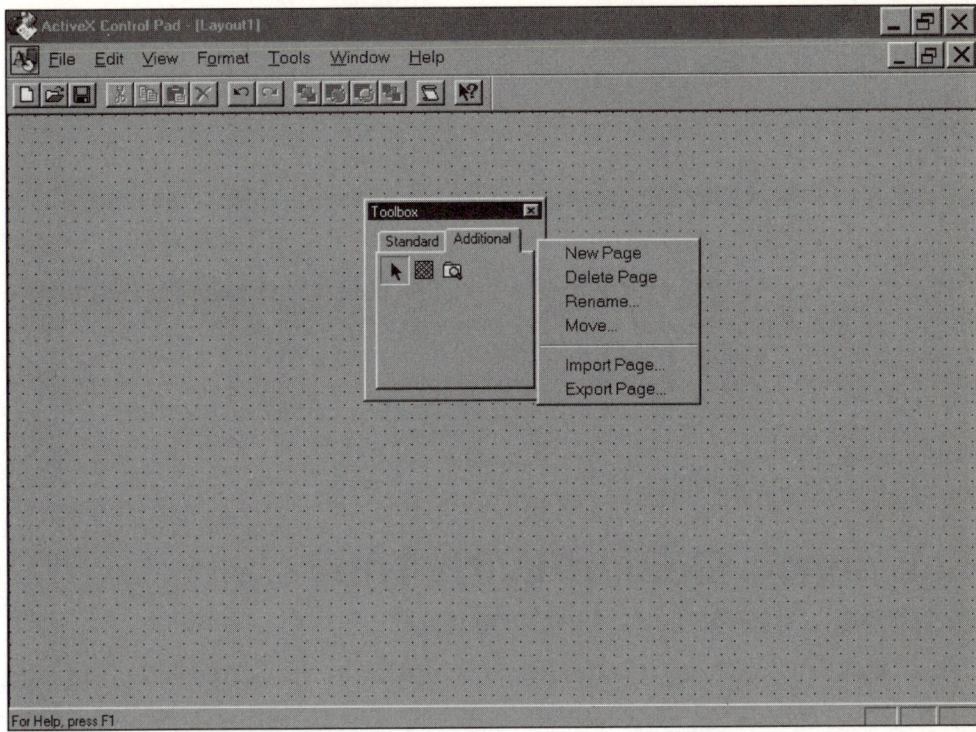

Figure 8.17
Preparing to add a new page to the Toolbox.

4. Select Additional Controls. The Additional Controls dialog box will appear, as shown in Figure 8.18. It lists the ActiveX controls available on your PC.

5. In the dialog box, select the checkbox next to the control you want to add to the Toolbox.

6. Click on OK. The new control appears in the blank Toolbox page.

Deleting Controls From The Toolbox

Deleting controls from the Toolbox is even easier than adding them. To delete a control, follow these steps:

1. Right-click on the control you want to delete from the Toolbox. A shortcut menu will appear. Two of the menu choices are to delete or to customize the control on which you clicked.

2. In the menu, select the Delete menu choice. The control is deleted from the Toolbox.

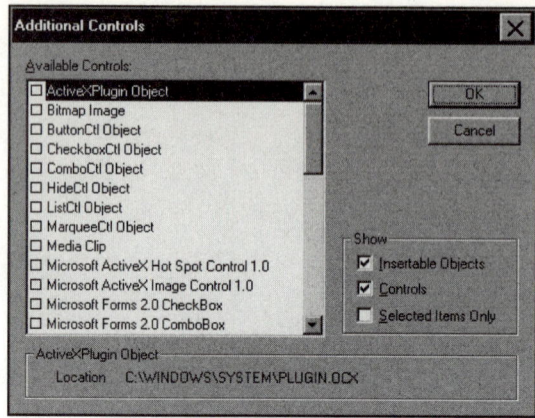

Figure 8.18
The Additional Controls dialog box.

Automatic Coding With The Script Wizard's List View

Earlier, you saw how easy it is to create event subs in the Script Wizard's Code View. But if you need to create an event sub that performs a very common VBScript task, there's an even easier way: Use the Script Wizard's List View.

Consider the example we created earlier in this chapter: a Web page with a command button that displays some text in a label control. The truly amazing VBScript programmers that we are, we had no trouble writing the appropriate line of code for the command button's **Click** event:

```
Label1.caption = "This text is displayed by a sub " & _
  "created in the Script Wizard."
```

But amazing as it might seem, the Script Wizard—through its List View—can even do *that* for us. To create the same sub code using the List View, we would follow these steps:

1. Open the Tools menu and select Script Wizard. The Script Wizard window appears. List View is actually the default.

2. In the list at the left, double-click on the control for which you want to create or edit an event sub. In this case, that's *CommandButton1*. A list of available events appears under the control name.

3. Click on the event for which you want to create a sub. In this case, that's the **Click** event.

4. In the list on the right, double-click on the control or object that the event sub should affect. In this case, that's the *Label1* control. A list of available properties appears under the control name, as shown in Figure 8.19.

5. In the property list, double-click on the property you want the event sub to affect. In this case, we double-click on the label control's **caption** property. A dialog box appears, asking for the new value of the property, as shown in Figure 8.20.

6. In the dialog box, enter the new value you want in the control's property. In this case, we'd enter "This text is displayed by a sub created in the Script Wizard." as the new caption of the label control.

7. Click on OK. The **caption** property change is added—in plain English—to the box showing the result of the sub selected in the left-hand list. This is shown in Figure 8.21.

8. Click on OK once more to close the Script Wizard.

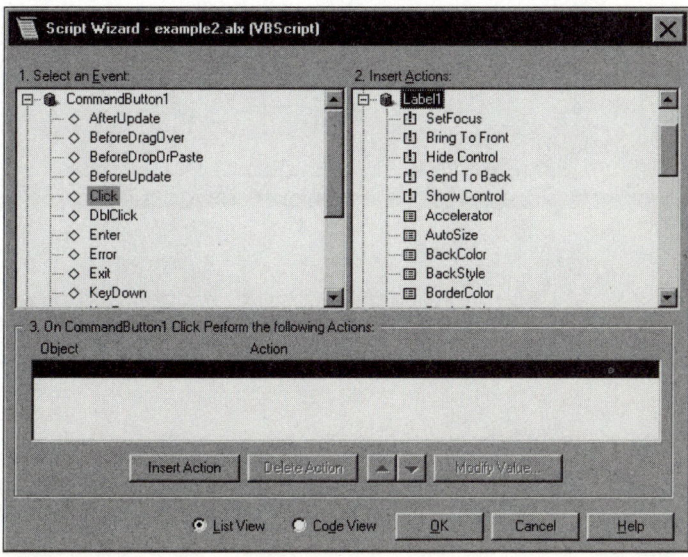

Figure 8.19
Preparing to create an event sub for the command button.

176   Chapter 8

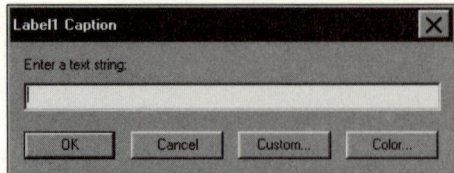

Figure 8.20
The Script Wizard asks for the new property value.

And that's it! The Script Wizard's List View gives you a simple point-and-shoot method of creating subs when you don't want to type the code. The only limitation is that because it deals with very common types of sub operations, it won't create highly specialized sub code for you. In those situations—and in most situations, as you become a highly proficient VBScript programmer—you'll find it more efficient simply to write the code on your own.

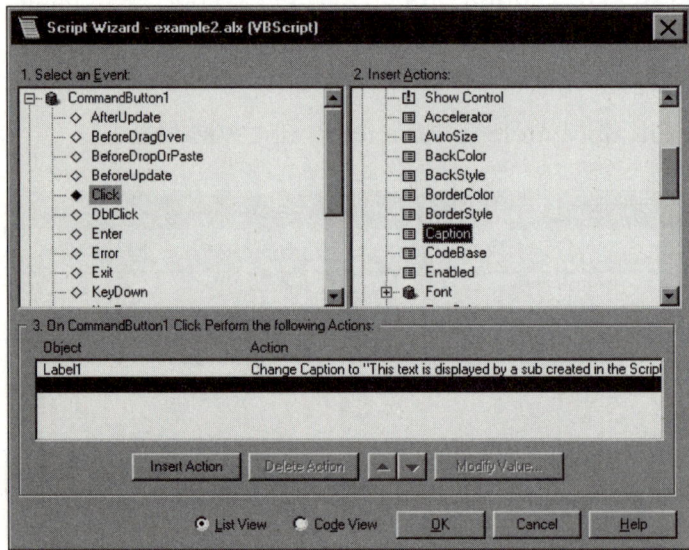

Figure 8.21
The Script Wizard has created the sub for you.

9

THE SCRIPTING OBJECT MODEL

Microsoft Internet Explorer's scripting object model is not just for VBScript. It lets your code communicate with different parts of the Web page and gives you the foundation for some pretty neat tricks.

If you're like most people—even most programmers, who are, of course, a different breed—your first question is, "What the heck is a scripting object model, anyway?" Your second question is, "Do I really need to know about this?"

In order, the answers to your questions are: Something Really Important, Yes, and 42. Oh, wait, you didn't ask about the ultimate question: Forget that third answer.

The scripting object model isn't part of VBScript: It's part of Microsoft Internet Explorer's Web browser. As a result, the scripting object model works equally well with VBScript and JavaScript, the other major scripting language for Web pages.

Objects, Properties, And Events

Internet Explorer treats each Web page as an object. But what is an object? An object is simply a thing that has properties and can react to certain external events. The ActiveX controls we've been using—and even the ordinary-seeming HTML controls—are objects. So are apples, bridges, PCs, and, at a higher level, human beings. Take your PC, for example. It has the following properties (among many others):

- Color
- Texture
- Weight
- Shape

A PC can also respond to certain external events, such as the following:

- Typing on the keyboard
- Electronic impulses from the modem
- Movements of the mouse over the mouse pad

On the other hand, there are also properties that your PC does *not* have and events to which it cannot respond. For example, your PC doesn't have blood pressure because it doesn't have any blood. Moreover, if you talk out loud to your PC, it will usually not react at all—at least, not in 1997.

Objects in the Internet Explorer scripting object model are almost exactly like that. They have certain properties and not others; they react to certain events and not others.

The Object Hierarchy

So what objects are we talking about here? Well, inasmuch as Internet Explorer is a Web browser, you might guess—correctly—that the relevant objects are Web pages and their contents. In essence, anything that can appear in a Web page is included in the scripting object model. In addition, the model includes a few other objects that are part of Internet Explorer itself. The objects are as follows:

- **Window.** This is the top-level object that holds everything else. You can think of it as the Web page itself.

- **Frame.** The main window can hold multiple, independent frames. The whole set of frames is kept in an array and stored in the window's **frames** property. Each frame can be referred to by its array index, starting with **frames[0]**.

- **History.** This object is used to get the history list from Internet Explorer in case you need to back up to a Web page the user visited earlier.

- **Navigator.** This object holds information about the browser program itself, i.e., about Internet Explorer.

- **Location.** This object holds the URL (Web address, or Uniform Resource Locator) of the current Web page.

- **Script.** This object holds any script code that's embedded in the current window.

- **Document.** This is the object you'll use most often. It's the "writing area" of the current window. If you want your Web page to change its background color or display new text in response to a user's actions, you can use the **document** object to accomplish those tasks—among many others.

- **Link.** This object is an array of links contained in the current document. It's part of the **document** object.

- **Anchor.** This object is an array of anchor tags (**<a>**) contained in the current document. It's part of the **document** object.

- **Form.** This object is a form (if any) contained in the current document. If you give the form a name in the **<form>** tag, you can refer to this object by name. It's part of the **document** object.

- **Element.** This object is a control contained in the current form or document. It can be either a standard HTML control (created with the **<input>** tag) or an ActiveX control. Depending on where the control is located—in a form, or just in the document outside of any form—it can be part of either the **form** or the **document** object.

The object hierarchy is shown in Figure 9.1.

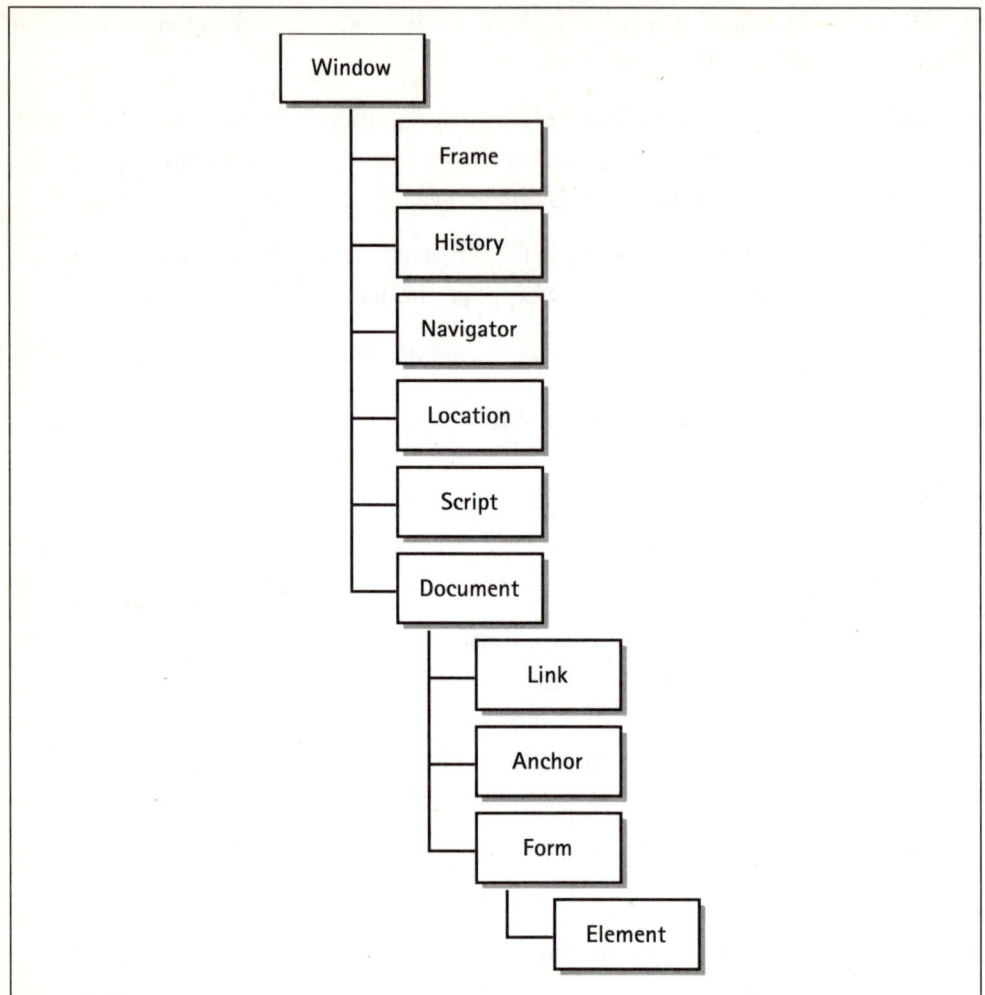

Figure 9.1
The scripting object hierarchy.

Attaching Scripts To Objects

Given that introduction, let's now take a look at how you can use VBScript (or JavaScript, if you are so inclined) with the various objects that can appear in a window. There are two main ways to attach script code to objects:

- Use the **script** element. This means using the HTML **<script>** tag exactly as we've been using it so far. The script code appears in its own separate section of the HTML document. Various event subs are linked to controls by their names, such as **CmdDoIt.Click**().

- Name a particular sub in the HTML tag for a form control. This means, for example, including an **OnClick** clause in the HTML tag for an input button.

Listing 9.1 shows the two methods for attaching script code to objects. Figure 9.2 shows the Web page created by the code in Listing 9.1, while Figure 9.3 shows the result of clicking on one of the buttons.

Listing 9.1 USING DIFFERENT METHODS TO ATTACH SCRIPT CODE TO OBJECTS.

```
<HTML>
<HEAD>
<TITLE>Different Ways Of Using Script Elements</TITLE>
</HEAD>
<H1>Two (And A Half) Ways Of Using Script Elements</H1>
<BODY>
<script language="vbs">
<!--
Sub MScript_OnClick
    msgbox "The matching sub has run.",,"Ways To Use Script Elements"
end sub

sub NSub
    msgbox "The named sub has run.",,"Ways To Use Script Elements"
end sub
-->
</script>
<pre>
<form name="SForm">
<input type="button" name="MScript" value="Matching Script Element"><br>
<input type="button" name="NScript" value="Named Script Element"
    onClick="NSub"><br>
<input type="button" name="BScript" value="Bundled Script Element"><br>
    <script for="BScript" event="onClick" language="VBScript">
    msgbox "The bundled sub has run.",,"Ways To Use Script Elements."
    </script>
</form>
</pre>

</BODY>
</HTML>
```

182   Chapter 9

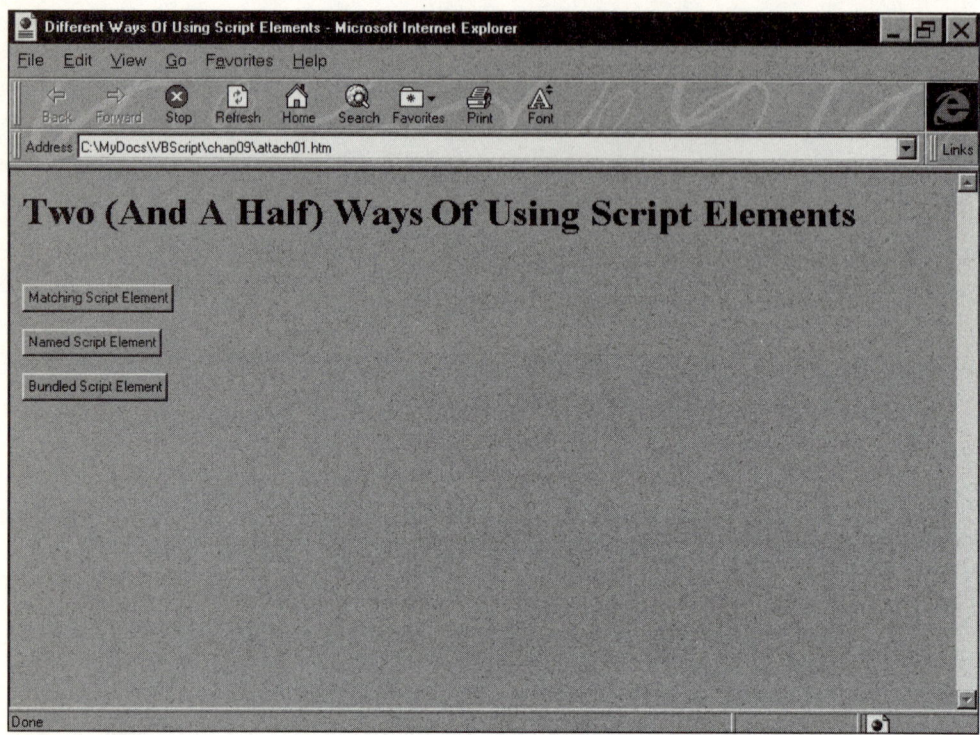

Figure 9.2
The Web page created by the code in Listing 9.1.

The first method matches the name of the VBScript sub to the control and event. That's the approach used by the following snippet from Listing 9.1:

```
<input type="button" name="MScript" value="Matching Script Element"><br>
Sub MScript_OnClick
    msgbox "The matching sub has run.",,"Ways To Use Script Elements"
end sub
```

It's pretty easy to see what's happening here. To match the sub to the control, you simply name the sub so that it combines the control name (**MScript**) with the event name (**OnClick**).

The second method comes in two varieties. The first, more familiar variety is shown in the following code snippet:

```
<input type="button" name="NScript" value="Named Script Element"
    onClick="NSub">
```

```
sub NSub
    msgbox "The named sub has run.",,"Ways To Use Script Elements"
end sub
```

In this case, the names don't match, but it doesn't matter. Inside the <input> tag, you've specified the name of the sub that should run when the user clicks on the button.

A variation on this method is to bundle the sub code right inside the HTML form, nestled snugly under the control tag that activates it. This is shown in the following code snippet:

```
<input type="button" name="BScript" value="Bundled Script Element"><br>
    <script for="BScript" event="onClick" language="VBScript">
    msgbox "The bundled sub has run.",,"Ways To Use Script Elements."
    </script>
```

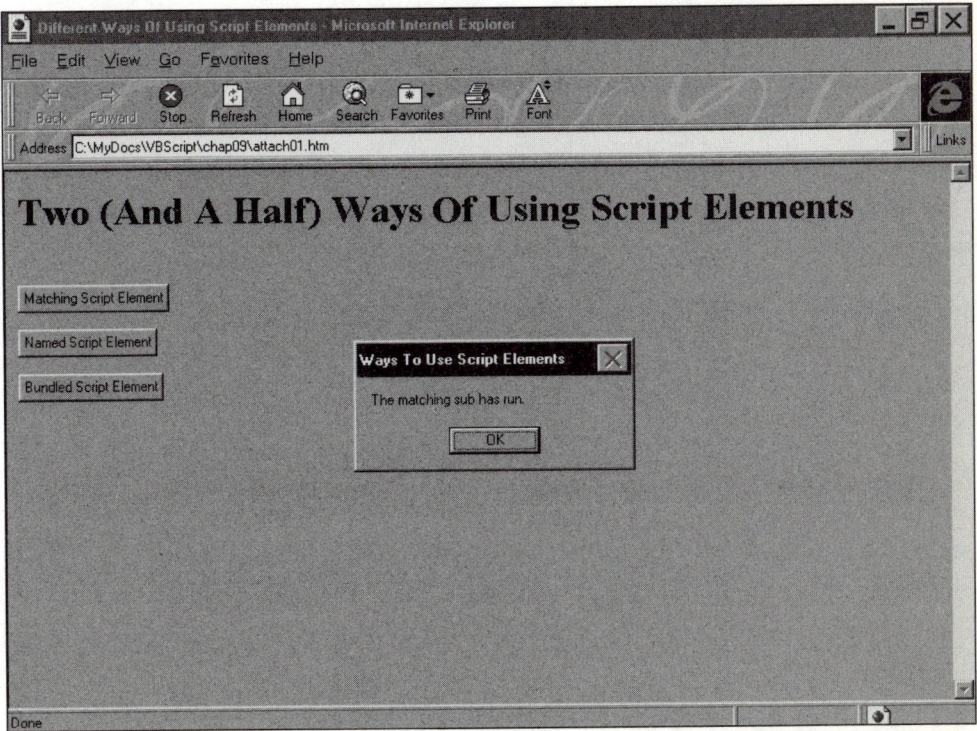

Figure 9.3
The result of clicking on a button on the Web page.

Referring To Objects

In your script code, you'll often need to refer to objects—getting values from them, assigning values to their properties, calling their built-in methods, and so on. The general way you refer to object properties and methods is as follows

```
ObjectName.property
```

or:

```
ObjectName.method
```

The main exception to this rule is when you need to refer to the **window** object of the current Web page. Because the **window** object is the top-level object that contains all the other objects, you can leave out the word "window" when you use it. For instance, with either of these code lines, you can get the name of the current window and assign it to the **NameString** variable:

```
NameString = window.name
NameString = name
```

If you want to refer to other objects, however, you need to include them in your code line. To call the **document** object's **writeln** method, for example, you'd use this code line:

```
document.writeln("Howdy, world.")
```

To assign a value to **Btn1** in a form that's contained in your document (contained in the main **window** object), you'd write

```
Document.FormName.Btn1.value = "New text in the button"
```

where **FormName** is the form name you assigned with the **<form>** tag. This is, of course, a way you'll use the object model very often: to refer to controls on your Web page.

The Objects Themselves

With that introduction, let's look at some of the things you can do with the objects themselves. This isn't meant to be an exhaustive reference to all the objects and their properties—it's merely to show you "how it's done," so you can experiment on your own. We'll look at a few of the more interesting and useful properties and methods.

The window Object

The **window** object is the top-level object that holds your Web page. It has two events—**OnLoad** and **OnUnload**—that you can use to do setup and shutdown work. Listing 9.2 shows an example of how to use these events, while Listing 9.3 shows code for an essentially blank Web page that just gives you a way to leave the first Web page. Figure 9.4 shows the result when the user loads the Web page created by Listing 9.2; the result of unloading is similar.

Listing 9.2 USING THE window OBJECT'S OnLoad AND OnUnload EVENTS.

```
<HTML>
<HEAD>
<TITLE> Window OnLoad Event Demonstration</TITLE>
</HEAD>

<H1>The Window OnLoad Event</H1>

<BODY language="vbs" onLoad="DisplayMsg" onUnLoad="ByeBye">

<p>The window object's OnLoad event can be used
to perform setup tasks when the user first loads your HTML
document into his/her Web browser. In this case, it displays
a simple message box.</p> <br><br>

<a href="Page2.htm">Go to a different page.</a>

<script language="vbs">

sub DisplayMsg
    msgbox "The window has loaded.",,"OnLoad Event Demonstration"
end sub

sub ByeBye
    msgbox "The window is unloading.",,"OnUnload Event Demonstration"
end sub

</script>

</BODY>
</HTML>
```

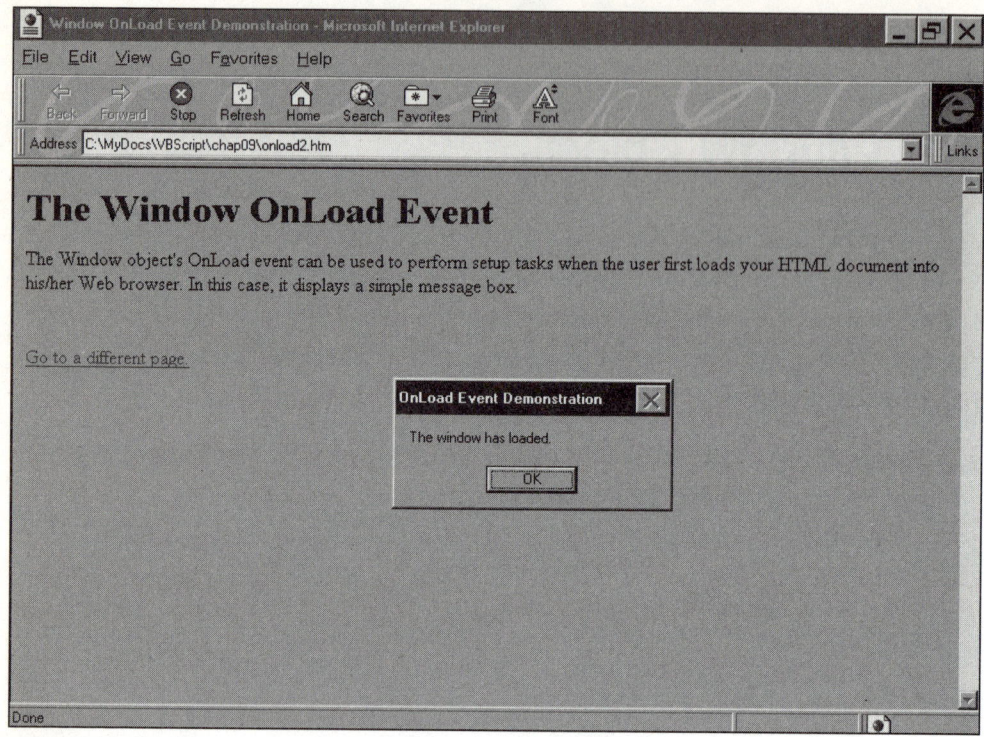

Figure 9.4
Using the **window** object's **OnLoad** event.

Listing 9.3 A BLANK WEB PAGE TO WHICH WE CAN JUMP.

```
<HTML>
<HEAD>
<TITLE> Page Two</TITLE>
</HEAD>
<H1>Page Two</H1>
<BODY>
<p>This page doesn't really do anything. It simply gives you a
way to leave the other page so you can see the sub run for the
window object's OnUnload event.</p><br><br>
<a href="onload1.htm">Go back to the original page.</a>
</BODY>
</HTML>
```

The relevant HTML code line in Listing 9.2 is the **<body>** tag, as follows:

```
<BODY language="vbs" onLoad="DisplayMsg" onUnload="ByeBye">
```

To use the **OnLoad** and **OnUnload** events, you add information to the HTML document's **<body>** tag: the scripting engine (VBScript), the sub to execute when the **OnLoad** event fires, and the sub to execute when the **OnUnload** event fires. Of course, you don't have to use both events: You can use only one if that's appropriate.

In Listing 9.2, the event subs simply display message boxes. But in real-world Web pages, you can make them declare variables, set initial values, or change the text in a Web page based on the value of an already-existing variable.

The **document** Object

You change document properties pretty much as you'd expect: by using the **document** object name and property in an assignment statement. Listing 9.4 shows an example of how you can change the color of your Web page by assigning a new value to the **document** object's background color. Figure 9.5 shows

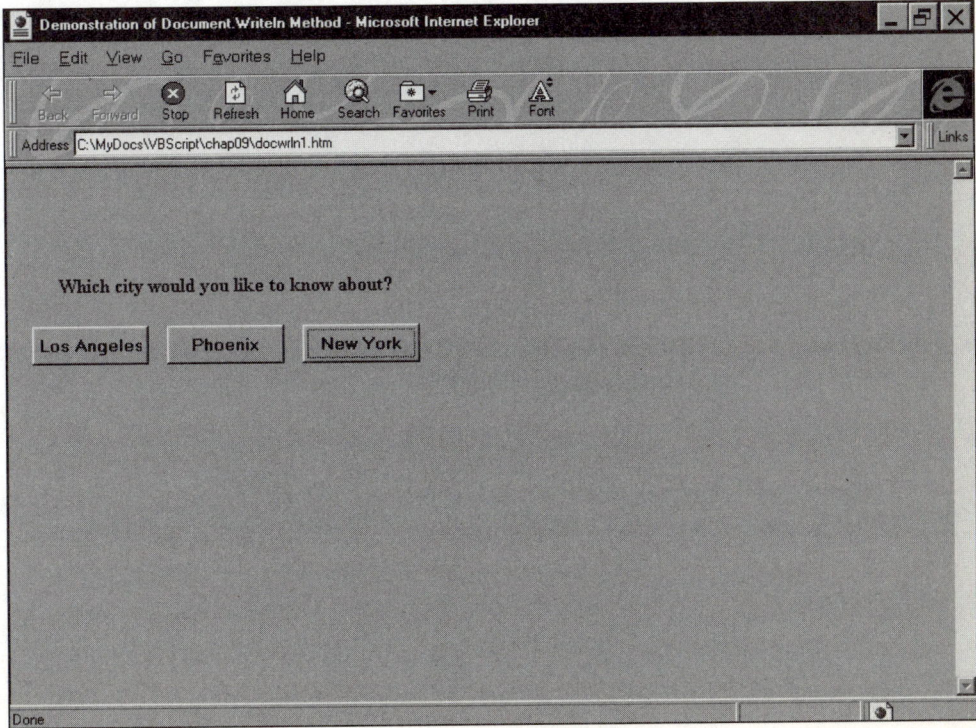

Figure 9.5
The Web page created by the code in Listing 9.5.

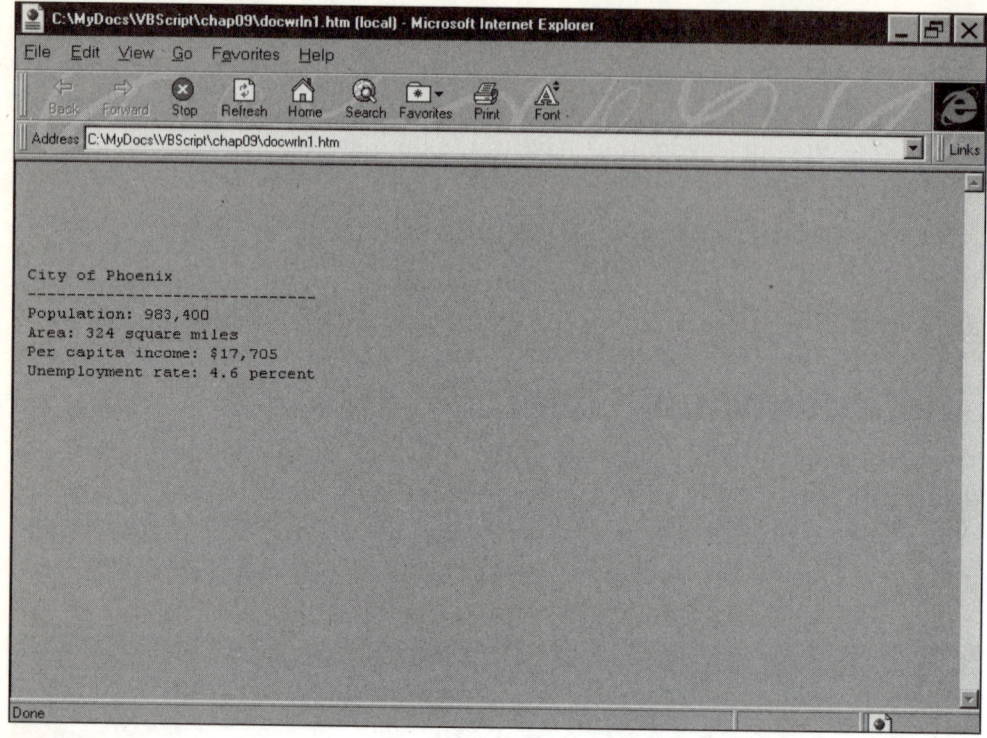

Figure 9.6
Information displayed by the **document.writeln** method.

the Web page created by the code in Listing 9.5, while Figure 9.6 shows the *new* Web page displayed by the **document.writeln** calls.

Listing 9.4 CHANGING THE document OBJECT'S BACKGROUND COLOR.

```
<HTML>
<HEAD>
<TITLE> type_Document_Title_here </TITLE>
</HEAD>
<BODY>
<script language="VBScript">
    sub Pressed
        document.bgColor = "Blue"
    end sub
</script>
<form>
<input type="button" value="Change Web page color" onclick="Pressed">
```

```
</form>
</BODY>
</HTML>
```

As you'd expect, in the **Pressed** sub, you specify the object (**document**), the property (**bgColor**), and assign the new value.

USING DOCUMENT METHODS

Using the **document** object's **write** or **writeln** methods is even more interesting. You can use these methods to write new text into your Web page's underlying HTML document. In response to user actions, you can display new text, or even new controls, on your Web page. Listing 9.5 shows an example of using ActiveX controls and the **document** object's **writeln** method to answer a user's question about Phoenix, Arizona.

Listing 9.5 USING THE **document** OBJECT'S **writeln** METHOD.

```
<HTML>
<HEAD>
<TITLE> Demonstration of Document.Writeln Method</TITLE>
</HEAD>
<BODY>
<pre>
<br><br><br>
<TABLE WIDTH=200 HEIGHT=100 CELLPADDING=5 CELLSPACING=5>
<CAPTION ALIGN=top>
    <b>Which city would you like to know about?</b></CAPTION>
<TR><TD>
<SCRIPT LANGUAGE="VBScript">
<!--
Sub CmdLA_Click()
document.open
document.writeln("<pre>")
document.writeln("<br><br><br><br>City of Los Angeles")
document.writeln("-----------------------------")
document.writeln("Population: 3.5 million")
document.writeln ("Area: 465 square miles")
document.writeln ("Per capita income: $19,906")
document.writeln ("Unemployment rate: 7.3 percent")
document.writeln("</pre>")
document.close
end sub
-->
```

```
        </SCRIPT>
            <OBJECT ID="CmdLA" WIDTH=96 HEIGHT=32
             CLASSID="CLSID:D7053240-CE69-11CD-A777-00DD01143C57">
                <PARAM NAME="Caption" VALUE="Los Angeles">
                <PARAM NAME="Size" VALUE="2540;846">
                <PARAM NAME="FontEffects" VALUE="1073741825">
                <PARAM NAME="FontHeight" VALUE="200">
                <PARAM NAME="FontCharSet" VALUE="0">
                <PARAM NAME="FontPitchAndFamily" VALUE="2">
                <PARAM NAME="ParagraphAlign" VALUE="3">
                <PARAM NAME="FontWeight" VALUE="700">
            </OBJECT>
</TD><TD>
<SCRIPT LANGUAGE="VBScript">
<!--
Sub CmdPhoenix_Click()
document.open
document.writeln("<pre>")
document.writeln("<br><br><br><br>City of Phoenix")
document.writeln("-----------------------------")
document.writeln("Population: 983,400")
document.writeln ("Area: 324 square miles")
document.writeln ("Per capita income: $17,705")
document.writeln ("Unemployment rate: 4.6 percent")
document.writeln("</pre>")
document.close
end sub
-->
</SCRIPT>
            <OBJECT ID="CmdPhoenix" WIDTH=96 HEIGHT=32
             CLASSID="CLSID:D7053240-CE69-11CD-A777-00DD01143C57">
                <PARAM NAME="Caption" VALUE="Phoenix">
                <PARAM NAME="Size" VALUE="2540;846">
                <PARAM NAME="FontEffects" VALUE="1073741825">
                <PARAM NAME="FontHeight" VALUE="200">
                <PARAM NAME="FontCharSet" VALUE="0">
                <PARAM NAME="FontPitchAndFamily" VALUE="2">
                <PARAM NAME="ParagraphAlign" VALUE="3">
                <PARAM NAME="FontWeight" VALUE="700">
            </OBJECT>
</TD><TD>
<SCRIPT LANGUAGE="VBScript">
<!--
Sub CmdNYC_Click()
document.open
document.writeln("<pre>")
document.writeln("<br><br><br><br>City of New York")
```

```
document.writeln("------------------------------")
document.writeln("Population: 7,325,000")
document.writeln ("Area: 301 square miles")
document.writeln ("Per capita income: $22,064")
document.writeln ("Unemployment rate: 7.4 percent")
document.writeln("</pre>")
document.close
end sub
-->
</SCRIPT>
    <OBJECT ID="CmdNYC" WIDTH=96 HEIGHT=32
     CLASSID="CLSID:D7053240-CE69-11CD-A777-00DD01143C57">
        <PARAM NAME="Caption" VALUE="New York">
        <PARAM NAME="Size" VALUE="2540;846">
        <PARAM NAME="FontEffects" VALUE="1073741825">
        <PARAM NAME="FontHeight" VALUE="200">
        <PARAM NAME="FontCharSet" VALUE="0">
        <PARAM NAME="FontPitchAndFamily" VALUE="2">
        <PARAM NAME="ParagraphAlign" VALUE="3">
        <PARAM NAME="FontWeight" VALUE="700">
    </OBJECT>
</TD></TR>
</TABLE>
</pre>
</BODY>
</HTML>
```

We're getting a little fancy with our HTML code—using a table instead of an ActiveX layout to position our ActiveX command buttons. The main point of the listing, however, is contained in the **Click** event subs for the command buttons, as follows:

```
Sub CmdPhoenix_Click()
document.open
document.writeln("<pre>")
document.writeln("<br><br><br><br>City of Phoenix")
document.writeln("------------------------------")
document.writeln("Population: 983,400")
document.writeln ("Area: 324 square miles")
document.writeln ("Per capita income: $17,705")
document.writeln ("Unemployment rate: 4.6 percent")
document.writeln("</pre>")
document.close
end sub
```

To write to a **document** object, you must first open it, much as—in a "regular" PC program—you would open a file before writing to it. Once you've opened the **document** object for writing, you insert a **<pre>** (preformatted text) tag. Without it, VBScript won't distinguish between the **document** object's **writeln** method, which inserts a line break at the end of each line, and the document object's **write** method, which doesn't.

After that, you make repeated calls to **document.writeln** to insert your text into the HTML document. Note that the text goes right into the HTML code, and therefore must be formatted with the appropriate HTML tags. If that seems like a pain, consider the result: You can insert not only text, but also **<input>** or **<object>** tags to display new controls on the rewritten Web page.

When you're finished, you call **document.close** to close the **document** object and update the Web page. If you forget this step, your new Web page won't display and the old one will just sit there.

The **form** Object

The next most important object in the scripting object model is the **form** object. If you want to submit data from your Web page to a server—for example, to allow users to order products—you'll need to use the **form** object and standard HTML form controls.

At this time, Internet Explorer and its scripting model do not allow you to submit values directly from ActiveX controls to a server via the HTML **submit** method. However, by a trick that combines standard form **<input>** controls with ActiveX controls, you can have the power and convenience of ActiveX controls and layouts while still using the **submit** method. All you need to do is refer to form elements. Creating such order forms—and using VBScript for client-side data validation—is the subject of Chapter 10.

10
CLIENT-SIDE DATA VALIDATION

In this chapter, you'll use the skills you've learned to combine HTML, Visual Basic Script, and ActiveX in one of the Web's most common needs: validating data from order forms. You can do it on the user's PC, with VBScript, or you can do it on your Web server, with CGI programs. The choice is yours.

One of the most common uses of the Web is to let customers order products from your Web page. But that entails a rather thorny problem: how to make sure that each customer enters all the data required to process his or her order. Moreover, you often need to make sure that the data is not only *present,* but that it also fits some general guidelines. For example, you need to make sure that the customer's last name isn't all digits, or that a customer's credit-card number is in the correct format.

Creating a Web-page order form with data validation is an ideal exercise because you'll use every concept and skill you've learned so far—as well as a few new ones:

- Creating an ActiveX layout
- Using the Internet Explorer scripting object model to access controls on the Web page

- Writing subs and functions to process the data on the order form
- Checking the data to make sure it's complete
- Sending data from a Web page to a Web server

Client-Side Vs. Server-Side Data Validation

If a user is going to send some data to your Web page—whether it's to order a product or for some other purpose—you can choose one of three strategies (shown in Figure 10.1) for checking the data:

- Don't check the data at all.
- Check the data after it gets to your Web server (server-side data validation).
- Check the data on the user's own machine, before it's submitted to your Web server (client-side data validation).

For serious Web applications, it's simply not an option to skip checking the data. That leaves only two choices: Either you check the data on your Web server, or you check it on the user's machine—the client.

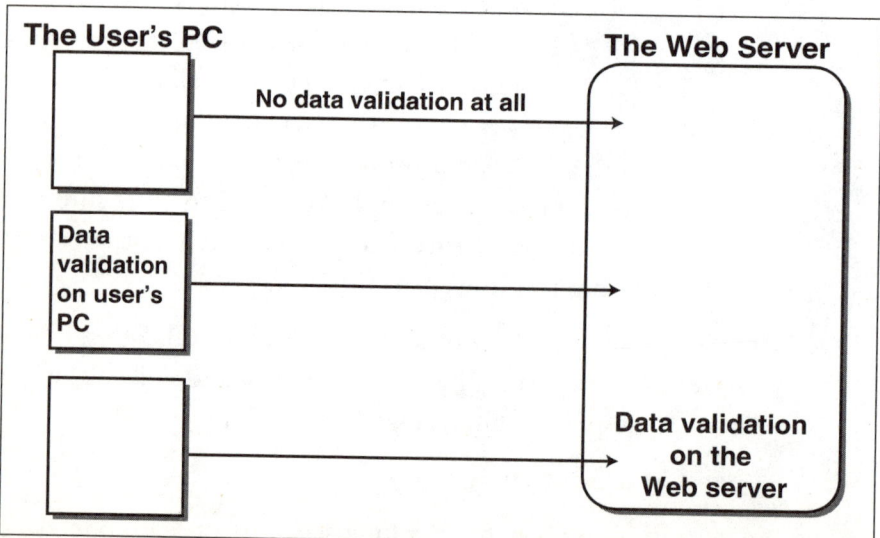

Figure 10.1
Strategies for Web data validation.

Historically, most Web ordering systems have used server-side data validation because that's what was available with current technology. To validate data when it gets to your Web server, you can write a CGI (Common Gateway Interface) program that actually runs on your Web server. Normally, this type of program will check the data, then process it to fulfill the customer's order. In Chapter 16, you'll learn how to use Visual Basic 5 to create this type of program and run it on your Web server.

VBScript, however, makes it easy to validate data on the client machine, before it ever gets to your Web server. If you're going to process a lot of orders, this can be a much more efficient way to check the data.

Client-Side Validation With VBScript And HTML

The simplest way to do client-side data validation is to use VBScript with standard HTML forms and controls. That's not nearly as easy or powerful as using an ActiveX layout and ActiveX controls, but it's much simpler, so it's a good place to start.

The concept is simple: Before you submit the data to the Web server, you run it through a few VBScript routines to check it. This approach is shown in Listing 10.1. As before, we had to break a few lines to fit the code into the page margins of this book. As a result, the material between the **<pre>** and **</pre>** (preformatted text) tags won't display properly on your screen unless you reformat it. The Web page created by the HTML code in Listing 10.1 is shown in Figure 10.2.

Listing 10.1 HTML code to create a Web page order form.

```
<HTML>
<HEAD>
<TITLE>Order Books from Coriolis!</TITLE>
<!--
    This version of the Web page order form shows the beginnings of how
    to incorporate error-checking into a simple HTML document without
    using an ActiveX layout or controls.
-->

<script language="VBS">
<!--
```

```
function DataOkay
   MsgBox "The data has been checked, and it's okay.",, _
      "Client-Side Data Validation"
end function

sub Btn_Order_onClick
   if DataOkay then OrderForm.Submit
end sub

-->
</script>

</HEAD>
<BODY>
<h1>Check the books you would like to order:</h1>
<FORM name="OrderForm" method=post
   ACTION="http://localhost/cgi-win/cgitest32.exe/Form">
<hr>
<ul><ul><ul><ul><ul>
<INPUT NAME="CB_VBScriptPrg" TYPE="CHECKBOX" VALUE="1"
   ALIGN=left>VBScript 2 and ActiveX Programming, $39.99<br>
<INPUT NAME="CB_DelphiExp" TYPE="CHECKBOX" VALUE="1"
   ALIGN=left>The New Delphi 2 Programming EXplorer, $44.99<br>
<INPUT NAME="CB_JavaApp" TYPE="CHECKBOX" VALUE="1"
   ALIGN=left>Writing Java Applets, $39.99<br>
<INPUT NAME="CB_Intranet" TYPE="CHECKBOX" VALUE="1"
   ALIGN=left>Developing Real-World Intranets, $39.99<br>
</ul></ul></ul></ul></ul>
<hr>
<pre>
Your Name:       <INPUT NAME="TB_Customer" TYPE="" SIZE="20"
   ALIGN=right><br>
Street Address: <INPUT NAME=
   "TB_Street" TYPE="" SIZE="25" ALIGN=right><br>
City:            <INPUT NAME="TB_City" TYPE="TEXT" SIZE="15"
   ALIGN=right> State: <INPUT NAME="TB_State" TYPE="TEXT"
   SIZE="5" ALIGN=right> Zip: <INPUT NAME="TB_Zip"
   TYPE="TEXT" SIZE="5" ALIGN=right>
<br>
Send your order today!  <INPUT NAME="Btn_Order" TYPE="Button"
   value="Submit Order" ALIGN=right >
</pre>
</FORM>

</BODY>
</HTML>
```

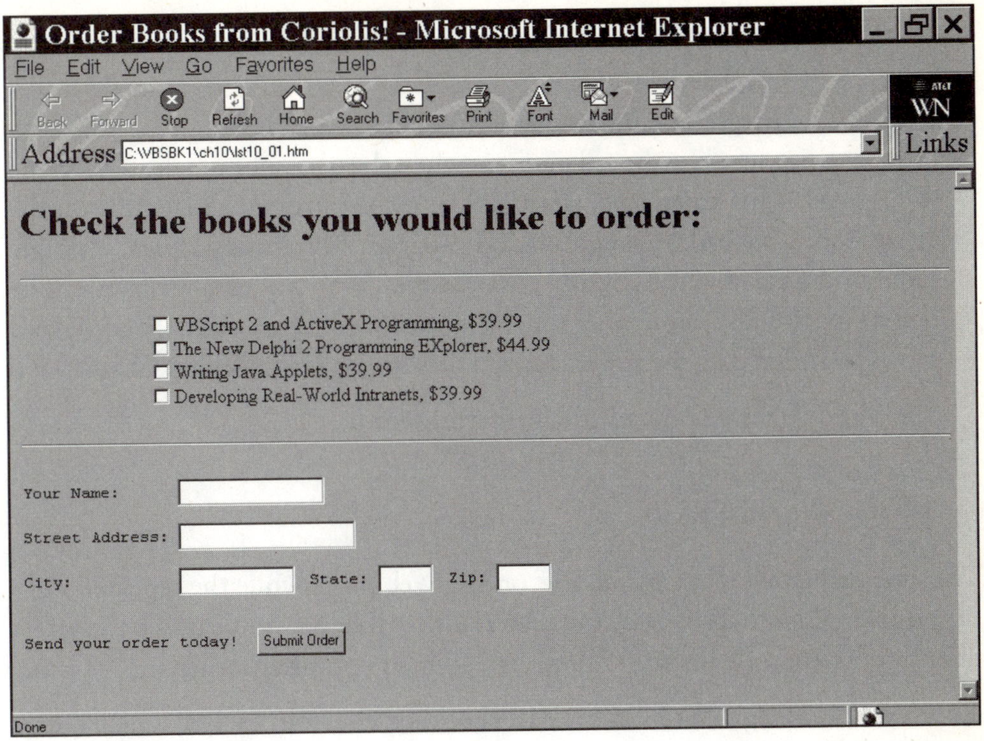

Figure 10.2
A Web page order form.

Stepping Through The Example Code

Before we construct a fully functional example, let's take a look at the broad outlines of what's going on in Listing 10.1. Later, when we do the same thing with an ActiveX layout, you'll need a firm understanding of these basic moves.

The first step in the Web page proper is to create an HTML form by using the **<form>** tag. The specific code that sets up the HTML form is as follows:

```
<FORM name="OrderForm" method=post
    ACTION="http://localhost/cgi-win/cgitest32.exe/Form">
```

This line does several jobs. First, of course, it tells the Web browser that this is the beginning of a form. Then, it does the following:

- **name="OrderForm"** tells the Web browser that the form is named *OrderForm*. You'll use that name to refer to the form and its controls later on.

- **method=post** tells the Web browser that this form will be used to send data to the Web server.

- **ACTION="http://localhost/cgi-win/cgitest32.exe/Form"** tells the Web browser what action it should perform when the user submits the data to the Web server. This action will normally be a CGI program that runs on the server. Here, instead of a regular CGI program, we're using *cgitest*, a simple program bundled with O'Reilly & Associates' Web site server software. The *cgitest* program just verifies that your Web page is sending data to the server and shows you what data the server received. It's explained in detail in Chapter 16.

The next code lines just do a little formatting for us:

```
<hr>
<ul><ul><ul><ul><ul>
```

The **<hr>** tag draws a horizontal line on the Web page, while the repeated **<ul>** (unnumbered list) tags indent the material that follows. You can see the effect of both of these code lines in Figure 10.2, which appeared earlier.

The next lines set up a series of HTML checkbox controls, each of which corresponds to a book that a Web page user might order from The Coriolis Group:

```
<INPUT NAME="CB_VBScriptPrg" TYPE="CHECKBOX" VALUE="1"
    ALIGN=left>VBScript 2 and ActiveX Programming, $39.99<br>
...and so on
```

The code is fairly self-explanatory, but there's one point worth noting if you haven't used HTML checkboxes very much: The **value** property is set to 1. This does *not* mean what you might expect: that the checkbox has a value of 1 as soon as it appears on the Web page. Instead, it means that if and when the user checks the checkbox, it *will* have a value of 1—in other words, 1 is the value of its "checked" state. By testing to see if a checkbox control has a value of 1, you can determine whether or not it has been checked.

The next code removes the indents created by the **<ul>** tags, draws another horizontal line, and tells the browser to display the next material as it's formatted in the HTML document:

```
</ul></ul></ul></ul></ul>
<hr>
<pre>
```

Following the <pre> tag, we use essentially the same techniques to create a series of labeled text boxes in which the user can enter his/her name and address for order shipment:

```
<INPUT NAME="CB_VBScriptPrg" TYPE="CHECKBOX" VALUE="1"
   ALIGN=left>VBScript 2 and ActiveX Programming, $39.99<br>
```
and so on.

As before, these are native HTML controls, not ActiveX controls. Next, we create a submit button. When the user clicks on this button, the data will be sent from the Web page to the server, where the order will be processed by a CGI program:

```
Send your order today!   <INPUT NAME="Btn_Order" TYPE="Button"
 value="Submit Order" ALIGN=right >
</pre>
</FORM>
```

Ordinarily, the type of this control would be **submit**, so that clicking it would automatically submit the data to the server. However, we're bundling the call to the **form.submit** method into the **OnClick** sub for the button control. Therefore, the button control is coded simply as a plain vanilla **button**. Bundling the call to **form.submit** into the sub is done to enable us to validate the data before submitting it.

Now that the HTML code is out of the way, let's take a look at the framework for our data-validation script:

```
<script language="VBS">
<!--
function DataOkay
   MsgBox "The data has been checked, and it's okay.",, _
      "Client-Side Data Validation"
end function

sub Btn_Order_onClick
   if DataOkay then OrderForm.Submit
end sub
-->
</script>
```

In the next version of our code, we'll build the actual data validation into the **DataOkay** function and we'll call that function in the **Btn_Order_onClick**

Figure 10.3
The VBScript data-checking framework is running.

sub. At present, there really isn't any data checking. However, if the user clicks on the submit button, a message box will appear, as shown in Figure 10.3. That, at least, shows us that the VBScript code framework is up and running.

Creating A Data-Checking Function

Our next step is to fill in the blanks that we left in Listing 10.1—mainly by writing the actual VBScript code that does the data checking. Listing 10.2 shows the modified HTML document with the data-checking code.

Listing 10.2 Data-checking code for the Web page.

```
<HTML>
<HEAD>
<TITLE>Order Books from Coriolis!</TITLE>
<!--
   This version of the Web page order form builds in some simple error-
   checking. The DataOkay function is activated when the user clicks on
   the button to submit the order to the Web server.
-->

<script language="VBS">
<!--

function DataOkay
   if (OrderForm.CB_VBScriptPrg.checked) or _
      (OrderForm.CB_DelphiExp.checked)  or _
      (OrderForm.CB_JavaApp.checked) or _
      (OrderForm.CB_Intranet.checked) then
      DataOkay = true
      MsgBox "The data has been checked, and it's okay.",, _
         "Client-Side Data Validation"
   else
      DataOkay = false
      MsgBox "The data isn't adequate to process the order.",, _
         "Client-Side Data Validation"
   end if
end function
```

```
sub Btn_Order_onClick
   If DataOkay then
      OrderForm.Submit
   else
      MsgBox "You haven't provided adequate data to process your" & _
         "order.",,"Client-Side Data Validation"
   end if
end sub

-->
</script>

</HEAD>
<BODY>
<h1>Check the books you would like to order:</h1>
<FORM name="OrderForm" method=post
   ACTION="http://localhost/cgi-win/cgitest32.exe/Form">
<hr>
<ul><ul><ul><ul><ul>
<INPUT NAME="CB_VBScriptPrg" TYPE="CHECKBOX" VALUE="1"
   ALIGN=left>VBScript 2 and ActiveX Programming, $39.99<br>
<INPUT NAME="CB_DelphiExp" TYPE="CHECKBOX" VALUE="1"
   ALIGN=left>The New Delphi 2 Programming EXplorer, $44.99<br>
<INPUT NAME="CB_JavaApp" TYPE="CHECKBOX" VALUE="1"
   ALIGN=left>Writing Java Applets, $39.99<br>
<INPUT NAME="CB_Intranet" TYPE="CHECKBOX" VALUE="1"
   ALIGN=left>Developing Real-World Intranets, $39.99<br>
</ul></ul></ul></ul></ul>
<hr>
<pre>
Your Name:      <INPUT NAME="TB_Customer" TYPE="" SIZE="20"
   ALIGN=right><br>
Street Address: <INPUT NAME=
   "TB_Street" TYPE="" SIZE="25" ALIGN=right><br>
City:           <INPUT NAME="TB_City" TYPE="TEXT" SIZE="15"
   ALIGN=right> State: <INPUT NAME="TB_State" TYPE="TEXT"
   SIZE="5" ALIGN=right> Zip: <INPUT NAME="TB_Zip"
   TYPE="TEXT" SIZE="5" ALIGN=right>
<br>
Send your order today!  <INPUT NAME="Btn_Order" TYPE="Button"
   value="Submit Order" ALIGN=right >
</pre>
</FORM>

</BODY>
</HTML>
```

Let's take a look at how the VBScript code works. The **OnClick** event code for the submit button consists of a simple **if...then...else** statement:

```
If DataOkay then
      OrderForm.Submit
   else
      MsgBox _
        "You haven't provided adequate data to process your order."_
        ,, "Client-Side Data Validation"
end if
```

The **if** statement checks to see if the data is okay—that is, if the **DataOkay()** function returns a value of **true**. If so, the **then** clause calls **OrderForm.Submit** to send the data to the Web server. If not, then the **else** clause displays a message box informing the user that there's a problem.

The **DataOkay()** function, too, is pretty straightforward. It consists of another **if...then...else** statement:

```
if (OrderForm.CB_VBScriptPrg.checked) or _
     (OrderForm.CB_DelphiExp.checked)  or _
     (OrderForm.CB_JavaApp.checked) or _
     (OrderForm.CB_Intranet.checked) then
     DataOkay = true
     MsgBox "The data has been checked, and it's okay.",,_
        "Client-Side Data Validation"
else
     DataOkay = false
     MsgBox "The data isn't adequate to process the order.",,_
        "Client-Side Data Validation"
end if
```

Notice that, in accordance with Internet Explorer's scripting object model, we refer to the checkboxes by prefacing each checkbox name with the name of the form in which it appears, for example:

```
OrderForm.CB_VBScriptPrg.checked
```

The **if** part of the statement checks to see that at least one of the checkboxes has been checked. If none has been checked, then the user didn't select any books to order and there's no point in sending the rest of the data (if any) to the server. If at least one book is being ordered, the order goes through, and the data is sent

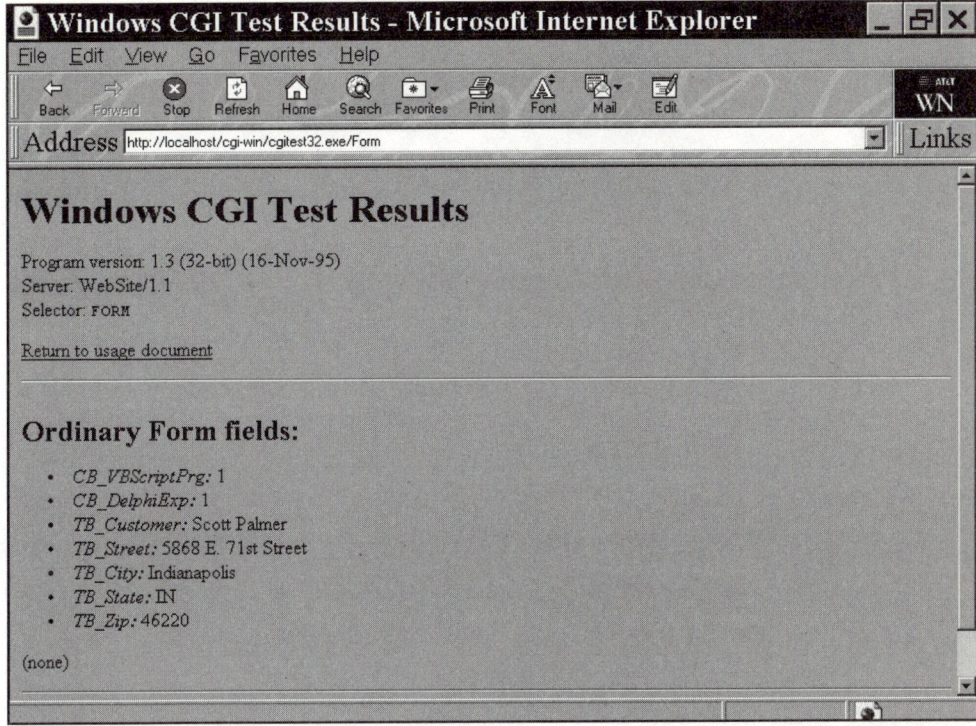

Figure 10.4
The order data was received by the Web server.

to the server. Figure 10.4 shows the report we get back from the Web site *cgitest* program if we order *VBScript 2 & ActiveX Programming* and *The New Delphi 2 Programming EXplorer.*

To keep things simple in this example, we only verified that at least one checkbox was checked. However, you can use the same techniques to build other data checks into the **DataOkay()** function.

Client-Side Data Validation With An ActiveX Layout

As noted earlier, the HTML-only implementation of client-side data validation has two very important virtues: First, it's simple; second, it works. But when you compare it to the attractive Web page layouts we can create with the ActiveX Control Pad, and the power we can get from ActiveX controls, it seems a bit lame.

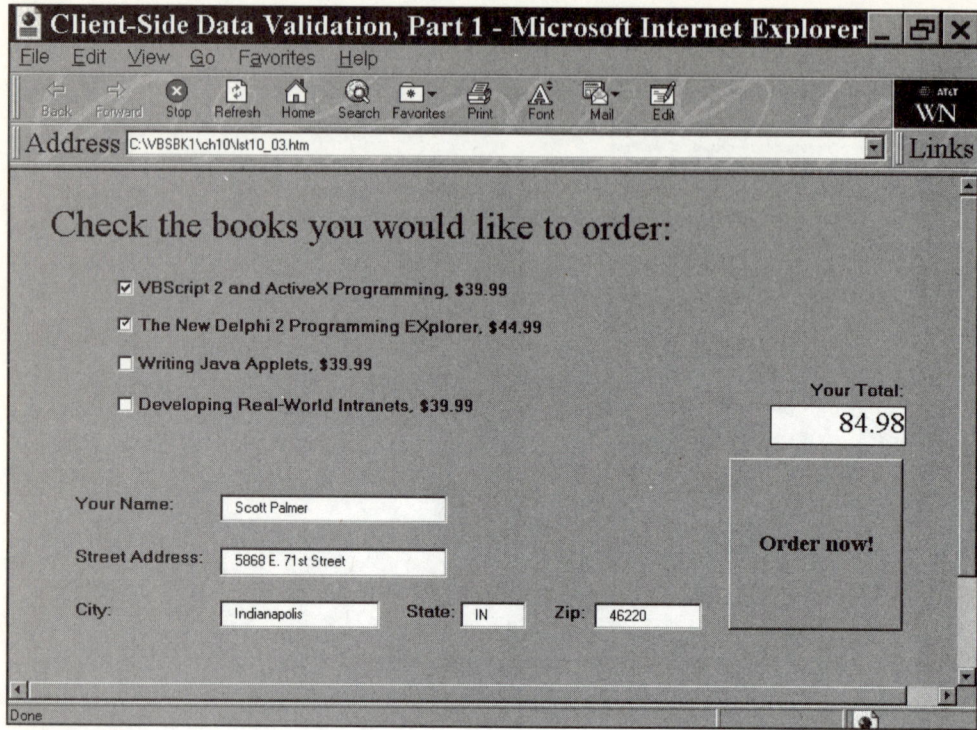

Figure 10.5
A Web order entry form that uses an ActiveX layout.

Doing client-side data validation with ActiveX layouts and controls is much more complicated than plain HTML data validation, but the results are spectacular—even amazing. And once you've mastered the necessary concepts and techniques, you'll be able to create better-looking order forms much faster than if you were hand-coding everything in HTML.

Let's take a "first pass" at creating an order entry form with the ActiveX Control Pad. It will do some basic data checking, but it won't yet submit the data to the Web server. The HTML container code is shown in Listing 10.3, while the ActiveX layout code is shown in Listing 10.4. The Web page created by Listings 10.3 and 10.4 is shown above in Figure 10.5.

Listing 10.3 HTML CODE FOR THE ORDER ENTRY FORM.

```
<HTML>
<HEAD>
<TITLE>Client-Side Data Validation, Part 1</TITLE>
</HEAD>
<BODY>
```

```
<OBJECT CLASSID="CLSID:812AE312-8B8E-11CF-93C8-00AA00C08FDF"
ID="ordrbk2_alx" STYLE="LEFT:0;TOP:0">
<PARAM NAME="ALXPATH" REF VALUE="ordrbk2.alx">
</OBJECT>
</BODY>
</HTML>
```

Listing 10.4 ActiveX layout for the order entry form.

```
<SCRIPT LANGUAGE="VBScript">
<!--
Sub CmdOrder_Click()
dim OrderComplete

if (CBApp or CBDelphi or CBIntra or CBVBS) then
   OrderComplete = true
else
   msgbox "You must select a book to order."
   OrderComplete = false
end if

if (TBName.text = "") or _
   (TBStreet.text = "") or _
   (TBCity.text = "") or _
   (TBState.text = "") or _
   (TBZip.text = "") then
   msgbox "You didn't fill in all the address information."
   OrderComplete = false
else
   OrderComplete = true
end if

If OrderComplete then
   MsgBox "Order accepted!"
else
   MsgBox "You didn't include all the necessary information."
end if

end sub
-->
</SCRIPT>
<SCRIPT LANGUAGE="VBScript">
<!--
Sub CBApp_Change()
if CBApp then
   LblTotal.caption = LblTotal.caption + 39.99
else
   LblTotal.caption = LblTotal.caption - 39.99
```

```
   end if
end sub
-->
</SCRIPT>
<SCRIPT LANGUAGE="VBScript">
<!--
Sub CBVBS_Change()
if CBVBS then
   LblTotal.caption = LblTotal.caption + 39.99
else
   LblTotal.caption = LblTotal.caption - 39.99
end if
end sub
-->
</SCRIPT>
<SCRIPT LANGUAGE="VBScript">
<!--
Sub CBIntra_Change()
if CBIntra then
   LblTotal.caption = LblTotal.caption + 39.99
else
   LblTotal.caption = LblTotal.caption - 39.99
end if
end sub
-->
</SCRIPT>
<SCRIPT LANGUAGE="VBScript">
<!--
Sub CBDelphi_Change()
if CBDelphi then
   LblTotal.caption = LblTotal.caption + 44.99
else
   LblTotal.caption = LblTotal.caption - 44.99
end if
end sub
-->
</SCRIPT>
<DIV ID="Layout1" STYLE="LAYOUT:FIXED;WIDTH:597pt;HEIGHT:370pt;">
    <OBJECT ID="Label1"
     CLASSID="CLSID:978C9E23-D4B0-11CE-BF2D-00AA003F40D0"
       STYLE="TOP:8pt;LEFT:17pt;WIDTH:396pt;HEIGHT:32pt;ZINDEX:0;">
       <PARAM NAME="Caption"
           VALUE="Check the books you would like to order:">
       <PARAM NAME="Size" VALUE="13970;1129">
       <PARAM NAME="FontName" VALUE="Times New Roman">
       <PARAM NAME="FontHeight" VALUE="480">
       <PARAM NAME="FontCharSet" VALUE="0">
```

```
        <PARAM NAME="FontPitchAndFamily" VALUE="2">
        <PARAM NAME="FontWeight" VALUE="0">
</OBJECT>

<OBJECT ID="CBVBS"
 CLASSID="CLSID:8BD21D40-EC42-11CE-9E0D-00AA006002F3"
 STYLE="TOP:50pt;LEFT:58pt;WIDTH:281pt;HEIGHT:22pt;
        TABINDEX:1;ZINDEX:1;">
    <PARAM NAME="BackColor" VALUE="2147483663">
    <PARAM NAME="ForeColor" VALUE="2147483666">
    <PARAM NAME="DisplayStyle" VALUE="4">
    <PARAM NAME="Size" VALUE="9913;776">
    <PARAM NAME="Value" VALUE="False">
    <PARAM NAME="Caption"
        VALUE="VBScript 2 and ActiveX Programming, $39.99">
    <PARAM NAME="FontEffects" VALUE="1073741825">
    <PARAM NAME="FontHeight" VALUE="200">
    <PARAM NAME="FontCharSet" VALUE="0">
    <PARAM NAME="FontPitchAndFamily" VALUE="2">
    <PARAM NAME="FontWeight" VALUE="700">
</OBJECT>

<OBJECT ID="CBDelphi"
 CLASSID="CLSID:8BD21D40-EC42-11CE-9E0D-00AA006002F3"
        STYLE="TOP:74pt;LEFT:58pt;WIDTH:281pt;HEIGHT:20pt;
        TABINDEX:2;ZINDEX:2;">
    <PARAM NAME="BackColor" VALUE="2147483663">
    <PARAM NAME="ForeColor" VALUE="2147483666">
    <PARAM NAME="DisplayStyle" VALUE="4">
    <PARAM NAME="Size" VALUE="9913;706">
    <PARAM NAME="Value" VALUE="False">
    <PARAM NAME="Caption"
        VALUE="The New Delphi 2 Programming EXplorer, $44.99">
    <PARAM NAME="FontEffects" VALUE="1073741825">
    <PARAM NAME="FontHeight" VALUE="200">
    <PARAM NAME="FontCharSet" VALUE="0">
    <PARAM NAME="FontPitchAndFamily" VALUE="2">
    <PARAM NAME="FontWeight" VALUE="700">
</OBJECT>

<OBJECT ID="CBApp"
 CLASSID="CLSID:8BD21D40-EC42-11CE-9E0D-00AA006002F3"
        STYLE="TOP:99pt;LEFT:58pt;WIDTH:281pt;HEIGHT:19pt;
        TABINDEX:3;ZINDEX:3;">
    <PARAM NAME="BackColor" VALUE="2147483663">
    <PARAM NAME="ForeColor" VALUE="2147483666">
    <PARAM NAME="DisplayStyle" VALUE="4">
```

```
        <PARAM NAME="Size" VALUE="9913;670">
        <PARAM NAME="Value" VALUE="False">
        <PARAM NAME="Caption"
            VALUE="Writing Java Applets, $39.99">
        <PARAM NAME="FontEffects" VALUE="1073741825">
        <PARAM NAME="FontHeight" VALUE="200">
        <PARAM NAME="FontCharSet" VALUE="0">
        <PARAM NAME="FontPitchAndFamily" VALUE="2">
        <PARAM NAME="FontWeight" VALUE="700">
</OBJECT>

<OBJECT ID="CBIntra"
 CLASSID="CLSID:8BD21D40-EC42-11CE-9E0D-00AA006002F3"
        STYLE="TOP:124pt;LEFT:58pt;WIDTH:281pt;HEIGHT:20pt;
        TABINDEX:4;ZINDEX:4;">
    <PARAM NAME="BackColor" VALUE="2147483663">
    <PARAM NAME="ForeColor" VALUE="2147483666">
    <PARAM NAME="DisplayStyle" VALUE="4">
    <PARAM NAME="Size" VALUE="9913;706">
    <PARAM NAME="Value" VALUE="False">
    <PARAM NAME="Caption"
        VALUE="Developing Real-World Intranets, $39.99">
    <PARAM NAME="FontEffects" VALUE="1073741825">
    <PARAM NAME="FontHeight" VALUE="200">
    <PARAM NAME="FontCharSet" VALUE="0">
    <PARAM NAME="FontPitchAndFamily" VALUE="2">
    <PARAM NAME="FontWeight" VALUE="700">
</OBJECT>

<OBJECT ID="Label2"
 CLASSID="CLSID:978C9E23-D4B0-11CE-BF2D-00AA003F40D0"
        STYLE="TOP:190pt;LEFT:33pt;WIDTH:66pt;
        HEIGHT:17pt;ZINDEX:5;">
    <PARAM NAME="Caption" VALUE="Your Name:">
    <PARAM NAME="Size" VALUE="2328;600">
    <PARAM NAME="FontEffects" VALUE="1073741825">
    <PARAM NAME="FontHeight" VALUE="200">
    <PARAM NAME="FontCharSet" VALUE="0">
    <PARAM NAME="FontPitchAndFamily" VALUE="2">
    <PARAM NAME="FontWeight" VALUE="700">
</OBJECT>

<OBJECT ID="Label3"
 CLASSID="CLSID:978C9E23-D4B0-11CE-BF2D-00AA003F40D0"
        STYLE="TOP:223pt;LEFT:33pt;WIDTH:83pt;
        HEIGHT:17pt;ZINDEX:6;">
    <PARAM NAME="Caption" VALUE="Street Address:">
    <PARAM NAME="Size" VALUE="2928;600">
```

```
        <PARAM NAME="FontEffects" VALUE="1073741825">
        <PARAM NAME="FontHeight" VALUE="200">
        <PARAM NAME="FontCharSet" VALUE="0">
        <PARAM NAME="FontPitchAndFamily" VALUE="2">
        <PARAM NAME="FontWeight" VALUE="700">
</OBJECT>

<OBJECT ID="Label4"
 CLASSID="CLSID:978C9E23-D4B0-11CE-BF2D-00AA003F40D0"
        STYLE="TOP:256pt;LEFT:33pt;WIDTH:33pt;
        HEIGHT:17pt;ZINDEX:7;">
    <PARAM NAME="Caption" VALUE="City:">
    <PARAM NAME="Size" VALUE="1164;600">
    <PARAM NAME="FontEffects" VALUE="1073741825">
    <PARAM NAME="FontHeight" VALUE="200">
    <PARAM NAME="FontCharSet" VALUE="0">
    <PARAM NAME="FontPitchAndFamily" VALUE="2">
    <PARAM NAME="FontWeight" VALUE="700">
</OBJECT>

<OBJECT ID="TBName"
 CLASSID="CLSID:8BD21D10-EC42-11CE-9E0D-00AA006002F3"
        STYLE="TOP:190pt;LEFT:124pt;WIDTH:140pt;
        HEIGHT:17pt;TABINDEX:8;ZINDEX:8;">
    <PARAM NAME="VariousPropertyBits" VALUE="746604571">
    <PARAM NAME="Size" VALUE="4939;600">
    <PARAM NAME="FontCharSet" VALUE="0">
    <PARAM NAME="FontPitchAndFamily" VALUE="2">
    <PARAM NAME="FontWeight" VALUE="0">
</OBJECT>

<OBJECT ID="TBStreet"
 CLASSID="CLSID:8BD21D10-EC42-11CE-9E0D-00AA006002F3"
        STYLE="TOP:223pt;LEFT:124pt;WIDTH:140pt;HEIGHT:18pt;
        TABINDEX:9;ZINDEX:9;">
    <PARAM NAME="VariousPropertyBits" VALUE="746604571">
    <PARAM NAME="Size" VALUE="4939;635">
    <PARAM NAME="FontCharSet" VALUE="0">
    <PARAM NAME="FontPitchAndFamily" VALUE="2">
    <PARAM NAME="FontWeight" VALUE="0">
</OBJECT>

<OBJECT ID="TBCity"
 CLASSID="CLSID:8BD21D10-EC42-11CE-9E0D-00AA006002F3"
        STYLE="TOP:256pt;LEFT:124pt;WIDTH:99pt;HEIGHT:17pt;
        TABINDEX:10;ZINDEX:10;">
    <PARAM NAME="VariousPropertyBits" VALUE="746604571">
    <PARAM NAME="Size" VALUE="3493;600">
```

```
            <PARAM NAME="FontCharSet" VALUE="0">
            <PARAM NAME="FontPitchAndFamily" VALUE="2">
            <PARAM NAME="FontWeight" VALUE="0">
    </OBJECT>

    <OBJECT ID="Label5"
     CLASSID="CLSID:978C9E23-D4B0-11CE-BF2D-00AA003F40D0"
            STYLE="TOP:256pt;LEFT:239pt;WIDTH:33pt;
            HEIGHT:17pt;ZINDEX:11;">
        <PARAM NAME="Caption" VALUE="State:">
        <PARAM NAME="Size" VALUE="1164;600">
        <PARAM NAME="FontEffects" VALUE="1073741825">
        <PARAM NAME="FontHeight" VALUE="200">
        <PARAM NAME="FontCharSet" VALUE="0">
        <PARAM NAME="FontPitchAndFamily" VALUE="2">
        <PARAM NAME="FontWeight" VALUE="700">
    </OBJECT>

    <OBJECT ID="TBState"
     CLASSID="CLSID:8BD21D10-EC42-11CE-9E0D-00AA006002F3"
            STYLE="TOP:256pt;LEFT:272pt;WIDTH:41pt;HEIGHT:16pt;
            TABINDEX:12;ZINDEX:12;">
        <PARAM NAME="VariousPropertyBits" VALUE="746604571">
        <PARAM NAME="Size" VALUE="1446;564">
        <PARAM NAME="FontCharSet" VALUE="0">
        <PARAM NAME="FontPitchAndFamily" VALUE="2">
        <PARAM NAME="FontWeight" VALUE="0">
    </OBJECT>

    <OBJECT ID="Label6"
     CLASSID="CLSID:978C9E23-D4B0-11CE-BF2D-00AA003F40D0"
            STYLE="TOP:256pt;LEFT:330pt;WIDTH:25pt;
            HEIGHT:17pt;ZINDEX:13;">
        <PARAM NAME="Caption" VALUE="Zip:">
        <PARAM NAME="Size" VALUE="882;600">
        <PARAM NAME="FontEffects" VALUE="1073741825">
        <PARAM NAME="FontHeight" VALUE="200">
        <PARAM NAME="FontCharSet" VALUE="0">
        <PARAM NAME="FontPitchAndFamily" VALUE="2">
        <PARAM NAME="FontWeight" VALUE="700">
    </OBJECT>

    <OBJECT ID="TBZip"
     CLASSID="CLSID:8BD21D10-EC42-11CE-9E0D-00AA006002F3"
            STYLE="TOP:256pt;LEFT:355pt;WIDTH:66pt;HEIGHT:16pt;
            TABINDEX:14;ZINDEX:14;">
        <PARAM NAME="VariousPropertyBits" VALUE="746604571">
        <PARAM NAME="Size" VALUE="2328;564">
```

```
        <PARAM NAME="FontCharSet" VALUE="0">
        <PARAM NAME="FontPitchAndFamily" VALUE="2">
        <PARAM NAME="FontWeight" VALUE="0">
</OBJECT>

<OBJECT ID="CmdOrder"
 CLASSID="CLSID:D7053240-CE69-11CD-A777-00DD01143C57"
        STYLE="TOP:165pt;LEFT:437pt;WIDTH:107pt;HEIGHT:107pt;
        TABINDEX:15;ZINDEX:15;">
    <PARAM NAME="Caption" VALUE="Order now!">
    <PARAM NAME="Size" VALUE="3775;3775">
    <PARAM NAME="FontName" VALUE="Times New Roman">
    <PARAM NAME="FontEffects" VALUE="1073741825">
    <PARAM NAME="FontHeight" VALUE="280">
    <PARAM NAME="FontCharSet" VALUE="0">
    <PARAM NAME="FontPitchAndFamily" VALUE="2">
    <PARAM NAME="ParagraphAlign" VALUE="3">
    <PARAM NAME="FontWeight" VALUE="700">
</OBJECT>

<OBJECT ID="Label7"
 CLASSID="CLSID:978C9E23-D4B0-11CE-BF2D-00AA003F40D0"
        STYLE="TOP:116pt;LEFT:470pt;WIDTH:74pt;
        HEIGHT:17pt;ZINDEX:16;">
    <PARAM NAME="Caption" VALUE="Your Total:">
    <PARAM NAME="Size" VALUE="2611;600">
    <PARAM NAME="FontEffects" VALUE="1073741825">
    <PARAM NAME="FontHeight" VALUE="240">
    <PARAM NAME="FontCharSet" VALUE="0">
    <PARAM NAME="FontPitchAndFamily" VALUE="2">
    <PARAM NAME="ParagraphAlign" VALUE="2">
    <PARAM NAME="FontWeight" VALUE="700">
</OBJECT>

<OBJECT ID="LblTotal"
 CLASSID="CLSID:978C9E23-D4B0-11CE-BF2D-00AA003F40D0"
        STYLE="TOP:132pt;LEFT:462pt;WIDTH:83pt;
        HEIGHT:25pt;ZINDEX:17;">
    <PARAM NAME="BackColor" VALUE="16777215">
    <PARAM NAME="Caption" VALUE="0.00">
    <PARAM NAME="Size" VALUE="2928;882">
    <PARAM NAME="BorderStyle" VALUE="1">
    <PARAM NAME="FontName" VALUE="Times New Roman">
    <PARAM NAME="FontHeight" VALUE="360">
    <PARAM NAME="FontCharSet" VALUE="0">
    <PARAM NAME="FontPitchAndFamily" VALUE="2">
    <PARAM NAME="ParagraphAlign" VALUE="2">
```

```
        <PARAM NAME="FontWeight" VALUE="0">
    </OBJECT>
</DIV>
```

Stepping Through The Example Code

Let's see how the code works. As usual, the HTML document itself functions as a container for the ActiveX layout, to which it's connected by the **<object>** tag for the HTML Layout control. The layout creates a Web page that's quite similar to the one we created earlier: There are checkboxes for the books, text boxes for the customer's name and address, and a command button to send the order. One new wrinkle is the addition of a dynamically updated label control that shows the current total due for the customer's order. We'll look at that first. The relevant VBScript code is as follows:

```
Sub CBApp_Change()
if CBApp then
    LblTotal.caption = LblTotal.caption + 39.99
else
    LblTotal.caption = LblTotal.caption - 39.99
end if

end sub

Sub CBVBS_Change()
if CBVBS then
    LblTotal.caption = LblTotal.caption + 39.99
else
    LblTotal.caption = LblTotal.caption - 39.99
end if
end sub

Sub CBIntra_Change()
if CBIntra then
    LblTotal.caption = LblTotal.caption + 39.99
else
    LblTotal.caption = LblTotal.caption - 39.99
end if
end sub

Sub CBDelphi_Change()
if CBDelphi then
    LblTotal.caption = LblTotal.caption + 44.99
```

```
else
   LblTotal.caption = LblTotal.caption - 44.99
end if
end sub
```

The various "CB" controls, of course, are the checkboxes, and the **Change** event is fired whenever the value of the check box *changes*. Inside the **Change** event code, each sub performs a check on the new value of the checkbox. If the checkbox is checked—which means that before, it *wasn't* checked—then the sub adds the appropriate dollar amount to the label that displays the order total. If the checkbox is unchecked—meaning that it *was* checked before—then the code subtracts the same amount from the total in the label control. This keeps the customer's current order total up to date.

Now, let's get back to our central problem: client-side data validation. The data-checking code is in the **Click** event sub for the command button, as follows:

```
Sub CmdOrder_Click()
dim OrderComplete

if (CBApp or CBDelphi or CBIntra or CBVBS) then
   OrderComplete = true
else
   msgbox "You must select a book to order."
   OrderComplete = false
end if

if (TBName.text = "") or _
   (TBStreet.text = "") or _
   (TBCity.text = "") or _
   (TBState.text = "") or _
   (TBZip.text = "") then
   msgbox "You didn't fill in all the address information."
   OrderComplete = false
else
   OrderComplete = true
end if

If OrderComplete then
   MsgBox "Order accepted!"
else
   MsgBox "You didn't include all the necessary information."
end if

end sub
```

First, we declare a variable called **OrderComplete**: This will indicate whether or not the user has provided the data needed to process the order. The value of **OrderComplete** is set by two **if...then** statements. The first **if...then** statement looks to see if at least one checkbox has been checked, indicating that at least one book is being ordered. The second **if...then** statement makes sure that *all* of the name and address blanks have been filled in—none of them is empty. If all the data has been provided, then **OrderComplete** is set to **true** and the order is accepted.

As before, this is fairly simple data checking. Using the same techniques, you can easily build in more sophisticated data validation for your Web order forms.

Another thing to notice is that, at this point, we're still talking only about the client side of things. We haven't yet attempted to *send* the data to the server. That's what we'll do in the next section.

Sending Data From An ActiveX Layout To The Web Server

There are two ways you might try to send data from an HTML document with an ActiveX layout. One is obvious, but doesn't work. The other one is tricky—and *does* work. Let's examine the obvious solution first: After that, it will be easier to understand the non-obvious (but correct) solution. The obvious solution is embodied in the Web page created by Listings 10.5 and 10.6, which constitute our "first draft" version of a Web page that sends data to the server. The Web page itself looks the same, as you can see in Figure 10.6.

Listing 10.5 HTML CODE FOR THE "FIRST DRAFT" DATA SUBMISSION.

```
<HTML>
<HEAD>
<TITLE>Client-Side Data Validation, Part 2</TITLE>
</HEAD>
<BODY>

<OBJECT CLASSID="CLSID:812AE312-8B8E-11CF-93C8-00AA00C08FDF"
ID="cantsubm_alx" STYLE="LEFT:0;TOP:0">
<PARAM NAME="ALXPATH" REF VALUE="cantsubm.alx">
</OBJECT>

</BODY>
</HTML>
```

Client-Side Data Validation 215

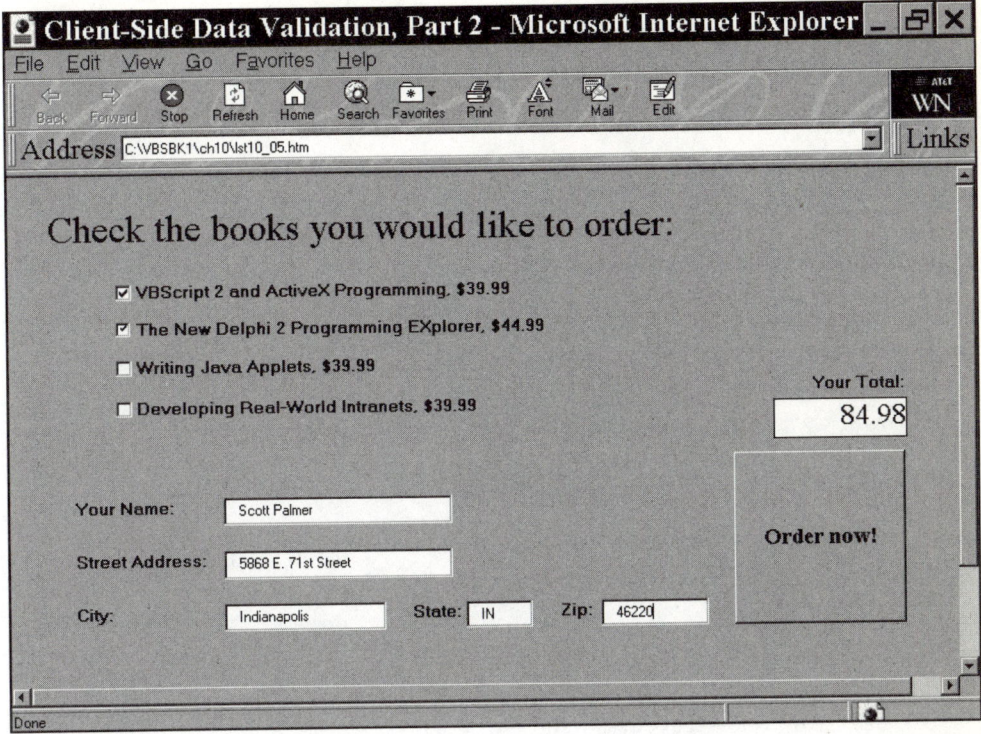

Figure 10.6
The Web page created by Listings 10.5 and 10.6.

Listing 10.6 ActiveX layout for the "first draft" data submission.

```
<SCRIPT LANGUAGE="VBScript">
<!--
Sub CmdOrder_Click()
dim OrderComplete
dim TheForm

if LblTotal.caption > 0 then
   OrderComplete = true
else
   msgbox "You must select a book to order."
   OrderComplete = false
end if

if (TBName.text = "") or _
   (TBStreet.text = "") or _
   (TBCity.text = "") or _
```

```
      (TBState.text = "") or _
      (TBZip.text = "") then
      msgbox "You didn't fill in all the address information."
      OrderComplete = false
   else
      OrderComplete = true
   end if

   If OrderComplete then
      MsgBox "Order accepted!"
      TheForm.submit
   else
      MsgBox "You didn't include all the necessary information."
   end if


end sub
-->
</SCRIPT>
<SCRIPT LANGUAGE="VBScript">
<!--
Sub CBApp_Change()
if CBApp then
   LblTotal.caption = LblTotal.caption + 39.99
else
   LblTotal.caption = LblTotal.caption - 39.99
end if


end sub
-->
</SCRIPT>
<SCRIPT LANGUAGE="VBScript">
<!--
Sub CBVBS_Change()
if CBVBS then
   LblTotal.caption = LblTotal.caption + 39.99
else
   LblTotal.caption = LblTotal.caption - 39.99
end if
end sub
-->
</SCRIPT>
<SCRIPT LANGUAGE="VBScript">
<!--
Sub CBIntra_Change()
```

```
    if CBIntra then
        LblTotal.caption = LblTotal.caption + 39.99
    else
        LblTotal.caption = LblTotal.caption - 39.99
    end if
end sub
-->
</SCRIPT>
<SCRIPT LANGUAGE="VBScript">
<!--
Sub CBDelphi_Change()
    if CBDelphi then
        LblTotal.caption = LblTotal.caption + 44.99
    else
        LblTotal.caption = LblTotal.caption - 44.99
    end if
end sub
-->
</SCRIPT>

<DIV ID="Layout1" STYLE="LAYOUT:FIXED;WIDTH:597pt;HEIGHT:370pt;">
    <OBJECT ID="Label1"
     CLASSID="CLSID:978C9E23-D4B0-11CE-BF2D-00AA003F40D0"
     STYLE="TOP:8pt;LEFT:17pt;WIDTH:396pt;HEIGHT:32pt;ZINDEX:0;">
        <PARAM NAME="Caption"
            VALUE="Check the books you would like to order:">
        <PARAM NAME="Size" VALUE="13970;1129">
        <PARAM NAME="FontName" VALUE="Times New Roman">
        <PARAM NAME="FontHeight" VALUE="480">
        <PARAM NAME="FontCharSet" VALUE="0">
        <PARAM NAME="FontPitchAndFamily" VALUE="2">
        <PARAM NAME="FontWeight" VALUE="0">
    </OBJECT>

    <OBJECT ID="CBVBS"
     CLASSID="CLSID:8BD21D40-EC42-11CE-9E0D-00AA006002F3"
     STYLE="TOP:50pt;LEFT:58pt;WIDTH:281pt;HEIGHT:22pt;
            TABINDEX:1;ZINDEX:1;">
        <PARAM NAME="BackColor" VALUE="2147483663">
        <PARAM NAME="ForeColor" VALUE="2147483666">
        <PARAM NAME="DisplayStyle" VALUE="4">
        <PARAM NAME="Size" VALUE="9913;776">
        <PARAM NAME="Value" VALUE="False">
        <PARAM NAME="Caption"
            VALUE="VBScript 2 and ActiveX Programming, $39.99">
        <PARAM NAME="FontEffects" VALUE="1073741825">
        <PARAM NAME="FontHeight" VALUE="200">
```

```
            <PARAM NAME="FontCharSet" VALUE="0">
            <PARAM NAME="FontPitchAndFamily" VALUE="2">
            <PARAM NAME="FontWeight" VALUE="700">
        </OBJECT>

        <OBJECT ID="CBDelphi"
         CLASSID="CLSID:8BD21D40-EC42-11CE-9E0D-00AA006002F3"
                STYLE="TOP:74pt;LEFT:58pt;WIDTH:281pt;HEIGHT:20pt;
                TABINDEX:2;ZINDEX:2;">
            <PARAM NAME="BackColor" VALUE="2147483663">
            <PARAM NAME="ForeColor" VALUE="2147483666">
            <PARAM NAME="DisplayStyle" VALUE="4">
            <PARAM NAME="Size" VALUE="9913;706">
            <PARAM NAME="Value" VALUE="False">
            <PARAM NAME="Caption"
                VALUE="The New Delphi 2 Programming EXplorer, $44.99">
            <PARAM NAME="FontEffects" VALUE="1073741825">
            <PARAM NAME="FontHeight" VALUE="200">
            <PARAM NAME="FontCharSet" VALUE="0">
            <PARAM NAME="FontPitchAndFamily" VALUE="2">
            <PARAM NAME="FontWeight" VALUE="700">
        </OBJECT>

        <OBJECT ID="CBApp"
         CLASSID="CLSID:8BD21D40-EC42-11CE-9E0D-00AA006002F3"
                STYLE="TOP:99pt;LEFT:58pt;WIDTH:281pt;HEIGHT:19pt;
                TABINDEX:3;ZINDEX:3;">
            <PARAM NAME="BackColor" VALUE="2147483663">
            <PARAM NAME="ForeColor" VALUE="2147483666">
            <PARAM NAME="DisplayStyle" VALUE="4">
            <PARAM NAME="Size" VALUE="9913;670">
            <PARAM NAME="Value" VALUE="False">
            <PARAM NAME="Caption"
                VALUE="Writing Java Applets, $39.99">
            <PARAM NAME="FontEffects" VALUE="1073741825">
            <PARAM NAME="FontHeight" VALUE="200">
            <PARAM NAME="FontCharSet" VALUE="0">
            <PARAM NAME="FontPitchAndFamily" VALUE="2">
            <PARAM NAME="FontWeight" VALUE="700">
        </OBJECT>

        <OBJECT ID="CBIntra"
         CLASSID="CLSID:8BD21D40-EC42-11CE-9E0D-00AA006002F3"
                STYLE="TOP:124pt;LEFT:58pt;WIDTH:281pt;HEIGHT:20pt;
                TABINDEX:4;ZINDEX:4;">
            <PARAM NAME="BackColor" VALUE="2147483663">
            <PARAM NAME="ForeColor" VALUE="2147483666">
```

```
        <PARAM NAME="DisplayStyle" VALUE="4">
        <PARAM NAME="Size" VALUE="9913;706">
        <PARAM NAME="Value" VALUE="False">
        <PARAM NAME="Caption"
            VALUE="Developing Real-World Intranets, $39.99">
        <PARAM NAME="FontEffects" VALUE="1073741825">
        <PARAM NAME="FontHeight" VALUE="200">
        <PARAM NAME="FontCharSet" VALUE="0">
        <PARAM NAME="FontPitchAndFamily" VALUE="2">
        <PARAM NAME="FontWeight" VALUE="700">
</OBJECT>

<OBJECT ID="Label2"
 CLASSID="CLSID:978C9E23-D4B0-11CE-BF2D-00AA003F40D0"
        STYLE="TOP:190pt;LEFT:33pt;WIDTH:66pt;
        HEIGHT:17pt;ZINDEX:5;">
    <PARAM NAME="Caption" VALUE="Your Name:">
    <PARAM NAME="Size" VALUE="2328;600">
    <PARAM NAME="FontEffects" VALUE="1073741825">
    <PARAM NAME="FontHeight" VALUE="200">
    <PARAM NAME="FontCharSet" VALUE="0">
    <PARAM NAME="FontPitchAndFamily" VALUE="2">
    <PARAM NAME="FontWeight" VALUE="700">
</OBJECT>

<OBJECT ID="Label3"
 CLASSID="CLSID:978C9E23-D4B0-11CE-BF2D-00AA003F40D0"
        STYLE="TOP:223pt;LEFT:33pt;WIDTH:83pt;
        HEIGHT:17pt;ZINDEX:6;">
    <PARAM NAME="Caption" VALUE="Street Address:">
    <PARAM NAME="Size" VALUE="2928;600">
    <PARAM NAME="FontEffects" VALUE="1073741825">
    <PARAM NAME="FontHeight" VALUE="200">
    <PARAM NAME="FontCharSet" VALUE="0">
    <PARAM NAME="FontPitchAndFamily" VALUE="2">
    <PARAM NAME="FontWeight" VALUE="700">
</OBJECT>

<OBJECT ID="Label4"
 CLASSID="CLSID:978C9E23-D4B0-11CE-BF2D-00AA003F40D0"
        STYLE="TOP:256pt;LEFT:33pt;WIDTH:33pt;
        HEIGHT:17pt;ZINDEX:7;">
    <PARAM NAME="Caption" VALUE="City:">
    <PARAM NAME="Size" VALUE="1164;600">
    <PARAM NAME="FontEffects" VALUE="1073741825">
    <PARAM NAME="FontHeight" VALUE="200">
    <PARAM NAME="FontCharSet" VALUE="0">
```

```
            <PARAM NAME="FontPitchAndFamily" VALUE="2">
            <PARAM NAME="FontWeight" VALUE="700">
</OBJECT>

<OBJECT ID="TBName"
 CLASSID="CLSID:8BD21D10-EC42-11CE-9E0D-00AA006002F3"
         STYLE="TOP:190pt;LEFT:124pt;WIDTH:140pt;
         HEIGHT:17pt;TABINDEX:8;ZINDEX:8;">
      <PARAM NAME="VariousPropertyBits" VALUE="746604571">
      <PARAM NAME="Size" VALUE="4939;600">
      <PARAM NAME="FontCharSet" VALUE="0">
      <PARAM NAME="FontPitchAndFamily" VALUE="2">
      <PARAM NAME="FontWeight" VALUE="0">
</OBJECT>

<OBJECT ID="TBStreet"
 CLASSID="CLSID:8BD21D10-EC42-11CE-9E0D-00AA006002F3"
 STYLE="TOP:223pt;LEFT:124pt;WIDTH:140pt;HEIGHT:18pt;
         TABINDEX:9;ZINDEX:9;">
      <PARAM NAME="VariousPropertyBits" VALUE="746604571">
      <PARAM NAME="Size" VALUE="4939;635">
      <PARAM NAME="FontCharSet" VALUE="0">
      <PARAM NAME="FontPitchAndFamily" VALUE="2">
      <PARAM NAME="FontWeight" VALUE="0">
</OBJECT>

<OBJECT ID="TBCity"
 CLASSID="CLSID:8BD21D10-EC42-11CE-9E0D-00AA006002F3"
 STYLE="TOP:256pt;LEFT:124pt;WIDTH:99pt;HEIGHT:17pt;
         TABINDEX:10;ZINDEX:10;">
      <PARAM NAME="VariousPropertyBits" VALUE="746604571">
      <PARAM NAME="Size" VALUE="3493;600">
      <PARAM NAME="FontCharSet" VALUE="0">
      <PARAM NAME="FontPitchAndFamily" VALUE="2">
      <PARAM NAME="FontWeight" VALUE="0">
</OBJECT>

<OBJECT ID="Label5"
 CLASSID="CLSID:978C9E23-D4B0-11CE-BF2D-00AA003F40D0"
 STYLE="TOP:256pt;LEFT:239pt;WIDTH:33pt;
         HEIGHT:17pt;ZINDEX:11;">
      <PARAM NAME="Caption" VALUE="State:">
      <PARAM NAME="Size" VALUE="1164;600">
      <PARAM NAME="FontEffects" VALUE="1073741825">
      <PARAM NAME="FontHeight" VALUE="200">
      <PARAM NAME="FontCharSet" VALUE="0">
      <PARAM NAME="FontPitchAndFamily" VALUE="2">
```

```
            <PARAM NAME="FontWeight" VALUE="700">
</OBJECT>

<OBJECT ID="TBState"
 CLASSID="CLSID:8BD21D10-EC42-11CE-9E0D-00AA006002F3"
        STYLE="TOP:256pt;LEFT:272pt;WIDTH:41pt;HEIGHT:16pt;
        TABINDEX:12;ZINDEX:12;">
    <PARAM NAME="VariousPropertyBits" VALUE="746604571">
    <PARAM NAME="Size" VALUE="1446;564">
    <PARAM NAME="FontCharSet" VALUE="0">
    <PARAM NAME="FontPitchAndFamily" VALUE="2">
    <PARAM NAME="FontWeight" VALUE="0">
</OBJECT>

<OBJECT ID="Label6"
 CLASSID="CLSID:978C9E23-D4B0-11CE-BF2D-00AA003F40D0"
        STYLE="TOP:256pt;LEFT:330pt;WIDTH:25pt;
        HEIGHT:17pt;ZINDEX:13;">
    <PARAM NAME="Caption" VALUE="Zip:">
    <PARAM NAME="Size" VALUE="882;600">
    <PARAM NAME="FontEffects" VALUE="1073741825">
    <PARAM NAME="FontHeight" VALUE="200">
    <PARAM NAME="FontCharSet" VALUE="0">
    <PARAM NAME="FontPitchAndFamily" VALUE="2">
    <PARAM NAME="FontWeight" VALUE="700">
</OBJECT>

<OBJECT ID="TBZip"
 CLASSID="CLSID:8BD21D10-EC42-11CE-9E0D-00AA006002F3"
        STYLE="TOP:256pt;LEFT:355pt;WIDTH:66pt;HEIGHT:16pt;
        TABINDEX:14;ZINDEX:14;">
    <PARAM NAME="VariousPropertyBits" VALUE="746604571">
    <PARAM NAME="Size" VALUE="2328;564">
    <PARAM NAME="FontCharSet" VALUE="0">
    <PARAM NAME="FontPitchAndFamily" VALUE="2">
    <PARAM NAME="FontWeight" VALUE="0">
</OBJECT>

<OBJECT ID="CmdOrder"
 CLASSID="CLSID:D7053240-CE69-11CD-A777-00DD01143C57"
        STYLE="TOP:165pt;LEFT:437pt;WIDTH:107pt;HEIGHT:107pt;
        TABINDEX:15;ZINDEX:15;">
    <PARAM NAME="Caption" VALUE="Order now!">
    <PARAM NAME="Size" VALUE="3775;3775">
    <PARAM NAME="FontName" VALUE="Times New Roman">
    <PARAM NAME="FontEffects" VALUE="1073741825">
    <PARAM NAME="FontHeight" VALUE="280">
```

```
            <PARAM NAME="FontCharSet" VALUE="0">
            <PARAM NAME="FontPitchAndFamily" VALUE="2">
            <PARAM NAME="ParagraphAlign" VALUE="3">
            <PARAM NAME="FontWeight" VALUE="700">
        </OBJECT>

        <OBJECT ID="Label7"
         CLASSID="CLSID:978C9E23-D4B0-11CE-BF2D-00AA003F40D0"
                STYLE="TOP:116pt;LEFT:470pt;WIDTH:74pt;
                HEIGHT:17pt;ZINDEX:16;">
            <PARAM NAME="Caption" VALUE="Your Total:">
            <PARAM NAME="Size" VALUE="2611;600">
            <PARAM NAME="FontEffects" VALUE="1073741825">
            <PARAM NAME="FontHeight" VALUE="240">
            <PARAM NAME="FontCharSet" VALUE="0">
            <PARAM NAME="FontPitchAndFamily" VALUE="2">
            <PARAM NAME="ParagraphAlign" VALUE="2">
            <PARAM NAME="FontWeight" VALUE="700">
        </OBJECT>

        <OBJECT ID="LblTotal"
         CLASSID="CLSID:978C9E23-D4B0-11CE-BF2D-00AA003F40D0"
                STYLE="TOP:132pt;LEFT:462pt;WIDTH:83pt;
                HEIGHT:25pt;ZINDEX:17;">
            <PARAM NAME="BackColor" VALUE="16777215">
            <PARAM NAME="Caption" VALUE="0.00">
            <PARAM NAME="Size" VALUE="2928;882">
            <PARAM NAME="BorderStyle" VALUE="1">
            <PARAM NAME="FontName" VALUE="Times New Roman">
            <PARAM NAME="FontHeight" VALUE="360">
            <PARAM NAME="FontCharSet" VALUE="0">
            <PARAM NAME="FontPitchAndFamily" VALUE="2">
            <PARAM NAME="ParagraphAlign" VALUE="2">
            <PARAM NAME="FontWeight" VALUE="0">
        </OBJECT>
</DIV>
```

The obvious solution is simply to do what you did before in the Web page that used only HTML controls: Call **form.submit** and thereby send the data in the various controls to the server. That's the approach taken in the **Click** event sub for the command button, as follows:

```
Sub CmdOrder_Click()
dim OrderComplete
dim TheForm
```

```
' …some code omitted here

If OrderComplete then
   MsgBox "Order accepted!"
   TheForm.submit
else
   MsgBox "You didn't include all the necessary information."
end if

end sub
```

The fact that the ActiveX-layout Web page looks similar to the HTML-only page suggests that this will work. But there's a problem in this approach: **form.submit** is a method supported by the Internet Explorer scripting object model for *HTML forms*. What you've got in your ActiveX layout is not an HTML form. The controls in your ActiveX layout are not HTML form controls. And in that situation, calling **form.submit** in your VBScript code won't do anything but generate an error message, as shown in Figure 10.7.

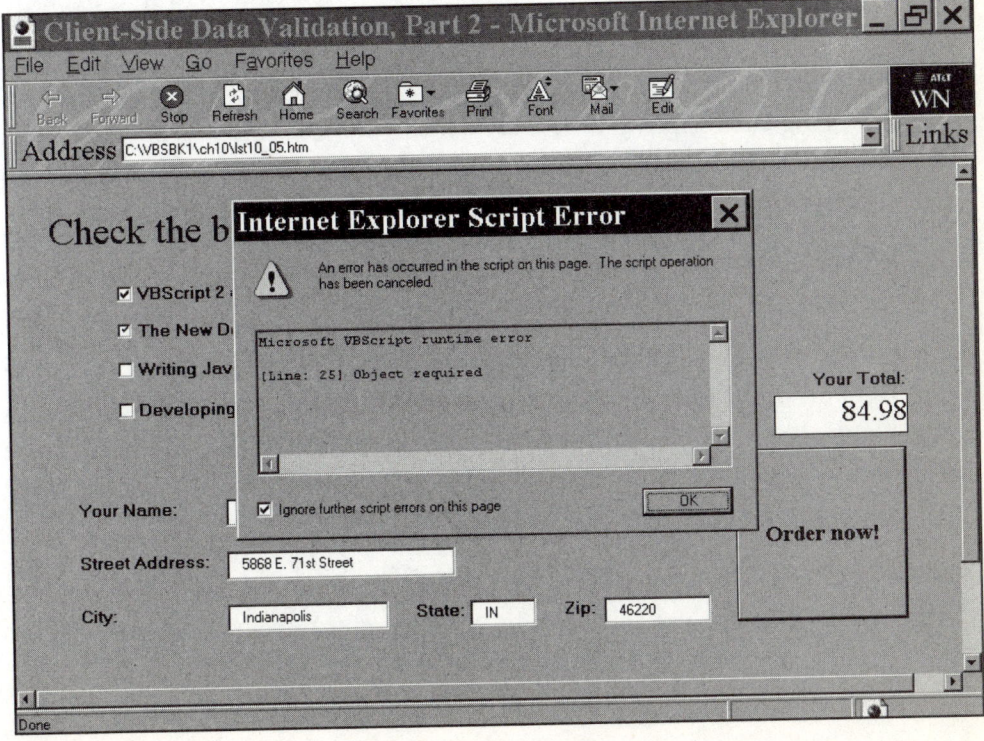

Figure 10.7
You can't use **form.submit** when there's no HTML form on your Web page.

Another problem is that your ActiveX layout is a separate file, inserted into the display of your Web page by the HTML Layout control. The ActiveX layout itself, however, is not part of your HTML document.

The *most* crucial question that needs to be answered is this: How can you make your ActiveX layout communicate with your HTML document?

The Secret Trick: Use The Scripting Object Model

The secret is to use what you learned in Chapter 9 about the Internet Explorer scripting object model. From your ActiveX layout code, you assign values to elements in the HTML document by indicating which objects contain them. That suggests a three-step process for sending validated data to the Web server:

1. On the containing HTML document, create an HTML form with hidden form controls—controls that aren't visible when the user displays the Web page. There should be one hidden control for each data item that needs to be sent from the ActiveX layout to the server.

2. In the ActiveX layout, write code to validate the data entered by the user. Then, using the scripting object model as your guide, copy the data from each ActiveX data-entry control (in this case, checkboxes and text boxes) to the corresponding form control in the containing HTML document.

3. Call **form.submit** to send the data from the HTML form controls to the Web server.

This approach is embodied in Listings 10.7 and 10.8, which create a fully functional ActiveX order form that can send data to the Web server. When you fill in the blanks and click on the command button—sending the data to the Web site *cgitest* program—you get a result that looks something like Figure 10.8. That indicates that your data arrived safely at the Web server.

Communication Goes Both Ways
From your ActiveX layout code, you can refer to controls in your HTML document by identifying which controls contain them. Likewise, from within your HTML document, you can refer to controls in your ActiveX layout by prefacing the control names with the name of your ActiveX layout.

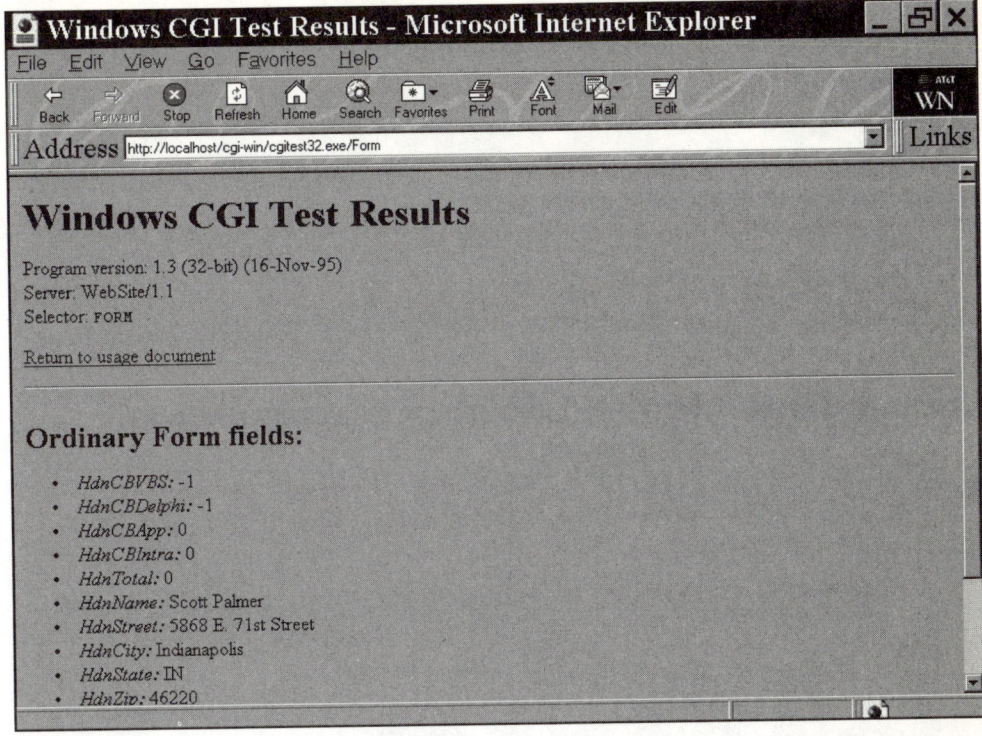

Figure 10.8
The cgitest program reports that your data was received by the Web server.

Listing 10.7 HTML CODE FOR SENDING DATA TO THE SERVER.

```
<HTML>
<HEAD>
<TITLE>Client-Side Data Validation, Part 2</TITLE>
</HEAD>
<BODY>
<FORM name="HiddenForm" METHOD="POST"
     ACTION="http://localhost/cgi-win/cgitest32.exe/Form">

<INPUT NAME="HdnCBVBS" TYPE="HIDDEN" VALUE="0">
<INPUT NAME="HdnCBDelphi" TYPE="HIDDEN" VALUE="0">
<INPUT NAME="HdnCBApp" TYPE="HIDDEN" VALUE="0">
<INPUT NAME="HdnCBIntra" TYPE="HIDDEN" VALUE="0">
<INPUT NAME="HdnTotal" TYPE="HIDDEN" VALUE="0">

<INPUT NAME="HdnName" TYPE="HIDDEN" VALUE="">
<INPUT NAME="HdnStreet" TYPE="HIDDEN" VALUE="">
<INPUT NAME="HdnCity" TYPE="HIDDEN" VALUE="""">
```

```
<INPUT NAME="HdnState" TYPE="HIDDEN" VALUE="""">
<INPUT NAME="HdnZip" TYPE="HIDDEN" VALUE="""">

</FORM>

<OBJECT CLASSID="CLSID:812AE312-8B8E-11CF-93C8-00AA00C08FDF"
ID="ordrbk2b_alx" STYLE="LEFT:0;TOP:0">
<PARAM NAME="ALXPATH" REF VALUE="ordrbk2b.alx">
</OBJECT>

</BODY>
</HTML>
```

Listing 10.8 ActiveX layout for sending data to the server.

```
<SCRIPT LANGUAGE="VBScript">
<!--
Sub CmdOrder_Click()
dim OrderComplete
dim TheForm
Set TheForm = window.Document.HiddenForm

if LblTotal.caption > 0 then
    OrderComplete = true
else
    msgbox "You must select a book to order."
    OrderComplete = false
end if

if (TBName.text = "") or _
   (TBStreet.text = "") or _
   (TBCity.text = "") or _
   (TBState.text = "") or _
   (TBZip.text = "") then
    msgbox "You didn't fill in all the address information."
    OrderComplete = false
else
    OrderComplete = true
end if

If OrderComplete then
    MsgBox "Order accepted!"
    window.Document.HiddenForm.HdnCBVBS.value = CBVBS.value
    window.Document.HiddenForm.HdnCBDelphi.value = CBDelphi.value
    window.Document.HiddenForm.HdnCBApp.value = CBApp.value
    window.Document.HiddenForm.HdnCBIntra.value = CBIntra.value
```

```
        window.Document.HiddenForm.HdnName.value = TBName.text
        window.Document.HiddenForm.HdnStreet.value = TBStreet.text
        window.Document.HiddenForm.HdnCity.value = TBCity.text
        window.Document.HiddenForm.HdnState.value = TBState.text
        window.Document.HiddenForm.HdnZip.value = TBZip.text
        TheForm.submit
else
        MsgBox "You didn't include all the necessary information."
end if

end sub
-->
</SCRIPT>
<SCRIPT LANGUAGE="VBScript">
<!--
Sub CBApp_Change()
if CBApp then
        LblTotal.caption = LblTotal.caption + 39.99
else
        LblTotal.caption = LblTotal.caption - 39.99
end if

end sub
-->
</SCRIPT>
<SCRIPT LANGUAGE="VBScript">
<!--
Sub CBVBS_Change()
if CBVBS then
        LblTotal.caption = LblTotal.caption + 39.99
else
        LblTotal.caption = LblTotal.caption - 39.99
end if
end sub
-->
</SCRIPT>
<SCRIPT LANGUAGE="VBScript">
<!--
Sub CBIntra_Change()
if CBIntra then
        LblTotal.caption = LblTotal.caption + 39.99
else
        LblTotal.caption = LblTotal.caption - 39.99
end if
end sub
-->
```

```
</SCRIPT>
<SCRIPT LANGUAGE="VBScript">
<!--
Sub CBDelphi_Change()
if CBDelphi then
    LblTotal.caption = LblTotal.caption + 44.99
else
    LblTotal.caption = LblTotal.caption - 44.99
end if
end sub
-->
</SCRIPT>

<DIV ID="Layout1" STYLE="LAYOUT:FIXED;WIDTH:597pt;HEIGHT:370pt;">
    <OBJECT ID="Label1"
      CLASSID="CLSID:978C9E23-D4B0-11CE-BF2D-00AA003F40D0"
      STYLE="TOP:8pt;LEFT:17pt;WIDTH:396pt;HEIGHT:32pt;ZINDEX:0;">
        <PARAM NAME="Caption"
            VALUE="Check the books you would like to order:">
        <PARAM NAME="Size" VALUE="13970;1129">
        <PARAM NAME="FontName" VALUE="Times New Roman">
        <PARAM NAME="FontHeight" VALUE="480">
        <PARAM NAME="FontCharSet" VALUE="0">
        <PARAM NAME="FontPitchAndFamily" VALUE="2">
        <PARAM NAME="FontWeight" VALUE="0">
    </OBJECT>

    <OBJECT ID="CBVBS"
      CLASSID="CLSID:8BD21D40-EC42-11CE-9E0D-00AA006002F3"
      STYLE="TOP:50pt;LEFT:58pt;WIDTH:281pt;HEIGHT:22pt;
            TABINDEX:1;ZINDEX:1;">
        <PARAM NAME="BackColor" VALUE="2147483663">
        <PARAM NAME="ForeColor" VALUE="2147483666">
        <PARAM NAME="DisplayStyle" VALUE="4">
        <PARAM NAME="Size" VALUE="9913;776">
        <PARAM NAME="Value" VALUE="False">
        <PARAM NAME="Caption"
            VALUE="VBScript 2 and ActiveX Programming, $39.99">
        <PARAM NAME="FontEffects" VALUE="1073741825">
        <PARAM NAME="FontHeight" VALUE="200">
        <PARAM NAME="FontCharSet" VALUE="0">
        <PARAM NAME="FontPitchAndFamily" VALUE="2">
        <PARAM NAME="FontWeight" VALUE="700">
    </OBJECT>
```

```
<OBJECT ID="CBDelphi"
 CLASSID="CLSID:8BD21D40-EC42-11CE-9E0D-00AA006002F3"
        STYLE="TOP:74pt;LEFT:58pt;WIDTH:281pt;HEIGHT:20pt;
        TABINDEX:2;ZINDEX:2;">
    <PARAM NAME="BackColor" VALUE="2147483663">
    <PARAM NAME="ForeColor" VALUE="2147483666">
    <PARAM NAME="DisplayStyle" VALUE="4">
    <PARAM NAME="Size" VALUE="9913;706">
    <PARAM NAME="Value" VALUE="False">
    <PARAM NAME="Caption"
        VALUE="The New Delphi 2 Programming EXplorer, $44.99">
    <PARAM NAME="FontEffects" VALUE="1073741825">
    <PARAM NAME="FontHeight" VALUE="200">
    <PARAM NAME="FontCharSet" VALUE="0">
    <PARAM NAME="FontPitchAndFamily" VALUE="2">
    <PARAM NAME="FontWeight" VALUE="700">
</OBJECT>

<OBJECT ID="CBApp"
 CLASSID="CLSID:8BD21D40-EC42-11CE-9E0D-00AA006002F3"
        STYLE="TOP:99pt;LEFT:58pt;WIDTH:281pt;HEIGHT:19pt;
        TABINDEX:3;ZINDEX:3;">
    <PARAM NAME="BackColor" VALUE="2147483663">
    <PARAM NAME="ForeColor" VALUE="2147483666">
    <PARAM NAME="DisplayStyle" VALUE="4">
    <PARAM NAME="Size" VALUE="9913;670">
    <PARAM NAME="Value" VALUE="False">
    <PARAM NAME="Caption"
        VALUE="Writing Java Applets, $39.99">
    <PARAM NAME="FontEffects" VALUE="1073741825">
    <PARAM NAME="FontHeight" VALUE="200">
    <PARAM NAME="FontCharSet" VALUE="0">
    <PARAM NAME="FontPitchAndFamily" VALUE="2">
    <PARAM NAME="FontWeight" VALUE="700">
</OBJECT>

<OBJECT ID="CBIntra"
 CLASSID="CLSID:8BD21D40-EC42-11CE-9E0D-00AA006002F3"
        STYLE="TOP:124pt;LEFT:58pt;WIDTH:281pt;HEIGHT:20pt;
        TABINDEX:4;ZINDEX:4;">
    <PARAM NAME="BackColor" VALUE="2147483663">
    <PARAM NAME="ForeColor" VALUE="2147483666">
    <PARAM NAME="DisplayStyle" VALUE="4">
    <PARAM NAME="Size" VALUE="9913;706">
    <PARAM NAME="Value" VALUE="False">
    <PARAM NAME="Caption"
```

```
              VALUE="Developing Real-World Intranets, $39.99">
     <PARAM NAME="FontEffects" VALUE="1073741825">
     <PARAM NAME="FontHeight" VALUE="200">
     <PARAM NAME="FontCharSet" VALUE="0">
     <PARAM NAME="FontPitchAndFamily" VALUE="2">
     <PARAM NAME="FontWeight" VALUE="700">
</OBJECT>

<OBJECT ID="Label2"
 CLASSID="CLSID:978C9E23-D4B0-11CE-BF2D-00AA003F40D0"
        STYLE="TOP:190pt;LEFT:33pt;WIDTH:66pt;
        HEIGHT:17pt;ZINDEX:5;">
     <PARAM NAME="Caption" VALUE="Your Name:">
     <PARAM NAME="Size" VALUE="2328;600">
     <PARAM NAME="FontEffects" VALUE="1073741825">
     <PARAM NAME="FontHeight" VALUE="200">
     <PARAM NAME="FontCharSet" VALUE="0">
     <PARAM NAME="FontPitchAndFamily" VALUE="2">
     <PARAM NAME="FontWeight" VALUE="700">
</OBJECT>

<OBJECT ID="Label3"
 CLASSID="CLSID:978C9E23-D4B0-11CE-BF2D-00AA003F40D0"
        STYLE="TOP:223pt;LEFT:33pt;WIDTH:83pt;
        HEIGHT:17pt;ZINDEX:6;">
     <PARAM NAME="Caption" VALUE="Street Address:">
     <PARAM NAME="Size" VALUE="2928;600">
     <PARAM NAME="FontEffects" VALUE="1073741825">
     <PARAM NAME="FontHeight" VALUE="200">
     <PARAM NAME="FontCharSet" VALUE="0">
     <PARAM NAME="FontPitchAndFamily" VALUE="2">
     <PARAM NAME="FontWeight" VALUE="700">
</OBJECT>

<OBJECT ID="Label4"
 CLASSID="CLSID:978C9E23-D4B0-11CE-BF2D-00AA003F40D0"
        STYLE="TOP:256pt;LEFT:33pt;WIDTH:33pt;
        HEIGHT:17pt;ZINDEX:7;">
     <PARAM NAME="Caption" VALUE="City:">
     <PARAM NAME="Size" VALUE="1164;600">
     <PARAM NAME="FontEffects" VALUE="1073741825">
     <PARAM NAME="FontHeight" VALUE="200">
     <PARAM NAME="FontCharSet" VALUE="0">
     <PARAM NAME="FontPitchAndFamily" VALUE="2">
     <PARAM NAME="FontWeight" VALUE="700">
</OBJECT>
```

```
<OBJECT ID="TBName"
 CLASSID="CLSID:8BD21D10-EC42-11CE-9E0D-00AA006002F3"
        STYLE="TOP:190pt;LEFT:124pt;WIDTH:140pt;
        HEIGHT:17pt;TABINDEX:8;ZINDEX:8;">
    <PARAM NAME="VariousPropertyBits" VALUE="746604571">
    <PARAM NAME="Size" VALUE="4939;600">
    <PARAM NAME="FontCharSet" VALUE="0">
    <PARAM NAME="FontPitchAndFamily" VALUE="2">
    <PARAM NAME="FontWeight" VALUE="0">
</OBJECT>

<OBJECT ID="TBStreet"
 CLASSID="CLSID:8BD21D10-EC42-11CE-9E0D-00AA006002F3"
        STYLE="TOP:223pt;LEFT:124pt;WIDTH:140pt;HEIGHT:18pt;
        TABINDEX:9;ZINDEX:9;">
    <PARAM NAME="VariousPropertyBits" VALUE="746604571">
    <PARAM NAME="Size" VALUE="4939;635">
    <PARAM NAME="FontCharSet" VALUE="0">
    <PARAM NAME="FontPitchAndFamily" VALUE="2">
    <PARAM NAME="FontWeight" VALUE="0">
</OBJECT>

<OBJECT ID="TBCity"
 CLASSID="CLSID:8BD21D10-EC42-11CE-9E0D-00AA006002F3"
        STYLE="TOP:256pt;LEFT:124pt;WIDTH:99pt;HEIGHT:17pt;
        TABINDEX:10;ZINDEX:10;">
    <PARAM NAME="VariousPropertyBits" VALUE="746604571">
    <PARAM NAME="Size" VALUE="3493;600">
    <PARAM NAME="FontCharSet" VALUE="0">
    <PARAM NAME="FontPitchAndFamily" VALUE="2">
    <PARAM NAME="FontWeight" VALUE="0">
</OBJECT>

<OBJECT ID="Label5"
 CLASSID="CLSID:978C9E23-D4B0-11CE-BF2D-00AA003F40D0"
        STYLE="TOP:256pt;LEFT:239pt;WIDTH:33pt;
        HEIGHT:17pt;ZINDEX:11;">
    <PARAM NAME="Caption" VALUE="State:">
    <PARAM NAME="Size" VALUE="1164;600">
    <PARAM NAME="FontEffects" VALUE="1073741825">
    <PARAM NAME="FontHeight" VALUE="200">
    <PARAM NAME="FontCharSet" VALUE="0">
    <PARAM NAME="FontPitchAndFamily" VALUE="2">
    <PARAM NAME="FontWeight" VALUE="700">
</OBJECT>
```

```
<OBJECT ID="TBState"
 CLASSID="CLSID:8BD21D10-EC42-11CE-9E0D-00AA006002F3"
        STYLE="TOP:256pt;LEFT:272pt;WIDTH:41pt;HEIGHT:16pt;
        TABINDEX:12;ZINDEX:12;">
    <PARAM NAME="VariousPropertyBits" VALUE="746604571">
    <PARAM NAME="Size" VALUE="1446;564">
    <PARAM NAME="FontCharSet" VALUE="0">
    <PARAM NAME="FontPitchAndFamily" VALUE="2">
    <PARAM NAME="FontWeight" VALUE="0">
</OBJECT>

<OBJECT ID="Label6"
 CLASSID="CLSID:978C9E23-D4B0-11CE-BF2D-00AA003F40D0"
        STYLE="TOP:256pt;LEFT:330pt;WIDTH:25pt;
        HEIGHT:17pt;ZINDEX:13;">
    <PARAM NAME="Caption" VALUE="Zip:">
    <PARAM NAME="Size" VALUE="882;600">
    <PARAM NAME="FontEffects" VALUE="1073741825">
    <PARAM NAME="FontHeight" VALUE="200">
    <PARAM NAME="FontCharSet" VALUE="0">
    <PARAM NAME="FontPitchAndFamily" VALUE="2">
    <PARAM NAME="FontWeight" VALUE="700">
</OBJECT>

<OBJECT ID="TBZip"
 CLASSID="CLSID:8BD21D10-EC42-11CE-9E0D-00AA006002F3"
        STYLE="TOP:256pt;LEFT:355pt;WIDTH:66pt;HEIGHT:16pt;
        TABINDEX:14;ZINDEX:14;">
    <PARAM NAME="VariousPropertyBits" VALUE="746604571">
    <PARAM NAME="Size" VALUE="2328;564">
    <PARAM NAME="FontCharSet" VALUE="0">
    <PARAM NAME="FontPitchAndFamily" VALUE="2">
    <PARAM NAME="FontWeight" VALUE="0">
</OBJECT>

<OBJECT ID="CmdOrder"
 CLASSID="CLSID:D7053240-CE69-11CD-A777-00DD01143C57"
        STYLE="TOP:165pt;LEFT:437pt;WIDTH:107pt;HEIGHT:107pt;
        TABINDEX:15;ZINDEX:15;">
    <PARAM NAME="Caption" VALUE="Order now!">
    <PARAM NAME="Size" VALUE="3775;3775">
    <PARAM NAME="FontName" VALUE="Times New Roman">
    <PARAM NAME="FontEffects" VALUE="1073741825">
    <PARAM NAME="FontHeight" VALUE="280">
    <PARAM NAME="FontCharSet" VALUE="0">
    <PARAM NAME="FontPitchAndFamily" VALUE="2">
```

```
            <PARAM NAME="ParagraphAlign" VALUE="3">
            <PARAM NAME="FontWeight" VALUE="700">
    </OBJECT>

    <OBJECT ID="Label7"
     CLASSID="CLSID:978C9E23-D4B0-11CE-BF2D-00AA003F40D0"
            STYLE="TOP:116pt;LEFT:470pt;WIDTH:74pt;
            HEIGHT:17pt;ZINDEX:16;">
        <PARAM NAME="Caption" VALUE="Your Total:">
        <PARAM NAME="Size" VALUE="2611;600">
        <PARAM NAME="FontEffects" VALUE="1073741825">
        <PARAM NAME="FontHeight" VALUE="240">
        <PARAM NAME="FontCharSet" VALUE="0">
        <PARAM NAME="FontPitchAndFamily" VALUE="2">
        <PARAM NAME="ParagraphAlign" VALUE="2">
        <PARAM NAME="FontWeight" VALUE="700">
    </OBJECT>

    <OBJECT ID="LblTotal"
     CLASSID="CLSID:978C9E23-D4B0-11CE-BF2D-00AA003F40D0"
            STYLE="TOP:132pt;LEFT:462pt;WIDTH:83pt;
            HEIGHT:25pt;ZINDEX:17;">
        <PARAM NAME="BackColor" VALUE="16777215">
        <PARAM NAME="Caption" VALUE="0.00">
        <PARAM NAME="Size" VALUE="2928;882">
        <PARAM NAME="BorderStyle" VALUE="1">
        <PARAM NAME="FontName" VALUE="Times New Roman">
        <PARAM NAME="FontHeight" VALUE="360">
        <PARAM NAME="FontCharSet" VALUE="0">
        <PARAM NAME="FontPitchAndFamily" VALUE="2">
        <PARAM NAME="ParagraphAlign" VALUE="2">
        <PARAM NAME="FontWeight" VALUE="0">
    </OBJECT>
</DIV>
```

Inside The Example Code

Let's take the technique one step at a time. The first step is to create a standard HTML form in the containing HTML document (Listing 10.7). The relevant code is as follows:

```
<FORM name="HiddenForm" METHOD="POST"
    ACTION="http://localhost/cgi-win/cgitest32.exe/Form">

<INPUT NAME="HdnCBVBS" TYPE="HIDDEN" VALUE="0">
<INPUT NAME="HdnCBDelphi" TYPE="HIDDEN" VALUE="0">
```

```
<INPUT NAME="HdnCBApp" TYPE="HIDDEN" VALUE="0">
<INPUT NAME="HdnCBIntra" TYPE="HIDDEN" VALUE="0">
<INPUT NAME="HdnTotal" TYPE="HIDDEN" VALUE="0">

<INPUT NAME="HdnName" TYPE="HIDDEN" VALUE="">
<INPUT NAME="HdnStreet" TYPE="HIDDEN" VALUE="">
<INPUT NAME="HdnCity" TYPE="HIDDEN" VALUE="""">
<INPUT NAME="HdnState" TYPE="HIDDEN" VALUE="""">
<INPUT NAME="HdnZip" TYPE="HIDDEN" VALUE="""">

</FORM>
```

Once again, we've created a form whose **action** property sends data to the Web site *cgitest* program. On the form, we've created one **<input>** control for each data item that needs to be transferred from the ActiveX layout to the Web server. Notice two things:

- The types of the controls are **hidden**. That's so they won't be visible on the Web page.

- As a result, none of the HTML form control types match the control types in your ActiveX layout. The data from all your ActiveX controls, whether they are checkboxes or text boxes, is sent to the **hidden**-type HTML form controls. This isn't a problem, because you're passing the data as text strings. For the Web server, you can write a CGI program (see Chapter 16) to interpret the data correctly.

Let's look at the VBScript code embedded in the ActiveX layout. The action takes place mainly in the **Click** event sub for the command button. The data validation code itself is the same as before. The first new piece of code is as follows:

```
Sub CmdOrder_Click()
    dim OrderComplete
    dim TheForm
    Set TheForm = window.Document.HiddenForm
```

Here, at the beginning of the **Click** sub, we declare the **OrderComplete** variable as well as **TheForm**, a variable by which our VBScript code will refer to the HTML form in the containing HTML document.

Having declared a variable for the form, we next set the variable's value so that it does, in fact, refer to the HTML form in the HTML document. We'll now be able to use the variable when we call the **form.submit** method.

The next step is to assign the values in the ActiveX controls to the corresponding form controls in the HTML document. That is accomplished by the following code:

```
If OrderComplete then
   MsgBox "Order accepted!"
   window.Document.HiddenForm.HdnCBVBS.value = CBVBS.value
   window.Document.HiddenForm.HdnCBDelphi.value = CBDelphi.value
   window.Document.HiddenForm.HdnCBApp.value = CBApp.value
   window.Document.HiddenForm.HdnCBIntra.value = CBIntra.value
   window.Document.HiddenForm.HdnName.value = TBName.text
   window.Document.HiddenForm.HdnStreet.value = TBStreet.text
   window.Document.HiddenForm.HdnCity.value = TBCity.text
   window.Document.HiddenForm.HdnState.value = TBState.text
   window.Document.HiddenForm.HdnZip.value = TBZip.text
```

Notice that each time we refer to a control on the form, we use the scripting object model to fully identify where the control is located. For example, the control for the first book's checkbox is named **HdnCBVBS** (for hidden checkbox, Visual Basic Script). It's on the hidden form, **HiddenForm**, which in turn is contained in the **Document** object, which in turn is contained in the **Window** object. Thus, the control is referred to like this:

```
window.Document.HiddenForm.HdnCBVBS.value = CBVBS.value
```

Once all the values have been copied from the ActiveX layout controls to the hidden HTML form controls, it's time for the final step: sending the data to the server. That's done with the following code line:

```
TheForm.submit
```

The result, as you saw earlier in Figure 10.8, is that the data is successfully transmitted to the Web server. Once it's on the Web server, you can subject it to further validation and processing as needed for your particular application.

You'll use this same general technique whenever you need to transfer data from an ActiveX layout to an HTML document, or from an HTML document to an ActiveX layout.

11

AN ACTIVEX MISCELLANY

You've seen how to use a few ActiveX controls so far—mainly labels, text boxes, and command buttons. In this chapter, you'll learn about some of the other controls.

Less than a year after the release of Internet Explorer 3.0—the first Web browser to support ActiveX—there were already well over a hundred ActiveX controls: one for every conceivable purpose. It's not marketing hype (for once) to say that ActiveX has taken the computing world by storm.

Most of the third-party ActiveX controls address specialized needs. If you want to keep up to date, the Microsoft Web site has a gallery of ActiveX controls, as well as links to other ActiveX sites. However, there are a few controls bundled with the ActiveX Control Pad that you'll use again and again in your Web projects. In this chapter, we'll take a look at those controls.

We've already seen many examples of the *most* often-used controls: labels, text boxes, command buttons, and checkboxes. Now, get ready to meet the list box, combo box, option button, toggle button, and scrollbar controls. All of our examples in this chapter will be set up with the ActiveX Control Pad, though we won't deal with the specifics of using the ActiveX Control Pad. If you're hazy on that part of the discussion, refer back to Chapter 8.

The List Box Control

The list box control lets you present the user with a list of text items. Depending on how you set up the list box, the user can select an item by clicking on it in the list box. Figure 11.1 shows a Web page with an ActiveX list box control. Listing 11.1 is the containing HTML document, while Listing 11.2 is the ActiveX layout code.

Listing 11.1   HTML DOCUMENT TO CONTAIN THE ACTIVEX LAYOUT.

```
<HTML>
<HEAD>
<TITLE>List Box Demonstration</TITLE>
</HEAD>
<BODY>

<OBJECT CLASSID="CLSID:812AE312-8B8E-11CF-93C8-00AA00C08FDF"
ID="listbox1_alx" STYLE="LEFT:0;TOP:0">
<PARAM NAME="ALXPATH" REF
    VALUE="file:C:\MyBooks\VBS\ch11\listbox1.alx">
</OBJECT>

</BODY>
</HTML>
```

Listing 11.2   ACTIVEX LAYOUT LIST BOX CONTROL AND VBSCRIPT CODE.

```
<SCRIPT LANGUAGE="VBScript">
<!--
Sub Layout1_OnLoad()
   ListBox1.AddItem "Drew Barrymore"
   ListBox1.AddItem "Alicia Silverstone"
   ListBox1.AddItem "Alyssa Milano"
   ListBox1.AddItem "Alyson Hannigan"
   ListBox1.AddItem "Kellie Martin"
end sub

Sub CmdLunch_Click()
   msgbox "Have lunch with " & ListBox1.value & ".",, _
       "Listbox Demonstration"
end sub
```

```
Sub CmdAddFriend_Click()
   dim NewFriend
   NewFriend = inputbox( _
      "Enter the name of your new friend:", _
      "Listbox Demonstration")
   ListBox1.AddItem NewFriend
end sub
-->
</SCRIPT>

<DIV ID="Layout1" STYLE="LAYOUT:FIXED;WIDTH:597pt;HEIGHT:370pt;">
   <OBJECT ID="Label1"
    CLASSID="CLSID:978C9E23-D4B0-11CE-BF2D-00AA003F40D0"
    STYLE="TOP:33pt;LEFT:198pt;WIDTH:198pt;HEIGHT:
          33pt;ZINDEX:0;">
       <PARAM NAME="Caption" VALUE="My Best Friends">
       <PARAM NAME="Size" VALUE="6985;1164">
       <PARAM NAME="FontName" VALUE="Times New Roman">
       <PARAM NAME="FontHeight" VALUE="480">
       <PARAM NAME="FontCharSet" VALUE="0">
       <PARAM NAME="FontPitchAndFamily" VALUE="2">
       <PARAM NAME="FontWeight" VALUE="0">
   </OBJECT>

   <OBJECT ID="CmdLunch"
    CLASSID="CLSID:D7053240-CE69-11CD-A777-00DD01143C57"
    STYLE="TOP:198pt;LEFT:305pt;WIDTH:132pt;HEIGHT:83pt;
          TABINDEX:2;ZINDEX:1;">
       <PARAM NAME="Caption" VALUE="Let's do lunch.">
       <PARAM NAME="Size" VALUE="4657;2928">
       <PARAM NAME="FontEffects" VALUE="1073741825">
       <PARAM NAME="FontHeight" VALUE="240">
       <PARAM NAME="FontCharSet" VALUE="0">
       <PARAM NAME="FontPitchAndFamily" VALUE="2">
       <PARAM NAME="ParagraphAlign" VALUE="3">
       <PARAM NAME="FontWeight" VALUE="700">
   </OBJECT>

   <OBJECT ID="CmdAddFriend"
    CLASSID="CLSID:D7053240-CE69-11CD-A777-00DD01143C57"
    STYLE="TOP:198pt;LEFT:157pt;WIDTH:132pt;HEIGHT:83pt;
          TABINDEX:3;ZINDEX:2;">
       <PARAM NAME="Caption" VALUE="Add a new friend">
       <PARAM NAME="Size" VALUE="4657;2928">
       <PARAM NAME="FontEffects" VALUE="1073741825">
       <PARAM NAME="FontHeight" VALUE="240">
       <PARAM NAME="FontCharSet" VALUE="0">
```

```
            <PARAM NAME="FontPitchAndFamily" VALUE="2">
            <PARAM NAME="ParagraphAlign" VALUE="3">
            <PARAM NAME="FontWeight" VALUE="700">
    </OBJECT>

    <OBJECT ID="Listbox1"
      CLASSID="CLSID:8BD21D20-EC42-11CE-9E0D-00AA006002F3"
      STYLE="TOP:74pt;LEFT:198pt;WIDTH:198pt;HEIGHT:111pt;
             TABINDEX:0;ZINDEX:3;">
            <PARAM NAME="ScrollBars" VALUE="3">
            <PARAM NAME="DisplayStyle" VALUE="2">
            <PARAM NAME="Size" VALUE="6985;3914">
            <PARAM NAME="MatchEntry" VALUE="0">
            <PARAM NAME="FontEffects" VALUE="1073741825">
            <PARAM NAME="FontHeight" VALUE="280">
            <PARAM NAME="FontCharSet" VALUE="0">
            <PARAM NAME="FontPitchAndFamily" VALUE="2">
            <PARAM NAME="FontWeight" VALUE="700">
    </OBJECT>
</DIV>
```

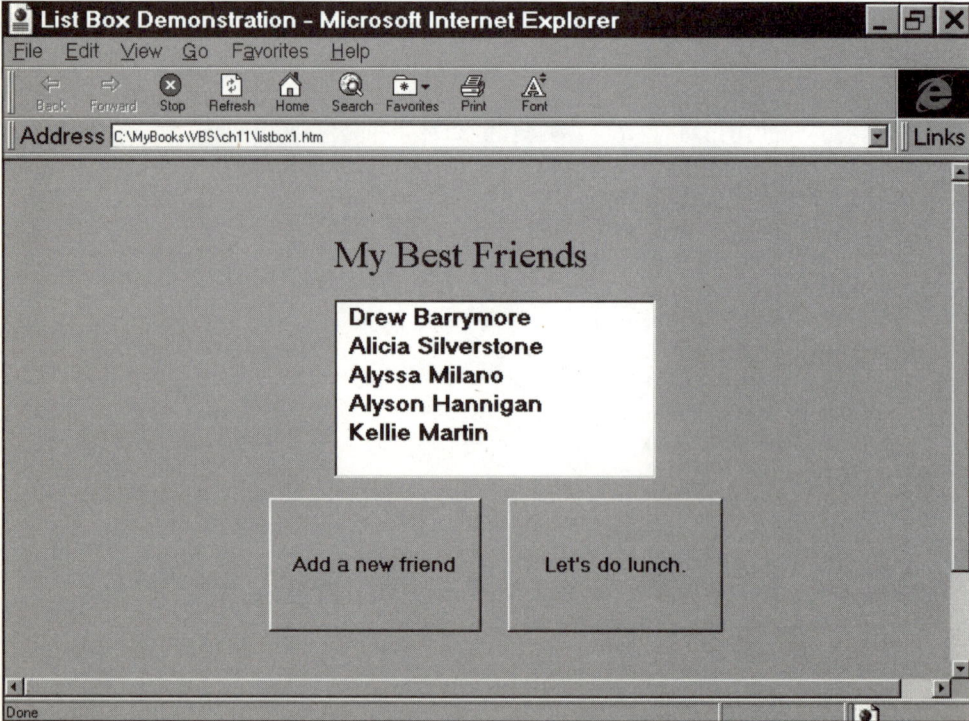

Figure 11.1
A Web page with a list box control.

Writing VBScript Code For The List Box Control

Of course, a list box control doesn't come with list items: You have to add them to the list. The most common time to do this is when your window or ActiveX layout loads. When the user loads your Web page into his or her browser, the **onLoad** event fires for both the containing Web page window and the ActiveX layout. Therefore, it's easy to put your initialization code in there. In this example, we loaded the list with the names of actresses who have fans in the Web-nerd community:

```
Sub Layout1_OnLoad()
   ListBox1.AddItem "Drew Barrymore"
   ListBox1.AddItem "Alicia Silverstone"
   ListBox1.AddItem "Alyssa Milano"
   ListBox1.AddItem "Alyson Hannigan"
   ListBox1.AddItem "Kellie Martin"
end sub
```

It's the list box control's **AddItem** method that does the work. To add an item to the list, you just call the **AddItem** method and give it the text for the new item. When the user clicks on an item in the list, that item is assigned to the list box control's **value** property. It's then quite easy to use that value in your VBScript code, as in the **Click** event sub for the "Let's do lunch" command button. As shown in Figure 11.2, this code displays a message box with the selected list item in the text:

```
Sub CmdLunch_Click()
   msgbox "Have lunch with " & Listbox1.value & ".",, _
      "Listbox Demonstration"
end sub
```

Of course, the **onLoad** event isn't the only time you can load new items into the list. As shown in Figure 11.3, the **Click** event sub for the other command button uses the VBScript **InputBox**() function to prompt the user for a new name to add to the list:

```
Sub CmdAddFriend_Click()
   dim NewFriend
   NewFriend = inputbox( _
      "Enter the name of your new friend:", _
      "Listbox Demonstration")
   ListBox1.AddItem NewFriend
end sub
```

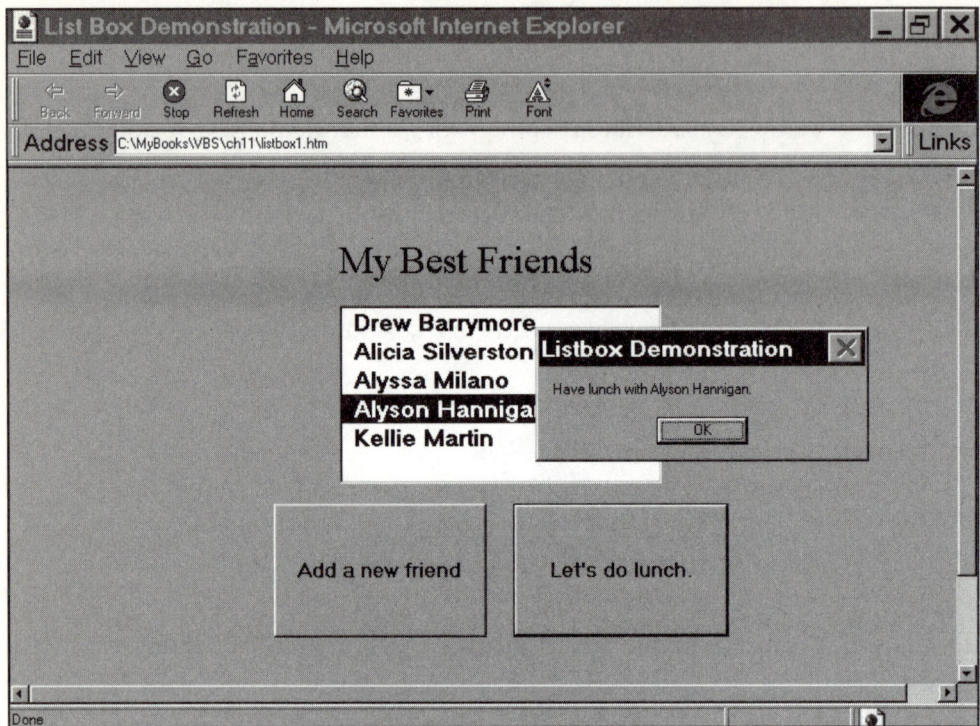

Figure 11.2
A message box with the selected list item in the text.

Once the user has entered the new name in the input box, the sub calls the list box's **AddItem** method and adds the new item to the list. It's that simple.

List boxes are appropriate when you want the user to choose from a predefined set of choices and do *not* want to allow a choice that isn't on the list. This contrasts with combo boxes, which are like list boxes but *do* allow the user to make a choice that isn't on the list.

The Combo Box Control

The combo box control is like a cross between a text box and a list box—in fact, it *is* a cross between a text box and a list box. At the top of a combo box is a text box in which the user can type an entry. Underneath, a drop-down list appears with the regular list items. This allows a user to either select an item from the list or type a new item in the text box.

An ActiveX Miscellany   243

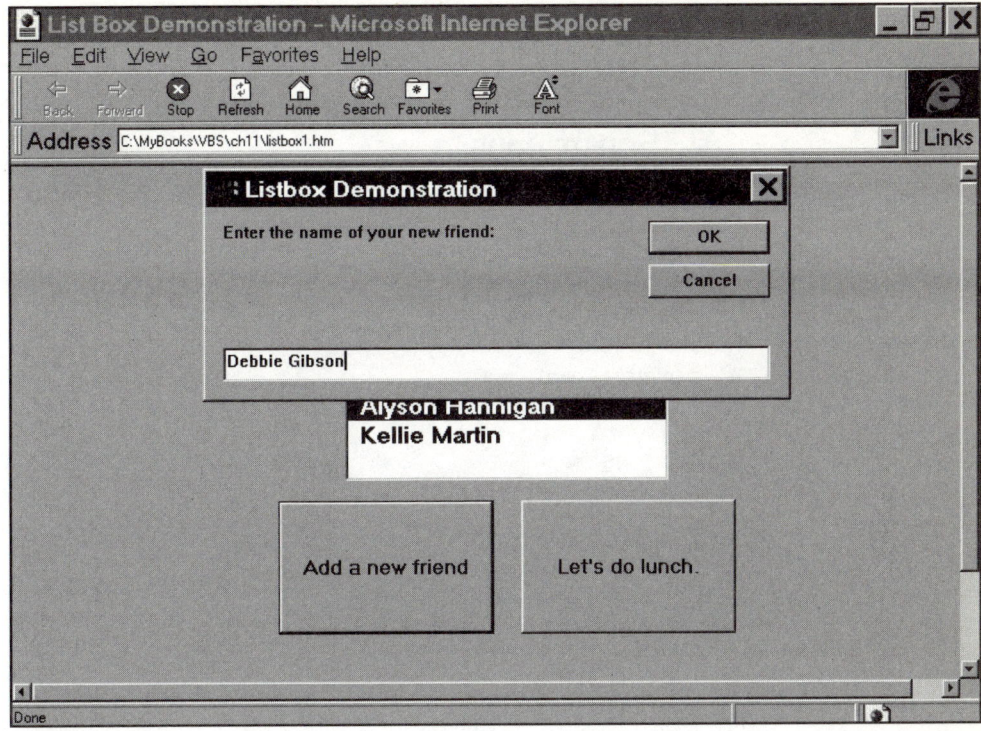

Figure 11.3
Adding a new item to the list box.

Figure 11.4 shows the combo-box version of our Web page, with names of people to call for lunch. Listing 11.3 shows the HTML container code for an ActiveX layout with a combo box, while Listing 11.4 shows the ActiveX layout and VBScript code.

Listing 11.3 HTML DOCUMENT TO CONTAIN THE LAYOUT WITH A COMBO BOX.

```
<HTML>
<HEAD>
<TITLE>Combo Box Demonstration</TITLE>
</HEAD>
<BODY>

<OBJECT CLASSID="CLSID:812AE312-8B8E-11CF-93C8-00AA00C08FDF"
ID="combobx1_alx" STYLE="LEFT:0;TOP:0">
<PARAM NAME="ALXPATH" REF
    VALUE="file:C:\MyBooks\VBS\ch11\combobx1.alx">
</OBJECT>
```

```
</BODY>
</HTML>
```

Listing 11.4 ACTIVEX LAYOUT WITH COMBO BOX AND VBSCRIPT CODE.

```
<SCRIPT LANGUAGE="VBScript">
<!--
Sub Layout1_OnLoad()
ComboBox1.AddItem "Drew Barrymore"
ComboBox1.AddItem "Alicia Silverstone"
ComboBox1.AddItem "Alyssa Milano"
ComboBox1.AddItem "Alyson Hannigan"
ComboBox1.AddItem "Kellie Martin"
end sub

Sub CmdLunch_Click()
msgbox "Have lunch with " & ComboBox1.value & ".",, _
   "Listbox Demonstration"
end sub

Sub CmdAddFriend_Click()
dim NewFriend
NewFriend = inputbox( _
   "Enter the name of your new friend:","Listbox Demonstration")
ComboBox1.AddItem NewFriend
end sub
-->
</SCRIPT>

<DIV ID="Layout1" STYLE="LAYOUT:FIXED;WIDTH:597pt;HEIGHT:370pt;">
   <OBJECT ID="Label1"
     CLASSID="CLSID:978C9E23-D4B0-11CE-BF2D-00AA003F40D0"
     STYLE="TOP:33pt;LEFT:198pt;WIDTH:198pt;
         HEIGHT:33pt;ZINDEX:0;">
       <PARAM NAME="Caption" VALUE="My Best Friends">
       <PARAM NAME="Size" VALUE="6985;1164">
       <PARAM NAME="FontName" VALUE="Times New Roman">
       <PARAM NAME="FontHeight" VALUE="480">
       <PARAM NAME="FontCharSet" VALUE="0">
       <PARAM NAME="FontPitchAndFamily" VALUE="2">
       <PARAM NAME="FontWeight" VALUE="0">
   </OBJECT>

   <OBJECT ID="CmdLunch"
     CLASSID="CLSID:D7053240-CE69-11CD-A777-00DD01143C57"
     STYLE="TOP:198pt;LEFT:305pt;WIDTH:132pt;
         HEIGHT:83pt;TABINDEX:1;ZINDEX:1;">
```

```
            <PARAM NAME="Caption" VALUE="Let's do lunch.">
            <PARAM NAME="Size" VALUE="4657;2928">
            <PARAM NAME="FontEffects" VALUE="1073741825">
            <PARAM NAME="FontHeight" VALUE="240">
            <PARAM NAME="FontCharSet" VALUE="0">
            <PARAM NAME="FontPitchAndFamily" VALUE="2">
            <PARAM NAME="ParagraphAlign" VALUE="3">
            <PARAM NAME="FontWeight" VALUE="700">
    </OBJECT>

    <OBJECT ID="CmdAddFriend"
     CLASSID="CLSID:D7053240-CE69-11CD-A777-00DD01143C57"
     STYLE="TOP:198pt;LEFT:157pt;WIDTH:132pt;
            HEIGHT:83pt;TABINDEX:2;ZINDEX:2;">
            <PARAM NAME="Caption" VALUE="Add a new friend">
            <PARAM NAME="Size" VALUE="4657;2928">
            <PARAM NAME="FontEffects" VALUE="1073741825">
            <PARAM NAME="FontHeight" VALUE="240">
            <PARAM NAME="FontCharSet" VALUE="0">
            <PARAM NAME="FontPitchAndFamily" VALUE="2">
            <PARAM NAME="ParagraphAlign" VALUE="3">
            <PARAM NAME="FontWeight" VALUE="700">
    </OBJECT>

    <OBJECT ID="ComboBox1"
     CLASSID="CLSID:8BD21D30-EC42-11CE-9E0D-00AA006002F3"
     STYLE="TOP:74pt;LEFT:182pt;WIDTH:231pt;
            HEIGHT:21pt;TABINDEX:3;ZINDEX:3;">
            <PARAM NAME="VariousPropertyBits" VALUE="746604571">
            <PARAM NAME="DisplayStyle" VALUE="3">
            <PARAM NAME="Size" VALUE="8149;741">
            <PARAM NAME="MatchEntry" VALUE="1">
            <PARAM NAME="ShowDropButtonWhen" VALUE="2">
            <PARAM NAME="FontEffects" VALUE="1073741825">
            <PARAM NAME="FontHeight" VALUE="240">
            <PARAM NAME="FontCharSet" VALUE="0">
            <PARAM NAME="FontPitchAndFamily" VALUE="2">
            <PARAM NAME="FontWeight" VALUE="700">
    </OBJECT>
</DIV>
```

When a user clicks on the down-arrow button at the right of the text box, a list appears underneath, as shown in Figure 11.5. If the user doesn't want to select any of the items in the list, he or she can type a new item in the text box and select it, as shown in Figure 11.6.

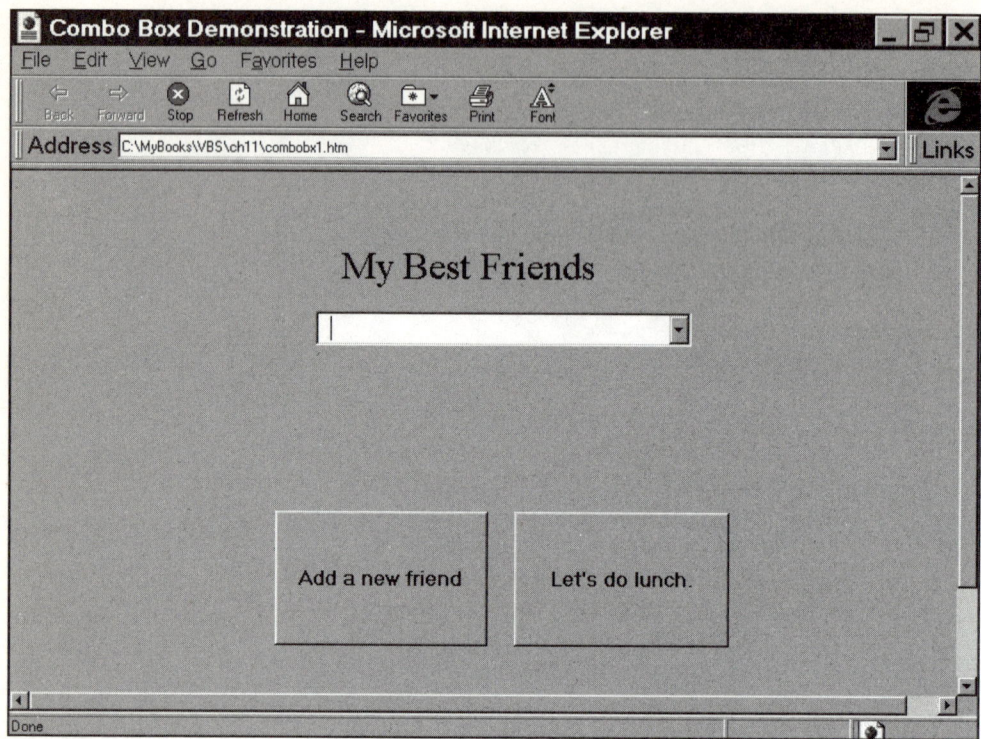

Figure 11.4
A combo box combines a text box with a drop-down list.

Writing VBScript Code For The Combo Box Control

As you can see from Listings 11.2 and 11.4, the VBScript code with a combo box works almost exactly the same as it does with a list box. The only real difference is in the way each control works: The combo box lets the user enter a choice that isn't on the list whereas the list box doesn't.

(Typing a new choice in the combo box's text box does not, by the way, add the new item to the list. That still has to be done by calling the combo box's **AddItem** method.)

The Option Button Control

Option buttons might *look* different from list boxes, but they really aren't that different. Option buttons are another way to present a list of choices to a user and require that he or she pick from that list. Figure 11.7 shows a simple Web

An ActiveX Miscellany   247

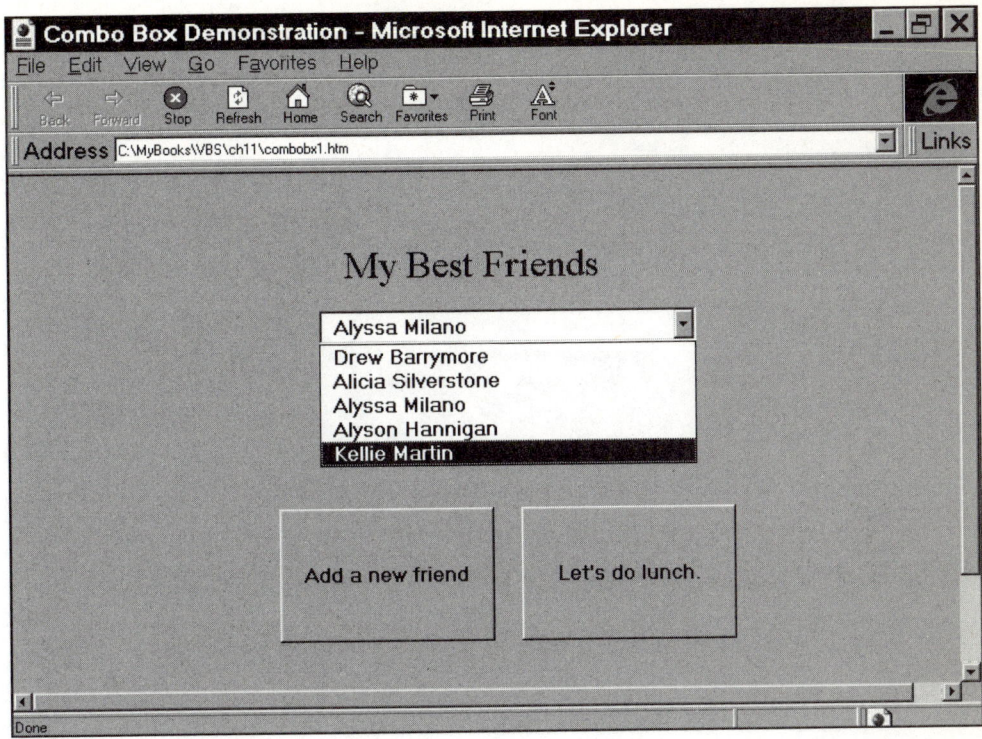

Figure 11.5
A list drops down underneath the text box.

page with three option buttons. Each option button corresponds to a CD that the user might want to play. Unlike checkboxes, only *one* of a group of option buttons can be selected at a time.

 Option Buttons Equal Radio Buttons, But Don't Call Them That

Option buttons are also sometimes called "radio buttons"—in fact, historically, that's what they were originally called. However, there's also a native HTML form control called a radio button, so it's probably a good idea to avoid calling ActiveX option button controls "radio buttons." That way, you avoid any potential confusion.

In spite of their functional similarity to list boxes, option buttons are coded quite differently in VBScript. Listing 11.5 shows the HTML container document for an ActiveX layout with option buttons, while Listing 11.6 shows the ActiveX layout and the VBScript code.

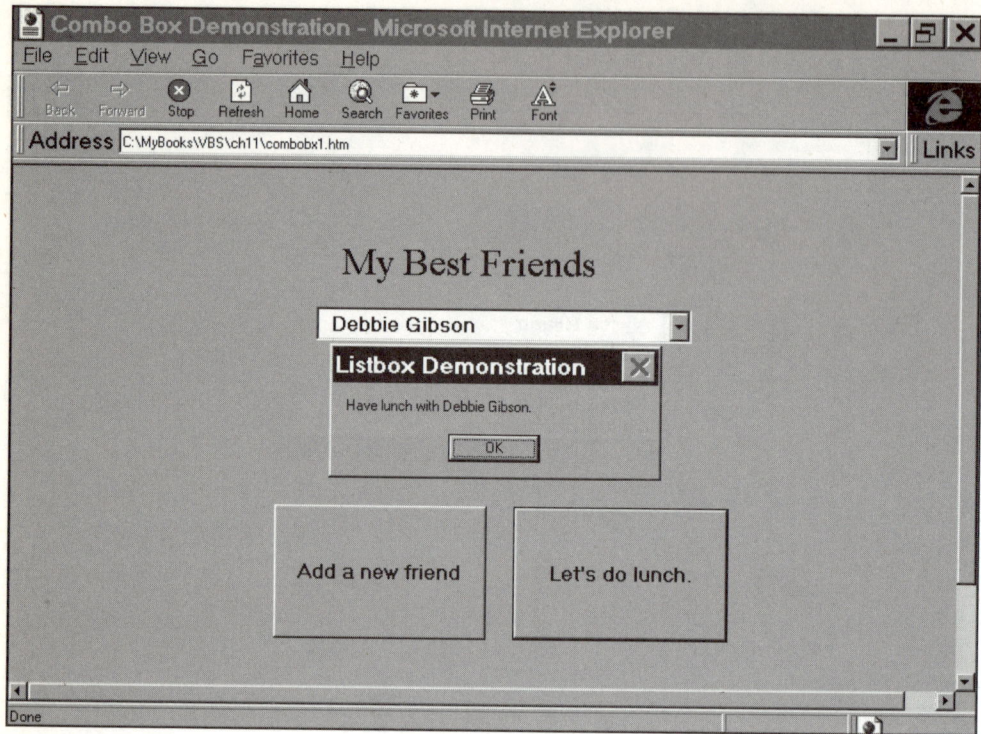

Figure 11.6
The user can type a new entry into the box.

Listing 11.5 HTML DOCUMENT FOR A LAYOUT WITH OPTION BUTTONS.

```
<HTML>
<HEAD>
<TITLE>Option Button Demonstration</TITLE>
</HEAD>
<BODY>

<OBJECT CLASSID="CLSID:812AE312-8B8E-11CF-93C8-00AA00C08FDF"
ID="opt_btn1_alx" STYLE="LEFT:0;TOP:0">
<PARAM NAME="ALXPATH" REF VALUE=
    "file:C:\MyBooks\VBS\ch11\opt_btn1.alx">
</OBJECT>

</BODY>
</HTML>
```

An ActiveX Miscellany   249

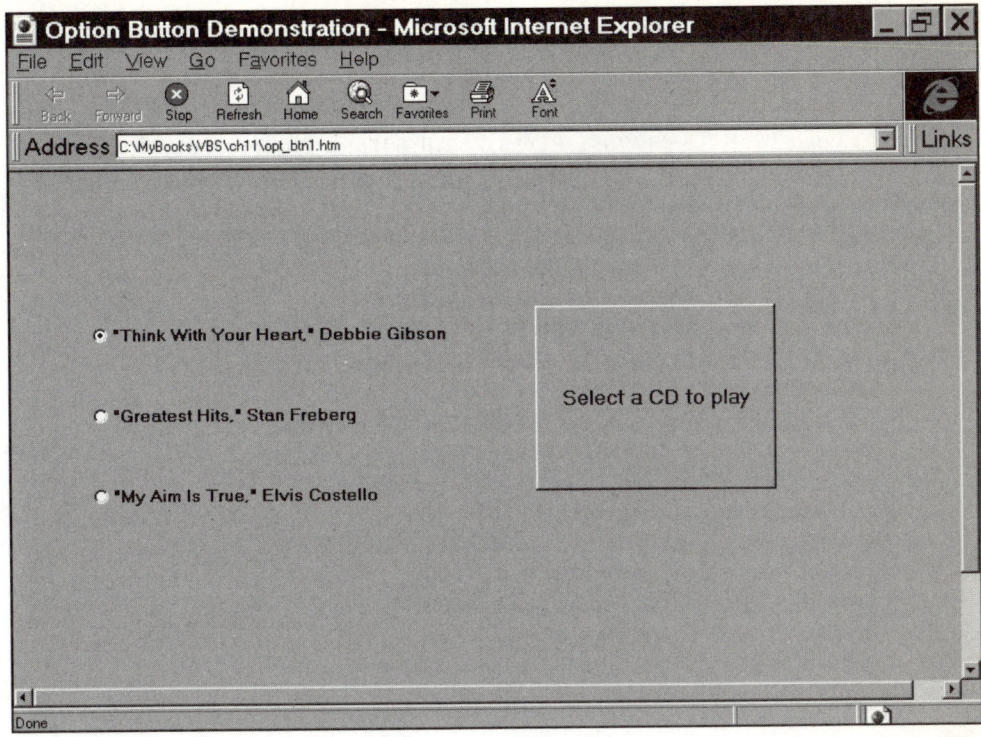

Figure 11.7
Using option buttons to pick a CD.

Listing 11.6 ACTIVEX LAYOUT WITH OPTION BUTTONS AND VBSCRIPT CODE.

```
<SCRIPT LANGUAGE="VBScript">
<!--
Sub CommandButton1_Click()
   If OptionButton1 then
      msgbox "Play " & OptionButton1.caption & ".",, _
         "Option Button Demonstration"
   end if

   If OptionButton2 then
      msgbox "Play " & OptionButton2.caption & ".",, _
         "Option Button Demonstration"
   end if

   If OptionButton3 then
      msgbox "Play " & OptionButton3.caption & ".",, _
         "Option Button Demonstration"
```

```
        end if
end sub
-->
</SCRIPT>
<DIV ID="Layout3" STYLE="LAYOUT:FIXED;WIDTH:597pt;HEIGHT:370pt;">

    <OBJECT ID="OptionButton1"
     CLASSID="CLSID:8BD21D50-EC42-11CE-9E0D-00AA006002F3"
     STYLE="TOP:74pt;LEFT:41pt;WIDTH:230pt;
            HEIGHT:34pt;TABINDEX:0;ZINDEX:0;">
        <PARAM NAME="BackColor" VALUE="2147483663">
        <PARAM NAME="ForeColor" VALUE="2147483666">
        <PARAM NAME="DisplayStyle" VALUE="5">
        <PARAM NAME="Size" VALUE="8114;1199">
        <PARAM NAME="Value" VALUE="True">
        <PARAM NAME="Caption"
            VALUE="&quot;Think With Your Heart,&quot; Debbie Gibson">
        <PARAM NAME="FontEffects" VALUE="1073741825">
        <PARAM NAME="FontHeight" VALUE="200">
        <PARAM NAME="FontCharSet" VALUE="0">
        <PARAM NAME="FontPitchAndFamily" VALUE="2">
        <PARAM NAME="FontWeight" VALUE="700">
    </OBJECT>

    <OBJECT ID="OptionButton2"
     CLASSID="CLSID:8BD21D50-EC42-11CE-9E0D-00AA006002F3"
     STYLE="TOP:124pt;LEFT:41pt;WIDTH:230pt;
            HEIGHT:35pt;TABINDEX:1;ZINDEX:1;">
        <PARAM NAME="BackColor" VALUE="2147483663">
        <PARAM NAME="ForeColor" VALUE="2147483666">
        <PARAM NAME="DisplayStyle" VALUE="5">
        <PARAM NAME="Size" VALUE="8114;1235">
        <PARAM NAME="Value" VALUE="False">
        <PARAM NAME="Caption"
            VALUE="&quot;Greatest Hits,&quot; Stan Freberg">
        <PARAM NAME="FontEffects" VALUE="1073741825">
        <PARAM NAME="FontHeight" VALUE="200">
        <PARAM NAME="FontCharSet" VALUE="0">
        <PARAM NAME="FontPitchAndFamily" VALUE="2">
        <PARAM NAME="FontWeight" VALUE="700">
    </OBJECT>

    <OBJECT ID="OptionButton3"
     CLASSID="CLSID:8BD21D50-EC42-11CE-9E0D-00AA006002F3"
     STYLE="TOP:173pt;LEFT:41pt;WIDTH:238pt;
            HEIGHT:37pt;TABINDEX:2;ZINDEX:2;">
        <PARAM NAME="BackColor" VALUE="2147483663">
```

```
            <PARAM NAME="ForeColor" VALUE="2147483666">
            <PARAM NAME="DisplayStyle" VALUE="5">
            <PARAM NAME="Size" VALUE="8396;1305">
            <PARAM NAME="Value" VALUE="False">
            <PARAM NAME="Caption"
                VALUE="&quot;My Aim Is True,&quot; Elvis Costello">
            <PARAM NAME="FontEffects" VALUE="1073741825">
            <PARAM NAME="FontHeight" VALUE="200">
            <PARAM NAME="FontCharSet" VALUE="0">
            <PARAM NAME="FontPitchAndFamily" VALUE="2">
            <PARAM NAME="FontWeight" VALUE="700">
    </OBJECT>

    <OBJECT ID="CommandButton1"
     CLASSID="CLSID:D7053240-CE69-11CD-A777-00DD01143C57"
     STYLE="TOP:74pt;LEFT:314pt;WIDTH:149pt;
         HEIGHT:116pt;TABINDEX:3;ZINDEX:3;">
        <PARAM NAME="Caption" VALUE="Select a CD to play">
        <PARAM NAME="Size" VALUE="5256;4092">
        <PARAM NAME="FontEffects" VALUE="1073741825">
        <PARAM NAME="FontHeight" VALUE="240">
        <PARAM NAME="FontCharSet" VALUE="0">
        <PARAM NAME="FontPitchAndFamily" VALUE="2">
        <PARAM NAME="ParagraphAlign" VALUE="3">
        <PARAM NAME="FontWeight" VALUE="700">
    </OBJECT>
</DIV>
```

When you first set up option buttons in the ActiveX Control Pad, you need to go into the Properties window and set the **value** property of one of the buttons to **true**. This will automatically set the values of the other buttons to **false**. When the user loads your Web page, the button whose initial value you set to **true** will be selected. The user can then accept it, or he or she can select one of the others by clicking on it.

Writing VBScript Code For Option Button Controls

Apart from its **caption** property, which is self-explanatory, the most important property of an option button is its **value** property. The **value** property is also the default property of an option button. If you refer to an option button control but don't specify a property, VBScript assumes you are talking about the default property—its value.

If the button is selected, then its value is **true**; otherwise, its value is **false**. In VBScript, **false** equals 0 (zero), while **true** is any non-zero integer value—usually –1. That makes it easy to write code that detects which option button is selected, as in this code snippet from Listing 11.6:

```
If OptionButton1 then
   msgbox "Play " & OptionButton1.caption & ".",, _
      "Option Button Demonstration"
end if
```

Notice that all the **if** clause says is "If OptionButton1." That's because if the control is selected, its **value** property is **true**. And when you refer to the control without specifying a property, you get the value property. It would work fine if you instead wrote

```
If OptionButton1.value = true then
   msgbox "Play " & OptionButton1.caption & ".",, _
      "Option Button Demonstration"
end if
```

but it wouldn't accomplish anything more, and would thus be a waste of time.

The Toggle Button Control

A toggle is essentially just an on-off switch, like a light switch. The ActiveX toggle button control works exactly as you'd expect: Each time it's clicked, it switches between "on" and "off." Because a toggle button is like a light switch, our example gives you a chance to turn the lights on or off at The Coriolis Group. When you first arrive, the lights are off, as shown in Figure 11.8. When you leave, like any thoughtful guest, you click on the toggle button to turn off the lights, as shown in Figure 11.9.

This Web page uses a few tricks in addition to the toggle button itself. The HTML code for the containing Web page is shown in Listing 11.7, while the ActiveX layout and the VBScript code are shown in Listing 11.8.

An ActiveX Miscellany

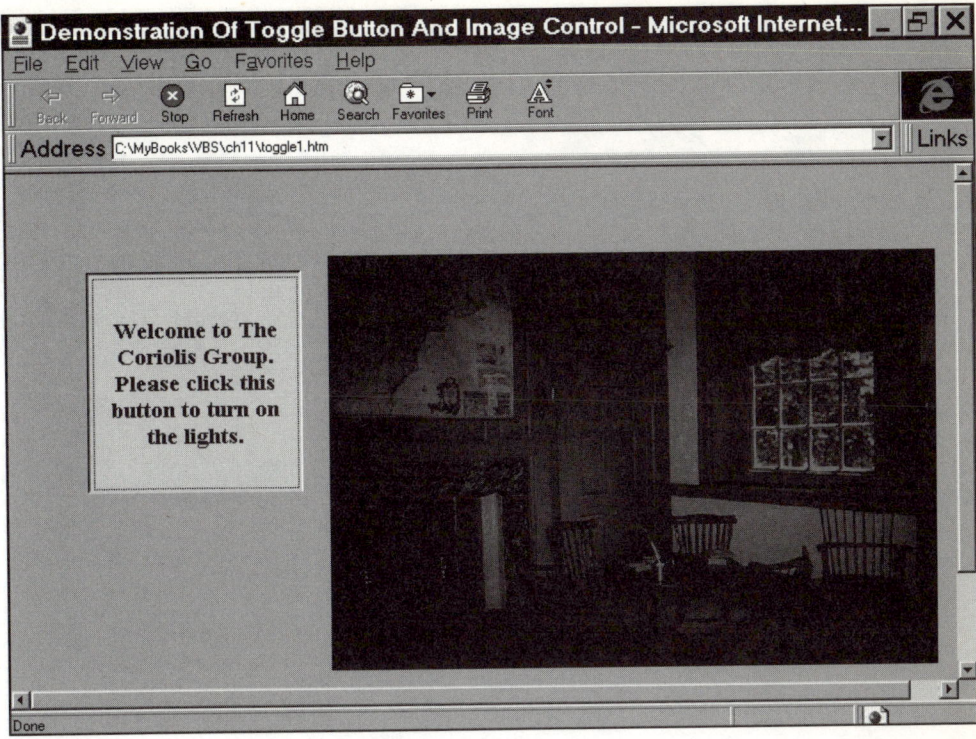

Figure 11.8
When you visit The Coriolis Group, turn on the lights.

Listing 11.7 HTML code for the containing Web page.

```
<HTML>
<HEAD>
<TITLE>Demonstration Of Toggle Button And Image Control</TITLE>
</HEAD>
<BODY>

<OBJECT CLASSID="CLSID:812AE312-8B8E-11CF-93C8-00AA00C08FDF"
ID="toggle1_alx" STYLE="LEFT:0;TOP:0">
<PARAM NAME="ALXPATH" REF VALUE=
    "toggle1.alx">
</OBJECT>

</BODY>
</HTML>
```

254 Chapter 11

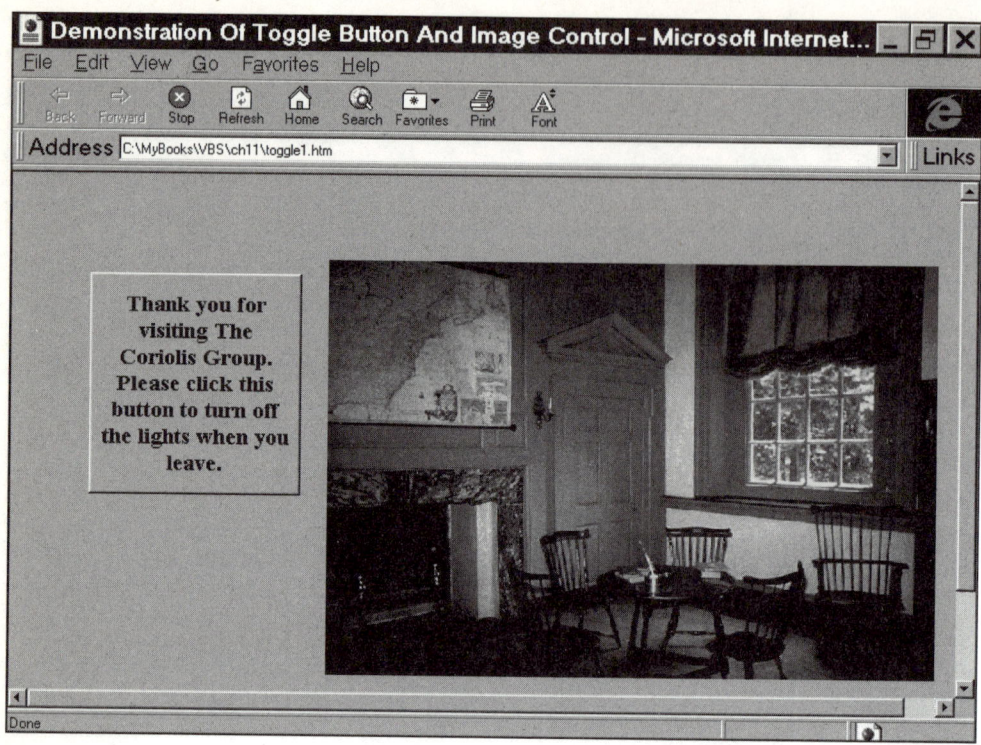

Figure 11.9
Please turn off the lights if you are the last to leave.

Listing 11.8 ACTIVEX LAYOUT WITH TOGGLE CONTROL, IMAGE CONTROL, AND VBSCRIPT CODE.

```
<SCRIPT LANGUAGE="VBScript">
<!--
Sub ToggleButton1_Click()
If ToggleButton1 then
   Image1.picturepath = "c:\mybooks\vbs\ch11\office2.bmp"
   ToggleButton1.caption = "Welcome to The Coriolis Group." & _
      "Please click this button to turn on the lights."
else
   Image1.picturepath = "c:\mybooks\vbs\ch11\office1.bmp"
   ToggleButton1.caption = "Thank you for visiting The " & _
      "Coriolis Group. Please click this button to turn off " & _
      "the lights when you leave."
end if

end sub
-->
</SCRIPT>
```

An ActiveX Miscellany

```
<DIV ID="Layout4" STYLE="LAYOUT:FIXED;WIDTH:597pt;HEIGHT:370pt;">

    <OBJECT ID="ToggleButton1"
      CLASSID="CLSID:8BD21D60-EC42-11CE-9E0D-00AA006002F3"
      STYLE="TOP:50pt;LEFT:41pt;WIDTH:132pt;HEIGHT:138pt;
            TABINDEX:0;ZINDEX:0;">
        <PARAM NAME="BackColor" VALUE="2147483663">
        <PARAM NAME="ForeColor" VALUE="4194368">
        <PARAM NAME="DisplayStyle" VALUE="6">
        <PARAM NAME="Size" VALUE="4657;4868">
        <PARAM NAME="Value" VALUE="True">
        <PARAM NAME="Caption"
            VALUE="Thank you for visiting The Coriolis Group.
                Please click this button to turn off the lights when
                you leave.">
        <PARAM NAME="FontName" VALUE="Times New Roman">
        <PARAM NAME="FontEffects" VALUE="1073741825">
        <PARAM NAME="FontHeight" VALUE="280">
        <PARAM NAME="FontCharSet" VALUE="0">
        <PARAM NAME="FontPitchAndFamily" VALUE="2">
        <PARAM NAME="ParagraphAlign" VALUE="3">
        <PARAM NAME="FontWeight" VALUE="700">
    </OBJECT>

    <OBJECT ID="Image1"
      CLASSID="CLSID:D4A97620-8E8F-11CF-93CD-00AA00C08FDF"
      STYLE="TOP:41pt;LEFT:190pt;WIDTH:375pt;
            HEIGHT:260pt;ZINDEX:1;">
        <PARAM NAME="PicturePath"
            VALUE="c:\mybooks\vbs\ch11\office1.bmp">
        <PARAM NAME="BorderStyle" VALUE="0">
        <PARAM NAME="SizeMode" VALUE="3">
        <PARAM NAME="Size" VALUE="13229;9172">
        <PARAM NAME="PictureAlignment" VALUE="0">
        <PARAM NAME="VariousPropertyBits" VALUE="19">
    </OBJECT>
</DIV>
```

As you might have guessed from the figures and confirmed by looking at the code, this example also uses an ActiveX image control. We'll cover the image control only in passing here. Chapter 12 discusses in more detail how to handle images in your Web documents.

Writing VBScript Code For The Toggle Button Control

The code for the toggle button control is as simple as the control itself. Just like an option button, a toggle button's default property is its **value** property, and its **value** property is either on (**true**) or off (**false**). Thus, inside the button's **Click** event, you set up a simple **if...then...else** statement, as follows:

```
Sub ToggleButton1_Click()
If ToggleButton1 then
   Image1.picturepath = "c:\mybooks\vbs\ch11\office2.bmp"
   ToggleButton1.caption = "Welcome to The Coriolis Group." & _
      "Please click this button to turn on the lights."
else
   Image1.picturepath = "c:\mybooks\vbs\ch11\office1.bmp"
   ToggleButton1.caption = "Thank you for visiting The " & _
      "Coriolis Group. Please click this button to turn off " & _
      "the lights when you leave."
end if
```

If the toggle button's value is already **true** when the user clicks on it, that means the lights are turned on at The Coriolis Group. Thus, **ToggleButton1** is **true** and the **then** part of the statement fires. This changes the image file name in the image control's **picturepath** property, causing a new image to display in the control.

If the toggle button's value is **false** when the button is clicked, then it means the lights are out. As a result, the **else** clause fires, using the same technique to swap a fully lit photograph into the image control's **picturepath** property.

How The Darkened Photo Was Created
To create the "dark" version of the office photo, I used JASC's Paint Shop Pro 4. By adjusting the brightness and contrast of the photo, I took a fully lit scene and made it look darker.

The Scrollbar Control

You use scrollbars all the time—in your word processor and in utility programs—any time there's some data that scrolls off the screen. What you might not realize is that scrollbars have other applications as well. They're a good way to let users visually change values in a program. Figure 11.10 shows a Web page with an

An ActiveX Miscellany 257

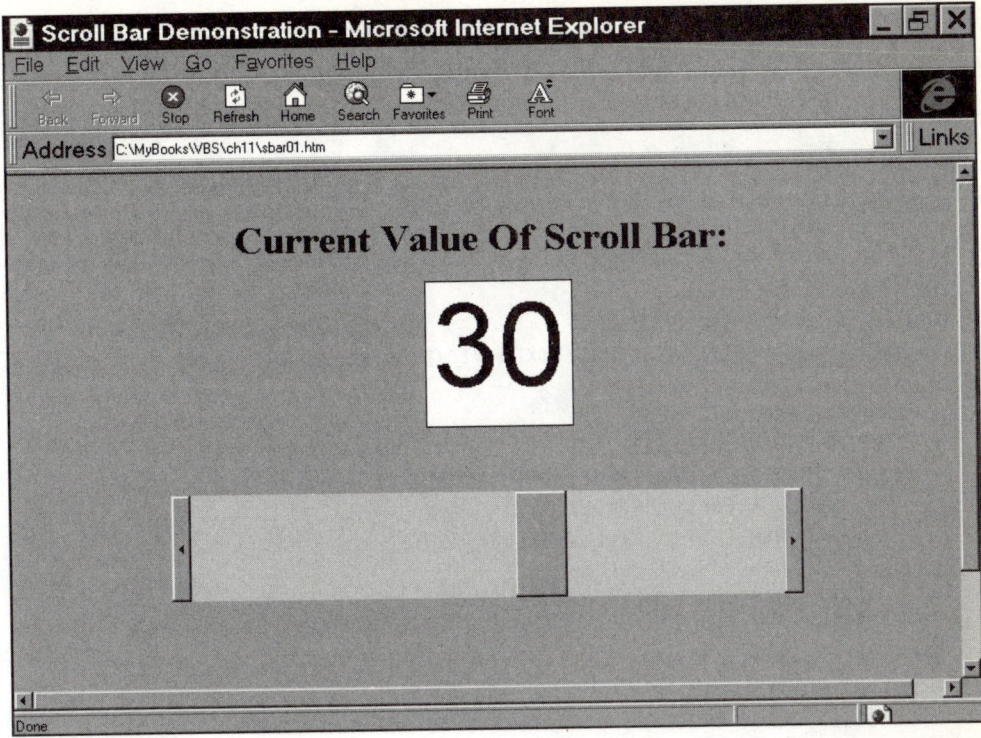

Figure 11.10
A Web page with a scrollbar control.

ActiveX scrollbar control that displays its current value in a label control. The HTML code for the containing document is shown in Listing 11.9, while the ActiveX layout and VBScript code is shown in Listing 11.10.

Listing 11.9 HTML CODE FOR THE SCROLLBAR LAYOUT.

```
<HTML>
<HEAD>
<TITLE>Scroll Bar Demonstration</TITLE>
</HEAD>
<BODY>

<OBJECT CLASSID="CLSID:812AE312-8B8E-11CF-93C8-00AA00C08FDF"
ID="sbar01_alx" STYLE="LEFT:0;TOP:0">
<PARAM NAME="ALXPATH" REF
    VALUE="file:C:\MyBooks\VBS\ch11\sbar01.alx">
</OBJECT>

</BODY>
</HTML>
```

Listing 11.10 ACTIVEX LAYOUT WITH SCROLLBAR CONTROL AND VBSCRIPT CODE.

```
<SCRIPT LANGUAGE="VBScript">
<!--
Sub ScrollBar1_Change()
    Label1.caption = ScrollBar1.value
end sub
-->
</SCRIPT>

<DIV ID="Layout1" STYLE="LAYOUT:FIXED;WIDTH:597pt;HEIGHT:370pt;">

    <OBJECT ID="ScrollBar1"
     CLASSID="CLSID:DFD181E0-5E2F-11CE-A449-00AA004A803D"
     STYLE="TOP:190pt;LEFT:91pt;WIDTH:388pt;
            HEIGHT:66pt;TABINDEX:0;ZINDEX:0;">
        <PARAM NAME="Size" VALUE="13688;2328">
        <PARAM NAME="Max" VALUE="50">
        <PARAM NAME="LargeChange" VALUE="5">
    </OBJECT>

    <OBJECT ID="Label1"
     CLASSID="CLSID:978C9E23-D4B0-11CE-BF2D-00AA003F40D0"
     STYLE="TOP:58pt;LEFT:248pt;WIDTH:91pt;
            HEIGHT:91pt;ZINDEX:1;">
        <PARAM NAME="BackColor" VALUE="16777215">
        <PARAM NAME="Caption" VALUE="0">
        <PARAM NAME="Size" VALUE="3210;3210">
        <PARAM NAME="BorderStyle" VALUE="1">
        <PARAM NAME="FontName" VALUE="Arial">
        <PARAM NAME="FontHeight" VALUE="1440">
        <PARAM NAME="FontCharSet" VALUE="0">
        <PARAM NAME="FontPitchAndFamily" VALUE="2">
        <PARAM NAME="ParagraphAlign" VALUE="3">
        <PARAM NAME="FontWeight" VALUE="0">
    </OBJECT>

    <OBJECT ID="Label2"
     CLASSID="CLSID:978C9E23-D4B0-11CE-BF2D-00AA003F40D0"
     STYLE="TOP:17pt;LEFT:132pt;WIDTH:314pt;
            HEIGHT:33pt;ZINDEX:2;">
        <PARAM NAME="Caption"
            VALUE="Current Value Of Scroll Bar:">
        <PARAM NAME="Size" VALUE="11077;1164">
        <PARAM NAME="FontName" VALUE="Times New Roman">
        <PARAM NAME="FontEffects" VALUE="1073741825">
        <PARAM NAME="FontHeight" VALUE="480">
```

```
        <PARAM NAME="FontCharSet" VALUE="0">
        <PARAM NAME="FontPitchAndFamily" VALUE="2">
        <PARAM NAME="FontWeight" VALUE="700">
    </OBJECT>
</DIV>
```

When you set up the scrollbar control in the ActiveX Control Pad, you need to know about its four most important properties:

- **SmallChange.** This is the amount by which the scrollbar's **value** property changes when a user clicks on one of the arrow buttons at either end of the scrollbar. Clicking once on the right-hand arrow button increases the value by **SmallChange**, while clicking once on the left-hand arrow button decreases the value by **SmallChange**.

- **LargeChange.** This is the amount by which the scrollbar's **value** property changes when a user clicks on the area *within* the scrollbar. Clicking to the right of the value indicator increases the value by **LargeChange**, while clicking to the left of the value indicator decreases the value by the same amount.

- **Min.** This is the minimum value of the control's **value** property—by default, this is 0 (zero).

- **Max.** This is the maximum value of the control's **value** property. If you're testing the control and clicking doesn't seem to have much effect, you might have left the **Max** property at its default setting, which is 32,767.

Writing VBScript Code For The Scrollbar Control

The most important event that happens to the scrollbar control is its **Change** event. Whenever the value of the scrollbar changes, its **Change** event fires. By putting your VBScript code into the scrollbar control's **Change** event, you can update any control with the scrollbar's new value. That's what was done in our example. The scrollbar control's **Change** event assigned a new value to the label control's **caption** property:

```
Sub ScrollBar1_Change()
    Label1.caption = ScrollBar1.value
end sub
```

There are many applications of scrollbars, and you'll often find them useful in your Web pages.

12

Images, Video, and Sound

There are plenty of ways to use images, video, and sound on your Web page—using ActiveX is only one of them. In this chapter, you'll learn the most important tricks of the trade.

Command buttons, text boxes, and other standard controls make your Web page *work*. Images, animations, video, and sound can make it *fun*. There are several controls and techniques you can use for various purposes. We'll start by looking at the ActiveX image control we discussed briefly in Chapter 11's toggle-button demonstration. Then, we'll look at some other ways you can incorporate images, video, and sound into your Web pages.

Using ActiveX Image Controls

If you recall from Chapter 11, the toggle-button demonstration used an ActiveX image control to show an office photograph from The Coriolis Group (at least, a fantasy version of the company's office). The Web page looked like Figure 12.1.

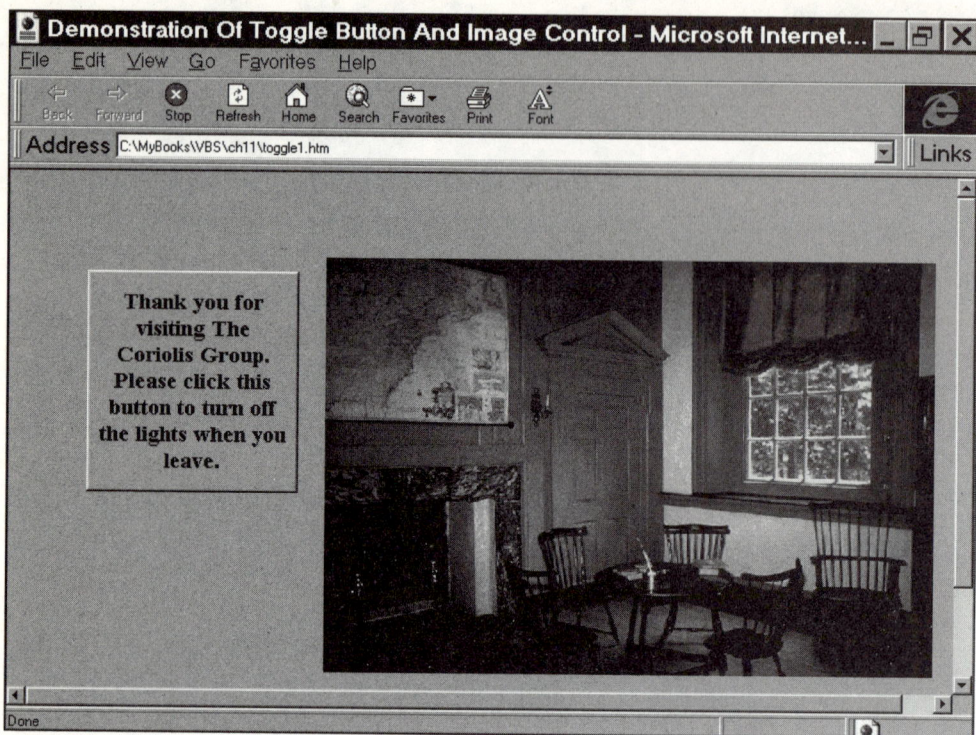

Figure 12.1
An image control displays a photo on the Web page.

Like any other control, an image control has some properties that you'll use all the time, and others that you'll use less often. The most important properties are as follows:

- **autosize.** This determines if the image control will resize itself to fit the picture that's loaded into it. If this property is set to **true**, then the image control will expand or shrink to fit the picture it contains. If the property is set to **false**, then the image control will remain the same size. If the image is bigger than the control, the right and bottom edges of the image will not be visible.

  Normally, you'll set the **autosize** property to **false**. Once you've created a Web page layout, you probably won't want it disrupted by an image control whose size on the page is unpredictable. On the other hand, if you're loading a series of pictures into the control and want to be sure that the picture edges don't get "clipped" by the control borders, then set **autosize** to **true** and plan for size changes when you design your Web page.

VBScript Vs. ActiveX

Don't get confused about what's in VBScript 2 and what's in ActiveX. The properties (and property values) of ActiveX controls are determined by the controls themselves, *not* by VBScript. Thus, even though VBScript 2 has **true** and **false** as named constants, they have nothing particular to do with the **true** and **false** values of the **autosize** property—or those of any other ActiveX control property.

- **borderstyle.** This determines whether or not the image control will have a visible border on your Web page. The default value is usually 0, or "none." The Microsoft image control only lets you have a single-line border, but other image controls might give you more choices.

- **id.** This, of course, is the name by which you refer to the image control in your VBScript code.

- **picturepath.** This is the location and file name of the picture that the image control should display. With the Microsoft image control, you type this directly into the **picturepath** line of the Properties window. With other image controls, you can often browse through your disk directories and select a file instead of typing the path and file name.

  The image control can display images from the following file types: GIF, JPEG, BMP, WMF, and WVLET. If you have an image in a different format, you need to convert it to a file type that the image control can use.

Try To Minimize Downloading Time For Images

No matter what file type you use for your images, you should try to keep your image files as small as possible because they'll have to load across the Web into the user's PC. Bigger files mean longer download times. One way to shrink the file size is to select a compressed file type, such as JPEG: A JPEG file takes up far less disk space than a BMP file of the same image. Another way to shrink the file size is to reduce the number of colors in the image. Paint Shop Pro and other image processing programs allow you to do this quite easily.

Some images will display fine with only 16 colors, whereas others require 256 or even 65,000 colors to display properly. But the thing to remember is a Web version of "Ockham's Razor": Don't multiply colors beyond necessity. (William of Ockham was a medieval philosopher who said that in explaining any phenomenon, we should not multiply entities beyond necessity—in other words, we should keep the explanation as simple as possible. Ditto for program code. Ditto for colors.)

The mechanics of writing VBScript code for the image control are similar to those for all other controls, as shown by this line, taken from Listing 11.8:

```
Image1.picturepath = "c:\mybooks\vbs\ch11\office2.bmp"
```

Most of the time, when you write code for an image control, it will be to assign a new picture file to the control's **picturepath** property. Of course, you can make other changes in the control, but that's the most common. The default event for the image control is the **Click** event: You can even use image controls as ersatz command buttons.

Other "Image Controls" Are Similar

In this chapter, we're primarily talking about the ActiveX image control from Microsoft. However, *all* image controls—whether they're called "image controls" or not, and whether they're from Microsoft or not—have the same basic properties in common. The reason is simple: They all do essentially the same thing, which is to display images on a Web page or program window.

As a result, don't be too worried if you end up working with a different image control than the one we discuss here. All the basic concepts, properties, and techniques you'll learn in this chapter should apply to the new control, too.

Using Images In HTML

ActiveX and VBScript aside, HTML itself gives you quite a bit of flexibility in displaying images on your Web page. There are two HTML tags supported by Internet Explorer that are of particular interest:

- The **<body>** tag. This has a property called **background** that lets you use an image file as wallpaper for your Web page.

- The **<img>** tag. This has a property called **src** ("source") that lets you display an image on your Web page—in much the same way as you would with an ActiveX image control. The difference, of course, is that an image displayed with the **<img>** tag can't react to events and execute VBScript code like an ActiveX image control.

Listing 12.1 shows the HTML code for a Web page that uses the **<body background>** and **<img>** tags. Figure 12.2 shows the Web page it creates.

Listing 12.1   HTML CODE SHOWING TWO WAYS TO USE IMAGES.

```
<HTML>
<HEAD>
<TITLE>Image And Web Page Wallpaper Demonstration</TITLE>
</HEAD>
<BODY background="orngbk1.gif">
<center>
<H1><STRONG>Low-Mileage Cars For Sale!</STRONG></H1>
<TABLE BORDER=5 WIDTH=250 HEIGHT=200 CELLPADDING=5 CELLSPACING=5>
<TR><TD><img src="car01.gif"></TD><TD><img src="car02.gif"></TD></TR>
<TR><TD><img src="car03.gif"></TD><TD><img src="car04.gif"></TD></TR>
</TABLE>
</center>

</BODY>
</HTML>
```

Compared to some of the code we've seen with ActiveX layouts, Listing 12.1 is remarkably simple. It does two things. First, it uses the **<body background=>** tag to load an image as Web-page wallpaper. The image is tiled so that it completely fills the Web page. The image itself is shown in Figure 12.3.

 Your Wallpaper Shouldn't Be Too "Busy"
Remember that people aren't visiting your Web page to look at the wallpaper. If your wallpaper has too many different colors or images, it will be hard for people to read the text in the *foreground* of your Web page. Thus, scenes of astronauts or rock stars, interesting as they are, make very bad wallpaper. Solid colors, weave patterns, and other innocuous images make the best wallpaper.

Notice that the file name loaded into the **background** property needs to be in quotation marks. If the image file is in the same directory as the Web page, you can

266   Chapter 12

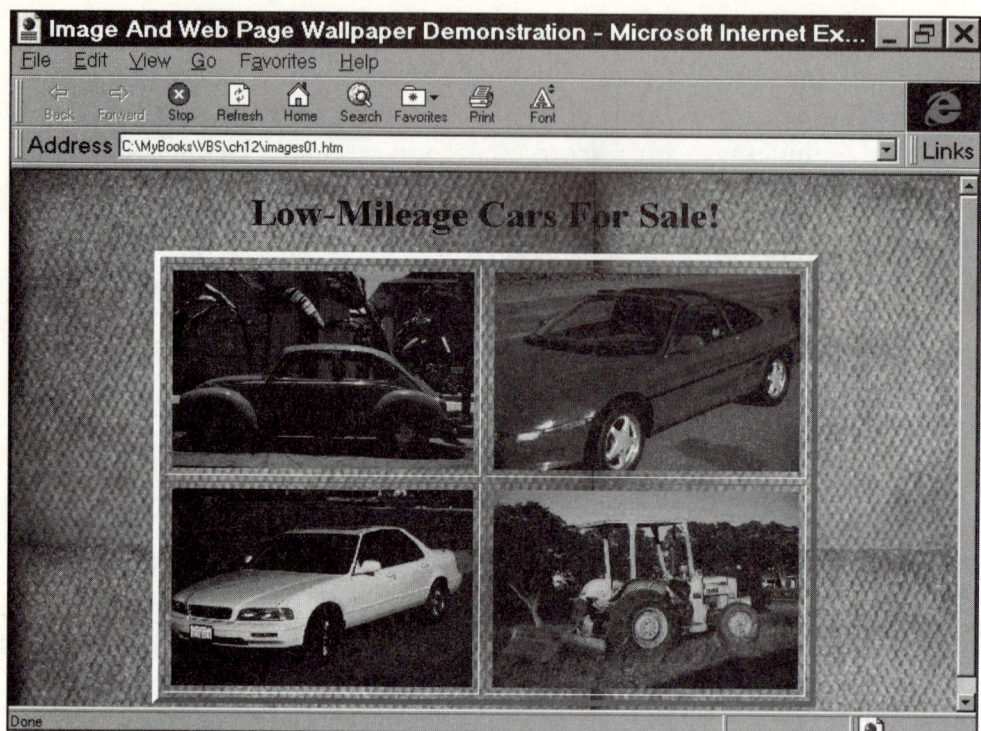

Figure 12.2
Selling cars on a Web page.

Figure 12.3
Background image for Web-page wallpaper.

simply use the file name, as I did in Listing 12.1. If the image file is in a different location, you need to include the complete directory path with the file name.

The second thing that happens in Listing 12.1 is that the HTML code sets up a table and uses the **<img src=>** tag to load a photo of a car into each cell of the table. As with the **<body>** tag's **background** property, you enclose the image file name in quotation marks and, if needed, give the full directory path of the file.

Playing Video With HTML

The HTML **<img>** tag is more powerful than you might expect. Not only does it allow you to display static images, but it also enables you to display video clips or virtual-reality simulations. The display isn't as flexible as what you get with ActiveX—as we'll see in the next part of the chapter—but it does work very well. Listing 12.2 shows the HTML code for a Web page that plays a video (AVI) clip, while Figure 12.4 shows the Web page that the HTML code creates. The video clip shown in the figure is from the movie *Eraser*, downloaded from the CompuServe ShowbizMedia Forum.

Listing 12.2 HTML CODE THAT PLAYS A VIDEO CLIP.

```
<HTML>
<HEAD>
<TITLE>HTML Video Tag Demonstration</TITLE>
</HEAD>
<BODY>
<br><br><br>
<center>

<img dynsrc="eraser03.avi" start="mouseover">

<br><br>

<font size="5">
<p>This page demonstrates how you can embed video in your Web
pages even without using ActiveX controls. The HTML <img> tag has
a property called "dynsrc" that lets you specify a video clip or
VRML world to play. The "start" property lets you specify when
you want the video or virtual reality to start playing. In this
case, we set the start property so that the video would begin
when the user moved the mouse over the image control.</p>

</center>
```

```
</BODY>
</HTML>
```

The video doesn't play when the Web page first loads—only when the user passes the mouse pointer over the control. The relevant line of code is as follows:

```
<img dynsrc="eraser03.avi" start="mouseover">
```

In this **<img>** tag, we've used two new properties designed for handling video, virtual-reality simulations, and other "dynamic" images:

- **dynsrc.** This stands for "dynamic source." The **dynsrc** property is to video clips what **src** is to static images. To load a video clip, animation, or virtual-reality world, you just assign the file name (and directory path, if needed) to the **dynsrc** property of the **<img>** tag.

- **start.** This determines when the video clip (etc.) should begin to play. The default value is **fileopen**, which causes the video to begin as soon as the Web

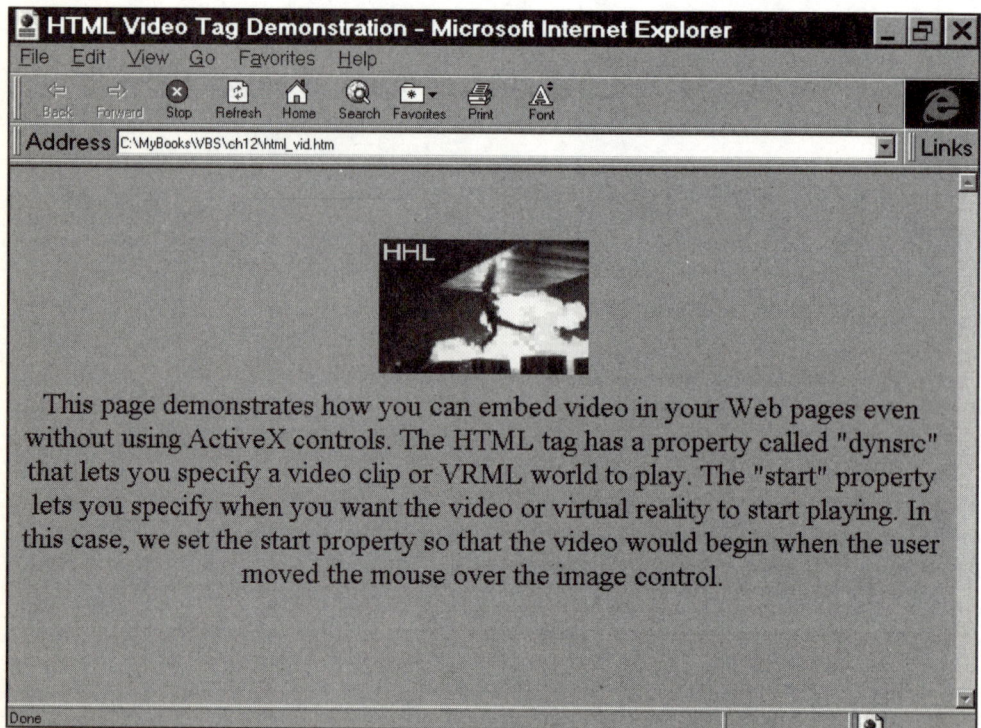

Figure 12.4
The HTML **<img>** tag can display video clips. The clip shown is from the movie *Eraser*, copyright 1996 by Warner Brothers.

page and video file have finished loading. In Listing 12.2, we used the other possible value, **mouseover**, which starts the video when the user passes the mouse pointer over the control on the Web page.

Playing Video With ActiveX

Just as with static images, ActiveX gives you a more flexible and powerful way to display video clips, animations, or virtual-reality worlds. Microsoft's ActiveMovie control (which you can download from http://www.microsoft.com) lets a user of your Web page:

- Start the video clip
- Stop the video clip
- Back up to a certain point in the video clip
- See the total length of the video clip and the current time elapsed

It also lets you, the programmer, choose the size, position, and other features of the video display. Listing 12.3 shows the HTML code for a Web page that contains an ActiveX layout with the ActiveMovie control, while Listing 12.4 shows the layout itself. Figure 12.5 shows the Web page with the video clip running. The video clip is from the movie *Eraser* and was downloaded from the CompuServe ShowbizMedia Forum.

Listing 12.3 HTML code for the Web page with the ActiveX layout.

```
<HTML>
<HEAD>
<TITLE>ActiveX Video Demonstration</TITLE>
</HEAD>
<BODY>

<OBJECT CLASSID="CLSID:812AE312-8B8E-11CF-93C8-00AA00C08FDF"
    ID="video01_alx" STYLE="LEFT:0;TOP:0">
<PARAM NAME="ALXPATH" REF
    VALUE="file:C:\MyBooks\VBS\ch12\video01.alx">
</OBJECT>

</BODY>
</HTML>
```

270 Chapter 12

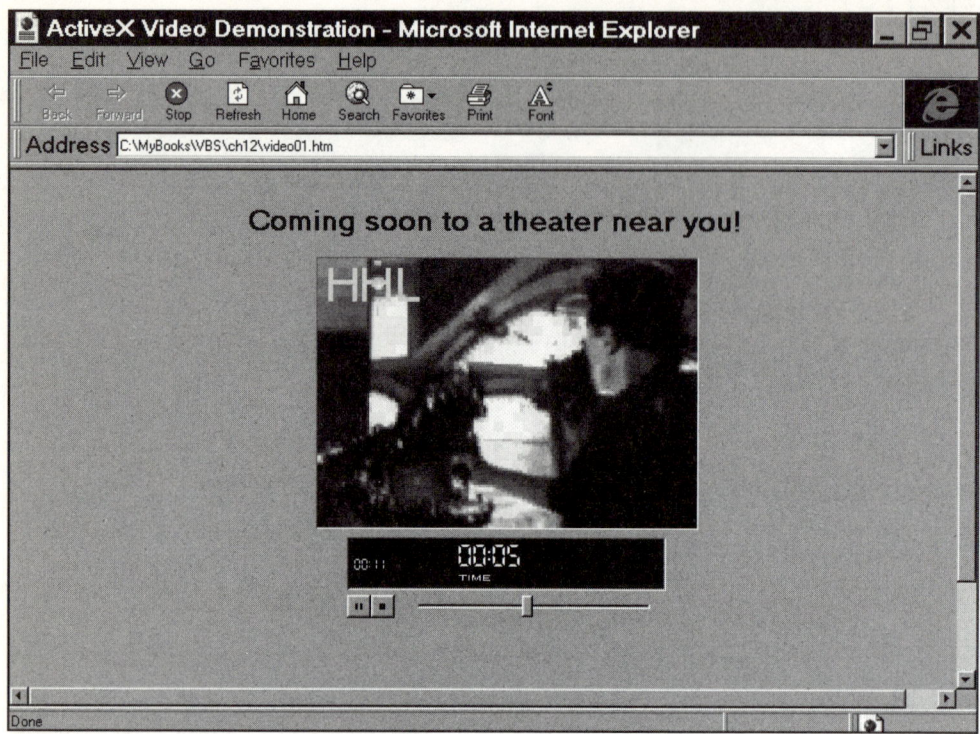

Figure 12.5
The ActiveMovie control can display video clips. The clip shown is from the movie *Eraser*, copyright 1996 by Warner Brothers.

Listing 12.4 ACTIVEX LAYOUT WITH THE ACTIVEMOVIE CONTROL.

```
<DIV ID="Layout1" STYLE="LAYOUT:FIXED;WIDTH:597pt;HEIGHT:370pt;">

    <OBJECT ID="Label1"
     CLASSID="CLSID:978C9E23-D4B0-11CE-BF2D-00AA003F40D0"
     STYLE="TOP:8pt;LEFT:140pt;WIDTH:314pt;HEIGHT:25pt;ZINDEX:0;">
        <PARAM NAME="Caption"
            VALUE="Coming soon to a theater near you!">
        <PARAM NAME="Size" VALUE="11077;882">
        <PARAM NAME="FontEffects" VALUE="1073741825">
        <PARAM NAME="FontHeight" VALUE="360">
        <PARAM NAME="FontCharSet" VALUE="0">
        <PARAM NAME="FontPitchAndFamily" VALUE="2">
        <PARAM NAME="FontWeight" VALUE="700">
    </OBJECT>
```

```
        <OBJECT ID="ActiveMovie1"
         CLASSID="CLSID:05589FA1-C356-11CE-BF01-00AA0055595A"
         STYLE="TOP:41pt;LEFT:182pt;WIDTH:237pt;
         HEIGHT:229pt;TABINDEX:1;ZINDEX:1;">
            <PARAM NAME="_ExtentX" VALUE="8361">
            <PARAM NAME="_ExtentY" VALUE="8070">
            <PARAM NAME="MovieWindowSize" VALUE="1">
            <PARAM NAME="MovieWindowWidth" VALUE="312">
            <PARAM NAME="MovieWindowHeight" VALUE="224">
            <PARAM NAME="FileName"
                VALUE="c:\mybooks\vbs\ch12\eraser03.avi">
            <PARAM NAME="Volume" VALUE="-1185">
            <PARAM NAME="Balance" VALUE="0">
        </OBJECT>
</DIV>
```

Setting up the ActiveMovie control on an ActiveX layout proceeds the same as with the image control. The main thing you need to specify is the name and location of the video clip file: You enter this information into the control's **filename** property. Beyond that, you can make the movie playback window bigger by adjusting the **moviewindowsize** property—making the window two, three, or four times the original size of the video clip image.

Playing Sound On Your Web Page

As far as sound and music go, ActiveX controls are still in their infancy. Several new ActiveX controls are being developed, such as DFL Software's Light Lib Multimedia Sound control. But the mainstay of your Web page sound and music, at least for the present, is likely to be—yes, you guessed it—HTML. The HTML **<bgsound>** tag lets you play background sound effects, spoken words, and music on your Web page.

Let's look at two simple examples. The first example will use **<bgsound>** to play a WAV file. The one I've chosen is a snippet of dialogue from the old *Dragnet* television series that I downloaded from the Web. You'll have to get your own WAV file to play, however, since I don't want to spend the next five years in court with the producers of *Dragnet*. The HTML code is shown in Listing 12.5.

Listing 12.5 USING <bgsound> TO PLAY A SIMPLE WAV FILE.

```
<HTML>
<HEAD>
<TITLE>Playing A Simple WAV Sound File</TITLE>
</HEAD>
<BODY>
<H1>Sgt. Friday speaks out on the dangers of marijuana</H1>
<bgsound src="harmless.wav">
</BODY>
</HTML>
```

There's really nothing to see, so we'll skip the usual figure showing the Web page. And since you can't *hear* the Web page talking from this book, you'll have to take it on faith that Sgt. Friday is really saying, "Marijuana is harmless." (I'm sure this was taken out of context, because Sgt. Friday would never have endorsed the use of marijuana!)

As with the **<img>** tag, you use the **src** property to specify the name of the file you want to play—adding the directory path if the file isn't in the same directory as your Web page.

The **<bgsound>** tag can also be used to play MIDI music files, as shown in Listing 12.6.

Listing 12.6 USING <bgsound> TO PLAY A MIDI FILE.

```
<HTML>
<HEAD>
<TITLE>Playing A Simple MIDI File</TITLE>
</HEAD>
<BODY>
<p>This plays the CANYON.MID sound file that comes with Windows 95.
<bgsound src="canyon.mid">
</BODY>
</HTML>
```

One other property of the **<img>** tag that you will probably want to use is the **loop** property. This property lets you specify how many times the sound file should be played. For example

```
<bgsound src="harmless.wav" loop=5>
```

will make the indefatigable Sgt. Friday say, "Marijuana is harmless" five times.

If you're playing a music file, you might want the music to play continuously as long as the user is viewing your Web page. To do that, you set the **loop** property either to **infinite** or to **–1**, as in the following:

```
<bgsound src="bach02.mid" loop="-1">
```

In either case, adding sound and music will add *a lot* of interest to your Web page.

13

A VBScript And ActiveX FAQ

Still have a question about VBScript or ActiveX? Here's where you might find the answer.

FAQ stands for Frequently Asked Questions. It's a list of questions and problems that come up over and over. In this chapter, you'll get answers to some of the questions that have been bugging VBScript users but haven't been answered in previous chapters. If you have additional questions you'd like answered in the next edition of this book, send them to me at the email address given in the Introduction.

Q: What's the difference between Visual Basic Script and Visual Basic?

A: Visual Basic Script is a subset of Visual Basic. It's designed to work inside a Web browser and work smoothly with HTML objects and controls. Because of this, it lacks the file I/O and some other advanced features offered by Visual Basic.

Q: My Web page loads too slowly. How can I speed it up?

A: Other than data transfer rates over the Web—which you can't do anything about—the most common reason for slow loading is that the Web page has too many images or the image files are too big. Try (a) cutting down on the number of images,

(b) reducing the size of the images themselves, and (c) reducing the number of colors in the image files. Any or all of those moves should considerably improve your loading time.

Q: Can I combine VBScript and JavaScript on the same Web page?

A: Yes. Just make sure that you use **<script language= "">** and **</script>** tags to enclose each separate block of script code. The **language** property is very important. If you have multiple **<script>...</script>** blocks in your HTML document and do *not* specify the language for each block, Internet Explorer assumes by default that the *first* script language you used in the document is the only one you're using. Each time you start a new **<script>** block, you must specify which script language you're using.

Q: Can I do file I/O operations in VBScript?

A: No. For reasons of Web security, VBScript doesn't support file I/O operations.

Q: How can I get the value of an HTML radio button and use it in VBScript code?

A: Just use the Internet Explorer scripting object model to guide how you refer to the radio button in VBScript. If the radio button is in an HTML form, preface the button name with the form name; if that doesn't work, try adding *document* before the form name.

Q: How can I access HTML controls from within an ActiveX layout and vice versa?

A: As before, use the Internet Explorer scripting object model to guide how you refer to controls in the HTML document and the ActiveX layout. Remember that an ActiveX layout has a name, just like an ActiveX control has a name or an HTML form can have a name. To refer to controls in an ActiveX layout from your HTML document, preface each control name with the name of the layout. To refer to controls in your HTML document from within the ActiveX layout, preface the control names with **window.document** and any other object names that are needed to locate the controls.

This same procedure, by the way, enables you to call subs and functions between HTML documents and ActiveX layouts. Just preface the name of the sub or function with the name of the object in which it resides.

Q: How can I make my Web page play a greeting based on the time of day?

A: Use the VBScript **hour()** function to identify the current system time. Then use an **if...then...else** statement to control which greeting is played for the user. For example:

```
dim Greeting
dim h

h=hour(now)

if h < 12 then
    Greeting = "sound1.wav"
else
    Greeting = "sound2.wav"
end if
document.write "<bgsound src=" & Greeting & ">"
```

Q: Can I play a WAV file when the user clicks on the Web page, but without using an ActiveX control?

A: Yes. Just embed the name of the WAV file in a hyperlink reference, as in the following code:

```
<a href="harmless.wav">Click this to hear something interesting.</a>
```

Q: How can I create a scrolling text marquee?

A: Use either the ActiveX Marquee control, included with the ActiveX Control Pad, or use the HTML **<marquee>** tag.

Q: How can I make an ActiveX layout initialize its controls and then make them perform actions?

A: Remember that, just like the **window** object in the Internet Explorer scripting object model, an ActiveX layout has an **OnLoad** event. You can put code in that event to initialize any controls in the layout and—once they're initialized—make them do things.

Q: VBScript 2 has a new function called *LoadPicture*. Do I use this function to load picture files into an ActiveX image control?

A: No, you don't need to use the **LoadPicture** function. If you're accustomed to programming in Visual Basic, you would probably expect to write code like that shown at the top of the next page.

```
imgThePicture.PicturePath = LoadPicture("myimage.bmp")
```

In VBScript, however, it is much simpler to load a picture file into an image control. Simply set the **picturepath** property of the control to the directory path (if needed) and the file name of the picture file, as follows:

```
imgThePicture.PicturePath = "myimage.bmp"
```

This code line assumes that your image file is in the same directory as your ActiveX layout and your HTML document. If the picture file is in a different location, you need to include the directory path in the text string you assign to the **picturepath** property, as follows:

```
imgThePicture.PicturePath = "f:\images\bitmaps\myimage.bmp"
```

14

A Multimedia Web Game, Part 1

VBScript isn't just for work—it's for fun. And Web games are where the fun is at.

One of the most popular types of Web page is the Web game. You've already created Trivia, Forsooth, a simple Web game that uses command buttons, label controls, and some relatively simple coding. Now, it's time to tackle a more ambitious project.

In this chapter, we'll walk through the design of a multimedia Web game called *The Haunted Mall*. You'll learn the basics of adventure game design, whether for the Web or some other medium, and will take a walk through the game we're creating here. In the next chapter, you'll learn the specific coding techniques needed to make the game come alive in the player's Web browser.

Designing The Game

The first step in creating an ambitious Web game like The Haunted Mall doesn't require a computer: You simply have to design your game. That means:

- Devising the game story.

- Laying out a map of the game rooms. This is standard in creating adventure games. Each new scene is a different "room" of the game, containing different objects and, sometimes, unexpected traps for the player.

- Determining what should happen in each room. This will depend on what the player has done, what game objects the player has in his/her possession, and the current state of the game program itself.

For The Haunted Mall, the story is simple. The player goes to meet a friend at the mall. When he/she arrives, however, the mall doors are locked. Through the glass panes in the doors, the player sees that the mall is dark and deserted. Just as the player is about to leave, a faint cry for help echoes from deep inside the darkened mall. It sounds like the player's friend.

The player must find a way to get into the mall and solve the mystery to rescue his/her friend. Along the way, there are treasures to collect and deadly traps to avoid.

Laying Out A Game Map

The next step is to lay out a game map. This map shows what each room contains, as well as what traps or treasures await the player. The player never sees this map, of course, though most experienced adventure game players will make their own maps as they play the game. The map of our mall is shown in Figure 14.1. Each room description includes the room number, a description of the room, a description of an object found in the room, and a description of a trap set in the room.

When you're coding an adventure game, a map like the one in Figure 14.1 is essential. The heart of The Haunted Mall, for example, is the **Move_Player** sub, which keeps track of the player's current room number. When the player moves—left, right, forward, or backward—the **Move_Player** sub changes the room number and calls another sub to display the new game room. Coding a sub like **Move_Player** is much easier when you have a map that shows you, at a glance, which room the player will occupy if he/she moves in a certain direction.

Doing A Walkthrough

One of the best ways to visualize your game is as a *storyboard*—essentially a comic strip that shows, in each panel, what you expect to happen and what the player is expected to see.

1. Mall entrance (doors locked).	2. Inside entrance (doors vanish).	3. Mallway (getting dark). You need light.	4. Mallway (pitch dark). Hole in floor: fall in=die.	5. CD store with CDs by Elvis Costello & The Violent Femmes.
6. Bushes by entrance (key in bushes).	7. Radio Shack (flashlight on sale).	8. Tux rental store ($40 on floor).	9. Mallway. Security guard. Shoplifted= die.	10. Joe's Hot Dogs (hot dog on sale).
11. Women's rest room (graffiti about the author).	12. Men's rest room (graffiti, flood).	13. Arcade with hot new game: Crowther's Castle.	14. Mallway.	15. Bookstore (*VBScript 2 & ActiveX Programming* on sale).
16. Mallway (sign on wall).	17. Mallway.	18. Mallway (live wire hangs from ceiling).	19. Mallway (guard dog: feed him or die).	20. Granny's Porno Palace.
21. Hardware store (rubber gloves on sale).	22. Aerobics studio.	23. Movie theatre ("Beaches" on five screens).	24. Donut shop.	25. Secret room.

Figure 14.1
The game map for The Haunted Mall.

Ordinarily, of course, your game won't be completed at this stage. In this case, however, the game is already done, so our storyboard will be a walkthrough of the entire game and will give us the same information as a well-thought-out storyboard. If you need to get your bearings as we walk through the game, refer to the game map in Figure 14.1.

Beginning The Game

At the beginning of the game, the player arrives at the mall and sees a welcome screen, shown in Figure 14.2.

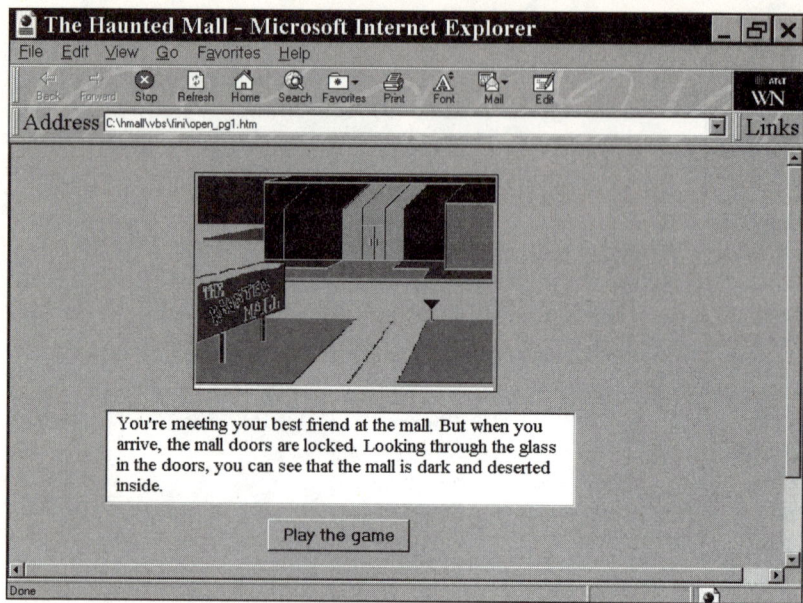

Figure 14.2
The opening screen of the game.

The layout of this screen differs somewhat from the main screen, so we'll need a separate Web page and HTML layout for it. The opening page shows a distant view of the mall and, in a text box, tells the *backstory* of the game—i.e., everything that's happened up to the time the player arrived at the mall. The backstory will display one paragraph at a time, so we'll use a timer control to display each paragraph and pause for a few seconds before displaying the next paragraph.

After the backstory is finished, the player clicks on the Play The Game button to load the Web page containing the main game screen, shown in Figure 14.3.

The room is displayed in the center of the Web page, with a text description underneath the picture. To perform an action, the player clicks on one of the buttons at the left. To move, the player clicks on one of the arrow buttons at the bottom. As the game progresses, the player's score, number of turns taken, and amount of cash are displayed at the lower left. Any game objects that the player picks up are displayed at the right, under *Inventory*.

When the game starts, the mall doors are locked. The player unsuccessfully tries to go forward, left, and backward; he/she can only go right, moving to Room 6,

A Multimedia Web Game, Part 1   283

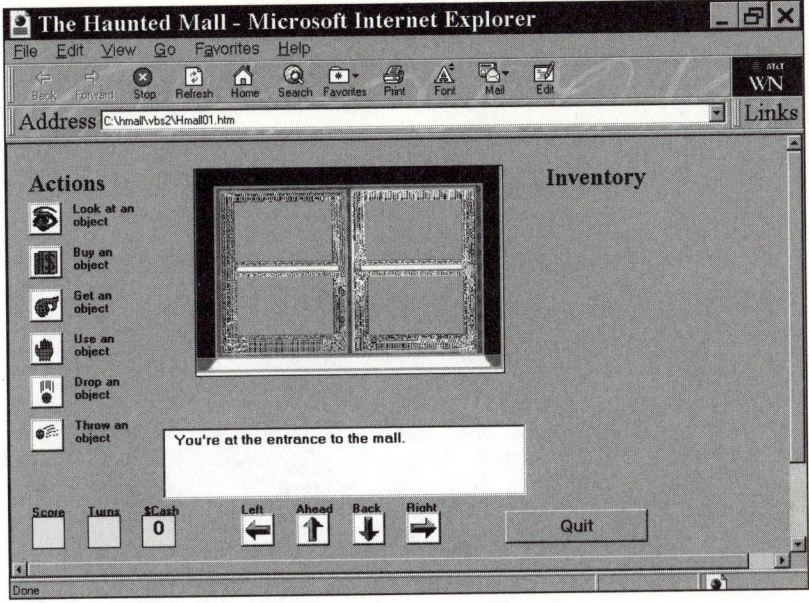

Figure 14.3
The main game screen in Room 1 of The Haunted Mall.

shown in Figure 14.4. Apart from Room 1, where the game begins, this is the only game room outside the mall.

There are a couple new things in this screen. First, both the Score and the Turns labels have been updated. The player has taken a turn, and, by moving to a previously unvisited room, has earned a point.

Second, and more obvious, there's a game object displayed under the room scene. To pick up this object, the player clicks on the Get An Object button at the left, then clicks on the object. When the player does this, the object disappears from the room and appears in the player's inventory, as shown in Figure 14.5. The player's score also increases by three points for picking up the object.

By clicking on the Look At An Object button, then on the object in inventory, the player gets a close-up view of the object he/she has just obtained, as shown in Figure 14.6. The object is displayed for five seconds, then the room scene reappears. (This process, as you might have guessed, is run by a timer control and associated VBScript embedded in the HTML layout.)

284 Chapter 14

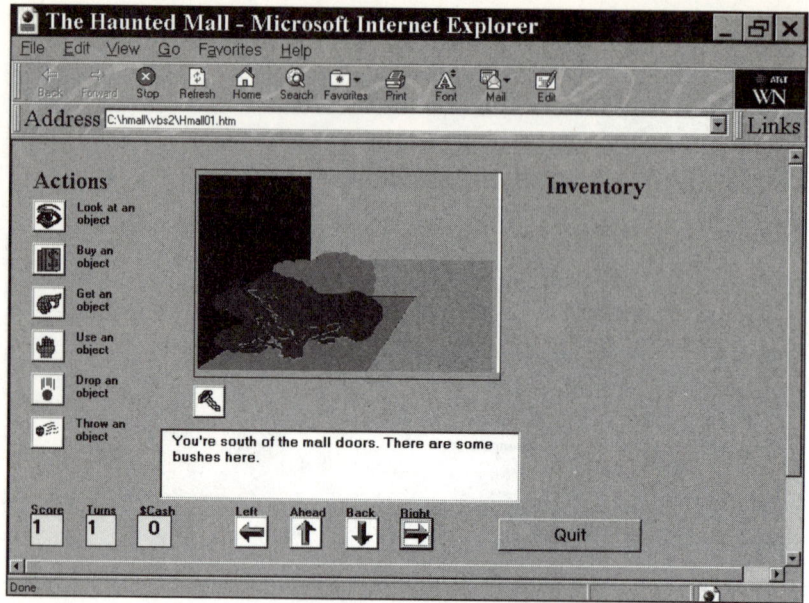

Figure 14.4
Room 6 of The Haunted Mall.

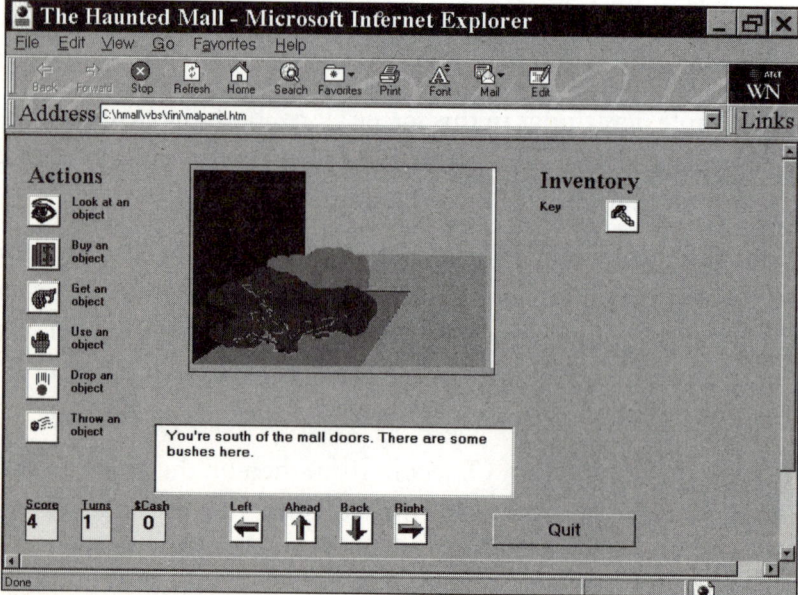

Figure 14.5
An object appears in the player's inventory.

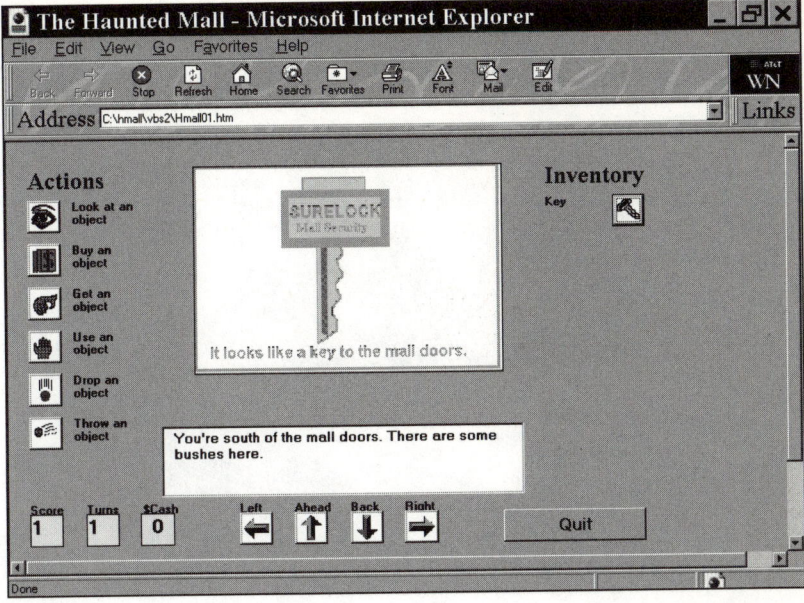

Figure 14.6
A close-up view of an inventory object.

The player then clicks the back-arrow button to return to Room 1. By clicking on the Use An Object button, then on the key in inventory, the player unlocks the mall doors.

Entering The Mall

The first mall room is in the deserted mallway, as shown in Figure 14.7. The text underneath the room informs the player that there is a Radio Shack to the south. At this point, the player can go into Radio Shack and take a flashlight—there's nobody around. However, taking a flashlight is shoplifting, and most computer games take a dim view of such activity. If the player shoplifts, a trap is triggered that, later in the game, proves fatal.

To escape the trap, the player must move forward one room, then turn right into a tuxedo rental shop. On the floor, someone has dropped a wad of cash, as shown in Figure 14.8. The player simply picks up the money, then returns to Radio Shack to buy the flashlight by clicking on the Buy An Object button, and then clicking on the flashlight underneath the room scene. Radio Shack is shown in Figure 14.9.

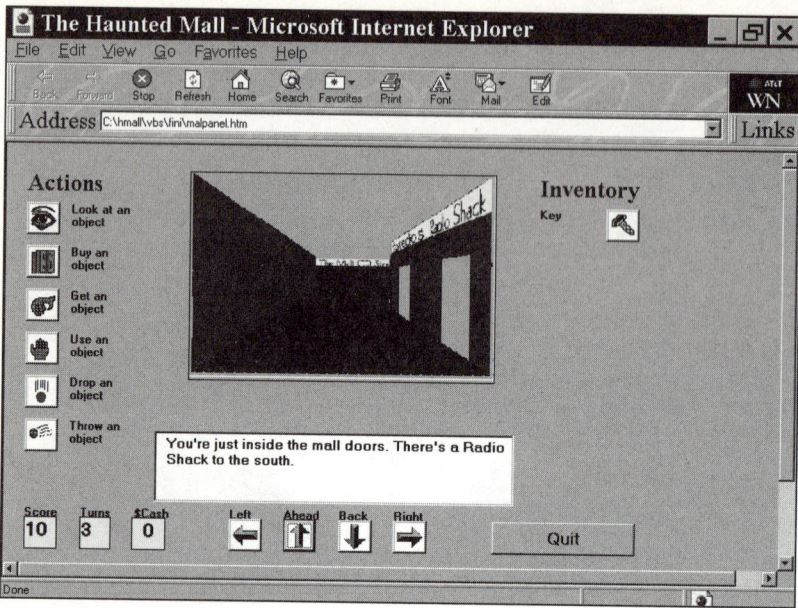

Figure 14.7
The first room inside the mall.

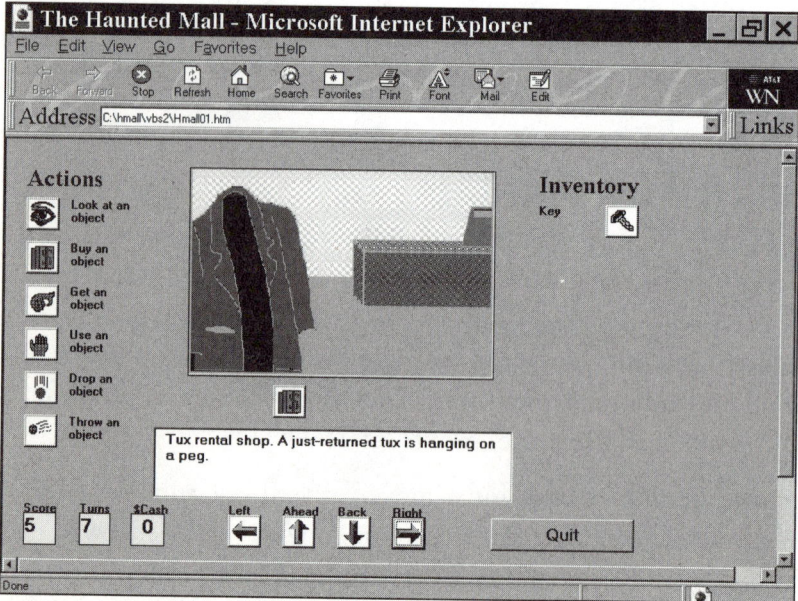

Figure 14.8
The tuxedo rental shop: Someone dropped a wad of cash!

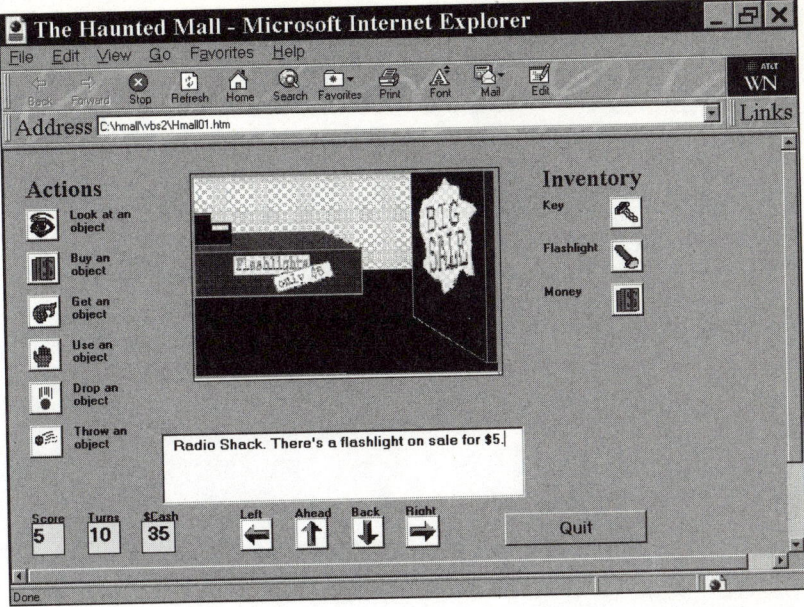

Figure 14.9
Back in Radio Shack to buy the flashlight.

Avoiding The Pit

Next, the player encounters the first trap in the game: a hole in the floor that opens down into a deadly pit. The player needed a flashlight to navigate the darkened mall, but *having* the flashlight isn't enough. To avoid the pit, the player must *use* the flashlight by clicking on the Use An Object button and then on the Flashlight inventory item. That turns on the flashlight, enabling the player to see and avoid the hole, shown in Figure 14.10.

The player must use the flashlight before he/she reaches Room 4. Otherwise, it's the pit, player dead, game over. A "crash" image appears in the room scene and "You're dead" appears in the text box under the scene.

If the player avoids the pit, then straight ahead is a CD store. Nothing much is happening in the CD store, so the player backs out of the store and goes south down the mallway. To the player's left is Joe's Hot Dogs, shown in Figure 14.11, where the player should buy a hot dog for $2.

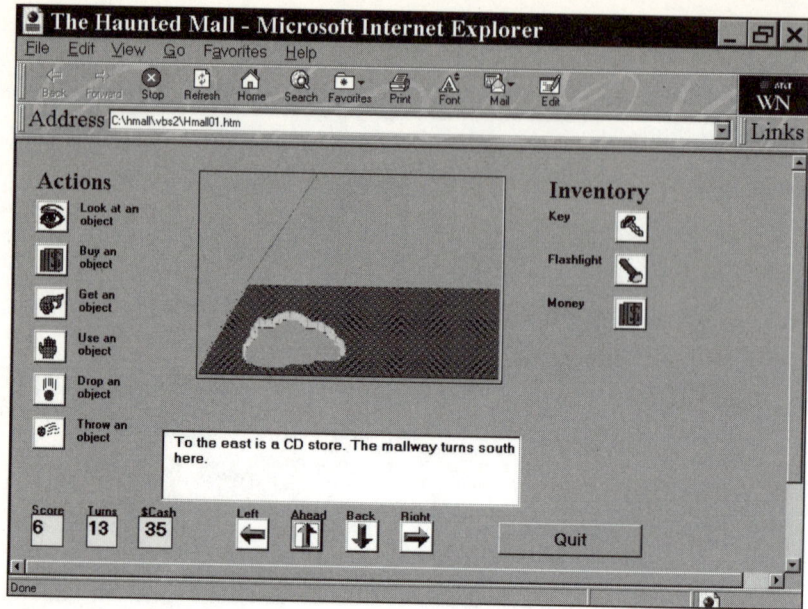

Figure 14.10
The game's first trap is a hole in the floor.

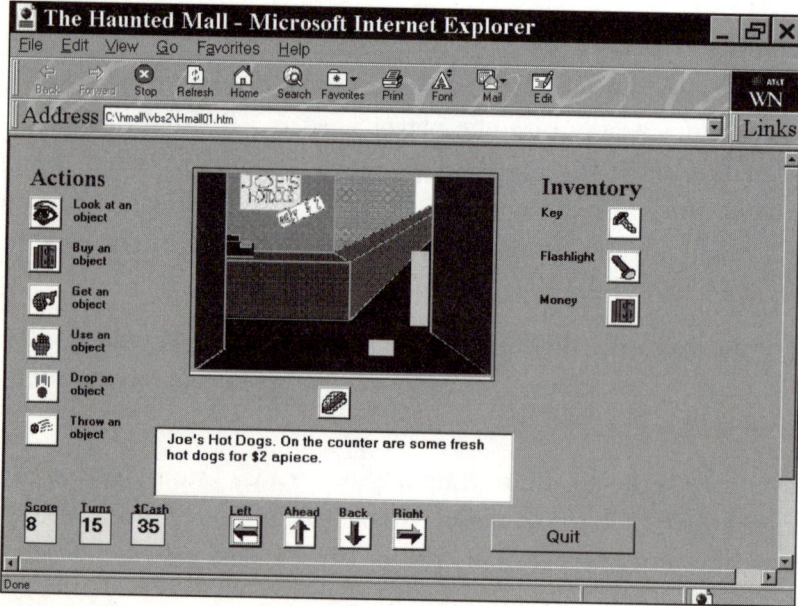

Figure 14.11
Joe's Hot Dogs, where the player buys a hot dog.

More Deadly Traps To Avoid

As the player tries to move from Room 9 south to Room 14, the game's second trap is triggered: a "ghostly security guard," shown in Figure 14.12. If the player simply *took* the flashlight from Radio Shack instead of paying for it, the security guard arrests the player for shoplifting. Unfortunately, this security guard has seen *Maniac Cop* 700 times and is, shall we say, a bit over-enthusiastic about his work. He does not just arrest the player, but he beats him/her to a bloody pulp, ending the game.

If the player paid for the flashlight, however, the security guard doesn't appear. The player can proceed to Room 14, the part of the mallway just outside the bookstore, shown in Figure 14.13. The bookstore is selling a hot new book called *VBScript 2 & ActiveX Programming*, which the player can see close up, as shown in Figure 14.14.

Because the player has already passed the ghostly security guard in Room 9, he/she can now simply take the book if needed. The book contains a hint about how to solve the game-within-a-game that's at the end of The Haunted Mall.

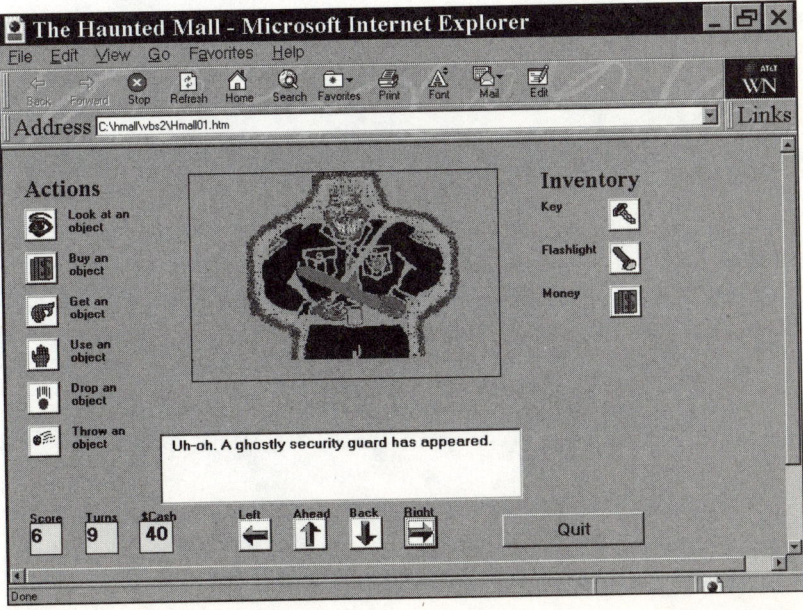

Figure 14.12
A ghostly security guard threatens the player.

290 Chapter 14

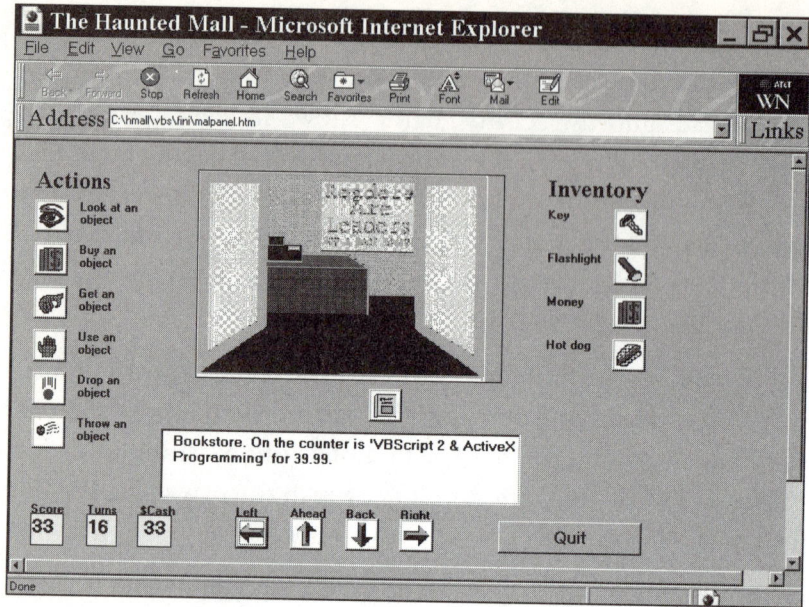

Figure 14.13
A bookstore that stocks only the best books.

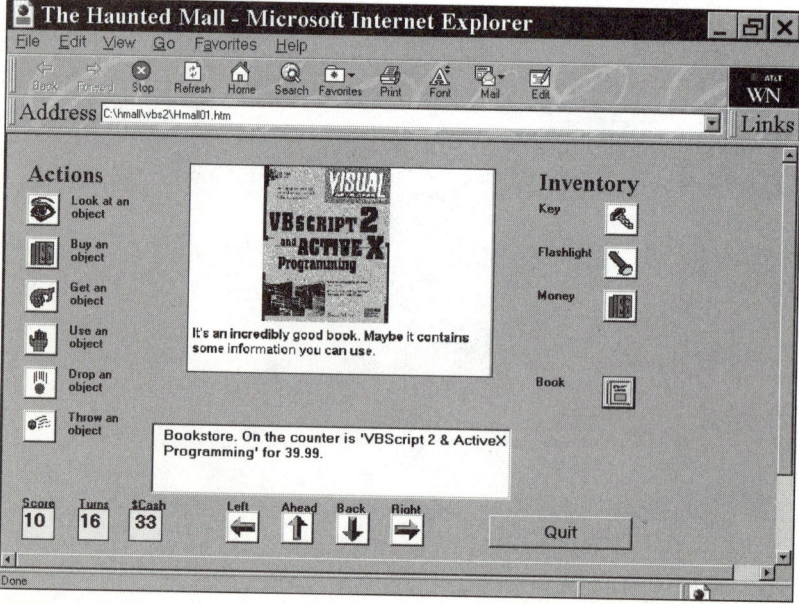

Figure 14.14
A close-up of the book you're reading.

After backing out of the bookstore, the player tries to proceed south to Room 19. But there's another hazard: a ghostly guard dog, shown in Figure 14.15, that won't let the player pass.

Once the guard dog is visible, the player can't move in any direction. No matter which way the player tries to move, the guard dog blocks the way, growling. If the player can't get rid of the guard dog, the game is over. However, if the player bought a hot dog at Joe's, he/she can feed it to the guard dog. After the guard dog is fed, he goes to sleep.

Proceeding south to Room 19, the player comes to the final bend in the mall. Ahead is a donut shop, while to the left is Granny's Porno Palace. If the player turns right, going around the bend in the mallway, he/she ends up in Room 18. A live electric wire hangs from the ceiling, as shown in Figure 14.16.

If the player tries to get the wire, the result is predictable: electrocution, shown in Figure 14.17. It seems that picking up a live electric wire barehanded is not such a good idea. The player must look further in the mall to find something with which to get the wire safely.

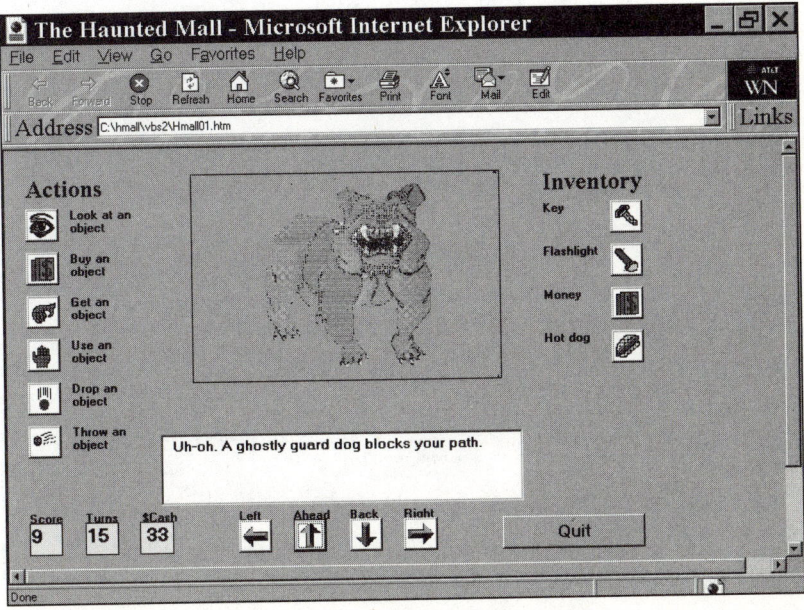

Figure 14.15
A ghostly guard dog blocks the way, growling.

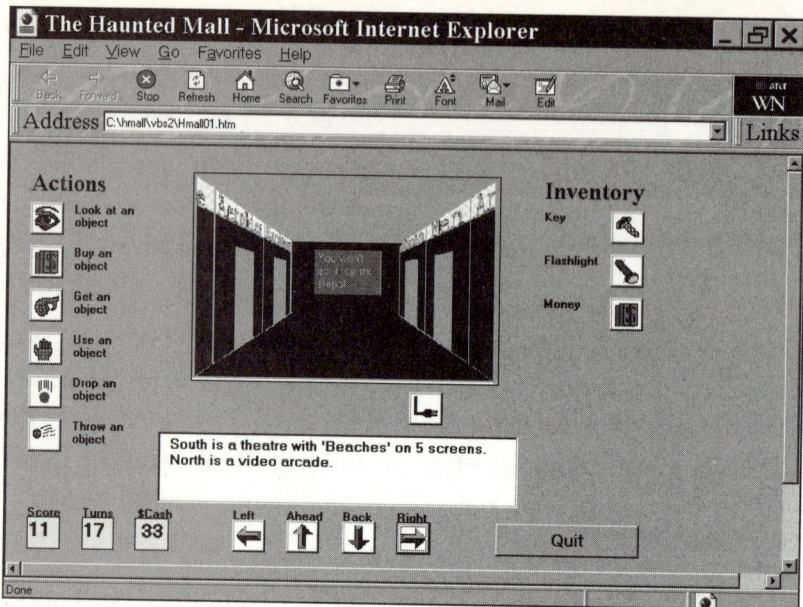

Figure 14.16
A live wire hangs from the ceiling.

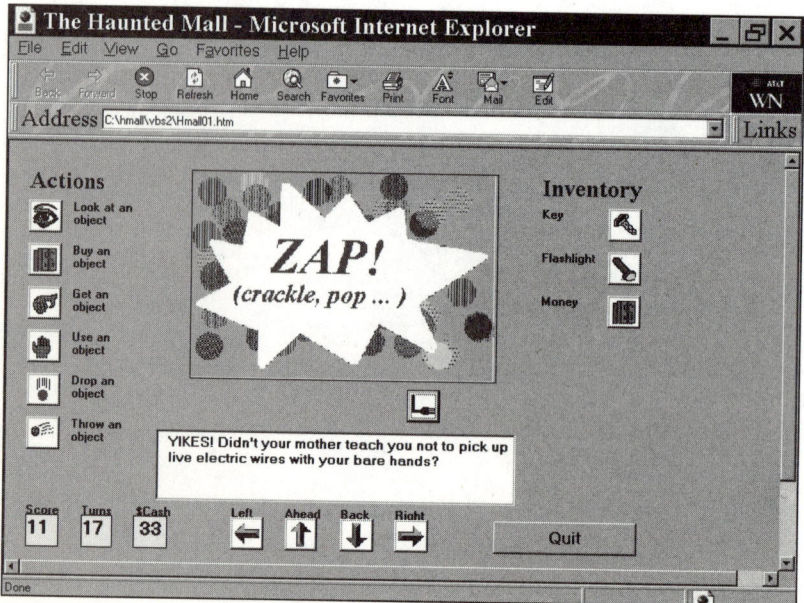

Figure 14.17
Even in a game, one shouldn't pick up live electric wires barehanded.

Winning The Game

If the player is smart enough to avoid picking up the wire, he/she can proceed west in the mallway to Room 16, a dead end, as shown in Figure 14.18. On the wall in front of the player is a sign that says, "You won't get it up the steps!" That's a homage to the grand-daddy of all adventure game programs, Will Crowther's classic 1970s text-only game, Adventure, which contains an identical sign.

To the south is a hardware store, shown in Figure 14.19. Luckily for the player, the store is selling rubber gloves—perfect for picking up the wire in Room 18. After buying or taking the gloves, the player must remember to use them before picking up the wire. When the player uses the gloves, the game displays a message: "You are now wearing rubber gloves."

The player then proceeds back to Room 18, a backward view of which is shown in Figure 14.20. Because this is a player-point-of-view game, many of the rooms have both forward and backward views. Which one displays on the player's screen depends on which way the player is facing in the mall.

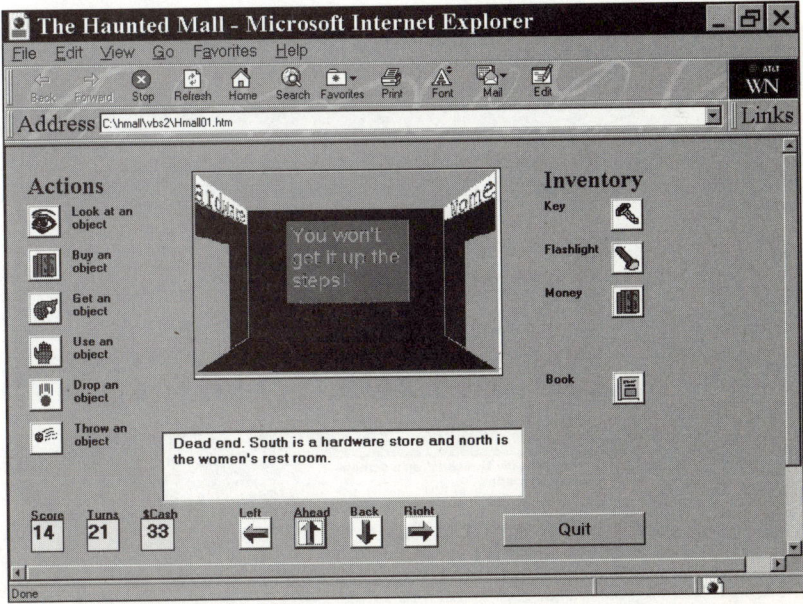

Figure 14.18
A dead end in the mallway.

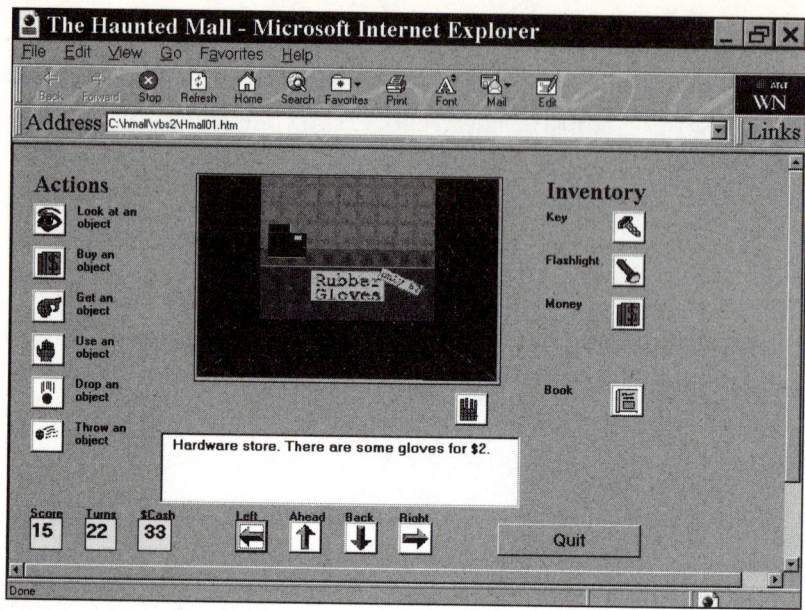

Figure 14.19
A hardware store that sells rubber gloves.

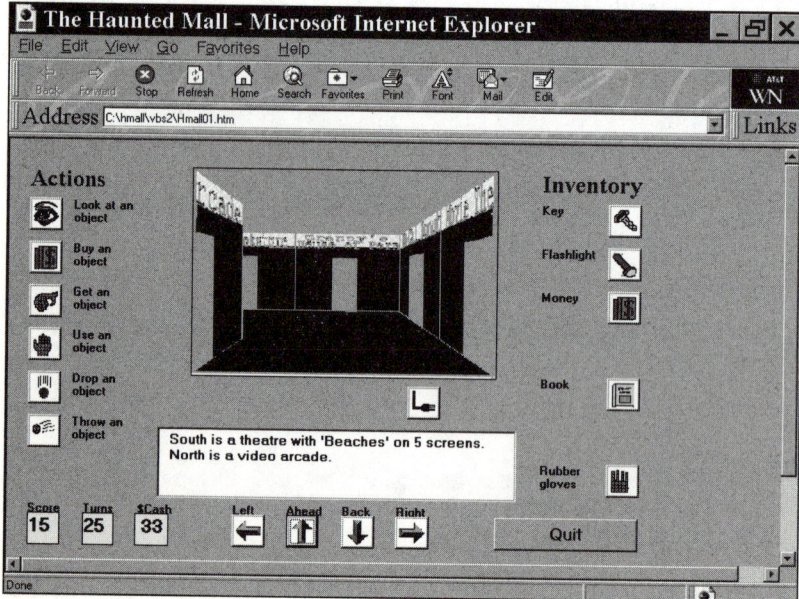

Figure 14.20
A backward view of Room 18. The player can now get the live wire.

A Multimedia Web Game, Part 1

The player can now pick up the live wire. But what good is it? That becomes evident when the player enters Room 13, a video arcade: The game Crowther's Castle is unplugged, as shown in Figure 14.21.

To play Crowther's Castle—which is the only way to win The Haunted Mall—the player must use the wire to plug in the video game. Then, the player must use money from inventory: The game costs $1 to play. When the player uses the money, Crowther's Castle begins, as shown in Figure 14.22.

In Crowther's Castle, the player starts in the Hall of the Mountain King, confronted by a huge green snake with giant fangs. This is another homage to the original Adventure game, which featured the same snake, albeit 20 years younger and a bit thinner. If the player is familiar with the original Adventure, he/she knows that the way to deal with the snake is to free the little bird, which in an astounding flurry attacks the snake and drives it away.

However, not everyone has played the original Adventure, so The Haunted Mall contains a hint. By using *VBScript 2 & ActiveX Programming,* the player can read a page from this book—in fact, this very page, as shown in Figure 14.23.

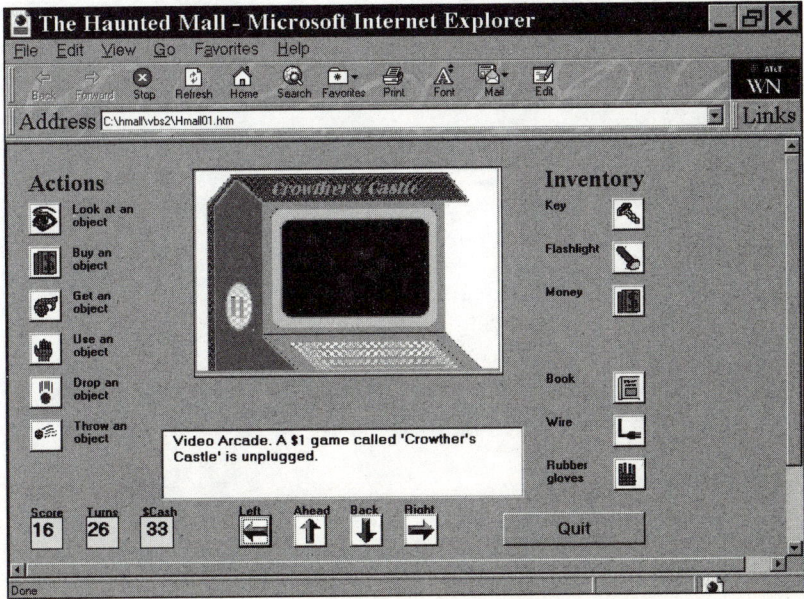

Figure 14.21
A new video game is unplugged.

296   Chapter 14

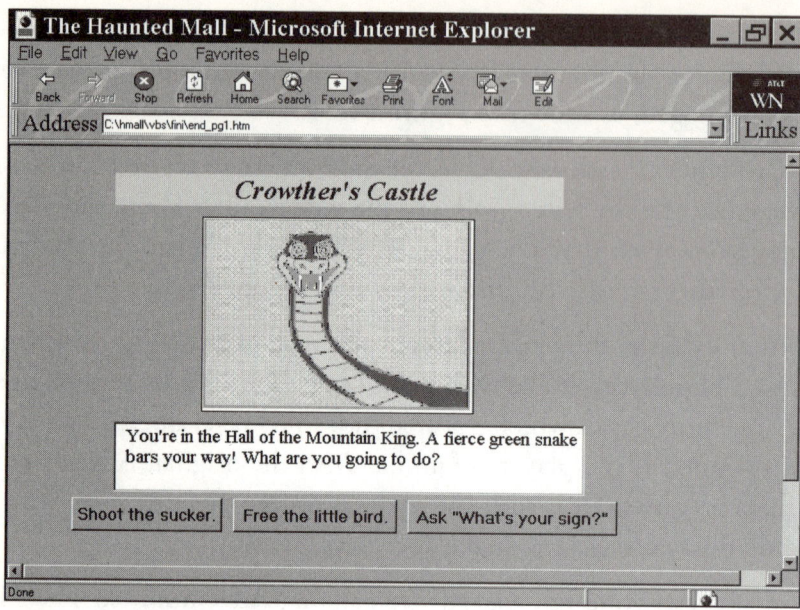

Figure 14.22
The Crowther's Castle game page.

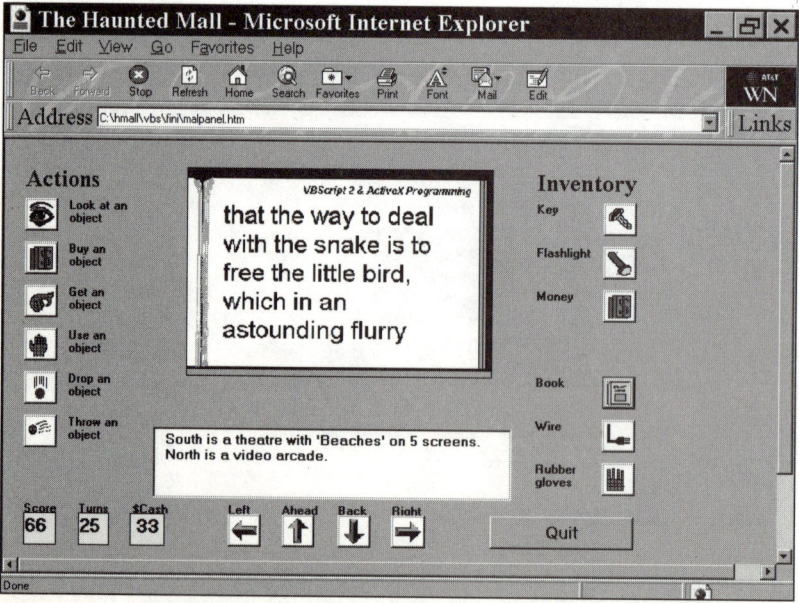

Figure 14.23
In the game, the player views the very page you just read.

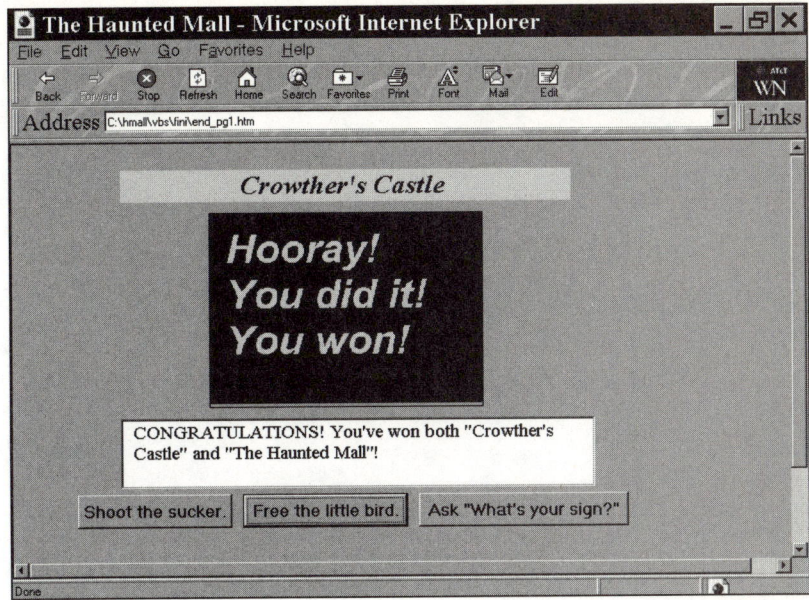

Figure 14.24
Congratulating the player for winning the game.

When the player finally vanquishes the snake, Crowther's Castle is won and the player sees the screen in Figure 14.24. In The Haunted Mall, a voice intones, "This is King Crowther speaking." The voice congratulates the player on solving the mystery of The Haunted Mall and winning the game.

Designing The Game Pages

That's the overall play structure of the game. To pull it off, we'll need three Web pages—as usual, HTML documents containing HTML layouts with ActiveX controls and VBScript code:

- A Web page to open and explain the game
- A Web page for the main game panel
- A Web page for the concluding sequence

In the next chapter, we'll see how to design and code these pages, making each load the next when needed. We'll also look at how to use timer controls to create slide shows and implement a **Move_Player** sub that can be modified for almost any Web adventure game.

15 Coding The Haunted Mall

The overall design got you started. Now, it's time to write the VBScript code that makes The Haunted Mall work.

Now that you've got the "lay of the land," so to speak, it's time to create the code that runs The Haunted Mall. The code will need to move the player from room to room, display appropriate room images, keep track of game objects, spring traps, and update the player's score.

In the course of creating the game code, you'll learn quite a bit about programming tricks with VBScript and, by extension, about Visual Basic generally. In particular, you'll learn how to:

- Create a large program project with VBScript
- Use multidimensional arrays to store and retrieve complex information
- Use timer controls to create slide shows with text and images
- Update Web page controls "on the fly" as your script runs
- Use multiple command buttons to create complex events

- Use the Microsoft Internet Explorer scripting object model to make an ActiveX control load a new Web page
- Use VBScript constants to make your program *much* easier to follow

Setting Up The Game Pages

The game pages are fairly easy to set up. As we discussed in Chapter 14, there are three pages:

- The intro page, which tells the backstory and opens the game
- The main game page, where the action of the game takes place
- The end-sequence page, where the player wins the game

Creating The Intro With The Timer And **Window.Location**

Let's look at each page in turn. The first is the intro page, shown in Figure 15.1.

This is a very simple ActiveX layout. It contains four controls:

- An image control to hold the picture of the mall
- A text box control to display the text that introduces the game
- A command button, which the user clicks to exit from the intro page and load the main game page
- A timer control, which controls the slide-show display of text that introduces the game

There's nothing remarkable about either the image control or the text box control. The command button and timer controls, however, are a little more interesting. The command button's **Click** event contains a single code line:

```
window.location = "malpanel.htm"
```

This line uses the browser window's **location** property to load a different HTML document into the Web browser. It can be used any time an ActiveX control needs to load a Web page different from the current one. All that's needed is to load the new URL into the **location** property. In this case, the URL is simply

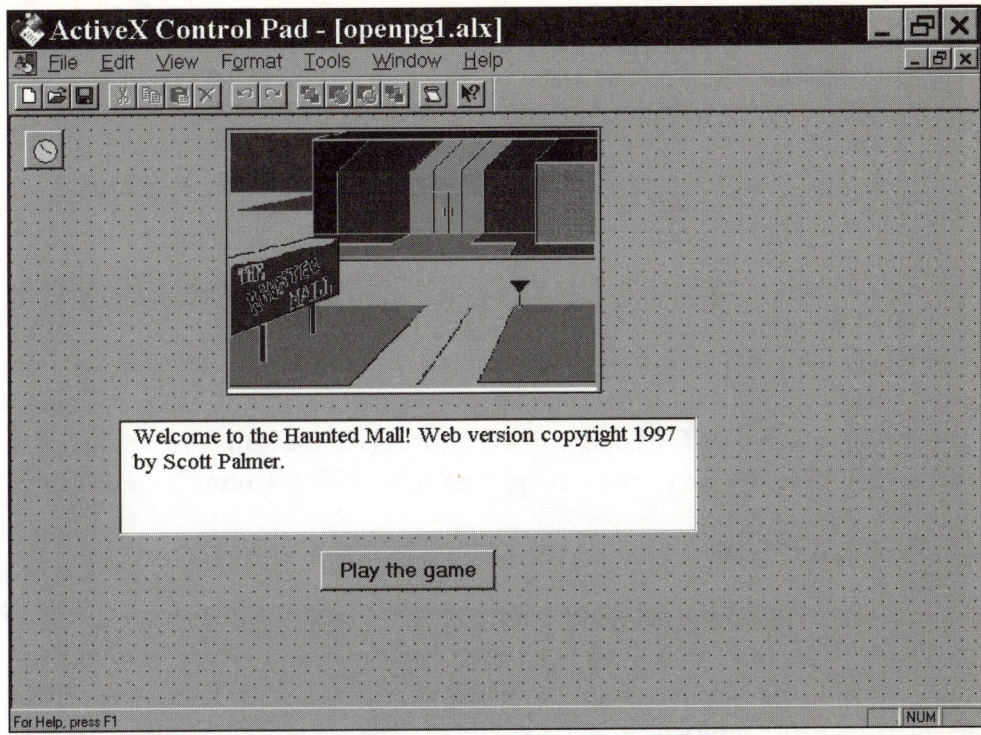

Figure 15.1
The Web page that introduces the game.

the name of a file in the same directory as the current Web page, so it's simpler than loading a page from a different Web site. Nonetheless, the same technique applies.

The timer—more formally, the **IeTimer** control—uses a technique that we'll see several more times in the course of the game. In case you need a quick refresher course about timer controls, the timer fires a "timer event" at intervals you specify in milliseconds. Thus, if you set the timer's **interval** property to 1500, the timer event will fire every 1.5 seconds, or 1,500 milliseconds. And every time the timer event fires, the code inside the event is executed. The code for the intro page timer is:

```
Sub IeTimer1_Timer()
    TimeCount = TimeCount + 1
    select case TimeCount
```

```
         case 1: tbScene = "You're meeting your best friend at the " & _
            "mall. But when you arrive, the mall doors are locked. " & _
            "Looking through the glass in the doors, you can see that " & _
            "the mall is dark and deserted inside."
         case 2: tbScene = "Just as you're about to leave, you " & _
            "hear a faint cry for help. It seems to come from " & _
            "deep inside the mall--and it sounds like your friend!"
            IeTimer1.enabled = false
      end select
end sub
```

The **TimeCount** variable is the key to our timer trick. It's declared outside the timer event sub so that it retains its value between calls to the sub. When the intro page first loads and its **OnLoad** event fires, it sets **TimeCount** to a value of 0. Then, each time the timer event fires, the value of **TimeCount** increases by 1:

```
TimeCount = TimeCount + 1
```

The current value of **TimeCount** controls which text is displayed in the intro page's text box. On the first pass through the timer event code, **TimeCount** equals 1, and the first paragraph is displayed. Five seconds later—we set the **IeTimer** control's **interval** property to 5000—the timer event fires again. The value of **TimeCount** is bumped up to 2, and the second paragraph displays. The last line of the **case 2** case sets the **IeTimer**'s **enabled** property to **false**, thereby turning off the timer and preventing any future ticks of the timer event.

At this point, the Web page just sits there, waiting for the user to click on the Play The Game button.

Creating The Main Game Page

The main game page has lots more controls than the intro page, but it isn't complicated in principle. The page is shown in Figure 15.2.

The first thing you might notice about the main game page is that each of the game object buttons appears twice: first under the room scene and then in the Inventory column. This reflects the way we put game objects in rooms and, if the player picks them up, "move" them to the player's inventory.

When the game page first loads, the **visible** property of all these game object buttons is set to **false**. When the player moves to a room where a game object is

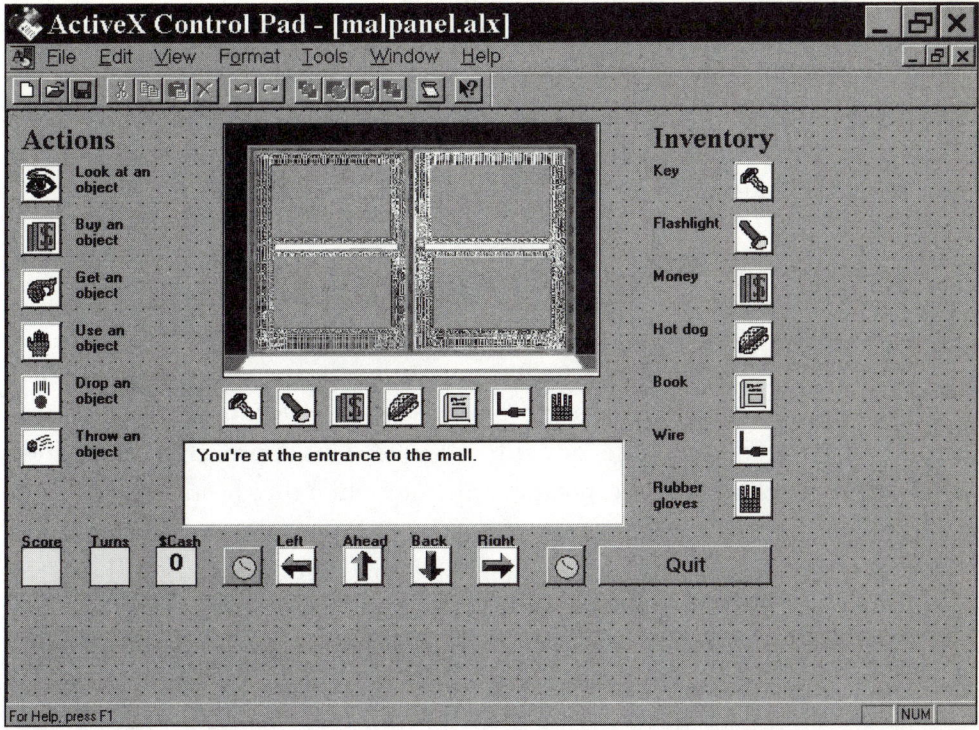

Figure 15.2
The main game page.

located, the program code sets the appropriate room object control's **visible** property to **true**. This causes the object to appear under the room scene. When the user gets the object, either by getting it or buying it, the room object control's **visible** property is set back to **false**, causing it to disappear from underneath the room scene. At the same time, the corresponding inventory object control's **visible** property is set to **true**, causing the object to appear in the player's inventory.

There are two timers on the game page. The first timer controls the various traps in the game, while the second controls the display of game objects in the room scene window when the player clicks on the Look At An Object button.

Two of the action buttons (Drop An Object and Throw An Object) and the Quit button aren't implemented here. They are left as an exercise for the reader. The logic of the Drop and Throw action buttons is the same as that for all the other action buttons; the Quit button can use the **window.location** property to load a different Web page.

Creating The End-Sequence Page

The end-sequence page, shown in Figure 15.3, has essentially the same design as the intro page. An image control displays the snake. When the player clicks a button, the timer control displays either the "You've won!" sequence or the "You're dead!" sequence.

Creating The Program Framework

The next step is to give the main game page some skeleton code to which you can add more substantive code, one sub at a time. This approach has a decided advantage: At each step, you can catch any bugs while they're still easy to find. If you know that the framework program is working right and adding a sub causes the program to malfunction, then you know that the flaw must be in the

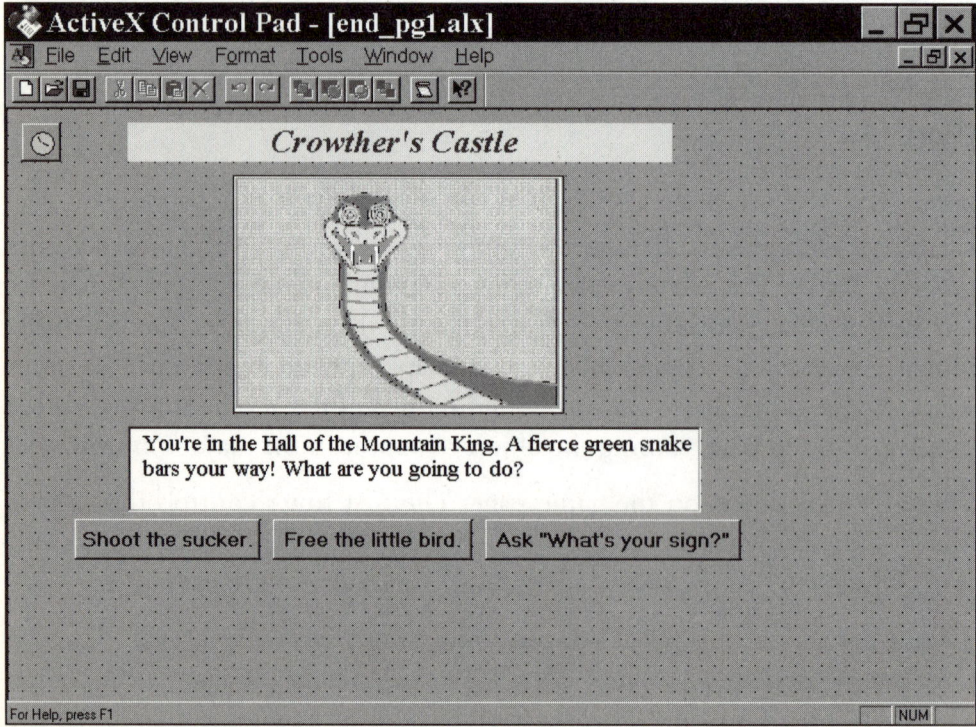

Figure 15.3
The end-sequence page.

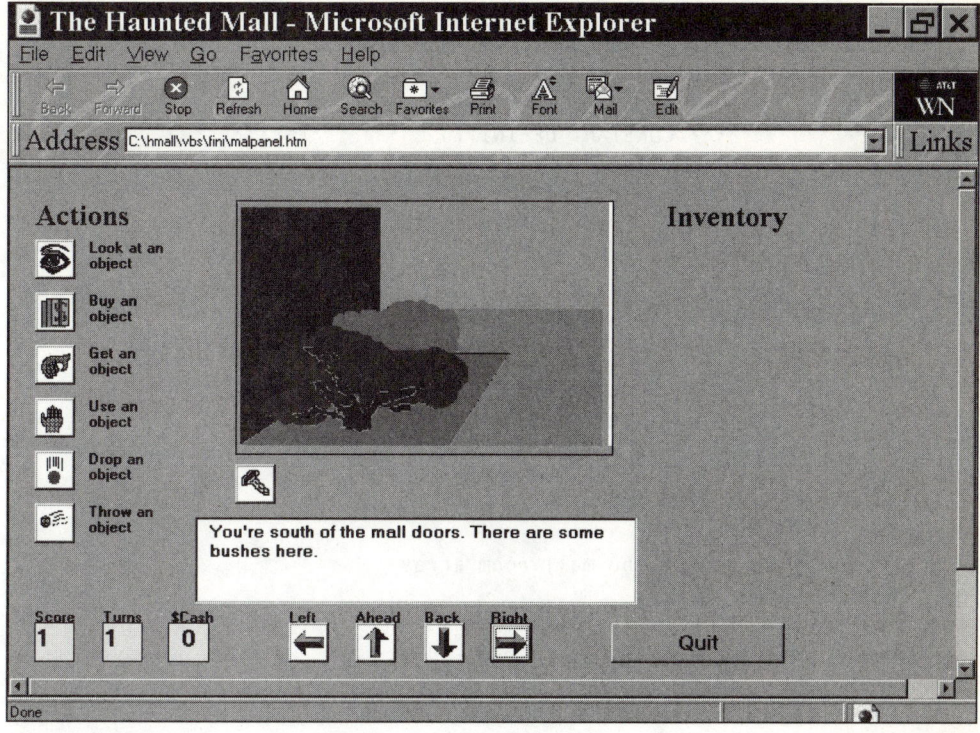

Figure 15.4
The main game page created by the framework layout.

new sub. As long as you add subs one at a time and test the program each time to verify that it still works, debugging your code will be easy.

Therefore, let's take a look at a code framework for the main game page. The VBScript code from the ActiveX layout is shown in Listing 15.1. The page created by the layout is shown in Figure 15.4.

Listing 15.1 FRAMEWORK CODE FOR THE MAIN GAME PAGE.

```
<!--Malpan01.ALX:
This version sets up the
game window layout and the
code framework for the game
script.
-->
<SCRIPT LANGUAGE="VBScript">
<!--
option explicit
```

```
' VARIABLE AND CONSTANT DECLARATIONS
' This script module declares public variables and
' constants for the game program.
'
' ********************* CONSTANT DEFINITIONS *****************
Const room_min = 1
Const room_max = 25
Const MaxInventory = 7
Const InInventory = 100

' Definitions for the slots of the player state array
Const score = 0
Const turns = 1
Const alive = 2
Const lit = 3
Const gloved = 4
Const shoplifted = 5
'
' Definitions for rows of the mall room array
Const RoomText = 0
Const RoomFView = 1
Const RoomBView = 2
Const RoomVisited = 3
'
' Definitions for the slots of the maze state array
Const DoorOpen = 0
Const dogfed = 1
Const gameon = 2
Const SecretDoorOpen = 3

' Definitions for the objects in the game
Const keys = 0
Const flashlight = 1
Const money = 2
Const hotdog = 3
Const book = 4
Const wire = 5
Const gloves = 6
'
'
' ************************ ROOM INFORMATION *****************
' In Visual Basic, we would use a TYPE...END TYPE declaration to create
' a data structure that would hold information about the rooms in the
' game. VBScript, however, does not support TYPE...END TYPE. Therefore,
' we will use a two-dimensional array to hold the room information. The
' first row of the array will contain text descriptions of each room. In
' the second and third rows, each array slot will contain the image file
```

```
' name for either the forward or backward view of the room. The final
' row contains a true/false slot indicating whether or not the player has
' visited the room.

' Rooms in the mall are arranged as follows:
'  1  2  3  4  5
'  6  7  8  9 10
' 11 12 13 14 15
' 16 17 18 19 20
' 21 22 23 24 25

dim MallArray(26,4)

' *********************** VARIABLE DECLARATIONS *****************
dim UserChoice
dim Action
dim GameObject
dim RoomNumber
dim Forward    ' T/F: Is player going forward in mall?
dim PicPath    ' holds the directory path for game images, if needed
dim TimeCount  ' counts ticks of the IeTimer event

' Boolean variables to show if an action button
' is currently being used. When the player clicks
' the action button, the variable is set to true.
' When the player clicks on the object of the action,
' the variable is set back to false.
dim LookAtObject
dim BuyAnObject
dim GetAnObject
dim UseAnObject
dim ThrowAnObject

' In VB, array slots can start at numbers other than 0.
' Thus, it was possible to start array slots at 1, using
' code such as dim Inventory(keys to gloves). In VBScript,
' however, all arrays start at 0, so we simply use the highest
' number in a group of objects to be the top slot in the array.
dim Inventory(10)
dim ObjectVisible(10)
dim GameObjLoc(7)
dim Maze(4)
dim Player(5)

-->
</SCRIPT>
<SCRIPT LANGUAGE="VBScript">
```

```
<!--
' GLOBAL SUBS AND FUNCTIONS
' DoSetup, Move, etc.
Sub DoSetup

' Declare local variables to control initialization loops.
Dim i, j

' *********** INITIALIZE GAME ROOM ARRAY ****************

' *********** INITIALIZE PLAYERSTATE() ARRAY ************

' *********** INITIALIZE MAZE() ARRAY *******************

' *********** INITIALIZE INVENTORY ARRAY ****************

' *********** INITIALIZE ObjectVisible ARRAY ************

' *********** INITIALIZE Action Button values ***********

' *********** SET STARTING LOCATION *********************

end sub

' THE MOVE_PLAYER SUB
Sub Move_Player (direction)
' This sub checks the current room number. Then, it checks to see
' which direction button the player clicked. Based on that data, it
' either moves the player to a new room and calls the NewRoom sub,
' or performs some other action, such as making the player fall into
' a pit.

    Select Case roomnumber
        Case 1:
        Case 2:
        Case 3:
        Case 4:
        Case 5:
        Case 6:
        Case 7:
        Case 8:
        Case 9:
        Case 10:
        Case 11:
        Case 12:
        Case 13:
        Case 14:
```

```
                Case 15:
                Case 16:
                Case 17:
                Case 18:
                Case 19:
                Case 20:
                Case 21:
                Case 22:
                Case 23:
                Case 24:
                Case Else
                    MsgBox "Error in Move routine!", , "The Haunted Mall"
        End Select
        MsgBox "The Move_Player sub has run.",,"The Haunted Mall"
End Sub

Sub NewRoom ()
' This sub should do several things:
'   1. Display the correct image in the ScenePicture control.
'   2. Display the room description in the Lbl_Scene control.
'   3. Display the new score in the Lbl_Score control.
'   4. Display the new number of turns taken in the Lbl_Turns control.
'   5. Update the score and number of turns?
'       The score only increases if the room hasn't yet been visited.
'       The number of turns should be updated in the command processor,
'       because each command takes a turn -- not just moving.

End Sub

-->
</SCRIPT>
<SCRIPT LANGUAGE="VBScript">
<!--
Sub Scene_MouseDown(Button, Shift, X, Y)
    msgbox "There's nothing you can get here.",,"The Haunted Mall"
end sub
-->
</SCRIPT>
<SCRIPT LANGUAGE="VBScript">
<!--
Sub cmdBuy_Click()
    MsgBox "The Buy An Object button has been clicked." _
        ,,"The Haunted Mall"
end sub
-->
</SCRIPT>
<SCRIPT LANGUAGE="VBScript">
```

```
<!--
Sub cmdBack_Click()
   MsgBox "The Back button has been clicked.",,"The Haunted Mall"
end sub
-->
</SCRIPT>
<SCRIPT LANGUAGE="VBScript">
<!--
Sub cmdAhead_Click()
   MsgBox "The Ahead button has been clicked.",,"The Haunted Mall"
end sub
-->
</SCRIPT>
<SCRIPT LANGUAGE="VBScript">
<!--
Sub cmdLook_Click()
   MsgBox "The Look At An Object button has been clicked." _
       ,,"The Haunted Mall"
end sub
-->
</SCRIPT>
<SCRIPT LANGUAGE="VBScript">
<!--
Sub cmdRight_Click()
   MsgBox "The Right button has been clicked.",,"The Haunted Mall"
end sub
-->
</SCRIPT>
<SCRIPT LANGUAGE="VBScript">
<!--
Sub cmdLeft_Click()
   MsgBox "The Left button has been clicked.",,"The Haunted Mall"
end sub
-->
</SCRIPT>
<SCRIPT LANGUAGE="VBScript">
<!--
Sub cmdQuit_Click()
   msgbox "The Quit button has been clicked.",,"The Haunted Mall"
end sub
-->
</SCRIPT>
<SCRIPT LANGUAGE="VBScript">
<!--
Sub cmdHelp_Click()
   msgbox "The Help button has been clicked.",,"The Haunted Mall"
end sub
```

```
-->
</SCRIPT>
<SCRIPT LANGUAGE="VBScript">
<!--
Sub cmdGet_Click()
    MsgBox "The Get An Object button has been clicked." _
        ,,"The Haunted Mall"
end sub
-->
</SCRIPT>
<SCRIPT LANGUAGE="VBScript">
<!--
Sub cmdDrop_Click()
    Msgbox "The Drop An Object button has been clicked.",,"The Haunted Mall"
end sub
-->
</SCRIPT>
<SCRIPT LANGUAGE="VBScript">
<!--
Sub cmdInventory03_Click()
    MsgBox "The Inventory03 button has been clicked.",,"The Haunted Mall"
end sub
-->
</SCRIPT>
<SCRIPT LANGUAGE="VBScript">
<!--
Sub cmdInventory02_Click()
    MsgBox "The Inventory02 button has been clicked.",,"The Haunted Mall"
end sub
-->
</SCRIPT>
<SCRIPT LANGUAGE="VBScript">
<!--
Sub cmdInventory01_Click()
    MsgBox "The Inventory01 button has been clicked.",,"The Haunted Mall"
end sub
-->
</SCRIPT>
<SCRIPT LANGUAGE="VBScript">
<!--
Sub cmdInventory07_Click()
    MsgBox "The Inventory07 button has been clicked.",,"The Haunted Mall"
end sub
-->
</SCRIPT>
<SCRIPT LANGUAGE="VBScript">
<!--
```

```
Sub cmdInventory06_Click()
    MsgBox "The Inventory06 button has been clicked.",,"The Haunted Mall"
end sub
-->
</SCRIPT>
<SCRIPT LANGUAGE="VBScript">
<!--
Sub cmdInventory05_Click()
    MsgBox "The Inventory05 button has been clicked.",,"The Haunted Mall"
end sub
-->
</SCRIPT>
<SCRIPT LANGUAGE="VBScript">
<!--
Sub cmdInventory04_Click()
    MsgBox "The Inventory04 button has been clicked.",,"The Haunted Mall"
end sub
-->
</SCRIPT>
<SCRIPT LANGUAGE="VBScript">
<!--
Sub cmdUse_Click()
    MsgBox "The Use An Object button has been clicked." _
        ,,"The Haunted Mall"
end sub
-->
</SCRIPT>
<SCRIPT LANGUAGE="VBScript">
<!--
Sub RoomObject03_Click()
    MsgBox "The RoomObject 3 button has been clicked."
end sub
-->
</SCRIPT>
<SCRIPT LANGUAGE="VBScript">
<!--
Sub RoomObject02_Click()
    MsgBox "The RoomObject 2 button has been clicked."
end sub
-->
</SCRIPT>
<SCRIPT LANGUAGE="VBScript">
<!--
Sub RoomObject01_Click()
    MsgBox "The RoomObject 1 button has been clicked."
end sub
```

```
-->
</SCRIPT>
<SCRIPT LANGUAGE="VBScript">
<!--
Sub RoomObject07_Click()
   MsgBox "The RoomObject 7 button has been clicked."
end sub
-->
</SCRIPT>
<SCRIPT LANGUAGE="VBScript">
<!--
Sub RoomObject06_Click()
   MsgBox "The RoomObject 6 button has been clicked."
end sub
-->
</SCRIPT>
<SCRIPT LANGUAGE="VBScript">
<!--
Sub RoomObject05_Click()
   MsgBox "The RoomObject 5 button has been clicked."
end sub
-->
</SCRIPT>
<SCRIPT LANGUAGE="VBScript">
<!--
Sub RoomObject04_Click()
   MsgBox "The RoomObject 4 button has been clicked."
end sub
-->
</SCRIPT>
<SCRIPT LANGUAGE="VBScript">
<!--
Sub Layout1_OnLoad()
     DoSetup
end sub
-->
</SCRIPT>
<SCRIPT LANGUAGE="VBScript">
<!--
Sub IeTimer1_Timer()
   MsgBox "The IeTimer1 Timer event has fired."
   IeTimer1.enabled = false
end sub
-->
</SCRIPT>
<SCRIPT LANGUAGE="VBScript">
<!--
```

```
Sub IeTimer2_Timer()
    MsgBox "The IeTimer2 Timer event has fired."
    IeTimer2.enabled = false
end sub
-->
</SCRIPT>
<DIV ID="Layout1" STYLE="LAYOUT:FIXED;WIDTH:597pt;HEIGHT:369pt;">
<!--
Here, we are omitting the object tags in the HTML layout.
They aren't relevant at this point.
-->
</DIV>
```

Declaring Variables And Constants

The code in Listing 15.1 is still largely empty of content: It simply shows where everything will fit. The first task is to declare global variables and constants in the game. To do that, we create a script at the top of the document, as shown in Listing 15.2.

Listing 15.2 DECLARING VARIABLES AND CONSTANTS.

```
' VARIABLE AND CONSTANT DECLARATIONS
' This script module declares public variables and
' constants for the game program.
'
' ******************* CONSTANT DEFINITIONS ****************
Const room_min = 1
Const room_max = 25
Const MaxInventory = 7
Const InInventory = 100

' Definitions for the slots of the player state array
Const score = 0
Const turns = 1
Const alive = 2
Const lit = 3
Const gloved = 4
Const shoplifted = 5
'
' Definitions for rows of the mall room array
Const RoomText = 0
Const RoomFView = 1
Const RoomBView = 2
Const RoomVisited = 3
'
' Definitions for the slots of the maze state array
```

```
Const DoorOpen = 0
Const dogfed = 1
Const gameon = 2
Const SecretDoorOpen = 3

' Definitions for the objects in the game
Const keys = 0
Const flashlight = 1
Const money = 2
Const hotdog = 3
Const book = 4
Const wire = 5
Const gloves = 6
'
'
' ************************ ROOM INFORMATION *****************
' In Visual Basic, we would use a TYPE...END TYPE declaration
' to create a data structure that would hold information about the
' rooms in the game. VBScript, however, does not support TYPE...END
' TYPE. Therefore, we will use a two-dimensional array to hold the
' room information. The first row of the array will contain text
' descriptions of each room. In the second and third rows, each
' array slot will contain the image file name for either the forward
' or backward view of the room. The final row contains a true/false
' slot indicating whether or not the player has visited the
' room.

' Rooms in the mall are arranged as follows:
'  1  2  3  4  5
'  6  7  8  9 10
' 11 12 13 14 15
' 16 17 18 19 20
' 21 22 23 24 25

dim MallArray(26,4)

' ************************ VARIABLE DECLARATIONS *****************
dim UserChoice
dim Action
dim GameObject
dim RoomNumber
dim Forward      ' T/F: Is player going forward in mall?
dim PicPath      ' holds the directory path for game images, if needed
dim TimeCount    ' counts ticks of the IeTimer event

' Boolean variables to show if an action button
' is currently being used. When the player clicks
```

```
' the action button, the variable is set to true.
' When the player clicks on the object of the action,
' the variable is set back to false.
dim LookAtObject
dim BuyAnObject
dim GetAnObject
dim UseAnObject
dim ThrowAnObject

' In VB, array slots can start at numbers other than 0.
' Thus, it was possible to start array slots at 1, using
' code such as dim Inventory(keys to gloves). In VBScript,
' however, all arrays start at 0, so we simply use the highest
' number in a group of objects to be the top slot in the array.
dim Inventory(10)
dim ObjectVisible(10)
dim GameObjLoc(7)
dim Maze(4)
dim Player(5)
```

The constants are declared mainly to make the code easier to write. For example, toward the end of the listing, we declare the array **Inventory(10)** to keep track of which game objects the player has in inventory. At the beginning of the game, the player has nothing, so we can initialize the array very intuitively as:

```
for i=keys to gloves do
    Inventory(i)
next
```

The variables perform a variety of functions, some of which are obvious (e.g., **RoomNumber**). The arrays keep track of information about the game: where objects are located, what file should be loaded into the scene image when the player is in a particular room, and so on. The only array that's a little different is the array for the mall rooms, which has two dimensions:

```
dim MallArray(26,4)
```

Personally, I detest multidimensional arrays, but this one is necessary. The game must keep track of four pieces of information about each room:

- The text description of the room

- The name of the image file for the forward view of the room

- The name of the image file for the backward view of the room
- Whether or not the player has visited the room

The extra array slot is included in case additional information about a particular room needs to be added. In Visual Basic, the obvious way to handle this situation would be with a record type. Instead of a multidimensional array, we'd use a one-dimensional array of room records. However, VBScript doesn't support the **type…end type** declarations needed to create record types, so we're stuck with using multidimensional arrays as a substitute.

The action variables are used in the coding trick we use to let the player get and use objects:

```
dim LookAtObject
dim BuyAnObject
dim GetAnObject
dim UseAnObject
dim ThrowAnObject
```

When the player clicks an action button (e.g., Get An Object), the corresponding action variable is set to **true**. Then, when the player clicks on the button for the object, the **Click** event code for the object checks to see which action variable is **true**. That enables the game to know what the player wants to do with the object.

Setting Up To Play

To do that, we use the **OnLoad** event of the HTML layout: When the game page loads into the user's Web browser, the **OnLoad** event fires. The code for the **OnLoad** event is very simple:

```
Sub Layout1_OnLoad()
    DoSetup
end sub
```

As you can see, it simply calls the **DoSetup** sub, which does the substantive work required. The **DoSetup** sub goes like this:

```
Sub DoSetup

' Declare local variables to control initialization loops.
Dim i, j
```

```
'  *********** INITIALIZE GAME ROOM ARRAY ***************

'  *********** INITIALIZE PLAYERSTATE() ARRAY ************

'  *********** INITIALIZE MAZE() ARRAY *******************

'  *********** INITIALIZE INVENTORY ARRAY ****************

'  *********** INITIALIZE ObjectVisible ARRAY ************

'  *********** INITIALIZE Action Button values ***********

'  *********** SET STARTING LOCATION *********************

end sub
```

Right now, this is just a framework, so it doesn't do much. As we fill in the code, it will load initial values into the room array, set the initial state of the player (alive, etc.), set certain maze variables (such as whether or not the mall doors are locked), set the locations of game objects in the **GameObjLoc** array, initialize the action buttons, and set the starting room number to 1.

Action, Inventory, And Room Object Buttons

At this stage, the action buttons all do the same thing. When you click them, they display a message box saying that they've been clicked, as shown in Figure 15.5:

```
Sub cmdBuy_Click()
   MsgBox "The Buy An Object button has been clicked." _
      ,,"The Haunted Mall"
end sub
```

The point of the message box is simply to verify that all the buttons are responding to **Click** events. Later, we'll fill in event code for one button at a time, verifying at each step that the button code is working as it should.

Figure 15.5
A message box shows that a button has been clicked.

Moving From Room To Room

The framework program doesn't do much, but it *does* give you a pretty clear idea of how the **Move_Player** sub works. As the player moves from one room to another, the **Move_Player** sub works with the **NewRoom** sub to display the correct room scene and text, spring traps, and display game objects in the rooms. The logic of the **Move_Player** sub is fairly simple, as you can see in Listing 15.3.

Listing 15.3 FRAMEWORK CODE FOR THE Move_Player SUB.

```
Sub Move_Player (direction)

    Select Case roomnumber
        Case 1:
        Case 2:
        Case 3:
        Case 4:
        Case 5:
        Case 6:
        Case 7:
        Case 8:
        Case 9:
        Case 10:
        Case 11:
        Case 12:
        Case 13:
        Case 14:
        Case 15:
        Case 16:
        Case 17:
        Case 18:
        Case 19:
        Case 20:
        Case 21:
        Case 22:
        Case 23:
        Case 24:
        Case Else
            MsgBox "Error in Move routine!", , "The Haunted Mall"
    End Select
    MsgBox "The Move_Player sub has run.",,"The Haunted Mall"
End Sub
```

When the player clicks one of the move buttons (left, right, ahead, or back), the **Move_Player** sub gets the direction as a parameter. That's where the game map comes in handy: Given a room number and a direction, you can see at a glance which room the player is trying to enter.

Based on the current value of the **RoomNumber** variable, **Move_Player** then executes one of the cases of the **select case** statement. If the player is able to move to a new room—it's not always possible, because the player might be caught in a trap—then the **case** code calls the **NewRoom** sub, shown in Listing 15.4.

Listing 15.4 THE FRAMEWORK CODE FOR THE NewRoom SUB.

```
Sub NewRoom ()

' This sub should do several things.
'    1. Display the correct image in the ScenePicture control.
'    2. Display the room description in the Lbl_Scene control.
'    3. Display the new score in the Lbl_Score control.
'    4. Display the new number of turns taken in the Lbl_Turns control.
'    The score only increases if the room hasn't yet been visited.

End Sub
```

As you can see, there's no code yet, but we have a very specific list of tasks that the **NewRoom** sub must accomplish. Based on the value of **RoomNumber**, it looks in the **MallArray** variable, using the room number as the first array coordinate, and then simply reads off the values (text description and image file name) from the array slots in that dimension. It checks a global control variable, **Forward**, to determine which direction the player is facing—and thus, which of the two scene image files it should load.

That's about as much as we can learn from the general code framework. Let's fill in the details so we can look at the guts of the program.

Coding The Game

Because of the size of the game—the code for the main game panel is 42 pages long—we won't reproduce the entire game panel listing here in the book. If you want to look at the whole thing, it's on the CD-ROM included with this book. If we included all the code here, we'd have a monster listing that dwarfed everything else in the chapter.

Using The **OnLoad** Event For Game Setup Tasks

When the game page loads, we must first initialize all the global variables used in the game. That's done by the HTML layout's **OnLoad** event, which calls the VBScript **DoSetup** sub. The **DoSetup** sub is shown in Listing 15.5.

Listing 15.5 THE **DoSetup** SUB.

```
Sub DoSetup

' Declare local variables to control initialization loops.
Dim i, j

' ********** INITIALIZE GAME ROOM ARRAY ********************
' Load room descriptions and picture file names into the
' mall room array. We're taking advantage of the fact that
' even though VBScript starts arrays at slot 0, it adds an
' "extra" slot at the end, so an array declared as MyArray(25)
' has 26 slots numbered 0 to 25. This allows us to "skip" the
' first, 0-numbered slot and have the array slot numbers correspond
' to the mall room numbers 1 to 25.

' For rooms that have only a forward view,
' the backward view uses the GIF file for the
' forward view.
MallArray(1, RoomText) = "You're at the entrance to the mall."
MallArray(1, RoomFView) = "room01f.gif"
MallArray(1, RoomBView) = "room01f.gif"

MallArray(2, RoomText) = "You're just inside the mall doors. " & _
    "There's a Radio Shack to the south."
MallArray(2, RoomFView) = "room02f.gif"
MallArray(2, RoomBView) = "room02b.gif"

MallArray(3, RoomText) = "You're in the mallway. There's a tux " & _
    "rental shop to the south."
MallArray(3, RoomFView) = "room03f.gif"
MallArray(3, RoomBView) = "room03b.gif"

MallArray(4, RoomText) = "To the east is a CD store. " & _
    "The mallway turns south here."
MallArray(4, RoomFView) = "room04f.gif"
MallArray(4, RoomBView) = "room04b.gif"

MallArray(5, RoomText) = "CD store. There's a rack with CDs by " & _
    "Elvis Costello and the Violent Femmes."
```

```
MallArray(5, RoomFView) = "room05f.gif"
MallArray(5, RoomBView) = "room05f.gif"

MallArray(6, RoomText) = "You're south of the mall doors. " & _
    "There are some bushes here."
MallArray(6, RoomFView) = "room06f.gif"
MallArray(6, RoomBView) = "room06f.gif"

MallArray(7, RoomText) = "Radio Shack. There's a flashlight on " & _
    "sale for $5."
MallArray(7, RoomFView) = "room07f.gif"
MallArray(7, RoomBView) = "room07f.gif"

MallArray(8, RoomText) = "Tux rental shop. A just-returned tux " & _
    "is hanging on a peg."
MallArray(8, RoomFView) = "room08f.gif"
MallArray(8, RoomBView) = "room08f.gif"

MallArray(9, RoomText) = "To the east is Joe's Hot Dogs."
MallArray(9, RoomFView) = "room09f.gif"
MallArray(9, RoomBView) = "room09b.gif"

MallArray(10, RoomText) = "Joe's Hot Dogs. On the counter are " & _
    "some fresh hot dogs for $2 apiece."
MallArray(10, RoomFView) = "room10f.gif"
MallArray(10, RoomBView) = "room10f.gif"

MallArray(11, RoomText) = "Women's rest room. Graffiti on the " & _
    "wall says 'Scott's such a stud!'"
MallArray(11, RoomFView) = "room11f.gif"
MallArray(11, RoomBView) = "room11f.gif"

MallArray(12, RoomText) = "Men's rest room. There's a sink " & _
    "and soap dispenser."
MallArray(12, RoomFView) = "room12f.gif"
MallArray(12, RoomBView) = "room12f.gif"

MallArray(13, RoomText) = "Video Arcade. A $1 game " & _
    "called 'Crowther's Castle' is unplugged."
MallArray(13, RoomFView) = "room13f.gif"
MallArray(13, RoomBView) = "room13f.gif"

MallArray(14, RoomText) = "To the east is a bookstore."
MallArray(14, RoomFView) = "room14f.gif"
MallArray(14, RoomBView) = "room14b.gif"

MallArray(15, RoomText) = "Bookstore. On the counter is " & _
    "'VBScript 2 & ActiveX Programming' for 39.99."
```

```
MallArray(15, RoomFView) = "room15f.gif"
MallArray(15, RoomBView) = "room15f.gif"

MallArray(16, RoomText) = "Dead end. South is a hardware store " & _
    "and north is the women's rest room."
MallArray(16, RoomFView) = "room16f.gif"
MallArray(16, RoomBView) = "room16b.gif"

MallArray(17, RoomText) = "South is an aerobics studio and " & _
    "north is the men's rest room."
MallArray(17, RoomFView) = "room17f.gif"
MallArray(17, RoomBView) = "room17b.gif"

MallArray(18, RoomText) = "South is a theatre with 'Beaches' on " & _
    "5 screens. North is a video arcade."
MallArray(18, RoomFView) = "room18f.gif"
MallArray(18, RoomBView) = "room18b.gif"

MallArray(19, RoomText) = "South is a donut shop. East is " & _
    "Granny's Porno Palace. North is the mallway."
MallArray(19, RoomFView) = "room19f.gif"
MallArray(19, RoomBView) = "room19b.gif"

MallArray(20, RoomText) = "Granny's Porno Palace. Porno is $10. " & _
    "There's a small slot in the south wall."
MallArray(20, RoomFView) = "room20f.gif"
MallArray(20, RoomBView) = "room20f.gif"

MallArray(21, RoomText) = "Hardware store. There are some " & _
    "gloves for $2."
MallArray(21, RoomFView) = "room21f.gif"
MallArray(21, RoomBView) = "room21f.gif"

MallArray(22, RoomText) = "Aerobics studio. You can almost hear " & _
    "the disco music."
MallArray(22, RoomFView) = "room22f.gif"
MallArray(22, RoomBView) = "room22f.gif"

MallArray(23, RoomText) = "Theatre. A ticket to 'Beaches' is " & _
    "$7. A box of Milk Duds is $2."
MallArray(23, RoomFView) = "room23f.gif"
MallArray(23, RoomBView) = "room23f.gif"

MallArray(24, RoomText) = "Donut shop. Coffee is $2, " & _
    "chocolate donuts are $1."
MallArray(24, RoomFView) = "room24f.gif"
MallArray(24, RoomBView) = "room24f.gif"
```

```
MallArray(25, RoomText) = "You're in the secret room."
MallArray(25, RoomFView) = "room25f.gif"
MallArray(25, RoomBView) = "room25f.gif"

' At the start of the game, no rooms have been visited yet,
' except for room 1, where the player starts out.
For j = room_min To room_max
    MallArray(j, RoomVisited) = False
Next
' The player is in room 1 when the game starts.
MallArray(1, RoomVisited) = True
Roomnumber = 1
ObjectsInRoom = 0

' Initialize the GameObjLoc array to put the game objects
' in their initial locations. The value in the array slot is the
' room number.
GameObjLoc(keys) = 6
GameObjLoc(flashlight) = 7
GameObjLoc(money) = 8
GameObjLoc(hotdog) = 10
GameObjLoc(book) = 15
GameObjLoc(wire) = 18
GameObjLoc(gloves) = 21

' *********** INITIALIZE PLAYERSTATE() ARRAY ***********
For i = score To shoplifted
    player(i) = False
Next
player(alive) = True

' *************** INITIALIZE MAZE() ARRAY ***************
For i = dooropen To SecretDoorOpen
    maze(i) = False
Next

' ********** INITIALIZE INVENTORY ARRAY *********************
' At the beginning of the game, the player has nothing. Therefore,
' the value "false" is put into each slot of the inventory array.
For i = keys To gloves
    inventory(i) = False
Next

' ********** INITIALIZE ObjectVisible ARRAY *********************
' At the beginning of the game, only the wire (object 5) is visible.
For i = keys To gloves
    ObjectVisible(i) = False
```

```
Next
ObjectVisible(wire) = True

' *********** INITIALIZE Action Button values ********************
' At the beginning of the game, none of the action buttons
' has been clicked on yet. Therefore, the control variables
' are all set to false. No control variables are needed for
' the Help and Talk buttons, because they don't require the
' user to click on an object in inventory. They have their
' own code that is executed immediately.
LookAtObject = False
BuyAnObject = False
GetAnObject = False
UseAnObject = False
ThrowAnObject = False

' *********** SET STARTING LOCATION ********************
' At the beginning of the game, the player is in Room 1
' (the mall entrance). He/she is moving forward.
roomnumber = 1
forward = True
TimeCount = 0

end sub
```

Let's see how this sub works. After declaring **i** and **j** as loop control variables, it proceeds to initialize the first three rows for all 25 rooms in the **MallArray**:

```
MallArray(1, RoomText) = "You're at the entrance to the mall."
MallArray(1, RoomFView) = "room01f.gif"
MallArray(1, RoomBView) = "room01f.gif"

MallArray(2, RoomText) = "You're just inside the mall doors. " & _
    "There's a Radio Shack to the south."
MallArray(2, RoomFView) = "room02f.gif"
MallArray(2, RoomBView) = "room02b.gif"
```

Each room gets a text description. Most rooms get the names of two image files: a forward view and a backward view. Rooms that have no backward view get the name of the forward-view file as their "backward view."

You might recall that each room gets *four* pieces of information, not three. The fourth piece of information is whether or not the room has been visited by the player. We need to keep track of this, because each time the player enters a room he/she hasn't previously visited, one point is added to the player's score.

However, because only one room has been visited at the beginning of the game, it's far simpler to initialize this row of the array by using a **for** loop:

```
For j = room_min To room_max
    MallArray(j, RoomVisited) = False
Next

' The player is in room 1 when the game starts.
MallArray(1, RoomVisited) = True
```

The loop traverses the whole row, setting all the **RoomVisited** values to **false**. Then, we go back to Room 1 and set its **RoomVisited** value to **true**.

Next, we initialize the **GameObjLoc** array to put the game objects in their starting locations:

```
GameObjLoc(keys) = 6
GameObjLoc(flashlight) = 7
GameObjLoc(money) = 8
GameObjLoc(hotdog) = 10
GameObjLoc(book) = 15
GameObjLoc(wire) = 18
GameObjLoc(gloves) = 21
```

Later, when we examine the **NewRoom** sub, we'll see how that sub checks the **GameObjLoc** array to determine which, if any, objects to display in a given room.

Next, we initialize the **PlayerState** array, which sets the attributes of the player at the beginning of the game:

```
For i = score To shoplifted
    player(i) = False
Next
player(alive) = True
```

You might recall from the global variable declarations that the player has several attributes:

```
Const score = 0
Const turns = 1
Const alive = 2
Const lit = 3
Const gloved = 4
Const shoplifted = 5
```

At the beginning, each of these attributes is set to **false**, except "alive." Therefore, we use the same trick we used earlier to set the **RoomVisited** property in the mall array: First traverse the array with a **for** loop, then go back and reset the single odd value.

Initializing the **Maze**, **Inventory**, and **ObjectVisible** arrays works in exactly the same way, so we won't belabor the point.

Then, we set all the action button values to **false**:

```
LookAtObject = False
BuyAnObject = False
GetAnObject = False
UseAnObject = False
ThrowAnObject = False
```

As explained earlier, when the player clicks an action button, its value is set to **true**. At the beginning of the game, however, none of the action buttons has been clicked.

Finally, we set the starting location (Room 1), set the **Forward** variable to **true** because the player is facing forward in Room 1, and set the **TimeCount** variable to 0 for the first use of our timer control.

Moving From Room To Room

Now, let's look at what is really the heart of the game: the code that moves the player from one room to the next. This movement is controlled by the **Move_Player** sub. Each time the **Move_Player** sub runs, however, it also calls the **NewRoom** sub to display appropriate images and information for the player's new location.

THE **Move_Player** SUB

When the player clicks on one of the movement buttons, four facts are relevant:

- The player is in a particular room of the game (**RoomNumber**).
- The player clicked the button to go in a particular direction (**Direction**).
- The player has certain attributes, such as having shoplifted or being "lit" (i.e., having turned on the flashlight).
- The maze itself has certain attributes, such as having its entry doors locked.

The **Move_Player** sub, shown in Listing 15.6, uses these four facts to determine what to do next. It only gets the direction as a parameter (and of course, structured programming purists will scream bloody murder about the fact that it directly accesses global variables). Nonetheless, a certain amount of casualness is appropriate in Visual Basic and VBScript programming: If you want to pass all the global variables as parameters, feel free.

Listing 15.6 THE **Move_Player** SUB.

```
Sub Move_Player (direction)

    Select Case roomnumber

        Case 1:
            If forward Then
              Select Case direction
                Case "B", "L":
                    MsgBox "No way to go in that direction." _
                        , , "The Haunted Mall"
                Case "A":
                if maze(dooropen) = false then
                    tbScene = "The doors are locked. You can't get in."
                else
                    roomnumber = 2
                        NewRoom
                end if
                  Case "R":
                    roomnumber = 6
                    NewRoom
            End Select
        Else
            ' Nothing here, because you can't go backward in room 1.
        End If

        Case 2:
            If forward Then
                ' REMEMBER to adjust the forward T/F value when needed.
                Select Case direction
                    Case "B", "L":
                        MsgBox "No way to go in that direction." _
                            , , "The Haunted Mall"
                    Case "A":
                        roomnumber = 3
                        NewRoom
                    Case "R":
                        roomnumber = 7
                        NewRoom
```

```
            End Select
        Else
            Select Case direction
                Case "A", "R":
                    MsgBox "No way to go in that direction." _
                        , , "The Haunted Mall"
                Case "B":
                    forward = True
                    roomnumber = 3
                    NewRoom
                Case "L":
                    forward = True
                    roomnumber = 7
                    NewRoom
            End Select
        End If

Case 3:
    If forward Then
        ' REMEMBER to adjust the forward T/F value when needed.
        Select Case direction
            Case "L": MsgBox "No way to go in that direction." _
                    , , "The Haunted Mall"
            Case "A":
            if Player(lit) then
                roomnumber = 4
                NewRoom
            else
                scenepicture.PicturePath = "crash2.gif"
                tbScene = _
                    "Yikes! You've fallen down a hole " & _
                        "in the floor!"
                timecount = 0
                IeTimer1.enabled = true
            end if

            Case "B":
                forward = False
                roomnumber = 2
                NewRoom
            Case "R":
                roomnumber = 8
                NewRoom
        End Select
    Else
        Select Case direction
```

```
                Case "R": MsgBox "No way to go in that direction." _
                    , , "The Haunted Mall"
                Case "A":
                    roomnumber = 2
                    NewRoom
                Case "B":
                    forward = True
                    roomnumber = 4
                    NewRoom
                Case "L":
                    forward = True
                    roomnumber = 8
                    NewRoom
            End Select
        End If

Case 4:
    If forward Then
        ' REMEMBER to adjust the forward T/F value when needed.
        Select Case direction
            Case "L":
                MsgBox "No way to go in that direction." _
                    , , "The Haunted Mall"
            Case "A":
                roomnumber = 5
                NewRoom
            Case "B":
                forward = False
                roomnumber = 3
                NewRoom
            Case "R":
              if Player(shoplifted) then
                ScenePicture.picturepath = "guard.gif"
                tbScene.text = "Uh-oh. A ghostly security " & _
                    "guard has appeared."
                TimeCount = 0
                IeTimer1.enabled = true
              else
                roomnumber = 9
                NewRoom
              end if
        End Select
    Else
        Select Case direction
            Case "A":
                MsgBox "No way to go in that direction." _
                    , , "The Haunted Mall"
```

```
                Case "B":
                    forward = True
                    roomnumber = 9
                    NewRoom
                Case "L":
                    roomnumber = 3
                    NewRoom
                Case "R":
                    forward = True
                    roomnumber = 5
                    NewRoom
            End Select
        End If

Case 5:
    If forward Then
        ' REMEMBER to adjust the forward T/F value when needed.
        Select Case direction
            Case "L", "R", "A":
                MsgBox "No way to go in that direction." _
                    , , "The Haunted Mall"
            Case "B":
                roomnumber = 4
                NewRoom
        End Select
    Else
        ' There's no way forward can be false in room 5.
        MsgBox "Program Error! Run for your life!"
    End If

Case 6:
    If forward Then
        ' REMEMBER to adjust the forward T/F value when needed.
        Select Case direction
            Case "A", "L", "R":
                MsgBox "No way to go in that direction." _
                    , , "The Haunted Mall"
            Case "B":
                roomnumber = 1
                NewRoom
        End Select
    Else
        ' No way forward can be false in Room 6.
        MsgBox "Program error! Run for your life!"
    End If
```

```
Case 7:
    If forward Then
      ' REMEMBER to adjust the forward T/F value when needed.
      Select Case direction
          Case "A", "L", "R":
              MsgBox "No way to go in that direction." _
                  , , "The Haunted Mall"
          Case "B":
              roomnumber = 2
              NewRoom
      End Select
    Else
      ' No way forward can be false in Room 7.
      MsgBox "Program error! Run for your life!"
    End If

Case 8:
    If forward Then
      ' REMEMBER to adjust the forward T/F value when needed.
      Select Case direction
          Case "A", "L", "R":
              MsgBox "No way to go in that direction." _
                  , , "The Haunted Mall"
          Case "B":
              roomnumber = 3
              NewRoom
      End Select
    Else
      ' No way forward can be false in Room 8.
      MsgBox "Program error! Run for your life!"
    End If

Case 9:
    If forward Then
      ' REMEMBER to adjust the forward T/F value when needed.
      Select Case direction
          Case "R":
              MsgBox "No way to go in that direction." _
                  , , "The Haunted Mall"
          Case "A":
              roomnumber = 14
              NewRoom
          Case "B":
              forward = False
              roomnumber = 4
              NewRoom
```

```
                Case "L":
                    roomnumber = 10
                    NewRoom
            End Select
        Else
            Select Case direction
                Case "L":
                    MsgBox "No way to go in that direction." _
                        , , "The Haunted Mall"
                Case "A":
                    roomnumber = 4
                    NewRoom
                Case "B":
                    forward = True
                    roomnumber = 14
                    NewRoom
                Case "R":
                    forward = True
                    roomnumber = 10
                    NewRoom
            End Select
        End If

    Case 10:
        If forward Then
            ' REMEMBER to adjust the forward T/F value when needed.
            Select Case direction
                Case "A", "L", "R":
                    MsgBox "No way to go in that direction." _
                        , , "The Haunted Mall"
                Case "B":
                    roomnumber = 9
                    NewRoom
            End Select
        Else
            ' No way forward can be false in Room 10.
            MsgBox "Program error! Run for your life!"
        End If

    Case 11:
        If forward Then
            ' REMEMBER to adjust the forward T/F value when needed.
            Select Case direction
                Case "A", "L", "R":
                    MsgBox "No way to go in that direction." _
                        , , "The Haunted Mall"
```

```
                    Case "B":
                         roomnumber = 16
                         NewRoom
               End Select
          Else
               ' No way forward can be false in Room 11
               MsgBox "Program error! Run for your life!"
          End If

     Case 12:
          If forward Then
               ' REMEMBER to adjust the forward T/F value when needed.
               Select Case direction
                    Case "A", "L", "R":
                         MsgBox "No way to go in that direction." _
                              , , "The Haunted Mall"
                    Case "B":
                         roomnumber = 17
                         NewRoom
               End Select
          Else
               ' No way forward can be false in Room 12
               MsgBox "Program error! Run for your life!"
          End If

     Case 13:
          If forward Then
               ' REMEMBER to adjust the forward T/F value when needed.
               Select Case direction
                    Case "A", "L", "R":
                         MsgBox "No way to go in that direction." _
                              , , "The Haunted Mall"
                    Case "B":
                         roomnumber = 18
                         NewRoom
               End Select
          Else
               ' No way forward can be false in Room 13
               MsgBox "Program error! Run for your life!"
          End If

     Case 14:
          If forward Then
          if ScenePicture.picturepath = "dog.gif" _
          and maze(dogfed) = false then
               tbScene = "The dog growls menacingly " & _
                    "and blocks your path."
```

```
            else
               Select Case direction
                     Case "R":
                        MsgBox "No way to go in that direction." _
                           , , "The Haunted Mall"
                     Case "A":
                  if maze(dogfed) = false then
                     ScenePicture.picturepath = "dog.gif"
                     tbScene = "Uh-oh. A ghostly guard dog " & _
                        "blocks your path."
                     timecount = 0
                     IeTimer1.enabled = true
                  else
                     roomnumber = 19
                     NewRoom
                  end if
                     Case "B":
                        forward = False
                        roomnumber = 9
                        NewRoom
                     Case "L":
                        roomnumber = 15
                        NewRoom
               End Select
            end if
         Else
            Select Case direction
                  Case "L":
                     MsgBox "No way to go in that direction." _
                        , , "The Haunted Mall"
                  Case "A":
                     roomnumber = 9
                     NewRoom
                  Case "B":
                     forward = True
                     roomnumber = 19
                     NewRoom
                  Case "R":
                     forward = True
                     roomnumber = 15
                     NewRoom
            End Select
         End If

Case 15:
   If forward Then
      ' REMEMBER to adjust the forward T/F value when needed.
```

```
            Select Case direction
                Case "A", "L", "R":
                    MsgBox "No way to go in that direction." _
                        , , "The Haunted Mall"
                Case "B":
                    roomnumber = 14
                    NewRoom
            End Select
        Else
            ' No way forward can be false in Room 13
            MsgBox "Program error! Run for your life!"
        End If

    Case 16:
        If forward Then
            ' REMEMBER to adjust the forward T/F value when needed.
            Select Case direction
                Case "A":
                    MsgBox "No way to go in that direction." _
                        , , "The Haunted Mall"
                Case "B":
                    forward = False
                    roomnumber = 17
                    NewRoom
                Case "L":
                    roomnumber = 21
                    NewRoom
                Case "R":
                    roomnumber = 11
                    NewRoom
            End Select
        Else
            ' No way forward can be false in Room 16
            MsgBox "Program error! Run for your life!"
        End If

    Case 17:
        If forward Then
            ' REMEMBER to adjust the forward T/F value when needed.
            Select Case direction
                Case "A":
                    roomnumber = 16
                    NewRoom
                Case "B":
                    forward = False
                    roomnumber = 18
                    NewRoom
```

```
            Case "L":
                roomnumber = 22
                NewRoom
            Case "R":
                roomnumber = 12
                NewRoom
        End Select
    Else
        Select Case direction
            Case "A":
                roomnumber = 18
                NewRoom
            Case "B":
                forward = True
                roomnumber = 16
                NewRoom
            Case "L":
                forward = True
                roomnumber = 12
                NewRoom
            Case "R":
                forward = True
                roomnumber = 22
                NewRoom
        End Select
    End If

Case 18:
    If forward Then
        ' REMEMBER to adjust the forward T/F value when needed.
        Select Case direction
            Case "A":
                roomnumber = 17
                NewRoom
            Case "B":
                forward = False
                roomnumber = 19
                NewRoom
            Case "L":
                roomnumber = 23
                NewRoom
            Case "R":
                roomnumber = 13
                NewRoom
        End Select
    Else
        Select Case direction
```

```
                Case "A":
                    roomnumber = 19
                    NewRoom
                Case "B":
                    forward = True
                    roomnumber = 17
                    NewRoom
                Case "L":
                    forward = True
                    roomnumber = 13
                    NewRoom
                Case "R":
                    forward = True
                    roomnumber = 23
                    NewRoom
            End Select
        End If

Case 19:
    If forward Then
      ' REMEMBER to adjust the forward T/F value when needed.
        Select Case direction
            Case "A":
                    roomnumber = 24
                    NewRoom
            Case "B":
                    forward = False
                    roomnumber = 14
                    NewRoom
            Case "L":
                    roomnumber = 20
                    NewRoom
            Case "R":
                    roomnumber = 18
                    NewRoom
        End Select
    Else
        Select Case direction
            Case "A":
                    roomnumber = 14
                    NewRoom
            Case "B":
                    forward = True
                    roomnumber = 24
                    NewRoom
            Case "L":
                    forward = True
```

```
                roomnumber = 18
                NewRoom
            Case "R":
                forward = True
                roomnumber = 20
                NewRoom
        End Select
    End If

Case 20:
    If forward Then
        ' REMEMBER to adjust the forward T/F value when needed.
        Select Case direction
            Case "A", "L", "R":
                MsgBox "No way to go in that direction." _
                    , , "The Haunted Mall"
            Case "B":
                roomnumber = 19
                NewRoom
        End Select
    Else
        ' No way forward can be false in Room 20
        MsgBox "Program error! Run for your life!"
    End If

Case 21:
    If forward Then
        ' REMEMBER to adjust the forward T/F value when needed.
        Select Case direction
            Case "A", "L", "R":
                MsgBox "No way to go in that direction." _
                    , , "The Haunted Mall"
            Case "B":
                roomnumber = 16
                NewRoom
        End Select
    Else
        ' No way forward can be false in Room 21
        MsgBox "Program error! Run for your life!"
    End If

Case 22:
    If forward Then
        ' REMEMBER to adjust the forward T/F value when needed.
        Select Case direction
            Case "A", "L", "R":
                MsgBox "No way to go in that direction." _
                    , , "The Haunted Mall"
```

```
                Case "B":
                    roomnumber = 17
                    NewRoom
            End Select
        Else
            ' No way forward can be false in Room 22
            MsgBox "Program error! Run for your life!"
        End If

    Case 23:
        If forward Then
            ' REMEMBER to adjust the forward T/F value when needed.
            Select Case direction
                Case "A", "L", "R":
                    MsgBox "No way to go in that direction." _
                        , , "The Haunted Mall"
                Case "B":
                    roomnumber = 18
                    NewRoom
            End Select
        Else
            ' No way forward can be false in Room 23
            MsgBox "Program error! Run for your life!"
        End If

    Case 24:
        If forward Then
            ' REMEMBER to adjust the forward T/F value when needed.
            Select Case direction
                Case "A", "L", "R":
                    MsgBox "No way to go in that direction." _
                        , , "The Haunted Mall"
                Case "B":
                    roomnumber = 19
                    NewRoom
            End Select
        Else
            ' No way forward can be false in Room 24
            MsgBox "Program error! Run for your life!"
        End If

    Case Else
        MsgBox "Error in Move routine!", , "The Haunted Mall"
End Select

End Sub
```

The **Move_Player** sub is essentially a big **select case** statement that, inside each of its cases, contains an **if...else** statement and a little **select case** statement. The big **select case** statement uses **RoomNumber** as its control variable. Inside each case, the **Direction** parameter is used as the control variable for the little **select case** statement. The case of **RoomNumber** = 19 is typical. First, we'll look at the broad outline of the code:

```
Sub Move_Player (direction)
    Select Case roomnumber
' ------ code omitted
Case 19:
            If forward Then
              Select Case direction
                Case "A":
                Case "B":
                Case "L":
                Case "R":
              End Select
            Else
              Select Case direction
                Case "A":
                Case "B":
                Case "L":
                Case "R":
              End Select
            End If
```

First, the big **select case** statement uses **RoomNumber** to determine which case should be executed. Inside the appropriate case (here, it's Room 19), the code first checks to see if the player is facing forward or backward in the mall. This is significant not merely because it must display the correct (forward or backward) room scene, but because it determines which room the player enters by moving in a certain direction.

Suppose, for example, that the player is in Room 14, facing forward. Moving straight ahead takes the player to Room 19, moving left goes into the bookstore, moving right hits a wall ("No way to go in that direction"), and moving back takes the player to Room 9.

If the player is in Room 14 facing backward, however, everything is different. Moving straight ahead takes the player to Room 9, turning left hits a wall, turning right enters the bookstore, and moving back enters Room 19. That's why the first task inside each case is to determine the direction in which the player is facing.

Once that issue is settled, the code drops into one of the little **select case** statements, where the direction is the controlling factor. Let's look at one of these little **select case** statements in detail:

```
Select Case direction
          Case "A":
                 roomnumber = 24
                 NewRoom
          Case "B":
                 forward = False
                 roomnumber = 14
                 NewRoom
          Case "L":
                 roomnumber = 20
                 NewRoom
          Case "R":
                 roomnumber = 18
                 NewRoom
     End Select
```

In each case, the pattern is the same: Assign the appropriate new value to the **RoomNumber** variable, then call the **NewRoom** sub to do the heavy lifting of displaying the new room. The one direction with an additional code line (in every room) is for the case in which the player moves backwards (case "B"). In that case, the player's forward/backward orientation must be reversed.

The **Move_Player** sub also has additional code for rooms in which the player encounters traps, but we'll cover that later in the chapter when we talk about how the traps work.

THE NewRoom SUB

Now, let's take a look at how the **NewRoom** sub works. Compared to the **Move_Player** sub, it's fairly short. The **NewRoom** sub is shown in Listing 15.7.

Listing 15.7 THE NewRoom SUB.

```
Sub NewRoom ()
' This sub should do several things.
'    1. Display the correct image in the ScenePicture control.
```

- 2. Display the room description in the Lbl_Scene control.
- 3. Display the new score in the Lbl_Score control.
- 4. Display the new number of turns taken in the Lbl_Turns control.

```
If MallArray(roomnumber, RoomVisited) = False Then
    player(score) = player(score) + 1
End If

player(turns) = player(turns) + 1

If forward Then
    scenepicture.PicturePath = MallArray(roomnumber, RoomFView)
Else
    scenepicture.PicturePath = MallArray(roomnumber, RoomBView)
End If

tbScene = MallArray(roomnumber, RoomText)

' Traverse the GameObjLoc array. If the
' current room number is found in one of
' the array slots, display the corresponding
' object in the room (i.e., as an icon in one
' of the RoomObject controls below the room scene.
if GameObjLoc(keys) = roomnumber then
   RoomObject01.visible = true
else
   RoomObject01.visible = false
end if

if GameObjLoc(flashlight) = roomnumber then
   RoomObject02.visible = true
else
   RoomObject02.visible = false
end if

if GameObjLoc(money) = roomnumber then
   RoomObject03.visible = true
else
   RoomObject03.visible = false
end if

if GameObjLoc(hotdog) = roomnumber then
   RoomObject04.visible = true
else
   RoomObject04.visible = false
end if
```

```
    if GameObjLoc(book) = roomnumber then
        RoomObject05.visible = true
    else
        RoomObject05.visible = false
    end if

    if GameObjLoc(wire) = roomnumber then
        RoomObject06.visible = true
    else
        RoomObject06.visible = false
    end if

    if GameObjLoc(gloves) = roomnumber then
        RoomObject07.visible = true
    else
        RoomObject07.visible = false
    end if

    lbScore.Caption = player(score)
    lbTurns.Caption = player(turns)
    MallArray(roomnumber, RoomVisited) = True

End Sub
```

The first thing that the **NewRoom** sub does is check to see if the player has visited the room:

```
If MallArray(roomnumber, RoomVisited) = False Then
        player(score) = player(score) + 1
End If

player(turns) = player(turns) + 1
```

If this is a room the player hasn't previously visited, then the player gets a point for visiting it. After adjusting the **score** slot of the **player** array, the code adds 1 to the array's **turns** slot because the player has taken another turn.

Next, the sub determines which room scene it should display in the game panel's image control:

```
If forward Then
        scenepicture.PicturePath = MallArray(roomnumber, RoomFView)
Else
        scenepicture.PicturePath = MallArray(roomnumber, RoomBView)
End If

tbScene = MallArray(roomnumber, RoomText)
```

As explained earlier, the player's orientation inside the mall is crucial. Depending on whether the player is facing forward or backward, the code executes either the **if** or the **else** clause. It loads the appropriate image by using the file name from the **MallArray** array, selecting either the forward or backward view. Because there's only one text description of each room, that description is loaded simply by using the room number to select the appropriate **MallArray** slot.

Next, the sub uses a series of **if...else** statements to determine which game objects should be displayed in the room:

```
if GameObjLoc(keys) = roomnumber then
        RoomObject01.visible = true
else
        RoomObject01.visible = false
end if
```

Finally, it updates the game panel labels showing the player's score and number of turns taken. It also marks the room as "visited":

```
lbScore.Caption = player(score)
lbTurns.Caption = player(turns)
MallArray(roomnumber, RoomVisited) = True
```

A Memory-Saving Trick

In the original, Visual Basic version of the game, each room had an associated record that included information about the room's contents. If a particular game object was located in the room, the record would indicate its presence: When a player entered the room, the object would appear.

That option isn't available to us now. As already noted, VBScript doesn't support user-defined types (records). But there's an even more significant reason: With 25 rooms and 10 or more game objects, it takes a fairly large array to hold all that information. When the game is simply loading from the player's hard disk, it's not an issue. When the game is loading over the Web, however, we don't want to go looking for slowdowns.

Fortunately, there's a simple solution that would have worked just as well in the Visual Basic version of the game. We'll create a one-dimensional **GameObjLoc** array with a slot for each object. Then, each time the player moves to a new room, we'll simply traverse the array looking for any object slot containing that room number. If an object's slot contains the number of the current room, then it's in the room. By this little trick, we've replaced what was in effect a 250-slot array with a 10-slot array.

Performing Game Actions

Now, let's examine what happens when the player performs actions in the game. For getting, buying, and using objects, the pattern is the same. For looking at objects, it's a little more complicated and uses a timer.

Getting, Buying, And Using Objects

The code that enables the player to get, buy, or use an object follows the same pattern. As you may recall, to perform an action the player first clicks on one of the action buttons, then on the object of the action. An example is shown in Figure 15.6, where the player could click on the Get An Object button, then on the key underneath the room scene.

When the player clicks on the action button—in this case, Get An Object—the **Click** event code sets the action button's control variable to **true**:

```
Sub cmdGet_Click()
    GetAnObject = true
end sub
```

Then, when the player clicks on the button for the object, the **Click** event code for the object button executes:

```
Sub RoomObject01_Click()
    if GetAnObject then
        cmdInventory01.visible = true
        lbKey.visible = true
        GetAnObject = false
        ' Remove the object from the current room
        GameObjLoc(keys) = 100
        Player(score) = Player(score) + 3
        lbScore = Player(score)
        RoomObject01.visible = false
    end if
end sub
```

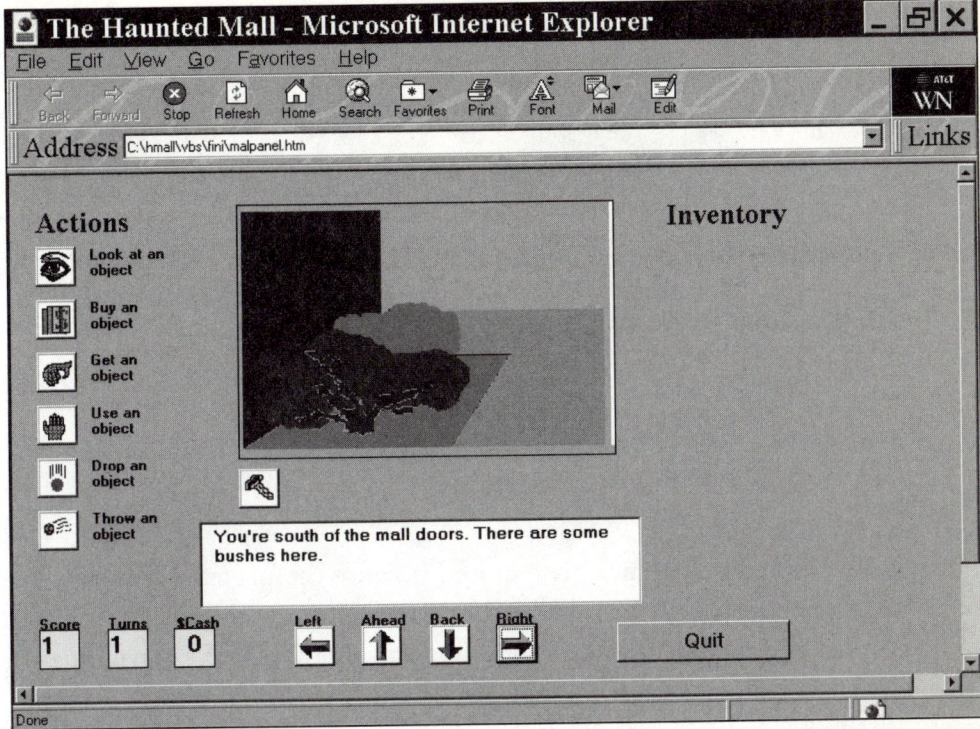

Figure 15.6
Example of getting an object.

When an object button is clicked, the first thing it does is check to see what action the user is trying to perform—i.e., which action variable has been set to **true**. The case of picking up the key in Room 6, as shown in the code snippet, is the simplest case. It makes the object disappear from the room by setting the appropriate **RoomObject**'s **visible** property to **false**. It then sets the action variable back to **false** so that when the user tries to perform a different action, the program won't try to perform both actions. It then adjusts the object's location in **GameObjLoc**, using 100 as the value for an object in inventory. And it adjusts the player's score: Getting most objects is worth 3 points.

The **Click** event code for most objects is a little more complex than the code for the key in Room 6. For example, the code for the flashlight in Room 7 has this general pattern:

```
Sub RoomObject02_Click()
```

```
if GetAnObject then
    ' Blah blah blah …
end if

if BuyAnObject then
    cmdInventory02.visible = true
    lbFlashlight.visible = true

    BuyAnObject = false
    ' Remove the object from the current room
    GameObjLoc(flashlight) = 100
    RoomObject02.visible = false
    ' Update the cash indicator
    lbCash.caption = lbCash.caption - 5
end if

end sub
```

Here, an additional **if** statement is required because the player might buy the object instead of simply getting it. The code for buying an object is very similar to that for getting an object: The main differences are that (a) the player doesn't get tagged as a shoplifter and thereby spring the trap of the ghostly security guard; (b) an appropriate amount is deducted from the player's cash supply to pay for the item; and (c) the player gets more points for buying an object than for simply getting it.

Using objects is a little different because certain objects can only be used profitably in certain rooms. For example:

- The hot dog can be used anywhere, but it only helps the player in Room 19, where he/she encounters the ghostly guard dog.
- The live wire can only be used in Room 13, to plug in Crowther's Castle.
- The money can only be used in Room 13, to pay for playing Crowther's Castle.

The code for using objects typically goes like this:

```
if UseAnObject then
    UseAnObject = false
    if roomnumber = 13 then
        ' turn on Crowther's Castle
        maze(gameon) = true
        tbScene = "The game is now turned on. Got some quarters?"
        Player(score) = Player(score) + 10
```

```
            lbScore = Player(score)
        end if
end if
```

As usual, the code first sets the action variable to **false**. Then, if the object can only be used in a certain room, the code checks the room number. If the player is in the correct room to use the object, then the program executes the code for using the object.

Looking At Objects

Looking at objects follows the same broad pattern as getting, buying, and using objects. However, it uses a timer to control how long the object is displayed.

When the player clicks the Look At An Object button, the **LookAtObject** variable is set to **true**. When the player then clicks on an object in inventory, a close-up view of the object is displayed in the image control that normally displays the room scene, as shown in Figure 15.7.

```
Sub cmdInventory04_Click()
    ' … Blah blah blah

    if LookAtObject then
        ScenePicture.picturepath = "look_hdg.gif"
        IeTimer2.enabled = true
    end if
end sub
```

After loading the close-up into the image control, the code activates the timer, meaning that timer events start to occur. Each time a timer event occurs, the code inside the event is executed:

```
Sub IeTimer2_Timer()
    If forward Then
        scenepicture.PicturePath = MallArray(roomnumber, RoomFView)
    Else
        scenepicture.PicturePath = MallArray(roomnumber, RoomBView)
    End If
        IeTimer2.enabled = false
end sub
```

In this case, merely to control how long the object close-up is displayed, we don't need much code. Before the timer is activated, the close-up is loaded into

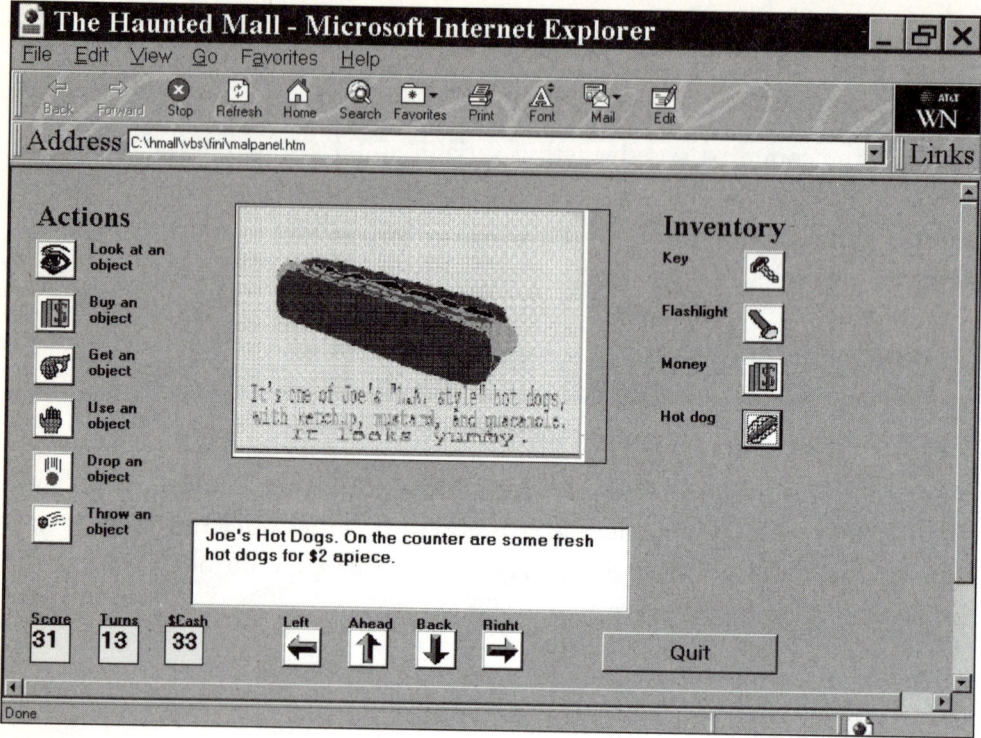

Figure 15.7
A close-up of the object displays in the image control.

the image control. Once the timer is activated, it will be *X* milliseconds until the timer event fires—where *X* is the number we plugged into the timer control's **interval** property. Once the timer event fires, the code executes. If the player is facing forward, the forward scene is reloaded for the current room; otherwise, the backward scene is reloaded.

To give the player time to look at the close-up, I set **IeTimer2**'s **interval** property to 5000—meaning that 5 seconds will elapse before the timer event fires and the room scene is reloaded.

Setting The Traps

The traps also use a timer control, but in a more complicated way than is used to look at objects. When a trap is activated, the **TimeCount** variable controls a slide show of text that tells the player what has happened as a result of falling into the trap.

Each trap is activated when the player tries to enter a certain room without having the required attribute, such as "being lit" by the flashlight. Consider what happens when the player is in Room 3, has not turned on the flashlight, and clicks the Ahead button to enter Room 4:

```
Case 3:
            If forward Then
               ' REMEMBER to adjust the forward T/F value when needed.
            Select Case direction
               Case "L": MsgBox _
                   "No way to go in that direction." _
                   , , "The Haunted Mall"
               Case "A":
                   if Player(lit) then
                      roomnumber = 4
                      NewRoom
                   else
                      scenepicture.PicturePath = "crash2.gif"
                      tbScene = "Yikes! You've fallen " & _
                         "down a hole in the floor!"
                      timecount = 0
                      IeTimer1.enabled = true
                   end if
   ' … Blah blah blah
```

First, the code loads an appropriately disastrous picture (such as "crash2.gif") into the image control. Then, it displays some initial text about the trap in the game panel text box. It sets the **TimeCount** variable to 0, then activates the timer. And the timer code looks like this:

```
Sub IeTimer1_Timer()
    TimeCount = TimeCount + 1

    select case roomnumber
       case 3: select case TimeCount
              case 1: tbScene = _
                 "Oh, I'm sorry. You seem to have got " & _
                 "yourself kilt (no point in skirting the issue)."
              case 2: tbScene = "Visit the mall again soon."
                 Player(alive) = false
                 IeTimer1.enabled = false
           end select
   ' … Blah blah blah
```

On each click of the timer event, the **TimeCount** variable is incremented by 1. Then, a **select case** statement checks the room number to determine which trap has been activated. Inside each **RoomNumber** case is, again, a smaller, embedded **select case** statement that uses **TimeCount** as its control variable. On each tick of the timer, it displays another text message about the player's predicament. When the last message is reached, the player is officially declared dead, and the timer control is turned off.

This same pattern of code—and, indeed, the same timer control—is used in all the game's traps.

Adding Music To The Game

Any true multimedia game should have music. Unfortunately, most music on the Web is copyrighted, so we couldn't include it in this book.

For use in your personal games, however, there are literally thousands of music samples (WAV and MIDI files) that you can plug into your game pages. As discussed in Chapter 12, the way to incorporate music into your game is to use the HTML <bgsound> tag, setting the **loop** property for continuous play of your music sample.

Bringing It All Together

And that's it. You've learned all the essential techniques used in creating The Haunted Mall. All you need now is practice and a little imagination. If you want to study the full code listing, it's on the CD-ROM included with this book. Happy game making!

16 Writing CGI Programs With Visual Basic 5

If you know Visual Basic Script, you know a lot about the "regular" kind of Visual Basic. In this chapter, you'll learn how you can use Visual Basic to create server-side CGI programs that can process a user's form data.

VBScript is a powerful tool for writing scripts that activate your Web pages. But for many purposes—perhaps most—your Web pages must interact with programs on a Web server. And VBScript by itself won't enable you to do that.

If you've had some exposure to books and articles about writing programs that run on Web servers—such as Coriolis's excellent *Serving the Web* (Robert Jon Mudry, 1996)—you're probably a little intimidated by the idea. Web servers usually run on Unix machines and run programs (or scripts) written in oddball languages like Perl. And then there's all that talk about CGI, as if you didn't have enough to learn already.

Well, you're in luck. If you know VBScript, you're already familiar with a lot of Microsoft's "regular" Visual Basic programming language. And if you know Visual Basic, you can write CGI programs, as long as your Web server is running compatible server software.

This isn't a book about CGI and Web servers, and we could easily fill up several chapters just giving you the fundamentals. To get you started as quickly as possible, we'll keep the technical details to a minimum and focus on the practical techniques you'll need. But you will need a little background information—otherwise, you'll have no idea what you're doing!

Web Servers And CGI: The Basics

In concept, the interaction between the Web browser on a user's PC and a CGI program on a Web server is a fairly simple process, as shown in Figure 16.1. The process has several steps:

1. The Web browser has an HTML document loaded. This document contains a form to get input from the user and submit it to the Web server.

2. The user sends the form information to the Web server by clicking on a Submit button.

3. The Web server software sends the information to a CGI program that's on the Web server computer.

4. The CGI program processes the information. If needed, it looks up the answer in an external database.

5. The CGI program creates an appropriate response for the user's data or query. Then, it sends the response back to the Web server software.

6. The Web server software forwards the response to the Web browser on the user's PC, where it displays as an HTML document.

Now, this simplicity masks a few unanswered questions. First, the Web server might have access to a large number of CGI programs. How does it know which program to run? Second, what data does the Web browser have to provide to the server, and in what form? Third, what data does the CGI program have to give back to the server, and in what form?

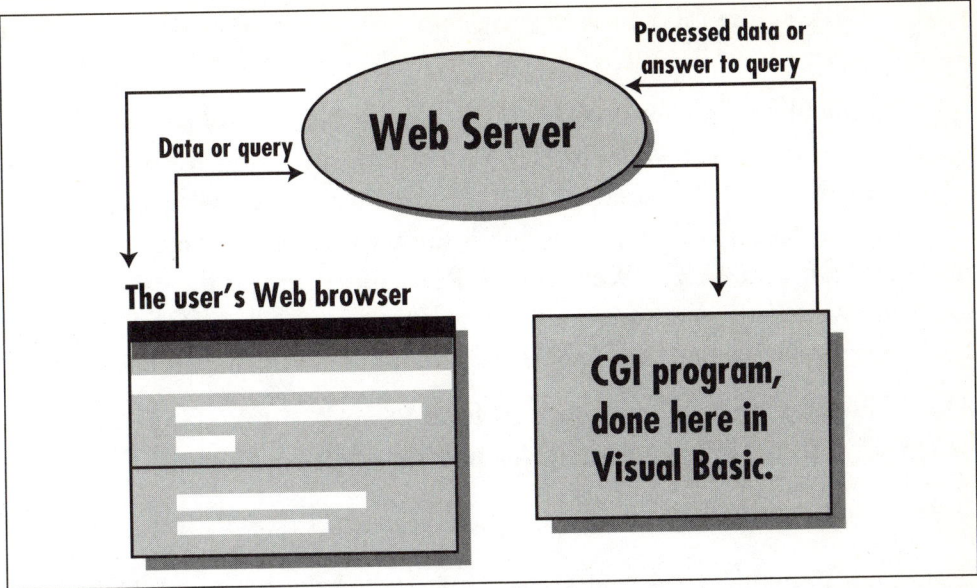

Figure 16.1
How a Web browser communicates with a CGI program.

All these questions are governed by HTTP, the Hypertext Transfer Protocol. It defines which information has to be provided, to whom, when, and in what form.

When you create a Web document and a CGI program that are meant to interact, you have to handle the arrangements for both ends of the conversation: from the user's Web browser to the CGI program on the server, and from the CGI program through the server back to the user's Web browser.

From The Web Browser To The Web Server

This is the easier side of the conversation to set up. When you create an HTML form, you should—if it's going to be useful for interacting with a Web server—provide several pieces of information:

- The form method. Normally, this will be **post**.

- The protocol governing the communication between your software and the server. This will usually be HTTP, but it can also be FTP (File Transfer Protocol) or some other protocol.

- The URL (Web address) of the Web server.

- The URL of the CGI program, meaning its location on the Web server computer.

If you think about this information, you can see that it answers some of our questions. **Post** tells the Web server what the browser means for it to do with the information from the user's HTML form. HTTP tells it what conventions the communication will follow, so that it knows what kind of message header information to expect. The Web server URL makes sure that the data is sent to the right Web server software on the right computer, and the CGI program's URL tells the Web server software where it should send the data it has received.

Thus, a bit later in the chapter, our first form to work with a CGI program will be started with the following tag in the user's HTML document:

```
<FORM method=post action="http://localhost/cgi-win/cgitest32.exe">
```

In the code line shown, the Web server's URL is *http://localhost*, while the location of the CGI program on the server computer is */cgi-win/cgitest32.exe*.

The CGI Program's URL Can Have Arguments At The End
Depending on which Web server software you're using, you can often add arguments (parameters) at the end of the CGI program's URL. These will be parsed by the server and passed to the CGI program. Normally, these arguments are preceded by a question mark. Different types of servers handle this information in slightly different ways, so you need to check the server documentation, and write your CGI program to receive the parameters in the server's particular format.

In the form itself, of course, you'll probably have input fields that get data for the CGI program to process. If you've created HTML forms already, that part is familiar. And if you code the HTML document correctly, the user's Web browser will handle the details of sending a message to the Web server in the appropriate form, with required header information and so forth.

In essence, what happens is this: For each input field in your HTML document, the user enters a particular piece of information, such as his/her name or email address. When the user clicks on the Submit button, the Web browser sends this information to the Web server as a set of *name=value* pairs. If you have one input field called *CustomerName* and the user enters the name *Sylvester Stallone*, the *name=value* pair sent to the server would be *CustomerName= "Sylvester Stallone"*.

The Web browser massages this data into a form that can be used by a CGI program. Then, it passes the data to the program. But everything is done behind the scenes: You don't have to worry too much about this part, as long as you set up your HTML form correctly in the first place.

From The CGI Program To The Web Server

It's on the other side of the conversation that you need slightly more knowledge of just how the server handles communication between the user's Web browser and the CGI program. The CGI program must give the server a message with an HTTP header indicating the type of data that the message contains. After that, the message might contain an HTML document like the ones we'll create with CGI programs in this chapter.

Setting Up To Test Your CGI Programs

If you want to write CGI programs in Visual Basic, the best Web server software to use is O'Reilly & Associates' WebSite. It runs under Windows 95 and Windows NT, has a Windows CGI interface for communicating with Windows CGI programs, and includes lots of CGI examples in Visual Basic. (It also includes a DOS CGI interface and a Standard CGI interface that lets you run programs in more traditional CGI languages, such as Perl.)

To run CGI programs with WebSite, you first need a CGI program to run. The program should, of course, be designed to work with the WebSite WebServer. This chapter will show you how to develop such programs. You'll also need an HTML document that submits data to be processed by the CGI program. After that, you follow these steps:

1. Install the WebSite software on your PC.

2. Open a TCP/IP connection. The WebSite WebServer software needs this connection open even if you're not going to be communicating over the Internet.

3. Start up the WebSite WebServer software.

4. Start your Web browser and load the HTML document that collects data for the CGI program.

5. Submit the data to the WebSite WebServer software.

6. Get the response from the CGI program.

Let's see how this process would work with a simple example. The WebSite package comes with a ready-to-use CGI program called *cgitest32.exe*. After we see how the overall process works, we'll be ready to create our own CGI programs in Visual Basic.

Testing The Form-CGI Connection

Let's create a basic HTML document that obtains the user's name and submits it to the Web server and then to a CGI program. First, create the HTML document shown in Listing 16.1. The document in Internet Explorer is shown in Figure 16.2.

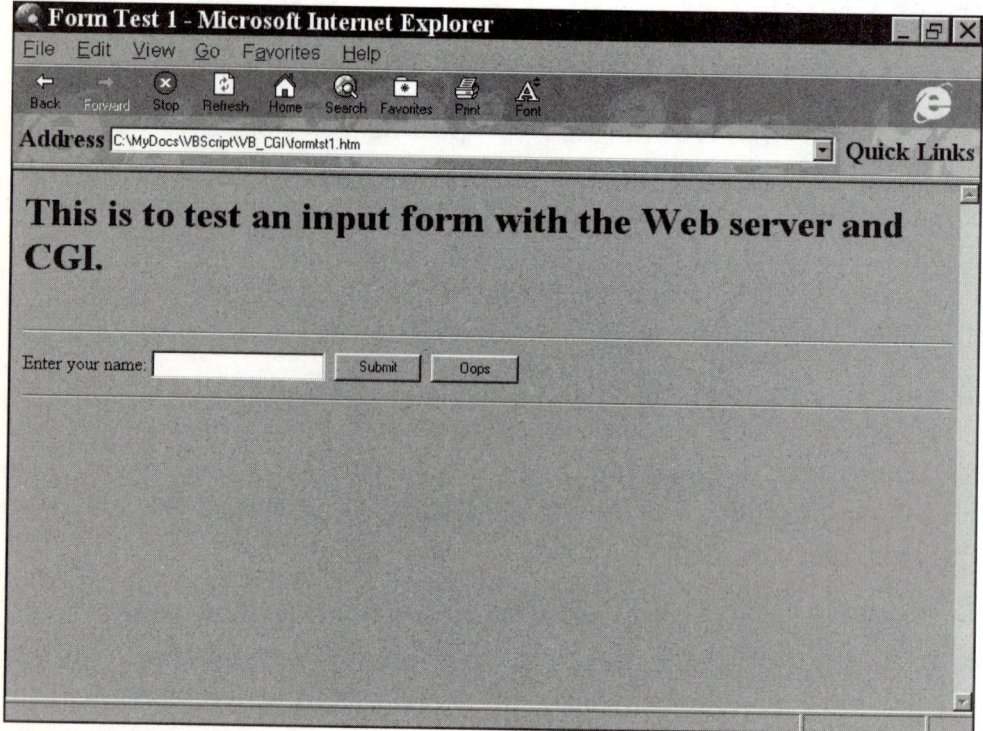

Figure 16.2
The HTML document loaded into Internet Explorer.

Listing 16.1 A simple HTML document to work with a CGI program.

```
<HTML>
<HEAD>
<TITLE> Form Test 1</TITLE>
</HEAD>
<BODY>
<h1>This is to test an input form with the Web server and CGI.</h1>
<br>
<hr>
<FORM METHOD="POST" ACTION="http://localhost/cgi-win/cgitest32.exe/Form">
Enter your name: <input type="text" name="UserName" size=25 value="">
<input type="submit" name="OK" value="Submit">
<input type="reset" name="Cancel" value="Oops">
</form>
<hr>
</BODY>
</HTML>
```

Most of the HTML code for the form will be familiar. Let's focus on the **<form>** tag itself. The form's method is **post**, and you should usually specify **post** as the method. The action part of the tag specifies the URL of the CGI program, as shown in this code line:

```
http://localhost/cgi-win/cgitest32.exe/Form
```

Let's dissect this URL. It consists of the following:

- **http:** tells the server what protocol is being used for the current message—i.e., the data being sent from the form to the CGI program.

- **//localhost** is the URL of the server itself. When WebSite WebServer software is running, it defines this as the directory where the WebSite software is installed.

- **/cgi-win/** is the subdirectory under the WebSite directory where the Windows CGI software is installed.

- **cgitest32.exe** is a ready-to-use CGI program that comes with WebSite. It was written in Visual Basic, and the Visual Basic project files are included as an example of CGI programming.

- **/Form** is a parameter that gets passed to the *cgitest32.exe* program, telling it about the format in which it should return data to the user's Web browser.

Note that this parameter is a little unusual, in that parameters at the end of a URL are normally preceded by a question mark.

Using The Forward Slash
It might have struck you as odd that the URL uses a path name with forward slash characters ("/") when Windows 95 uses the backward slash ("\") to separate directories. However, the WebSite WebServer software "maps" standard Windows directory names onto the forward-slash expressions so that you can use the forward slash character, which is standard in URL notation.

If you load the HTML document from Listing 16.1 into a Web browser, then start up your TCP/IP connection and load the WebServer software, you can submit data from the HTML document to the *cgitest32.exe* program. The program, in turn, will send an HTML document back to your Web browser. It will look something like Figure 16.3.

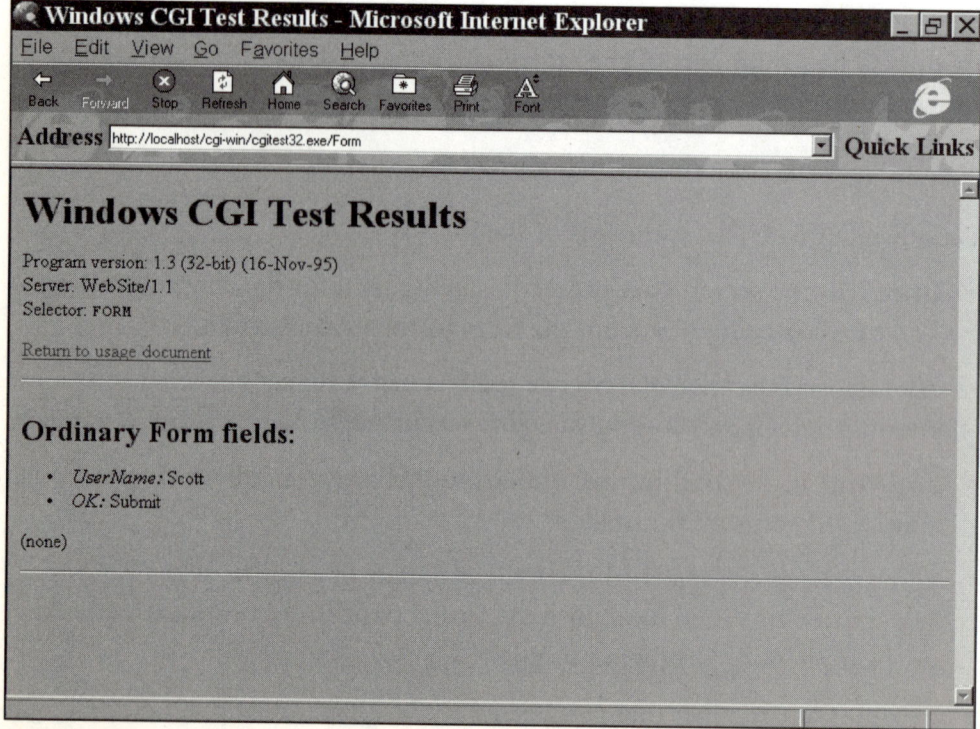

Figure 16.3
The *cgitest32.exe* program reports on what it received from your Web browser.

In this case, the CGI program tells you that it received data from two form fields: *UserName,* which in the figure is matched with the value "Scott," and *OK,* which is the name of the Submit button—with a value, appropriately enough, of "Submit."

Assuming that you already know how to create forms, the *cgitest32.exe* program is a good way to verify that you have your WebServer software set up and running properly. Once you've done that, you can go on to create your own CGI programs. If something doesn't work right, you'll know that the problem is with your program, not with the way that the Web server software is set up.

Writing A Simple CGI Program In Visual Basic

Now, let's create a simple—but practical—CGI program in Visual Basic. This program will process orders for Coriolis Group books. It will work with an HTML document that displays as an order form when loaded into a Web browser.

We're not going to tarry too long with the details of the HTML document, inasmuch as our main objective is to learn how to write a CGI program that will work with it. However, the HTML code is shown in Listing 16.2, while the Web page it creates is shown in Figure 16.4.

Listing 16.2 HTML CODE TO CREATE THE ORDER FORM IN FIGURE 16.4.

```
<HTML>
<HEAD>
<TITLE>Order Books from Coriolis!</TITLE>
</HEAD>
<BODY>
<h1>Check the books you would like to order:</h1>
<FORM method=post action="http://localhost/cgi-win/orderbk1.exe">
<hr>
<ul><ul><ul><ul><ul>
<INPUT NAME="CB_VBScriptPrg" TYPE="CHECKBOX" VALUE="1"
       ALIGN=left>VBScript 2 & ActiveX Programming, $39.99<br>
<INPUT NAME="CB_DelphiExp" TYPE="CHECKBOX" VALUE="1"
       ALIGN=left>The New Delphi 2 Programming EXplorer, $44.99<br>
<INPUT NAME="CB_JavaApp" TYPE="CHECKBOX" VALUE="1"
       ALIGN=left>Writing Java Applets, $39.99<br>
```

362   Chapter 16

```
<INPUT NAME="CB_Intranet" TYPE="CHECKBOX" VALUE="1"
       ALIGN=left>Developing Real-World Intranets, $39.99<br>
</ul></ul> </ul></ul></ul>
<hr>
<pre>
Your Name:     <INPUT NAME="TB_Customer" TYPE="" SIZE="20"
       ALIGN=right><br>
Street Address: <INPUT NAME="TB_Street" TYPE="" SIZE="25"
       ALIGN=right><br>
City:          <INPUT NAME="TB_City" TYPE="TEXT" SIZE="15"
       ALIGN=right> State: <INPUT NAME="TB_State" TYPE="TEXT" SIZE="5"
       ALIGN=right> Zip: <INPUT NAME="TB_Zip" TYPE="TEXT" SIZE="5"
       ALIGN=right><br>

Send your order today!  <INPUT NAME="Btn_Order"
    TYPE="SUBMIT" ALIGN=right>
</pre>
</FORM>
</BODY>
</HTML>
```

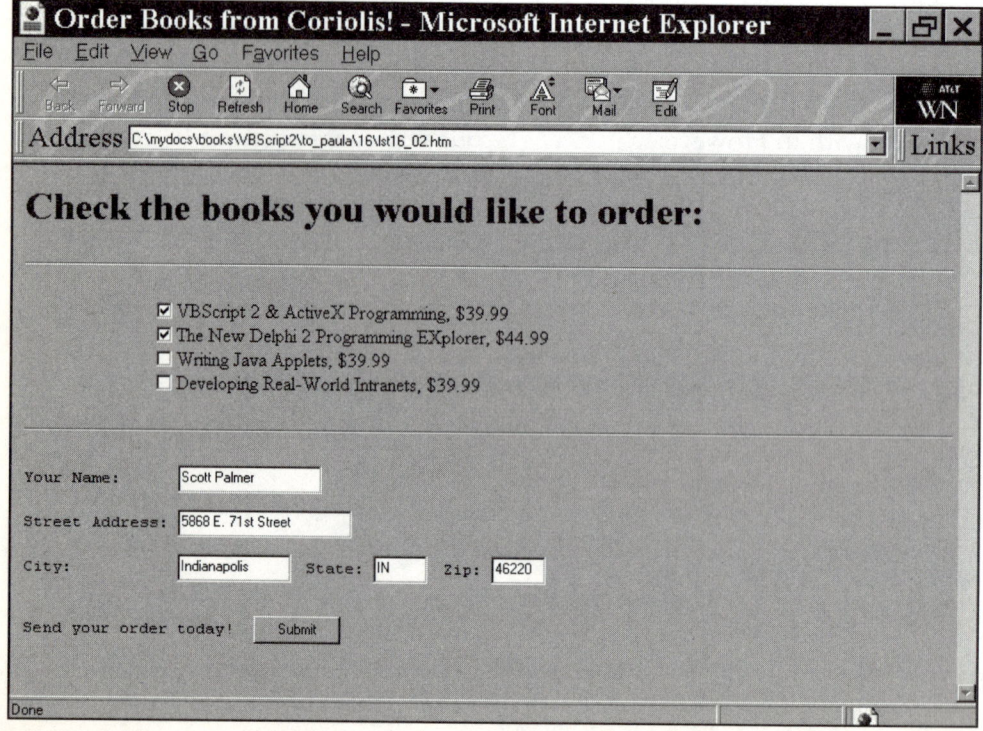

Figure 16.4
The Web page created by Listing 16.2.

As you can see, the HTML code in Listing 16.2 sets up a form with four checkboxes, each of which can be used (in theory) to order a book from The Coriolis Group. At the bottom of the form are text boxes for the customer's name and address.

The **action** part of the form tag specifies the usual URL path. Then, it specifies *orderbk1.exe*, the CGI program to process the form data—the CGI program we're now going to create.

Creating The CGI Program Itself

A CGI program needs routines to communicate with the server. In particular, it needs routines to:

- Get the names and values of various form fields passed to it by the server
- Determine if certain fields are present in the data stream or not
- Send data back to the server in a format appropriate to the original request made by the Web browser

That list, of course, is a bare minimum. Even so, if you had to write all those routines yourself, CGI programming would be a daunting task indeed.

WebSite, however, includes a ready-to-use Visual Basic code module called *cgi32.bas*. It defines all the procedures and functions you need to communicate with the WebSite WebServer software. That includes all three routines listed above, and quite a bit more. To use those routines, you need only add the *cgi32.bas* code module to your Visual Basic program project.

With that little bit of introduction, let's go step by step through the creation of an order-processing CGI program with Visual Basic. Follow these steps:

1. Create a directory for your CGI programs.

2. Start up Visual Basic 5.

    You can create CGI programs with Visual Basic 3, but you need a different version of WebSite. You can also create CGI programs with Visual Basic 4, though the procedure differs very slightly from what's presented here for Visual Basic 5—mainly in the steps you take to remove unwanted components and references from the project.

3. Delete the form from the program project.

   Highlight the form in the Project window, open the Project menu, and select Remove Form1.

4. Add the *cgi32.bas* code module to your program project.

   WebSite installs the *cgi32.bas* file in the directory \Website\cgi-src\: The "cgi-src" is for "CGI source code." To add the file to your project, open the Project menu and select Add Module. This opens the Add Module dialog box, as shown in Figure 16.5. Click on the Existing tab, and then browse to the appropriate directory, where you can highlight and select the file.

5. Open the Project menu, select References, and remove the reference to OLE Automation.

6. Open the Project menu, select Add Module, and click on the Open button.

   This creates a new Visual Basic code module and adds it to your program project. Save the module as *orderbk1.bas*.

7. Finally, save the whole project as *orderbk1.vbp*.

That gets you started. One thing you might do right now—it's optional, but you'll find it a deeply rewarding and spiritual experience—is peruse the code inside *cgi32.bas*. It defines all the routines your program will use to communicate with the Web server.

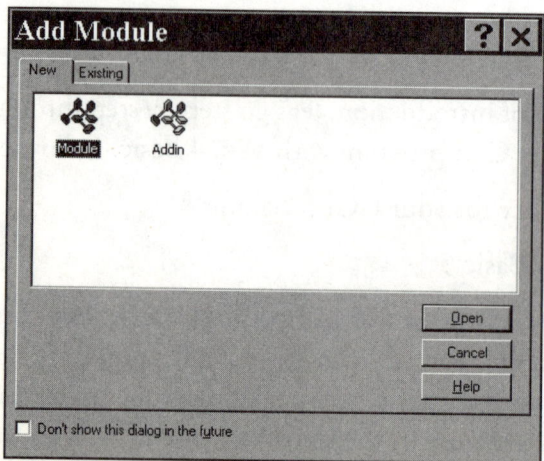

Figure 16.5
The Add Module dialog box.

Once you've set up the Orderbk1 program project, you need to add three procedures to the orderbk1.bas code module:

- **CGI_Main()**. This is the main control procedure for the program. It's a lot like the **main()** function in a C program, in that it doesn't do much itself except call other routines that do the work of the program.

- **Inter_Main()**. Even though you're going to create an executable (.EXE) program, it will only do meaningful work when it's interacting with the Web server software. If someone tries to start the program from the Windows File Manager, this procedure will display a short message explaining the purpose of the program.

- **ProcessOrder()**. This is the routine that does the application-specific stuff. It gets the data from the server, processes it, and sends a response back to the server.

The complete code for the orderbk1.bas module is shown in Listing 16.3. Look over the listing to get a bird's-eye view: We'll discuss the details in a moment.

Listing 16.3 THE ORDERBK1.BAS CODE MODULE.

```
'-----------------------------------------------------------
' Orderbk1: example of writing a CGI program in Visual Basic.
' This simple program gets data from an HTML book-order form.
' It adds up the total amount owed by the customer, then sends an
' HTML document back to the user's Web browser. The HTML document
' shows the total amount owed, as well as the customer's name and
' address. It shows how a Visual Basic CGI program can get data from
' an HTML form and send data back to it.
'-----------------------------------------------------------
Option Explicit


'-----------------------------------------------------------
' This is the CGI_Main() sub. It's very much like the main() function
' in a C program: Its purpose is to call other subs that do the
' substantive work of the program.
'-----------------------------------------------------------
Sub CGI_Main()
        ProcessOrder
        Beep
End Sub
```

```
'--------------------------------------------------------------------
' This gets the data from the various fields in the customer's order form.
' It then adds up the total amount due and sends a report to the customer
' in the form of an HTML document, which appears in his/her Web browser.
'--------------------------------------------------------------------
Sub ProcessOrder()

    Dim CustName, Street, City, State, Zip As String
    Dim Subtotal, Tax, Total As Single
    Dim VBScriptPrg, DelphiExp, JavaApp, Intranet As Boolean

    Subtotal = 0
    Tax = 0
    Total = 0

    VBScriptPrg = False
    DelphiExp = False
    JavaApp = False
    Intranet = False

    ' Get data from order form
    CustName = GetSmallField("TB_Customer")
    Street = GetSmallField("TB_Street")
    City = GetSmallField("TB_City")
    State = GetSmallField("TB_State")
    Zip = GetSmallField("TB_Zip")

    If FieldPresent("CB_VBScriptPrg") Then
        Subtotal = Subtotal + 39.99
        VBScriptPrg = True
    End If

    If FieldPresent("CB_DelphiExp") Then
        Subtotal = Subtotal + 44.99
        DelphiExp = True
    End If

    If FieldPresent("CB_JavaApp") Then
        Subtotal = Subtotal + 39.99
        JavaApp = True
    End If

    If FieldPresent("CB_Intranet") Then
        Subtotal = Subtotal + 39.99
        Intranet = True
    End If
```

```vb
    ' Compute the final amount.
    Tax = Subtotal * 1.5
    Total = Subtotal + Tax



    ' Report to the user on which books were ordered,
    ' where they will be sent, and how much he/she will
    ' be charged for them.

    Send ("Content-type: text/html")
    Send ("")
    Send ("<html><head><title>Thanks for your order!</title></head>")
    Send ("<body><h1>Books you will receive:</h1>")
    Send ("<ul><pre>")

    If VBScriptPrg Then
        Send ("<li>VBScript 2 & ActiveX Programming        $39.99")
    End If

    If DelphiExp Then
        Send ("<li>The New Delphi 2 Programming EXplorer   $44.99")
    End If

    If JavaApp Then
        Send ("<li>Writing Java Applets                    $39.99")
    End If

    If Intranet Then
        Send ("<li>Developing Real-World Intranets         $39.99")
    End If
    Send ("                                     ----------")
    Send ("Subtotal:                            $" & Subtotal)
    Send ("<br>Tax:                             $" & Tax)
    Send ("                                     ----------")
    Send ("Total amount billed:                 $" & Total)

    Send ("</ul><hr>")
    Send ("<h1>Books will be shipped to:</h1>")
    Send ("Name:    " & CustName)
    Send ("Address: " & Street)
    Send ("City:    " & City & "   State: " & State & _
          "Zip:    " & Zip)

    Send ("</pre></body></html>")

End Sub
```

```
'----------------------------------------------------------------
' Inter_Main: Because this is a CGI program designed to work with the
' Web server, it makes no sense for someone to run it directly from the
' Windows File Manager. If someone attempts to run the program directly,
' this sub displays a message box explaining what kind of program it is.
'----------------------------------------------------------------
Sub Inter_Main()
    MsgBox "This is a CGI program for the Web server.", 16, "Order Books"
End Sub
```

Inside The Orderbk1.bas Code Module

As noted earlier, there are only three procedures in the orderbk1.bas code module: **CGI_Main()**, **Inter_Main()**, and **ProcessOrder()**. Let's start with the first two, which are quite simple.

CGI_Main(), true to its mission as a control routine that simply calls other procedures, is only four lines long:

```
Sub CGI_Main()
        ProcessOrder
        Beep
End Sub
```

After calling the **ProcessOrder()** sub, it uses the Visual Basic **beep** statement to make the PC's speaker emit a tone. Then it terminates. In the next part of the chapter, we'll expand this procedure slightly to add server-side data validation.

Inter_Main() is similarly short and simple:

```
Sub Inter_Main()
    MsgBox "This is a CGI program for the Web server.", 16, "Order Books"
End Sub
```

It uses the Visual Basic **msgbox** statement to display a message box in case anyone tries to run the program independently of a conversation with the Web server.

Now, let's get to the real heart of the program: the **ProcessOrder()** sub. The first thing it does is declare some local variables: one for each of the fields in the order form, plus a couple of extras:

```
Dim CustName, Street, City, State, Zip As String
Dim Subtotal, Tax, Total As Single
Dim VBScriptPrg, DelphiExp, JavaApp, Intranet As Boolean
```

Once the variables are declared, the control variables are set to their initial values, as shown in the code snippet below. The variables for the money amounts in the order are set to zero. The boolean variables that show if particular books have been ordered are set to **false**.

```
Subtotal = 0
Tax = 0
Total = 0

VBScriptPrg = False
DelphiExp = False
JavaApp = False
Intranet = False
```

When the procedure gets the data from the form's text fields, it will put each data item into the variable that corresponds to its form field. To get the data from a text field, the program uses the **GetSmallField**() function defined in the *cgi32.bas* code module, as shown in this code snippet:

```
CustName = GetSmallField("TB_Customer")
Street = GetSmallField("TB_Street")
City = GetSmallField("TB_City")
State = GetSmallField("TB_State")
Zip = GetSmallField("TB_Zip")
```

The code is pretty easy to understand. If you look at the HTML document in Listing 16.2, you can see that *TB_Customer, TB_Street,* and so on are the names of the text box controls in the HTML form. Take one of the names, put it in quotation marks, pass it to the **GetSmallField**() function as a parameter, and the function returns whatever the form's user typed into that text box. Then, you just use a Visual Basic assignment statement to copy the value into the appropriate local variable.

Checkboxes, however, are handled differently. If the user checks a particular checkbox on the order form, then the checkbox's name-value pair will be passed by the server to the CGI program. However, if a particular checkbox is *not* checked, then it won't (like a text box control) have its name-value pair (with a null value) sent to the CGI program. If a particular checkbox is unchecked, then its name-value pair won't be sent to the CGI program at all. In that situation, trying to get its value by using **GetSmallField**() would cause a run-time error.

Fortunately, there's a simple and elegant solution. The value of a checkbox is really irrelevant in this context. If a checkbox is checked, then the WebServer software will send its name-value pair to the CGI program. If it's not checked, then its name-value pair will be absent from the data stream. As a result, you can use the **FieldPresent**() boolean function to see if a checkbox was checked, as shown in this code snippet:

```
If FieldPresent("CB_VBScriptPrg") Then
        Subtotal = Subtotal + 39.99
        VBScriptPrg = True
End If
```

This **if** statement uses **FieldPresent**() to determine if a book's checkbox was checked. If it was checked, then the next line adds the price of the book to the *subtotal* variable. Finally, the boolean variable for that book is set to **true**, indicating that the book has been ordered by the customer. At the end of this process, the *subtotal* variable will have the sum of the prices for the books the customer has ordered.

Sending A Report Back To The Customer's Web Browser

The final part of **ProcessOrder**() creates an HTML document with information about the customer's order. It then sends the document, with the required header information, back to the customer's Web browser. To do this, it uses the **Send**() procedure defined in cgi32.bas. **Send**() simply transmits a text string over the server to the user's Web browser.

The header information is absolutely required if the server is to get the message back to the customer's Web location. Two lines are mandatory: a content/type line and a blank line to separate it from the body of the message. Other lines can be used for special cases, but we won't discuss them in this book. The two mandatory lines are shown in this code snippet:

```
Send ("Content-type: text/html")
Send ("")
```

In this case, the content type line indicates that the CGI program is sending an HTML document back to the user. The blank line—well, it's a blank line. If you don't understand the concept, Zen meditation might help.

Next, the procedure sends the header information for an HTML document, along with some other initial formatting tags:

```
Send ("<html><head><title>Thanks for your order!</title></head>")
Send ("<body><h1>Books you will receive:</h1>")
Send ("<ul><pre>")
```

The **<ul>** tag, of course, marks the beginning of an unnumbered list in the HTML document. Then, the procedure uses successive **if** statements to test each boolean variable corresponding to a book that the customer might have ordered:

```
If VBScriptPrg Then
     Send ("<li>VBScript 2 & ActiveX Programming         $39.99")
End If

If DelphiExp Then
     Send ("<li>The New Delphi 2 Programming EXplorer   $44.99")
End If
… and so on.
```

For each boolean variable with a value of **true**, the procedure sends a list item with the title and price of the corresponding book. After listing all the books ordered, the procedure sends the subtotal, tax, and total amount that will be billed to the customer. Note the use of the ampersand (**&**) to concatenate text strings and numeric values:

```
Send ("                                   ----------")
Send ("Subtotal:                          $" & Subtotal)
Send ("<br>Tax:                           $" & Tax)
Send ("                                   ----------")
Send ("Total amount billed:               $" & Total)
```

Finally, the procedure sends back the name and address to which the books will be shipped, along with tags that mark the end of the HTML document:

```
Send ("</ul><hr>")
Send ("<h1>Books will be shipped to:</h1>")
Send ("Name:     " & CustName)
Send ("Address: " & Street)
Send ("City:     " & City & "   State: " & State & _
     "Zip:      " & Zip)

Send ("</pre></body></html>")
```

Use Of The Line Continuation Character "_"

In the listing, we've used the Visual Basic line continuation character "_" to keep the code lines from running too long for the book page margins. Obviously, in your own code, it's entirely optional. Use it only if you want to do so.

The HTML document sent back to the customer's Web browser is shown in Figure 16.6.

Adding Server-Side Data Validation

Earlier in the book, you saw how to use VBScript to handle client-side data validation—i.e., to build a few simple error traps right into the Web page that appears in the user's Web browser. Sometimes, however, you'd like to do server-side

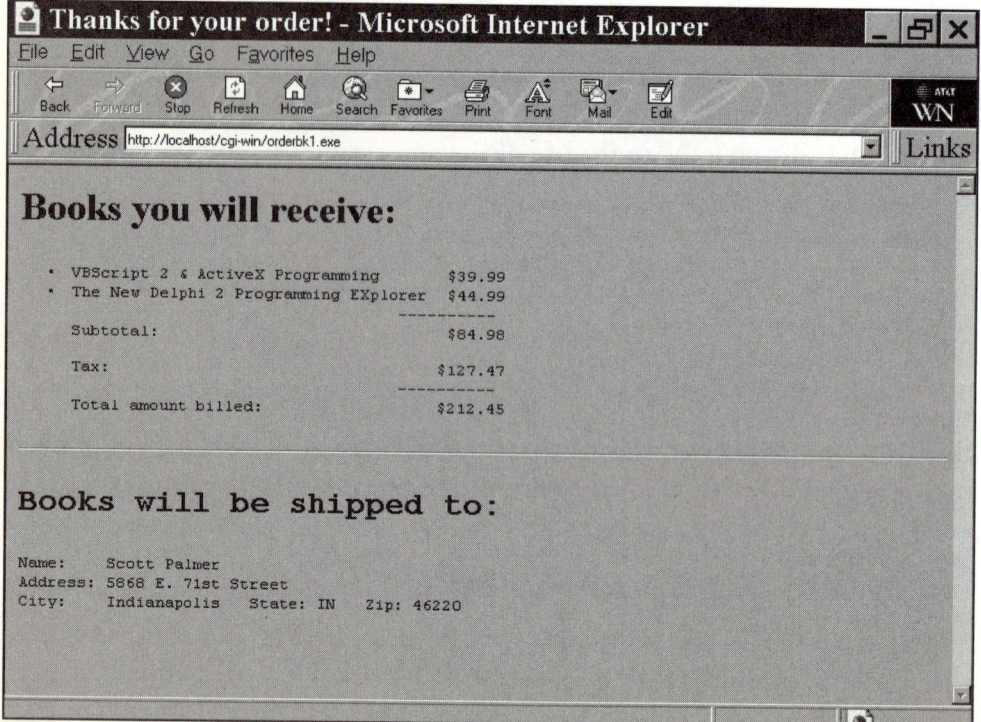

Figure 16.6
The HTML document sent back to the user by the CGI program.

data validation. You can accomplish that with a fairly easy modification of the *Orderbk1* program project and the HTML document with which the user places his/her order.

In essence, all you'll do is add two new routines to the CGI program:

- A boolean function called **OrderInfoPresent**(). This function will verify that in the order entry Web page, the user has filled in all the information required to process the order.

- A procedure called **RedisplayOrderForm**(). If any information is missing, this sub will send an HTML document back to the user's Web browser. This document will redisplay the order form, along with a message explaining that some of the required information was missing from the original transmission.

The simplest part of the exercise is to modify the HTML document to work with the new CGI program, which we'll call *Orderbk2*. All you need to change is the name of the program in the **action** part of the form tag, as shown in Listing 16.4.

Listing 16.4 CHANGING THE CGI PROGRAM CALLED BY THE HTML FORM.

```
<HTML>
<HEAD>
<TITLE>Order Books from Coriolis!</TITLE>
</HEAD>
<BODY>
<h1>Check the books you would like to order:</h1>
<FORM method=post action="http://localhost/cgi-win/orderbk2.exe">
<hr>
… and so on.
```

The next task is to change the orderbk1.bas code module so that it contains and uses the new routines. The updated module, which you might want to save under the name of *orderbk2.bas*, is shown in Listing 16.5.

Listing 16.5 THE ORDERBK2.BAS CODE MODULE, WITH SERVER-SIDE DATA VALIDATION.

```
'-----------------------------------------------------------------
' Orderbk2: Demonstrates how to add server-side data validation
' to the CGI program in Orderbk1.
'-----------------------------------------------------------------
Option Explicit
```

```
'-----------------------------------------------------------------
' This is the CGI_Main() sub. It's very much like the main() function
' in a C program: Its purpose is to call other subs that do the
' substantive work of the program.
'-----------------------------------------------------------------
Sub CGI_Main()
    If OrderInfoPresent Then
        ProcessOrder
    Else
        RedisplayOrderForm
    End If
End Sub


'-----------------------------------------------------------------
' This gets the data from the various fields in the customer's order
' form. It then adds up the total amount due and sends a report to
' the customer in the form of an HTML document that appears in
' his/her Web browser.
'-----------------------------------------------------------------
Sub ProcessOrder()

    Dim CustName, Street, City, State, Zip As String
    Dim Subtotal, Tax, Total As Single
    Dim VBScriptPrg, DelphiExp, JavaApp, Intranet As Boolean

    Subtotal = 0
    Tax = 0
    Total = 0

    VBScriptPrg = False
    DelphiExp = False
    JavaApp = False
    Intranet = False

    ' Get data from order form
    CustName = GetSmallField("TB_Customer")
    Street = GetSmallField("TB_Street")
    City = GetSmallField("TB_City")
    State = GetSmallField("TB_State")
    Zip = GetSmallField("TB_Zip")

    If FieldPresent("CB_VBScriptPrg") Then
        Subtotal = Subtotal + 39.99
        VBScriptPrg = True
    End If
```

```
    If FieldPresent("CB_DelphiExp") Then
        Subtotal = Subtotal + 44.99
        DelphiExp = True
    End If

    If FieldPresent("CB_JavaApp") Then
        Subtotal = Subtotal + 39.99
        JavaApp = True
    End If

    If FieldPresent("CB_Intranet") Then
        Subtotal = Subtotal + 39.99
        Intranet = True
    End If

    ' Compute the final amount.
    Tax = Subtotal * 1.5
    Total = Subtotal + Tax

    ' Report to the user on which books were ordered,
    ' where they will be sent, and how much he/she will
    ' be charged for them.

    Send ("Content-type: text/html")
    Send ("")
    Send ("<html><head><title>Thanks for your order!</title></head>")
    Send ("<body><h1>Books you will receive:</h1>")
    Send ("<ul><pre>")

    If VBScriptPrg Then
        Send ("<li>VBScript 2 & ActiveX Programming          $39.99")
    End If

    If DelphiExp Then
        Send ("<li>The New Delphi 2 Programming EXplorer    $44.99")
    End If

    If JavaApp Then
        Send ("<li>Writing Java Applets                      $39.99")
    End If

    If Intranet Then
        Send ("<li>Developing Real-World Intranets           $39.99")
    End If
    Send ("                                        ---------")
    Send ("Subtotal:                               $" & Subtotal)
    Send ("<br>Tax:                                $" & Tax)
```

```
        Send ("                              ----------")
        Send ("Total amount billed:              $" & Total)

        Send ("</ul><hr>")
        Send ("<h1>Books will be shipped to:</h1>")
        Send ("Name:     " & CustName)
        Send ("Address: " & Street)
        Send ("City:    " & City & "   State: " & State & _
              "Zip:    " & Zip)

        Send ("</pre></body></html>")

End Sub


'-------------------------------------------------------------------
' Inter_Main: Because this is a CGI program designed to work with the
' Web server, it makes no sense for someone to run it directly from the
' Windows File Manager. If someone attempts to run the program directly,
' this sub displays a message box explaining what kind of program it is.
'-------------------------------------------------------------------
Sub Inter_Main()
    MsgBox "This is a CGI program for the Web server.", 16, "Order Books"
End Sub


'-------------------------------------------------------------------
' RedisplayOrderForm: If the user doesn't provide all the required data,
' this procedure returns the order form with a "try again" message.
'-------------------------------------------------------------------
Public Sub RedisplayOrderForm()

    ' Send the header information.
    Send "Content-type: text/html"

    ' Here's the obligatory blank line
    ' to separate the header info from
    ' the body of the message.
    Send ""

    ' Redisplay the order form.
    Send ("<html><head><title>Order Books from Coriolis!")
    Send ("</title></head><body>")
    Send ("You didn't fill out the form completely. Try again.<br>")
    Send ("<h1>Check the books you would like to order:</h1>")
    Send ("<form method=post action=
      ""http://localhost/cgi-win/orderbk2.exe"">")
```

```vb
' You can use the <ul> tag to indent text on a Web page.
Send ("<hr><ul><ul><ul><ul>")

' Send the checkboxes.
' HTML lines are broken up here to fit in
' the margins of this book. The user's Web
' browser doesn't care.
Send ("<input name=""CB_VBScriptPrg"" type=""checkbox"" ")
Send ("value=""1"" align=left> ")
Send ("VBScript 2 & ActiveX Programming, $39.99<br>")

Send ("<input name=""CB_DelphiExp"" type=""checkbox"" ")
Send ("value=""1"" align=left> ")
Send ("The New Delphi 2 Programming EXplorer, $44.99<br>")

Send ("<input name=""CB_JavaApp"" type=""checkbox"" ")
Send ("value=""1"" align=left> ")
Send ("Writing Java Applets, $39.99<br>")

Send ("<input name=""CB_Intranet"" type=""checkbox"" ")
Send ("value=""1"" align=left> ")
Send ("Developing Real-World Intranets, $39.99<br>")

' Unindent and send a horizontal line. Use the
' <pre>formatted-text tag to make sure everything
' aligns as you want.
Send ("</ul></ul></ul></ul><hr><pre>")

' Send back the customer information fields.
Send ("Your Name:     <input name=""TB_Customer"" ")
Send ("type=""text"" size=""20"" align=right><br>")

Send ("Street Address: <input name=""TB_Street"" ")
Send ("type=""text"" size=""25"" align=right>")

' For the book's program listing ONLY, preformatted
' text needs to be turned off here. Otherwise, the
' hard carriage returns in the VB code will be included
' in the HTML document, and the City, State, and Zip
' fields will be displayed on separate lines. When you
' create a routine like this on your own, simply take out
' the next line ("Send("</pre>")") and send the City, State,
' and Zip fields in a single Send line. Then, turn off the
' preformatted-text tag at the end of the HTML form.
Send ("</pre>")
Send ("City: <input name=""TB_City"" ")
Send ("type=""text"" size=""15"" align=right>")
```

```
            Send ("State: <input name=""TB_State"" ")
            Send ("type=""text"" size=""5"" align=right>")

            Send ("Zip: <input name=""TB_Zip"" ")
            Send ("type=""text"" size=""5"" align=right><br><br>")

            Send ("Send your order today! <input name=""Btn_Order"" ")
            Send ("type=""submit"" align=right>")
            Send ("</form></body></html>")


End Sub

' ----------------------------------------------------------------------
' OrderInfoPresent: This checks to see if the customer has sent all the
' information needed to process his/her order.
' ----------------------------------------------------------------------
Public Function OrderInfoPresent()

        ' Set the function's value to false.
        ' The order will be processed ONLY IF
        ' all the required conditions are fulfilled,
        ' in which case, the function's value is set
        ' to true.
        OrderInfoPresent = False

        ' Notice that because we're using the "_" line
        ' continuation character, this is actually a
        ' single-line IF statement and doesn't require
        ' an ENDIF at the end.

        ' At least one of the book checkboxes must be checked.
        ' Therefore, we use OR here.
        If (FieldPresent("CB_VBScriptPrg") _
            Or FieldPresent("CB_DelphiExp") _
            Or FieldPresent("CB_JavaApp") _
            Or FieldPresent("CB_Intranet")) _

        ' And ALL of the customer information has to be present.
        ' Therefore, we use AND here.
            And GetSmallField("TB_Customer") <> "" _
            And GetSmallField("TB_Street") <> "" _
            And GetSmallField("TB_City") <> "" _
            And GetSmallField("TB_State") <> "" _
            And GetSmallField("TB_Zip") <> "" Then OrderInfoPresent = True

End Function
```

Changing The CGI_Main() Procedure

Apart from the addition of the two new routines, which we'll get to in a moment, the first and most obvious change is in the **CGI_Main()** procedure, shown in this code snippet:

```
Sub CGI_Main()
    If OrderInfoPresent Then
        ProcessOrder
    Else
        RedisplayOrderForm
    End If
End Sub
```

Previously, the **CGI_Main()** sub only called the **ProcessOrder()** routine. Now, it uses the **OrderInfoPresent()** function in an **if** statement to determine if the customer provided all the information needed to process the order. If so, then the program goes ahead with **ProcessOrder**, just as before. If not, then it calls the **RedisplayOrderForm()** sub.

Checking The Order Data

The **OrderInfoPresent()** function does only a basic data check: It ensures that all the required data is present. In this case, that's all we really need. If a user were submitting more complex information, we might easily build in more extensive error trapping, such as making sure some of the values fell into a certain range.

Here, however, we're keeping it simple. The first thing that **OrderInfoPresent** does is to set itself to the value **false**. Only if all the required information is present will the function's value be set to **true**.

After that, there are two distinct steps in the data check. The first step verifies that at least one of the order form's book-order checkboxes has been checked. This is shown in this code snippet:

```
If (FieldPresent("CB_VBScriptPrg") _
    Or FieldPresent("CB_DelphiExp") _
    Or FieldPresent("CB_JavaApp") _
    Or FieldPresent("CB_Intranet")) _
```

If no checkboxes are checked, then nothing has been ordered. Thus, only *one* of the checkboxes needs to be checked for this to be a valid order. We use parentheses to bundle together all four checkbox tests into a single expression. Inside the expression, we use **or** so that if the user checked at least one of the checkboxes, then the whole expression returns a value of **true**. As before, we use the line-continuation character to keep the Visual Basic code lines within the page margins of this book: For your own code, the line-continuation characters are totally optional.

The second step in the data check is to make sure that *all* of the customer information fields (name, street address, city, state, and ZIP code) have been filled in. To do that, we use the **and** operator so that the function will get a value of **true** only if all the blanks are filled in. This is shown in this code snippet:

```
And GetSmallField("TB_Customer") <> "" _
    And GetSmallField("TB_Street") <> "" _
    And GetSmallField("TB_City") <> "" _
    And GetSmallField("TB_State") <> "" _
    And GetSmallField("TB_Zip") <> "" Then OrderInfoPresent = True
```

Redisplaying The Order Form

The procedure to redisplay the order form uses the same approach as is used in the **ProcessOrder**() sub to send an order report back to the user. It starts out with the message header (content line, then a blank line). After that, it's just a matter of sending the appropriate text and HTML tags to redisplay the order form.

The only tricky part is using double and triple quotation marks. Visual Basic strings are delimited by quotation marks. Therefore, if you need to display a quotation mark inside a Visual Basic string, you use two consecutive quotation marks for each single quotation mark you want to display. Yes, it's a simple idea, but it gets pretty messy in the code, as shown in this line:

```
Send ("<form method=post action=
   ""http://localhost/cgi-win/orderbk2.exe"">")
```

Where does that > go, again? Is it after all three quotation marks at the end of the line, or between the second and third quotation marks? You can answer those questions, but if you aren't careful, it's very easy to mess things up. Fortunately, a Web browser generally doesn't care how HTML code is formatted, so the messy-looking HTML document generated by the **RedisplayOrderForm**() sub works just fine. It's shown in Listing 16.6. The order form it displays in the Web browser is shown in Figure 16.7.

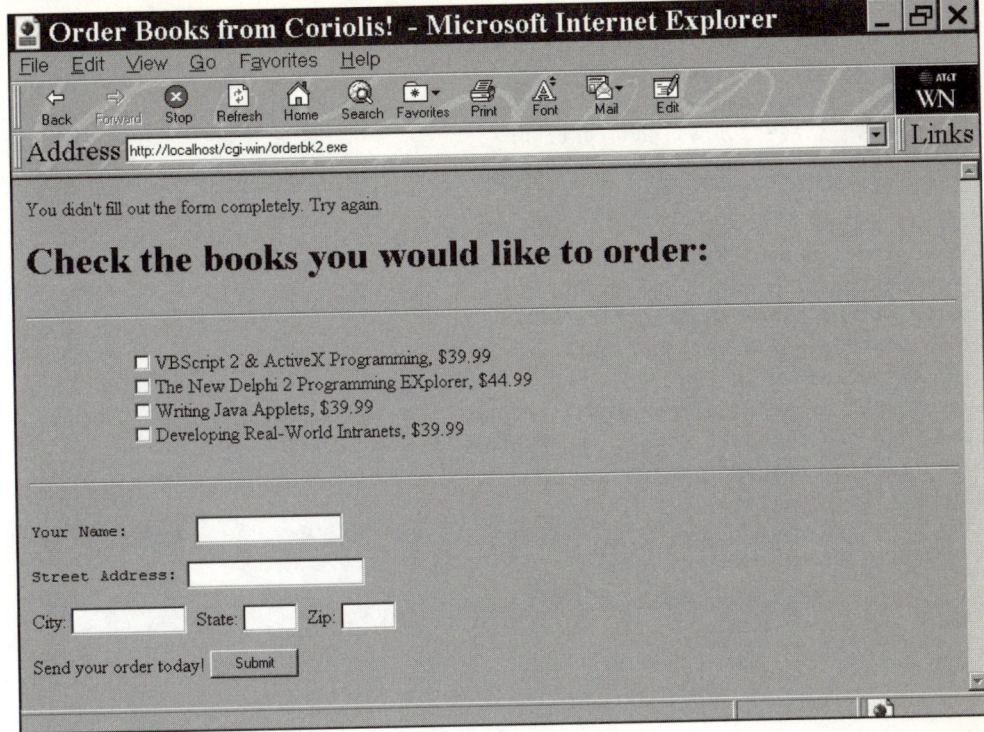

Figure 16.7
The redisplayed order form, sent from the CGI program to the user's Web browser.

Listing 16.6 THE HTML CODE SENT BY RedisplayOrderForm().

```
<html><head><title>Order Books from Coriolis!
</title></head><body>
You didn't fill out the form completely. Try again.<br>
<h1>Check the books you would like to order:</h1>
<form method=post action="http://localhost/cgi-win/orderbk2.exe">
<hr><ul><ul><ul><ul>
<input name="CB_VBScriptPrg" type="checkbox"
value="1" align=left>
VBScript 2 & ActiveX Programming, $39.99<br>
<input name="CB_DelphiExp" type="checkbox"
value="1" align=left>
The New Delphi 2 Programming EXplorer, $44.99<br>
<input name="CB_JavaApp" type="checkbox"
value="1" align=left>
Writing Java Applets, $39.99<br>
<input name="CB_Intranet" type="checkbox"
```

```
value="1" align=left>
Developing Real-World Intranets, $39.99<br>
</ul></ul></ul></ul></ul><hr><pre>
Your Name: <input name="TB_Customer"
type="text" size="20" align=right><br>
Street Address: <input name="TB_Street"
type="text" size="25" align=right>
</pre>
City: <input name="TB_City"
type="text" size="15" align=right>
State: <input name="TB_State"
type="text" size="5" align=right>
Zip: <input name="TB_Zip"
type="text" size="5" align=right><br><br>
Send your order today! <input name="Btn_Order"
type="submit" align=right>
</form></body></html>
```

17
USING COOKIES WITH VBSCRIPT

Cookies enable you to save information across multiple HTML documents—an essential feat for Web-based shopping cart systems.

VBScript, ActiveX, and HTML are great tools for creating interactive Web pages. In Chapters 10 and 16, you've already seen how to create Web-based order forms.

Suppose, however, that you want to create a multipage Web shopping cart system. In such a system—one of the most popular new Web site applications—each page contains information about a specific product, such as a book. At the bottom of the page, the user can click on a button to add the book to his or her "shopping cart." When finished, the user clicks another button, usually labeled Go To Checkout. At the checkout page, the purchases are displayed, the total added, and the user gives his or her credit card number.

A complete shopping cart system, including the security measures needed for safe transmission of credit card numbers over the Web, is beyond the scope of this book. However, Web shopping cart systems have one requirement that's more general and applies to other Web applications: the need to save data from one Web page to another.

HTTP, the communications protocol used to transmit Web pages over the Internet, is a "stateless" protocol. This means a lot of things, but the relevant meaning here is that whatever happens in one Web page will disappear as soon as you move to another Web page. If you're creating a Web shopping cart application—or any Web application in which data has to be kept as the user moves from one page of the application to another—you've got a problem.

The solution to the problem is to use *cookies*. A cookie is an ASCII text string that stores data in the user's PC memory as the user moves around your site; if you put an expiration date on the cookie, you can even store it in the Windows\Cookies directory of the user's PC. This isn't a security problem because cookies are just text files and can't execute programs on the user's PC. If an expiration date is not included, the cookie disappears as soon as the user shuts down Microsoft Internet Explorer.

Cookies Work Only From A Web Server
The cookie examples in this chapter will work only when the Web pages are loaded from a Web site. If you try to run this code just on your own PC, you won't create any cookies.

Creating Cookies In Your Code

In the cookie file, data is stored as a sequence of name-value pairs, with each pair separated from the next by a semicolon.

Creating a cookie is very simple in concept. You just use the Internet Explorer scripting object model to set the **cookie** property of the current document object, as follows:

```
Document.Cookie = CookieName & "=" & CookieValue
```

That's all you need to do in order to store the cookie. What you then do with the cookie data will depend on your specific application. Let's look at part of a simple shopping cart system that uses cookies. Figure 17.1 shows one Web page that gives information about a particular product on sale: In this case, it's one of Robert B. Parker's "Spenser" detective novels.

When the user first loads this page, no cookies are created. A cookie is created only when the user clicks on the Order This Book button. When the user clicks

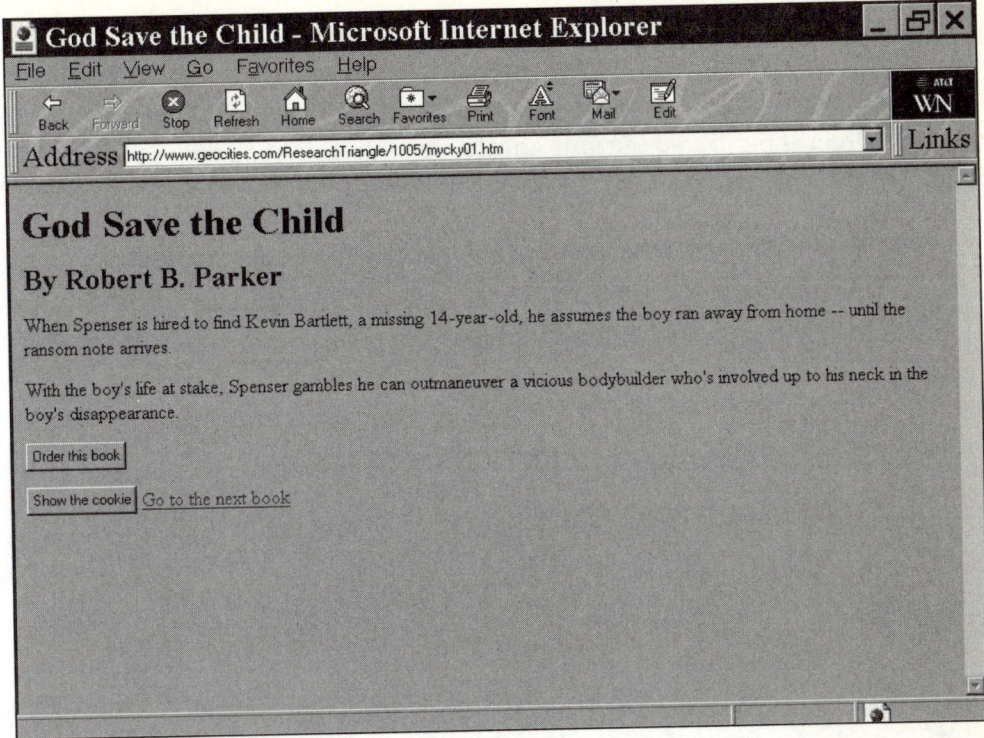

Figure 17.1
The first page of a simple shopping cart system.

on the button, Internet Explorer (if it's set to a high security level) displays the message box shown in Figure 17.2, alerting the user that the Web page has sent him/her a cookie.

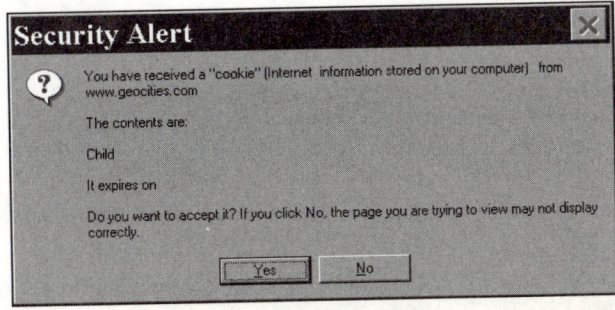

Figure 17.2
The Web page sent the user a cookie.

If the user accepts the cookie, then the cookie is stored in memory on the user's PC. The user can then move to the next Web page, which displays information about the classic novel *Silas Marner*, as shown in Figure 17.3. If the user clicks on the Order This Book button, another cookie alert appears, as shown in Figure 17.4.

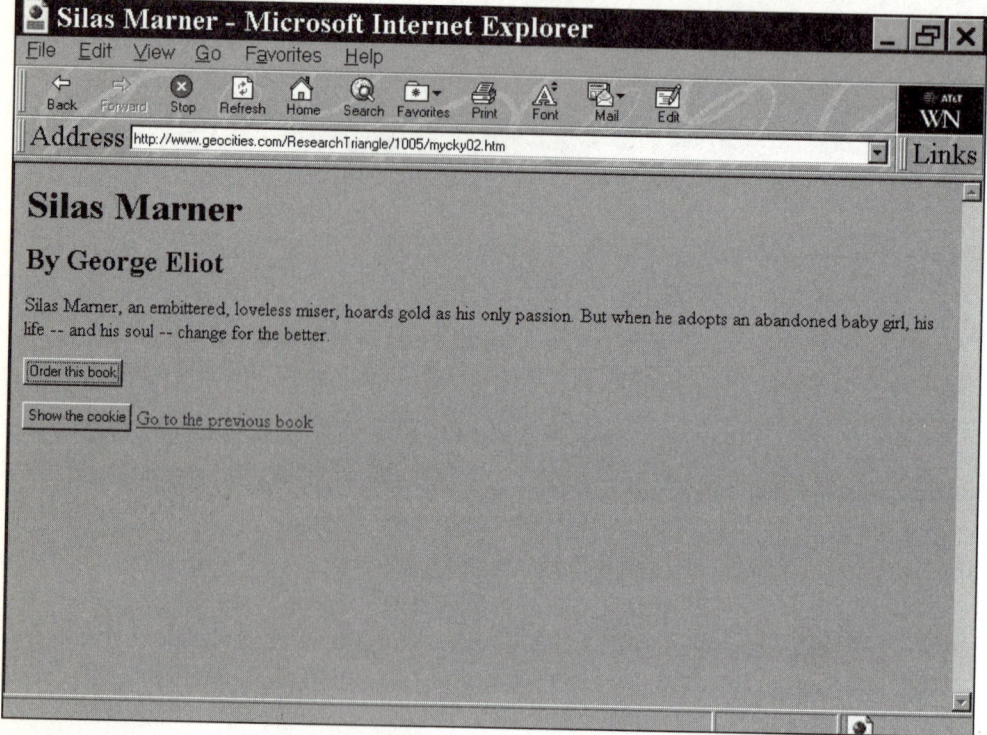

Figure 17.3
A second Web page with information about another book.

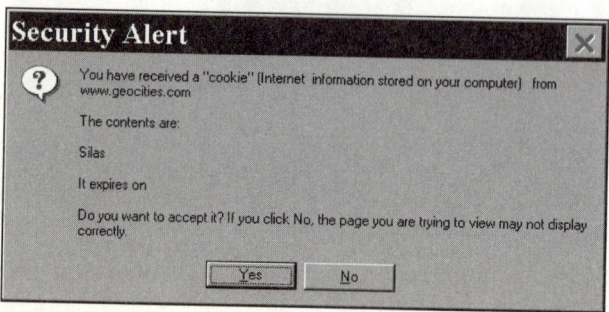

Figure 17.4
The second Web page sent the user a cookie.

Figure 17.5
The cookie has data from both Web pages.

But what happened to the data sent by the first Web page? It's still there, stored as a name-value pair inside the cookie with the data from the second Web page. If the user clicks on the Show The Cookie button, a message box displays the current contents of the cookie, as shown in Figure 17.5.

Inside The Cookie Code

Now that you've seen how our simple cookie system works, let's look at the code. Listings 17.1 and 17.2 show the HTML code for two Web pages we set up.

Listing 17.1 A BOOK ORDER PAGE THAT CREATES A COOKIE.

```
<HTML>
<HEAD>
<TITLE>God Save the Child</TITLE>
<script language="VBScript">
<!--
dim strCookieName
strCookieName = "Book"

Sub SetVariable(strVariableName, varVariableValue)
    Document.Cookie = strVariableName & "=" & varVariableValue
End Sub

sub OrderBtn_OnClick()
    dim BookName
    BookName = "Child"
    SetVariable strCookieName, BookName
end sub

sub DisplayCookie_OnClick()
    MsgBox Document.Cookie
end sub

-->
</script>
```

```
</HEAD>

<BODY>
<H1>God Save the Child</H1>
<H2>By Robert B. Parker</H2>

<p>When Spenser is hired to find Kevin Bartlett,
a missing 14-year-old, he assumes the boy ran away
from home -- until the ransom note arrives.</p>

<p>With the boy's life at stake, Spenser gambles
he can outmaneuver a vicious bodybuilder who's involved
up to his neck in the boy's disappearance.</p>

<FORM NAME="BookOrder">
<INPUT NAME="OrderBtn" TYPE="BUTTON" VALUE="Order this book"><br><br>
<INPUT NAME="DisplayCookie" TYPE="BUTTON" VALUE="Show the cookie">
<a href="mycky04.htm">Go to the next book</a>
</FORM>
</BODY>

</HTML>
```

Listing 17.2 THE SECOND BOOK ORDER PAGE THAT CREATES A COOKIE.

```
<HTML>
<HEAD>
<TITLE>Silas Marner</TITLE>
<script language="VBScript">
<!--
dim strCookieName
strCookieName = "Book"

Sub SetVariable(strVariableName, varVariableValue)
    Document.Cookie = strVariableName & "=" & varVariableValue
End Sub

sub OrderBtn_OnClick()
    dim BookName
    BookName = "Silas"
    SetVariable strCookieName, BookName
end sub

sub DisplayCookie_OnClick()
    MsgBox Document.Cookie
end sub
```

```
-->
</script>
</HEAD>

<BODY>
<H1>Silas Marner</H1>
<H2>By George Eliot</H2>

<p>Silas Marner, an embittered, loveless
miser, hoards gold as his only passion. But
when he adopts an abandoned baby girl, his
life -- and his soul -- change for the better.</p>

<FORM NAME="BookOrder">
<INPUT NAME="OrderBtn" TYPE="BUTTON" VALUE="Order this book"><br><br>
<INPUT NAME="DisplayCookie" TYPE="BUTTON" VALUE="Show the cookie">
<a href="mycky03.htm">Go to the previous book</a>
</FORM>
</BODY>

</HTML>
```

The code in both pages works essentially the same way, but there are a couple of surprises. We'll start with Listing 17.1. First, we name the cookie:

```
dim strCookieName
strCookieName = "Book"
```

Recall that a cookie is a series of name-value pairs: The cookie name is the first term of the pair. When the user clicks on the Order This Book button, the **OnClick** event code is executed:

```
sub OrderBtn_OnClick()
    dim BookName
    BookName = "Child"
    SetVariable strCookieName, BookName
end sub
```

This code creates a local variable for the book's cookie value ("Child"), then calls the **SetVariable** sub to set the value in the book:

```
Sub SetVariable(strVariableName, varVariableValue)
    Document.Cookie = strVariableName & "=" & varVariableValue
End Sub
```

SetVariable simply assigns a name-value pair to the **cookie** property of the document currently loaded into the user's Web browser: This caused the cookie to be downloaded into the PC's memory. The value is stored in the form:

```
BookCookie=Child;
```

The name is separated from its value by an equal sign (=), and if multiple cookie values are loaded, they are separated from each other by semicolons.

When the user moves to the next book's Web page, the process is repeated. Here's where a surprise comes in. If the user clicks on the Order This Book button for *Silas Marner*, the **OnClick** event sub calls the **SetVariable** sub, exactly the same as before:

```
SetVariable strCookieName, BookName
```

The **SetVariable** sub, in turn, assigns a new value to the document's **cookie** property:

```
Document.Cookie = strVariableName & "=" & varVariableValue
```

In most programming, this would mean that whatever value previously resided in the **cookie** property would be overwritten by the new value. But that's not what happens: Instead, the new value is simply *concatenated* with the old value, as shown in Figure 17.6.

That gives you all the basic techniques you need to get started using cookies in your Web applications. If you'd like to pursue the matter in depth, you can visit either of the following Web sites, where you'll find extensive technical discussions of cookies, along with many different cookie examples:

- http://www.microsoft.com/vbscript/us/samples/cookies/extcookie.htm
- http://www.yahoo.com/computers_and_internet/internet/world_wide_web/http/protocol_specification/persistent_cookies/

Figure 17.6
The new cookie value is added onto the end of the old value.

18
Web Database Publishing Made Easy

Putting your databases on the Web doesn't have to be difficult—as long as you have the right tools and know the right tricks.

To judge by some of the weighty tomes that have been written about it, putting databases on the Web is hard. *Really* hard. So hard that you don't even want to *think* about trying it (unless you're a 10-year MIS veteran with a solid working knowledge of SQL, high-end database managers such as Oracle or SQL Server, and plenty of time on your hands).

But putting databases on the Web doesn't have to be that difficult. In fact, there's an easy trick you can use to publish your database data on a Web site. Realistically, it won't be as impressive looking or as interactive as one of those SQL-CGI combos, which require you to be a Web database specialist. It will, however, do everything you need, and you can set up the whole thing in an afternoon.

How Web Database Publishing Ought To Work

Most of the time, VBScript works pretty much like Visual Basic proper. And knowing that, you might get a bright idea about how to put database data on a Web page. To do it in Visual Basic, you simply:

1. Drop a data control on a form.
2. Connect the data control to the database.
3. Drop data-aware components (such as text boxes or grid controls) on the form.
4. Connect the data-aware components to the data control.
5. Compile the program, and you're done. The result might look something like Figure 18.1.

If you assume that VBScript will work just like Visual Basic, the strategy is obvious. The ActiveX Control Pad works very much like the Visual Basic development environment, allowing you to drop controls on an HTML layout as if it were a Visual Basic form. So it could work like this:

1. Using the ActiveX Control Pad, drop a data control on an HTML layout.
2. Connect the data control to the database.
3. Drop data-aware components on the HTML layout.
4. Connect the data-aware components to the data control.
5. Insert the HTML layout into an HTML containing document, and you're done. The result—if you could really do it this way—would look like Figure 18.2.

Unfortunately, this doesn't work. You can indeed drop some third-party data controls on an HTML layout, but you can't connect them to anything. The only alternative is to buy one of those "Web database" books and prepare to spend some heavy-duty time on the problem.

Or is there another alternative?

Web Database Publishing Made Easy 393

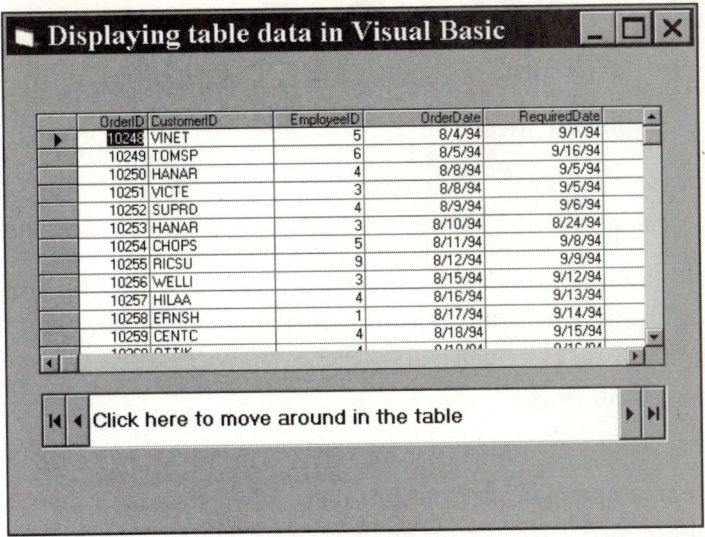

Figure 18.1
Displaying database data on a Visual Basic form.

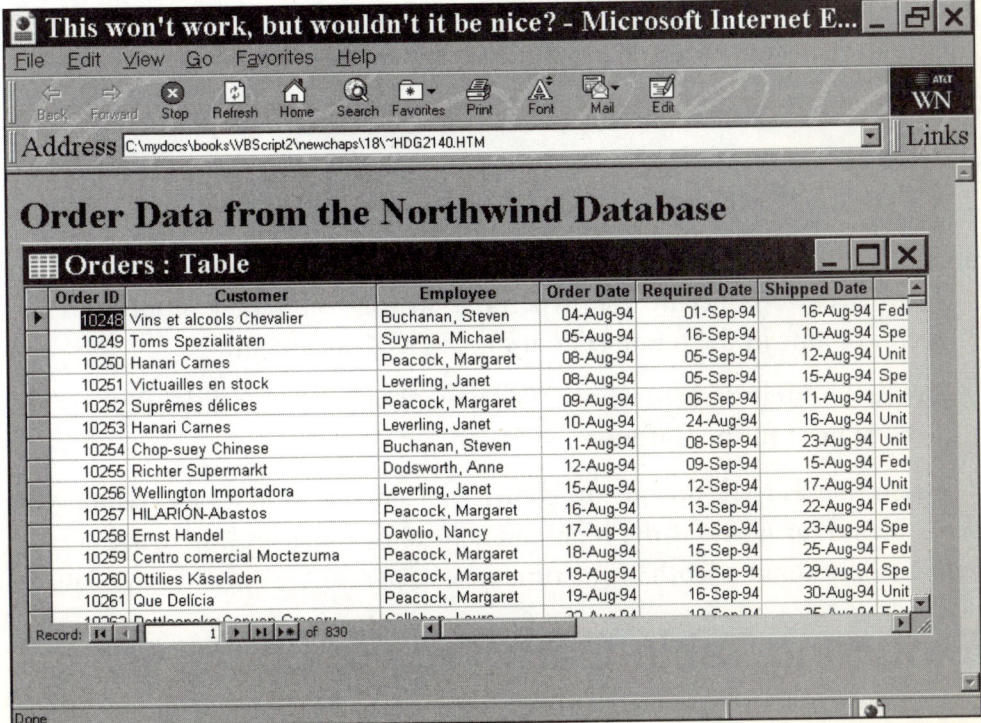

Figure 18.2
How Web database publishing *should* work with VBScript and ActiveX—but doesn't.

The Easy Way To Publish Data

The first step in solving almost any problem is to define clearly what the problem *is*. In the case of publishing database data on the Web, it's something like this:

To present database tables on a Web page so that the user can select which table to view and can scroll through the table to view all of its fields and records.

For most Web database publishing, this is all you need to do. The only thing that's missing in our problem definition is that users should be able to *change* the data displayed on the Web page. That's something for which you would need a high-end solution.

For most Web database publishing, however, you just want to *present* the data, not allow users to change it. If your company has a product catalog on its Web site, for example, you want customers to be able to view your product information but *not* be able to change it. The same applies to most other Web database publishing applications.

That's precisely what you can do, simply and quickly, with an easy Web-page trick and Microsoft Access 97. In outline, the procedure goes like this:

1. In Microsoft Access 97, export each table you want to publish as an HTML table.

2. Create an HTML document that contains three frames.

3. In the first frame, insert hyperlinks to each HTML table document exported from Access 97. Set up the hyperlinks so that the **target** property is the second frame in the frame-containing HTML document.

4. In the third frame, show whom Web users should contact if they have problems or need further information.

The resulting HTML document, shown in Figure 18.3, does everything you need. It's not as glitzy as the high-end solutions, but it is easy to create and requires only about a tenth of the time to set up.

Exporting Table Data From Access 97

Your first step is to export your data from Access 97 in the form of HTML tables. The steps are as follows:

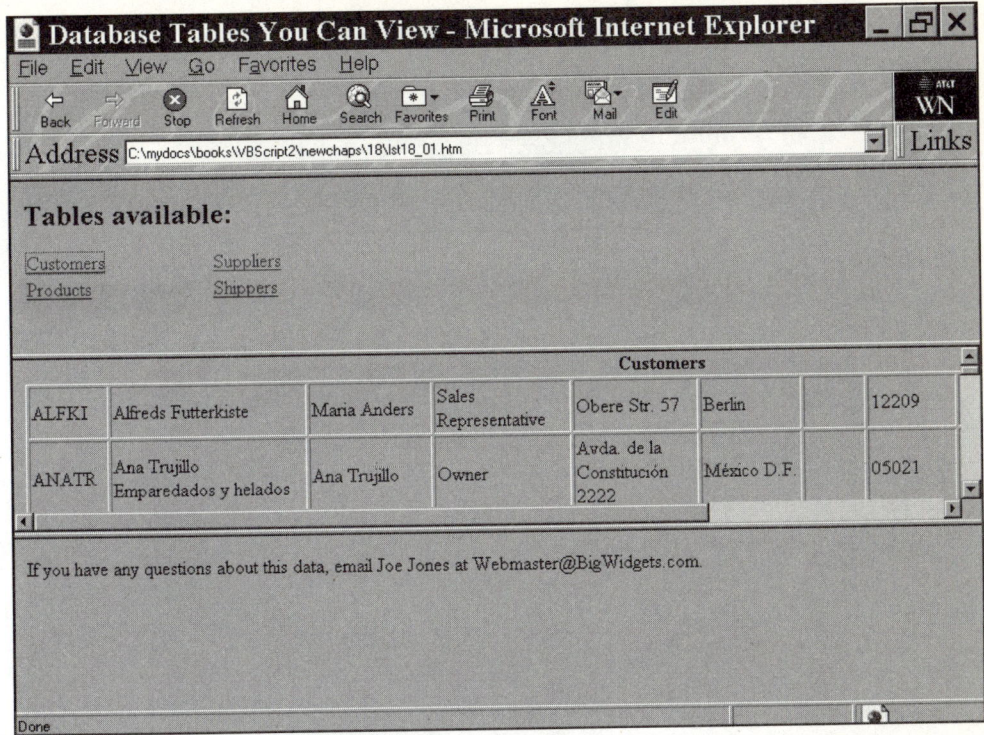

Figure 18.3
Publishing a database on the Web, the easy way. The figure shows data from the Northwind database included as a sample database with Microsoft Access 97.

1. In Access 97, load the database whose data you want to publish.
2. In the Tables card, click on the database table you want to export.

   The table name should now be highlighted on the Tables card.
3. Open the File menu and select Save As/Export.

   The Save As/Export dialog box appears, as shown in Figure 18.4.
4. Click on the OK button.

   The Save Table In dialog box appears, as shown in Figure 18.5.
5. Browse to the directory where your Web HTML files will be located.
6. Open the Save As Type list box and select *HTML documents (*.html, *.htm)*.
7. Click on the Export button.

   Access 97 saves the database table data as a table in an HTML document.

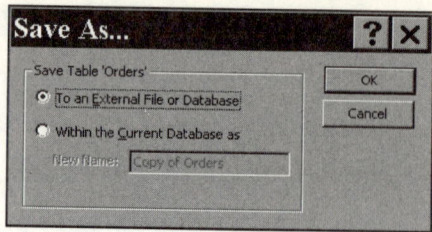

Figure 18.4
The Save As/Export dialog box.

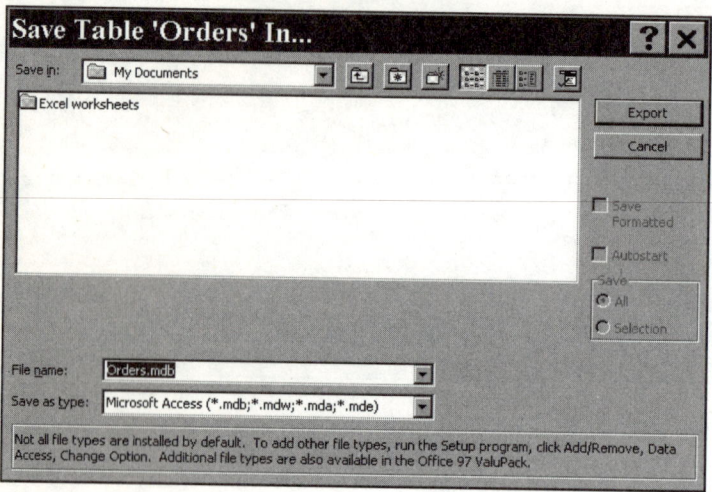

Figure 18.5
The Save Table In dialog box.

Repeat these steps for each table you want to publish on your Web site. Once you've created all the HTML tables you need, you're ready to create your containing HTML frameset document.

Creating The Database Frameset Document

To publish your database tables, you next need to create an HTML frameset document. This frameset document will have three frames, each of which will display another HTML document. The HTML code for the frameset document is shown in Listing 18.1.

Listing 18.1 THE FRAMESET DOCUMENT FOR THE DATABASE PAGE.

```
<HTML>
<HEAD>
<TITLE> Database Tables You Can View</TITLE>
</HEAD>
<frameset rows="*,*,*">
<frame name="frame1" src="lst18_02.htm">
<frame name="frame2" src="">
<frame name="frame3" src="datapub1.htm">
</frameset>
</HTML>
```

As you can see, this is remarkably simple. The **<frameset>** tag tells Internet Explorer to create three frames of equal size, dividing the Web page horizontally into three sections. Between the **<frameset>** and **</frameset>** tags, you insert the **<frame>** tags for all of the frames. The first frame uses its **src** (source) property to load an HTML document containing hyperlinks to the tables you want to display. The HTML code for this document is shown in Listing 18.2.

Listing 18.2 HTML CODE TO LOAD THE TABLE LIST.

```
<HTML>
<HEAD>
<TITLE> Database tables you can view at this Web site</TITLE>
</HEAD>
<BODY>
<font size=+3><b>
<h2>Tables available:</h2>
<table width=300 cellpadding=1 cellspacing=1>
<tr>
    <td><a href="customer.htm" target="frame2">Customers</a></td>
    <td><a href="supplier.htm" target="frame2">Suppliers</a></td>
</tr>
<tr>
    <td><a href="products.htm" target="frame2">Products</a></td>
    <td><a href="shippers.htm" target="frame2">Shippers</a></td>
</tr>
</table>
</b></font>
</BODY>
</HTML>
```

We've put the hyperlinks in an HTML table simply to arrange them neatly on the Web page, but it's the hyperlinks themselves that are the important part. Let's take a closer look at the first hyperlink:

```
<a href="customer.htm" target="frame2">Customers</a>
```

This is a standard HTML link, using the <a>...</a> (anchor) tag. The **href** property is set to the table that should be loaded into frame 2 of the frameset document. The **target** property is set to the name of frame 2, which is, appropriately enough, *frame2*.

As you can see, the HTML document in Listing 18.2 lists the HTML-exported versions of four Access 97 tables: These tables were exported from the Northwind database included as a sample with Access 97. When a Web user clicks on one of the hyperlinks, Internet Explorer loads the appropriate table document into frame 2. If scroll bars are needed, they appear automatically. No further work is needed on your part to make it work.

In the third frame, you can put contact or help information for using the database. If you prefer, you can omit the third frame altogether by creating a frameset document with only two frames:

```
<frameset rows="*,*">
```

And with those quite simple techniques, you've accomplished what others spend hours or weeks trying to do: You've published your database data on your Web site.

A

What's New In VBScript 2?

When the original version of VBScript was released, it was rumored—probably without foundation—that it had been hacked together by "a couple of Microsoft programmers in a weekend." Whether or not the story is true, what *is* true is that the original version of VBScript lacked some fairly important features, such as real constants as opposed to VBScript variables that merely "pretended" to be constants.

VBScript 2 corrects these shortcomings, and offers so many new features that it almost transcends its status as a Web scripting language. The most significant of these features are explained and demonstrated in the chapters of this book; in this appendix, I'll provide a summary and overview of each. Example code is given for some of the most important new features. It should be noted that in the syntax definitions, material in square brackets ([]) is optional.

Declaring Identifiers

- The **const** keyword—In the original version of VBScript, constants had to be "faked" by declaring variables, assigning initial values to them, and never changing the values. This left program constants vulnerable to accidental change, with potentially catastrophic results. VBScript 2's **const** keyword allows you to declare real program constants whose values can't be changed by the program. The syntax is:

```
[public | private] const ConstantName = Expression
```

By default, constants are public. They follow the same naming and scoping rules as all other program identifiers. Examples are:

```
const MaxTemp = 100
const pi = 3.14159
const Publisher = "The Coriolis Group"
const Name1 = "John", Name2 = "Jane", Name3 = "Jorge"
```

- The **private** keyword—Each pair of <script>...</script> tags in an HTML file delimits an individual script, and a Web page can have more than one script. If you declare an identifier with the **private** keyword, it is available only in the script where you declared it. When you're declaring variables, **private** substitutes for **dim**. When you're declaring constants, **private** modifies **const**. Of course, normal scoping rules apply, too. Examples are:

```
private SecretVariable   ' Declares a private variable
private SecretArray()    ' Declares a private dynamic array
private const TheAnswer = 42 ' Declares a private constant
```

- The **public** keyword—As you might have guessed, this is the opposite of the **private** keyword. If you declare an identifier with the **public** keyword, that identifier is available to all scripts in your project. This makes it possible for you to organize your VBScript code: for example, putting all your global variable and constant declarations into a single script module. Examples are:

```
public TellTheWorld         ' Declares a public variable
public const States = 50    ' Declares a public constant
```

Control Structures

- The **for each...next** statement—This statement enables you to traverse an array. (In Visual Basic proper, it lets you traverse both arrays and collections, but collections are not supported by VBScript.) It applies the statements inside the **for each** clause to each element of the array. For arrays of known size, this is essentially equivalent to **for...next**. The advantage of **for each...next** is that it can be used with arrays of unknown size, such as dynamic arrays, while **for...next** requires you to know the size of the array. Here's an example of a **for each...next** statement:

```
dim Thingie, RAIndex
RAIndex = 0
for each Thingie in MyArray
   if MyArray(RAIndex) = "VBScript" then
      Listbox1.additem "Slot number: " & RAIndex
   end if
   RAIndex = RAIndex + 1
next
```

Array Handling

- The **Array** function—This function takes values separated by commas and returns an array containing those values in its slots. It's not really creating a dynamic array, though it's pretty close. Here's an example:

```
Dim UserNames, SomeName
UserNames = Array("Jim","Sally")
SomeName = UserNames(1)
```

Dates And Times

The date and time functions get a little involved. There are four new date and time functions: **DateAdd**, **DateDiff**, **DatePart**, and **Weekday**. Let's look at each of them in detail.

The **DateAdd** Function

This function returns a date to which an additional time interval has been added. It takes three parameters: a string representing the type of interval to add (years, months, days, minutes, etc.), a numeric expression representing the number of units of the interval to add, and a variant representing the date to which the value should be added. The syntax is:

```
DateAdd(interval, number, date)
```

The different interval types are shown in Table A.1.

An example of the **DateAdd** function is:

```
NewDate = DateAdd("m", 1, "17-Oct-97")
```

The DateDiff Function

This function returns the number of intervals between two dates. It takes three required parameters and has two optional parameters. The required parameters are the interval, the starting date, and the ending date. The optional parameters only apply when the interval is in weeks or years. In the former case, the parameter specifies which day of the week to use; in the latter case, it specifies which week of the year to use. The syntax is:

```
DateDiff(interval, date1, date2 [,dayofweek[, firstweekofyear]])
```

TABLE A.1
INTERVAL TYPE STRINGS FOR THE **DateAdd** FUNCTION.

String	Interval Type
yyyy	Year
q	Quarter
m	Month
y	Day of year
d	Day
w	Weekday
ww	Week of year
h	Hour
m	Minute
s	Second

The **DateDiff** function uses the same interval constants as the **DateAdd** function; these are shown in Table A.1. The day of week constants are **vbSunday** through **vbSaturday**. The week of year constants give you a little less flexibility: You can pick the week containing January 1 (**vbFirstJan1**), the first week with at least four days in the new year (**vbFirstFourDays**), or the first full week of the new year (**vbFirstFullWeek**).

The **DatePart** Function

The **DatePart** function, as its name implies, returns part of a date: the year, month, day, and so on. It has two required parameters: the interval, indicating which part of the date you want to extract, and the date itself. The optional parameters apply only when the interval is in weeks or years. In the former case, the parameter specifies which day of the week to use; in the latter case, it specifies which week of the year to use. The syntax is:

```
DatePart(interval, date[, dayofweek[, firstweekofyear]])
```

The interval, day, and week constants are the same as those used for the **DateDiff** function.

The **Weekday** Function

The **Weekday** function takes a date as its only required parameter and returns a number indicating the day of the week for that date. An optional parameter indicates the day on which the week should start; if this parameter is left out, VBScript assumes that the week starts on Sunday. The syntax is:

```
Weekday(date, [firstdayofweek])
```

The return values of the **Weekday** function are shown in Table A.2.

String Formatting

There are four new string formatting functions, each of which formats a different kind of number when that number appears as a text string. The new functions are **FormatCurrency**, **FormatDateTime**, **FormatNumber**, and **FormatPercent**.

TABLE A.2

RETURN VALUES OF THE Weekday FUNCTION.

Constant	Value	Meaning
VbSunday	1	Sunday
VbMonday	2	Monday
VbTuesday	3	Tuesday
VbWednesday	4	Wednesday
VbThursday	5	Thursday
VbFriday	6	Friday
VbSaturday	7	Saturday

The FormatCurrency Function

The **FormatCurrency** function returns a number formatted as currency, using the currency system specified on the user's PC. The syntax is:

```
FormatCurrency(Expression[,NumDigitsAfterDecimal _
    [,IncludeLeadingDigit [,UseParensForNegativeNumbers _
    [,GroupDigits]]]])
```

The parameters are explained in Table A.3.

TABLE A.3

PARAMETERS OF THE FormatCurrency FUNCTION.

Parameter	Required?	Meaning
Expression	Yes	The string to format.
NumDigitsAfterDecimal	No	Numeric value indicating how many digits should be displayed to the right of the decimal point. By default, this is -1, which makes the value display according to the regional settings on the user's PC.
IncludeLeadingDigit	No	A constant that indicates whether or not a leading zero should be displayed for fractional values. Possible values of this constant are TriStateTrue (-1), TriStateFalse (0), and TriStateUseDefault (-2), which means to use the regional settings on the user's PC.

(continued)

TABLE A.3
PARAMETERS OF THE **FormatCurrency** FUNCTION (CONTINUED).

Parameter	Required?	Meaning
UseParensForNegativeNumbers	No	A constant that indicates whether negative values should be placed within parentheses. Possible values of this constant are TriStateTrue (-1), TriStateFalse (0), and TriStateUseDefault (-2), which means to use the regional settings on the user's PC.
GroupDigits	No	A constant that indicates whether or not numbers should be grouped with the group delimiter in the regional settings of the user's PC. Possible values of this constant are TriStateTrue (-1), TriStateFalse (0), and TriStateUseDefault (-2), which means to use the regional settings on the user's PC.

The FormatDateTime Function

The **FormatDateTime** function formats a date string to display as one of VBScript's date/time subtypes. It only requires one parameter: the date string that is to be formatted. Optionally, you can include the name of the format you want. If you don't specify a format, VBScript formats it as a "general date." The syntax is:

```
FormatDateTime(Date[,NamedFormat])
```

The available date formats are shown in Table A.4.

TABLE A.4
DATE FORMAT CONSTANTS FOR THE **FormatDateTime** FUNCTION.

Constant	Numeric Value	Meaning
VbGeneralDate	0	Display date and/or time. If there is a date part, display as a short date. If there is a time part, display as a long time. If both parts are present, they are displayed.
VbLongDate	1	Display a date using the long date format specified in the regional settings of the user's PC.

(continued)

TABLE A.4

DATE FORMAT CONSTANTS FOR THE **FormatDateTime** FUNCTION (CONTINUED).

Constant	Numeric Value	Meaning
VbShortDate	2	Display a date using the short date format specified in the regional settings of the user's PC.
VbLongTime	3	Display a time using the time format specified in the regional settings of the user's PC.
VbShortTime	4	Display a time using the 24-hour format (hh:mm).

The **FormatNumber** Function

The **FormatNumber** function returns a string expression formatted as a number. The syntax is:

```
FormatNumber(Expression[,NumDigitsAfterDecimal _
    [,IncludeLeadingDigit [,UseParensForNegativeNumbers _
    [,GroupDigits]]]])
```

The parameters are explained in Table A.5.

The **FormatPercent** Function

The **FormatPercent** function formats a string expression as a percentage, with a trailing percent sign (%). The syntax is:

```
FormatPercent(Expression[,NumDigitsAfterDecimal _
    [,IncludeLeadingDigit [,UseParensForNegativeNumbers _
    [,GroupDigits]]]])
```

The parameters are the same as those for the **FormatNumber** function, explained in Table A.5.

General String Handling

- The **Filter** function—This function searches an array of strings for a specific substring, returning a new array containing the search array's elements (strings) that contained the desired substring. The syntax is:

```
Filter( InputStrings, Value[, Include[, Compare]])
```

TABLE A.5 PARAMETERS OF THE **FormatNumber** FUNCTION.

Parameter	Required?	Meaning
Expression	Yes	The string to format.
NumDigitsAfterDecimal	No	Numeric value indicating how many digits should be displayed to the right of the decimal point. By default, this is -1, which makes the value display according to the regional settings on the user's PC.
IncludeLeadingDigit	No	A constant that indicates whether or not a leading zero should be displayed for fractional values. Possible values of this constant are TriStateTrue (-1), TriStateFalse (0), and TriStateUseDefault (-2), which means to use the regional settings on the user's PC.
UseParensForNegativeNumbers	No	A constant that indicates whether negative values should be placed within parentheses. Possible values of this constant are TriStateTrue (-1), TriStateFalse (0), and TriStateUseDefault (-2), which means to use the regional settings on the user's PC.
GroupDigits	No	A constant that indicates whether or not numbers should be grouped with the group delimiter in the regional settings of the user's PC. Possible values of this constant are TriStateTrue (-1), TriStateFalse (0), and TriStateUseDefault (-2), which means to use the regional settings on the user's PC.

The only two required parameters are **InputStrings** (the array to be searched) and **Value** (the string to search for). The **Include** parameter is a boolean value (True or False): If it's True, then the **Filter** function returns all the search array elements (strings) that *do* contain the desired substring; if it's False, then the function returns all the search array elements that *do not* contain the desired substring. The **Compare** parameter specifies whether the search comparison should be binary (bit-for-bit, **vbBinaryCompare**, value 0) or text (letter-for-letter, **vbTextCompare**, value 1).

- The **InStrRev** function—If you're familiar with the Visual Basic **InStr** function, you can easily guess the purpose of this new function. The **InStrRev** function returns the position of a substring within a search string. Unlike Visual Basic's **InStr**, which moves forward from the beginning, **InStrRev** moves backward from the end. The syntax is:

  ```
  InstrRev(String1, String2[, Start[, Compare]])
  ```

  The required parameters are **String1** (the string being searched) and **String2** (the string for which the search is being conducted). The optional **Start** parameter is used if you want the search to begin at a location other than the last slot in the string. The **Compare** parameter specifies whether the search comparison should be binary (bit-for-bit, **vbBinaryCompare**, value 0) or text (letter-for-letter, **vbTextCompare**, value 1).

- The **Join** function—This function traverses an array of strings and concatenates all its elements into one big string. The syntax is:

  ```
  Join(List[, Delimiter])
  ```

  The required parameter **List** is the array of strings to be searched. The optional **Delimiter** parameter specifies a character to separate the individual elements of the array in the big concatenated string with which you end up.

- The **Replace** function—This function searches a string for a substring, replaces the substring with another string, then returns the result. The syntax is:

  ```
  Replace(Expression, Find, Replacewith[, Start[, Count[, Compare]]])
  ```

  The required parameters are **Expression**, which is the string to be searched; **Find**, which is the string for which you're searching; and **Replacewith**, which is the string with which the searched-for string should be replaced. The **Start** parameter, which indicates at what point in the string to begin the search, is optional; if you leave it out, the search begins at slot 1 of the string. The **Count** parameter, which is also optional, indicates how many occurrences of the searched-for string should be replaced; if you leave it out, all occurrences will be replaced. The **Compare** parameter specifies whether the search comparison should be binary (bit-for-bit, **vbBinaryCompare**, value 0) or text (letter-for-letter, **vbTextCompare**, value 1).

- The **Split** function—This function is the opposite of the **Join** function. It takes a big string, splits it into substrings, pops each substring into a slot of an array, and returns the array. The syntax is:

```
Split(Expression[, Delimiter[, Count[, Compare]]])
```

The required **Expression** parameter is the string to be split up. The optional **Delimiter** parameter specifies the character (such as a comma or tab) that separates one substring from another; if you leave it out, the space character is assumed to be the delimiter. The optional **Count** parameter indicates the number of substrings to be returned in the array; if you leave it out, all the substrings in the big string will be returned. Finally, as usual, the optional **Compare** parameter specifies whether the search comparison should be binary (bit-for-bit, **vbBinaryCompare**, value 0) or text (letter-for-letter, **vbTextCompare**, value 1).

- The **StrReverse** function—This function takes a string as its only parameter and reverses the string. The syntax is:

```
StrReverse(String1)
```

For example, if Superman needed to get rid of Mr. Mxyzptlk, his magical nemesis from the fifth dimension, he could use **StrReverse**("Mxyzptlk") to return the value "kltpzyxM"—thereby forcing Mr. Mxyztplk to go back where he came from.

System I/O And Object Handling

- The **LoadPicture** function—This function loads a picture file at runtime. The syntax is:

```
LoadPicture(Filename)
```

The file can be a bitmap (.BMP), icon (.ICO), run-length encoded (.RLE), Windows metafile (.WMF), enhanced metafile (.EMF), GIF (.GIF), or JPEG (.JPG).

- The **CreateObject** function—This function creates an automation object for OLE automation. The syntax is:

```
CreateObject(Class)
```

The required **Class** parameter specifies the type of object to create, such as a Microsoft Excel worksheet. For example:

```
Dim TheWorkSheet
Set TheWorkSheet = CreateObject("Excel.Sheet")
```

- The **Dictionary** object—This object is used to store pairs of data items and keys, and is the VBScript equivalent of a Perl associative array. It's also something like a Visual Basic **collection** or a 2D array. The syntax is:

```
Scripting.Dictionary
```

Each pair in the **Dictionary** object consists of a data item, which can be anything, and an associated key, such as a letter of the alphabet.

- The **FileSystemObject** object—This object allows VBScript to read from and write to the file system of the user's PC. The syntax is:

```
Scripting.FileSystemObject
```

For example, the following code creates a **FileSystemObject**, then uses it to create a text file, write a line of text to the file, and finally close the file:

```
Set uzrfs = CreateObject("Scripting.FileSystemObject")
Set a = uzrfs.CreateTextFile("c:\vbscript.txt", True)
a.WriteLine("VBScript can write to files.")
a.Close
```

- The **TextStream** object—This object enables sequential access to a file on the user's computer. In the following code

```
Set uzrfs = CreateObject("Scripting.FileSystemObject")
Set a = uzrfs.CreateTextFile("c:\vbscript.txt", True)
a.WriteLine("VBScript can write to files.")
a.Close
```

the **CreateTextFile** function returns a **TextStream** object and assigns it to the variable **a**. **WriteLine** and **Close** are methods of the **TextStream** object.

Data Types

- The **TypeName** function—This function returns a string containing the name of a variable's data subtype. Recall that even though VBScript has only one "official" data type—the **variant** type—that official type is divided into several subtypes. The **TypeName** function, as you'd guess, returns the name of the data subtype for a particular variable. The syntax is:

`TypeName(Variable)`

The single parameter, **Variable**, is naturally the variable whose type you want the function to return. The possible return values of the function are shown in Table A.6.

TABLE A.6

RETURN VALUES OF THE **TypeName** FUNCTION.

Return Value	Meaning
Byte	Byte value
Integer	Integer value
Long	Long integer value
Single	Single-precision floating-point value
Double	Double-precision floating-point value
Currency	Currency value
Decimal	Decimal value
Date	Date or time value
String	Character string value
Boolean	Boolean value; True or False
Empty	Uninitialized
Null	No valid data
<object type>	Actual type name of an object
Object	Generic object
Unknown	Unknown object type
Nothing	Object variable that doesn't yet refer to an object instance
Error	Error

Miscellaneous Functions

- The **Round** function—This function rounds a number to a specified number of decimal places and returns the result. The syntax is:

  ```
  Round(Expression[, Numdecimalplaces])
  ```

  The **Expression** parameter is required and contains the number to be rounded. The **Numdecimalplaces** parameter is optional and contains the number of decimal places to include in the result; if you leave this out, **Round** returns an integer value.

- The **ScriptEngine** function—This function returns a string with the name of the scripting engine in use. The possible return values are VBScript, JScript (Javascript), and VBA (Visual Basic for Applications).

- The **ScriptEngineBuildVersion** function—This function returns the build version number of the scripting engine in use.

- The **ScriptEngineMajorVersion** function—This function returns the major version number of the scripting engine in use. If the version number is 5.3, this function will return the value 5.

- The **ScriptEngineMinorVersion** function—This function returns the minor version number of the scripting engine in use. If the version number is 5.3, this function will return the value 3.

VBScript 2 For Visual Basic Users

Knowing Visual Basic means you're already familiar with VBScript 2. However, there are a few important differences.

If you already know Visual Basic, you're way ahead of the game in using VBScript 2. Most of the actual language is the same; the differences are mainly in areas where VBScript had to be limited for security reasons.

Because of the great similarity between Visual Basic and VBScript, it's also easy to "port" Visual Basic applications from Windows to the Web. All you need to do is adapt the Visual Basic forms and code to use Web pages and VBScript.

In this appendix, we'll look at the major issues you have to confront in moving from Visual Basic to VBScript—whether you're moving an application, or just your expertise.

Handling Forms

In VBScript, you can't use standard Visual Basic forms to set up your application interface. However, you can easily create Web pages with ActiveX layouts that correspond very closely to Visual Basic forms. Consider The Haunted Mall, the game we developed in Chapters 14 and 15. That was originally developed in standard Visual Basic and ported to VBScript for this book. Figure B.1 shows the original Visual Basic form in which the game action took place. Figure B.2 shows its Web/VBScript equivalent.

Apart from a few minor differences in coding technique—dictated by the controls used and some limitations of VBScript—the Visual Basic form is virtually identical to the Web page with the ActiveX layout. So the basic rule is: *Replace Visual Basic forms with Web pages that use ActiveX layouts.*

Handling Data Types

As far as data types go, the principal difference between Visual Basic and VBScript is that Visual Basic has data types while VBScript, in effect, doesn't. VBScript has only the **variant** type and, although there are **variant** subtypes, the lack of distinct data types means that all Visual Basic types must be replaced by **variant**s.

This is a trifle inefficient, both in terms of memory and execution speed, but there's nothing we can do about it.

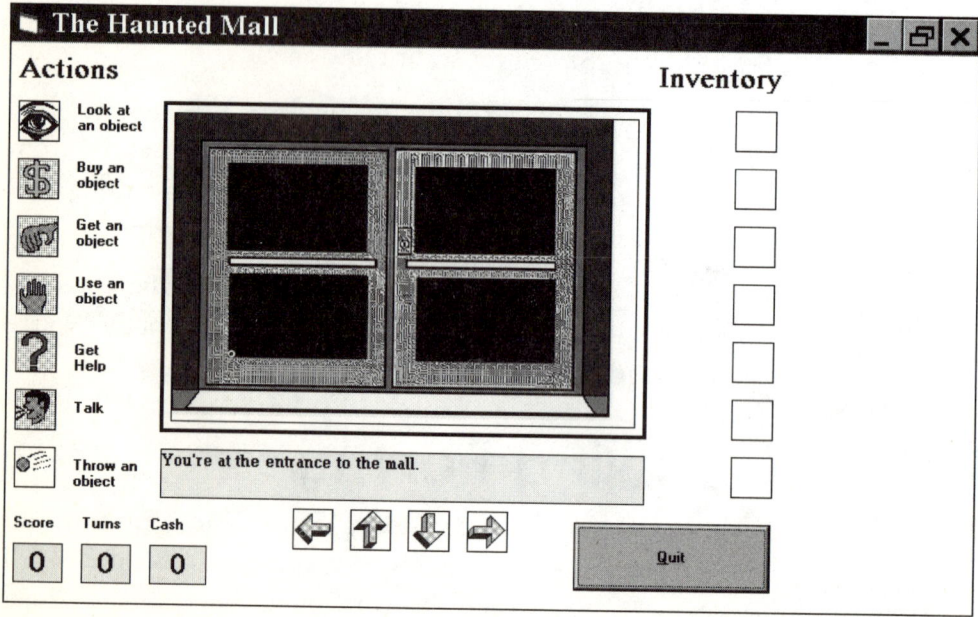

Figure B.1
The main Visual Basic form of The Haunted Mall.

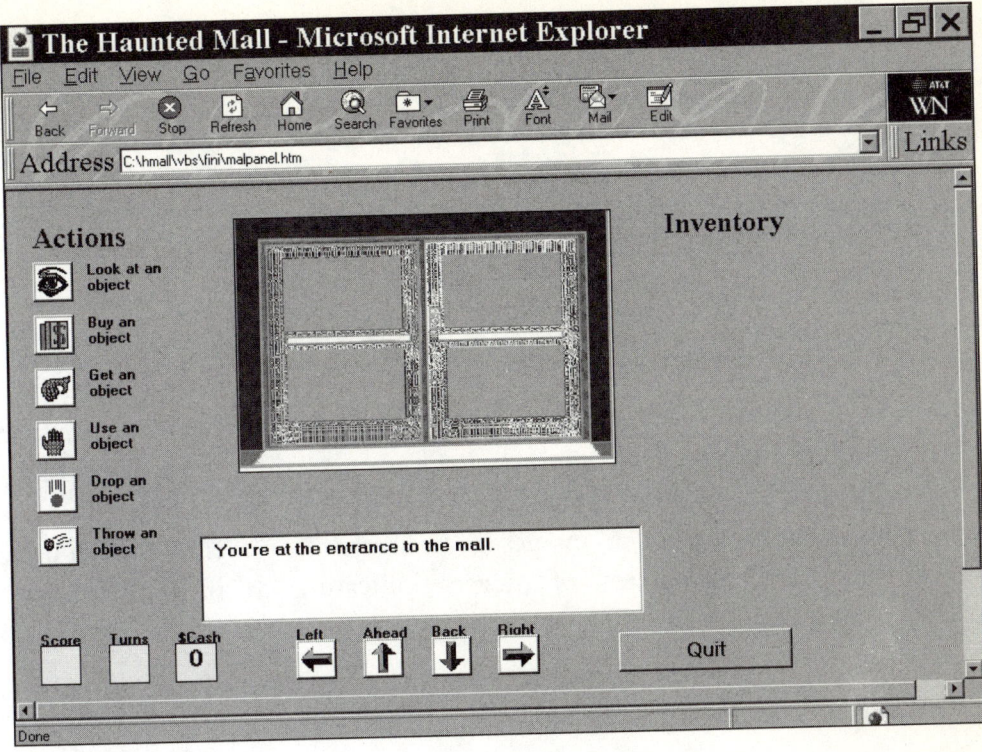

Figure B.2
The main Web page of The Haunted Mall.

Handling Record Data

The problem of handling record-type data is a little more interesting than that of changing all Visual Basic data types to **variant**s. Records enable you to combine multiple data items of different types in a single variable. In Visual Basic, you create them by using the **type...end type** construct. VBScript, however, doesn't support **type...end type**, so you can't create records at all.

The solution, as we saw in coding The Haunted Mall, is to use a multidimensional array, with each column of the array standing in for a single field of the record. If we were using distinct data types, this would impose a limitation because we couldn't combine different data types in the same array. However, this is one case in which VBScript's lack of support for multiple data types works to our advantage. All data items are **variant**s, so we can just throw everything into the array and let VBScript sort it out for us.

Let's look at how room data was handled in the Visual Basic version of The Haunted Mall; then let's compare it with how we tackled the exact same problem in the VBScript version. The Visual Basic type declaration is as follows:

```
Type room
    LDescription As String ' The long text description
    SDescription As String ' The short text description
    FScene As String ' File name for "forward" bitmap
    BScene As String ' File name for "backward" bitmap, if any
    Visited As Integer ' A T/F value
    Objects(keys to gloves) As Integer ' What objects are in room?
End Type
```

Here, we created a **room** type that included four text strings (long description of room, short description of room, forward-view image file name, and backward-view image file name), an integer (indicating if the player had previously visited the room), and an array of integers (indicating which, if any, objects were present in the room).

It's not as tidy in VBScript, but we accomplished the same tasks by using two arrays and some mnemonic constant names. The relevant code is:

```
' Definitions for rows of the mall room array
Const RoomText = 0
Const RoomFView = 1
Const RoomBView = 2
Const RoomVisited = 3

dim MallArray(26,4)

dim GameObjLoc(7)
```

Here, you can see essentially the same logic at work. Each row of the **MallArray** contains data about a particular attribute of the room: text description, forward-view image file name, backward-view image file name, and if the player has visited the room. As for which game objects were in the room, we broke that out into a separate array, **GameObjLoc**, which enabled us—at a slight cost in code clarity—to save a fair amount of memory and make the game load faster over the Web.

So the rule of thumb for handling record-type data is: *Use multidimensional arrays (even if you hate them).*

Using Separate Modules (Not) And Option Explicit

In Visual Basic, it's very common to put definitions of global variable, constant, sub, and function in a separate program module with the .bas extension. Unfortunately, you can't do that in VBScript. What you *can* do is put all your global declarations in a separate script, delimited by the HTML <script>...</script> tags, which is for all practical purposes a program module anyway.

One disadvantage of this approach is that an **option explicit** statement, which protects you from "accidental" variable declarations, only applies within the script in which it occurs. To use **option explicit** effectively, you must include the statement at the top of every pair of <script>...</script> tags.

Controls You Can Use— And Some You Can't

The controls you can use with VBScript in Web pages (whether or not they use ActiveX layouts) are largely the same as those you can use in Visual Basic forms. Exceptions are dictated by the security limitations built into VBScript and ActiveX layouts. You can use any normal user-interface controls, such as:

- Command buttons
- Timers
- Image controls
- Radio buttons
- Checkboxes
- List boxes

What you *can't* use are controls that would compromise security—either of the user's PC or of the Web server itself. Those controls include:

- The data control (see Chapter 18)
- File list box controls
- Directory list box controls

- Controls that perform dynamic data exchange with other programs on the user's PC
- Controls that access the user's hard disk

Visual Basic Features Left Out Of VBScript 2

There are quite a few language features in Visual Basic and Visual Basic for Applications (VBA) that were left out of VBScript. In general, you either don't need these for Web page scripts, or (as with **type...end type**) you can work around the limitation by using a different technique.

However, you do need to know what's left out. Table B.1 provides a list of Visual Basic and VBA features not found in VBScript.

TABLE B.1

VISUAL BASIC/VBA FEATURES LEFT OUT OF VBSCRIPT.

Category	Feature(s) Left Out
Arrays	Option base statement
Collections	All
Conditional compilation	#Const
	#If...Then...#Else
Control structures	DoEvents
	GoSub...Return
	GoTo
	On Error Goto
	On...GoSub
	On...GoTo
	Line numbers and labels
	With...End With
Type conversion (because there are no distinct types to convert)	CVar
	CVDate
	Str
	Val

(continued)

TABLE B.1

VISUAL BASIC/VBA FEATURES LEFT OUT OF VBSCRIPT (CONTINUED).

Category	Feature(s) Left Out
Data types	All intrinsic data types except variants
	Type...End Type
Date/Time	Date
	Time
	Timer
Dynamic Data Exchange	All
Debugging	Debug.Print
	End
	Stop
Declaration	Declare (for using DLLs)
	New
	Optional
	ParamArray
	Property Get
	Property Let
	Property Set
	Static
Error handling	Erl
	Error
	On Error...Resume
	On Error...Resume Next
File I/O	All
Financial functions	All
Object manipulation	TypeOf
Objects	Clipboard
	Collection
Operators	Like

(continued)

TABLE B.1

VISUAL BASIC/VBA FEATURES LEFT OUT OF VBSCRIPT (CONTINUED).

Category	Feature(s) Left Out
Options	Deftype
	Option Base
	Option Compare
	Option Private Module
Text strings	Fixed-length strings
	LSet
	RSet
	Mid
	StrConv
Using objects	Collection access

INDEX

Symbols

& (ampersand), 23, 26, 371
<= (less than or equal to), 85
<> (inequality), 85
< (less than), 85
= (equal sign), 25, 85
> (greater than), 85
/ (forward slash), 360
\ (backslash), 360
,, (two commas), 128
' (apostrophe), 8, 19

A

Access 97 (Microsoft), exporting table data from, 394-396, 398
ActiveMovie control, 269, 271
Active scripting, defined, 16
ActiveVRML control, 13
ActiveX (Microsoft), 12
   client-side data validation, 203-235
   command button, 20
   HTML control access, 276
   image controls, 254, 255, 261-264
   Marquee control, 277
   scripting object model, 224-235
   video with, 269-271
ActiveX Control Lister (ACList), 63
ActiveX Control Pad, 2, 13, 63, 64, 156, 237-238
   client-side data validation, 204-214
   database publishing, 392
   features, 157-158
   font property, 150
   free download, 156
   HTML layout with, 158-166
   layout, inserting in HTML document, 169-170
   option button, 251
   order entry form, 204-214
   properties window, 163-166
   tips and techniques, 170-175
   toolbox, 159-161, 170-173
ActiveX controls, 2, 12-13, 237
   activating, 277
   changing size or position, 161-163
   checkbox control, 153, 154
   combo box control, 242-246
   command button control, 151, 152
   defined, 26-27
   label controls, 29, 30, 150-151, 163, 164
   list box control, 238-242
   object tags for, 63
   option button control, 151, 153, 246-252
   properties, 149-150, 168-169, 263
   scrollbar control, 256-259
   sound, 271-273
   spin button control, 153-154, 155
   text box control, 150, 152, 163
   timer control, 29-30
   toggle button control, 252-256
   use with VBScript, 147-156
   VBScript subs used with, 26-31
ActiveX layout, Visual Basic and, 414
AddItem method, 241, 242, 246
Addition operator, 58, 60-62
Adventure (game), 293
ALX file, 167
Ampersand (&), 23, 26, 371
anchor object, 179, 180

Anchor tags, 179
And, logical operator, 75
Apostrophe ('), 8, 19
Arguments, 58
Arithmetic operators, 58, 59-60
    addition, 58, 60-62
    concatenation, 60
    division, 58, 60, 66-69
    exponentiation, 60
    integer division, 60, 66, 68, 69
    modulus, 60, 70-74
    multiplication, 60, 65
    negation, 58, 60
    subtraction, 60, 65
array function, VBScript 2, 401
Arrays
    coding, 54-56
    defined, 49
    demonstration of, 52-54
    looping statements, 88, 89
    multidimensional, 317, 415, 416
    using, 149-156
    Visual Basic features omitted from, 418
Array slots, 49
    assigning values, 51
    changing values, 51
    numbering, 50-51, 101
Arrow, changing the mouse
    pointer back to, 161
Assignment operator, 25, 51
autosize property, 262
AVI files, 267

B

backcolor property, 165
background attribute, 264, 265, 267
Backstory, games, 282
<bgsound> tag, 271-273, 352
Binary operator, 58
BMP file, 263
<body> tag, 187, 264, 265, 267
Bogovich's corollary, 16
Boolean value, defined, 45
Boolean variable, 371
borderstyle property, 165, 263
Branching statements, 88-101
break statement, 113
Button control, 30

Buttons
    in a Message Box, 122-130
    Web games, 302-304, 309-314, 318
Buzzword, 16
Byte, defined, 45

C

caption property, 34, 150, 163, 164, 166
case else clause, 112
Case sensitivity, 25, 48
"Case" statement, 108
cgi32.bas module, 363, 364, 370
CGI_Main() procedure, 365, 368, 379
CGI programs, 11, 195
    client-side data validation with,
        195, 198, 199, 203
    program basics, 363
    server-side data validation,
        194-195, 372-378
    testing, 357-358
    URL, CGI program, 356, 359, 360
    Visual Basic CGI program,
        357, 363-370
    Web browser communication, 354-355
    Web server communication,
        354, 355-357
    Website software, 357-358
cgitest32.exe program, 194, 196, 203, 224,
    225, 234, 359-361
Change event, 259
Chart control, 12
Checkbox, HTML form, 369
Checkbox control, 153, 154, 198, 213, 235
chr function, 144
Class parameter, 410
Click event sub, 20, 122, 140
ClickNum variable, 31-34
Client-side data validation, 192, 193-195
    with an ActiveX layout, 203-235
    HTML, 225-226, 234
    with VBScript and HTML, 195-203
    Web page, 192, 193-235
Close method, 410
codebase line, 29
Coding
    data checking, 200-203
    The Haunted Mall (game), 320-352,
        413-414, 416

HTML form, 195-203, 222, 233-235, 361-363, 373, 381-382
Trivia, Forsooth (game), 91-102, 108, 113-120, 279
Collections, Visual Basic features omitted from, 420
Combo box, 242, 246
Combo box control, 242-246
Command button, 20, 122, 300
Command button control, 151, 152
Commas, two commas, 128
Comment delimiters, 18
Comments
 single-line, 18, 25
 in VBScript, 19
Comment tags, VBScript code inside of, 7-8, 11
Commerce. *See* Shopping.
Common Gateway Interface. *See* CGI programs.
Compare parameter, 407, 408
Comparison operators, 85
Concatenation operator, 60
Conditional compilation, Visual Basic features omitted from VBScript, 418
Conjunction, 75, 79-83
Conjunctive expression, 79, 80
Constants
 declaring, 47
 game framework program, 306
 scope, 48, 49
 Web game, 314-317
const keyword, VBScript 2, 400
Control structures, 87-120, 417
 branching statements, 88-101
 examples, 89-102
 if statements, 88, 89-91
 looping statements, 88, 89, 102-108
 select case statements, 88, 108-120
 types, 88-89
 VBScript, 417-418
 VBScript 2, 401, 417-418
 Visual Basic, 417-418
 Visual Basic features omitted from VBScript, 418
Cookies
 defined, 383
 described, 384-387
 HTML code, 387
 URLs for discussions, 390

Cooper's law, 16
Count parameter, 408, 409
CreateObject function, VBScript 2, 409-410
CreateTextFile function, VBScript 2, 410
Crescent Software, 156
Critical Message icon, 128

D

Data, 36-45, 74
 arrays, 49-56
 record data, 415-416
 subtypes, 45
 types, 37-44
 variant data, 10, 37-40, 411, 414-416
 VBScript, 415-416
 Visual Basic, 414, 415
 Visual Basic features omitted, 419
Databases, Web publishing, 391-398
Data-checking function, 200-203
DataOkay function, 199, 202
Data Validation. *See* Client-side data validation; Server-side data validation.
Date
 defined, 45
 Visual Basic features omitted, 419
DateAdd function, VBScript 2, 401-402
DateDiff function, VBScript 2, 402-403
DatePart function, VBScript 2, 403
Debugging, Visual Basic features omitted, 419
Decision making, control structures, 87
Delimiter parameter, 409
Dictionary object, VBScript 2, 410
dim statement, 10, 24-25, 36, 40, 46, 50-51
Disjunction, defined, 75
Disjunction expression, 75, 79
Division operator, 58, 60, 66-69
document.close, 192
document object, 179, 180, 187-192
document.writeln method, 188-192
do...loop statement, 89, 107-108
Downloading time, images, 263-264
dynsrc property, 268

E

element object, 179, 180
Empty value, defined, 45
enabled property, 150

end function, 140
endif, 30-31
Equality operator (=), 85
Equal sign (=), 25, 85
Equivalence operator, 75, 84
Error handling, Visual Basic features omitted, 419
Exclusive "or," 75, 84
Explicit variable declaration, 46, 54
Exponentiation operator, 60
Expression parameter, 408, 409, 412
Expressions, 58, 59

F

FieldPresent() function, 370
File formats, images, 263
File I/O operations, VBScript, 276, 419
fileopen value, 269
FileSystemObject object, VBScript 2, 410
Filter function, VBScript 2, 406-407
font property, 150
for each...next statement, 89, 401
for loop, 88, 89, 102-107
FormatCurrency function, VBScript 2, 403, 404-405
FormatDateTime function, VBScript 2, 403, 405-406
FormatNumber function, VBScript 2, 403, 406, 407
form object, 179, 180, 192
Forms
   CGI programs, 192, 195-203
   checkboxes, 369
   HTML, 355, 356
   Visual Basic and, 3-5, 413-414
form.submit method, 199, 222-224, 234
<**form**> tag, 7, 179, 197
for...next statement, 51, 88, 401
Forward slash (/), 360
frame object, 179, 180
Frameset document, 396-398
<**frameset**> tag, 397
Framework program, Web game, 304-320
FrontPage (Microsoft), 12
fullname variable, 44
Functions, 121-122
   adding, 31-34
   array, 401
   CreateObject, 409-410
   CreateTextFile, 410
   creating, 136-141
   data-checking, 200-203
   DataOkay, 199, 202
   DateAdd, 401-402
   DateDiff, 402-403
   DatePark, 403
   defined, 31, 121
   End, 140
   FieldPresent(), 370
   Filter, 406-407
   FormatCurrency, 403, 404-405
   FormatDateTime, 403, 405-406
   FormatNumber, 403, 406, 407
   GetSmallField(), 369
   Hour, 277
   InputBox, 135-136, 241
   InStr, 145, 408
   InStrRev, 408
   IsMoreThan9, 33, 34
   Join, 408, 409
   LoadPicture, 277-278, 409
   Mid, 145-146
   MsgBox, 22, 122-130, 136
   OrderInfoPresent(), 373, 379
   Replace, 408
   Round, 402
   ScriptEngine, 412
   ScriptEngineBuildVersion, 412
   ScriptEngineMajorVersion, 412
   ScriptEngineMinorVersion, 412
   Split, 409
   sqr(), 122
   StrRev, 409
   TypeName, 411
   Weekday, 403

G

Game map, 280, 281
Games, 279
   Adventure, 293
   backstory, 282
   coding, 91-102, 108, 113-120, 299-352
   designing, 279, 297
   game map, 280, 281
   The Haunted Mall, 279-352
   storyboard, 280-297
   Trivia, Forsooth, 91-103, 108, 113-120, 279
   Web pages needed, 91, 297, 300
GetSmallField() function, 369

Index 425

Global variable, 54, 417
Greater than or equal to operator (>=), 85
Greater than operator (>), 85
GroupDigits parameter, 405, 407

H

The Haunted Mall (game), 279, 415
   backstory, 282
   beginning, 281-286
   coding, 320-352, 413-414, 416
   Crowther's Castle, 293, 295-297
   declaring variables and constants, 314-317
   designing, 279, 297
   end sequence page, 304
   framework code, 304-320
   game map, 280, 281
   introductory page, 300-302
   main game page, 302-303, 415
   music, 352
   performing game actions, 346-350
   storyboard, 280-297
   traps, 287-292, 350-352
   Visual Basic form, 413-414
   walkthrough, 280-297
   Web pages needed, 297, 300
   winning, 293-297
Hello program, 5-7, 15-18, 22-26
HiddenForm control, 235
history object, 179, 180
HotDog (Sausage Software), 12
hour() function, 277
<hr> tag, 198
HTML, 264
   books about, 11
   client-side data validation, 195-203, 225-226, 234
   comment tags, 7-8, 11, 18
   form information, 192, 195-203
   frameset document, 396-398
   intrinsic controls, 13
   for .MIDI, 272-273
   sound and, 271-273
   VBScript, use with, 3-12, 17
   video with, 267-269
   Web page set up, 133-134, 139-140, 143-144
HTML controls, from within ActiveX, 276

HTML document
   CGI script and, 195-196, 355, 356, 357-359, 361-363
   order form, 197-200, 204, 222, 233-235, 361-363, 373, 381-382
HTML form
   CGI script, 192, 195-203, 355, 356
   checkboxes, 369
   HTML layout, 63-64
   with ActiveX Control Pad, 158-166
   database publishing, 392-398
   order form, 212
   with Script Wizard, 167-169
HTML Layout control, 169
HTTP (Hypertext Transfer Protocol), defined, 355, 359

I

Identifiers, declaring, VBScript 2, 400
id line, 29
ID property, 149, 263
IeTimer control, 301-302
if clause, 33-34
if...elseif statement, 88
if...else statement, 56, 88, 91
if statements, 88
   examples, 89-102
   multiple-line, 89-90
   single-line, 89
if...then...else statement, 202, 418
if...then statement, 87
Image control
   ActiveX, 254, 255, 261-264
   game page, 300
   other than Microsoft, 264
Images
   downloading time, 263-264
   file formats, 263
   in HTML, 264-267
   loading speed, 275-276
<img> tag, 265, 267
   video with, 267-269
Implication operator, 58, 59, 75, 84
Implicit variable declarations, 46, 47
IncludeLeadingDigit parameter, 404, 407
Include parameter, 407
Inequality operator (<>), 85
InputBox() function, 135-136, 241
<input> control, 234
InputStrings parameter, 407

<input> tag, 20, 24, 183, 192
InStr function, 145, 408
InStrRev function, VBScript 2, 408
Integer, defined, 45
Integer division, 60, 66, 68-70
Inter_Main() procedure, 365, 368
Internet Explorer (Microsoft), 2, 11
    cookies, 384-387
    database publishing, 397
    object hierarchy, 178-181
    scripting object model, 177-192, 224
Intrinsic controls, 12
IsMoreThan9() function, 33, 34

J

JavaScript, use with VBScript, 276
Join function, VBScript 2, 408, 409
JPEG file, 263

L

Label control, 12, 29, 30, 150-151, 163, 164
LargeChange property, 259
Less than or equal to operator (<=), 85
Less than operator(<), 85
Link object, 179, 180
List box, 242, 246
List box control, 238-242
List parameter, 408
LoadPicture function, 277-278, 409
Location object, 179, 180
Logical conjunction, 75, 79-83
Logical disjunction, 75-79
Logical equivalence, 75, 84
Logical exclusion, 75, 84
Logical implication, 75, 84
Logical negation, 74, 75
Logical operators, 58, 74-84
Long integer, defined, 45
loopcounter variable, 55
Looping statements, 102
    do loops, 88, 107-108
    for loops, 88, 89, 102-107
loop property, 272

M

<marquee> tag, 277
Max property, 259

Message box, 10, 20-22
    inserting a line break in text, 144
    using variables with, 26
    values displaying buttons or icons, 128-130
Mid function, 145-146
MIDI file, HTML code to play, 272-273
Min property, 259
mod operator, 60, 70
Modulus operator, 70-74
Monadic operator, 58
mouseover value, 269
moviewindowsize property, 271
MsgBox function, 22, 122-130, 136
MsgBox statement, 10, 20-22, 26, 44, 56, 122-128, 141
Multidimensional arrays, 317, 415, 416
Multiline comments, 18
Multimedia games. *See* Games.
Multiplication operator, 60, 65
Music, 271-273, 352

N

Navigator object, 179, 180
Negation operator, 58, 74
New item control, 12
Not, logical operator, 75
Null value, defined, 45
Numdecimalplaces parameter, 412
NumDigitsAfterDecimal parameter, 404, 407

O

Object equivalence operator, 85
Objects, 147, 178, 184-185
    anchor, 179, 180
    attaching scripts to, 180-183
    defined, 45
    dictionary, 410
    document, 179, 180, 187-192
    element, 179, 180
    FileSystemObject, 410
    form, 179, 180, 192
    frame, 179, 180
    hierarchies, 178, 184
    hierarchy, 178-181
    history, 179, 180
    link, 179, 180

location, 179, 180
navigator, 179, 180
  referring to, 184
script, 179, 180
TextStream, 410
  Visual Basic features omitted from
    VBScript, 419, 420
window, 179, 180, 184, 185-187, 277
<object> tag, 13, 29, 63-64, 158, 192, 212
Ockham's Razor, 263-264
OCX controls, 12, 27, 154-156, 170
OnClick event, 20, 40, 41, 43, 54
One-line comment, 18, 25
OnLoad event, 185-187, 241, 277
OnUnload event, 185-187
Operators
  arithmetic operators, 58, 59-74
  comparison operators, 85
  logical operators, 58, 74-84
  relational operators, 58, 85
  Visual Basic features omitted from
    VBScript, 419
Option button, 246-247, 251
Option button control, 151, 153, 246-252
option explicit statement, 46-47, 54, 417
Options, Visual Basic features omitted from
  VBScript, 420
OrderComplete variable, 214, 234
Order form, 361-382
  ActiveX layout, 204-214
  CGI script, 355, 356, 357-359, 361-363
  HTML code, 195-196, 197-200, 204,
    222, 233-235
  sending data from to server, 214-233
  shopping cart system, 383-390
OrderInfoPresent() function, 373, 379
Or operator, 75

P

Parentheses, in VBScript, 135
picturepath property, 256, 263, 264, 278
post method, 355, 356, 359
Preloader control, 13
<pre> tag, 192, 195, 199
private keyword, VBScript 2, 400
ProcessOrder() procedure, 365, 370, 379
Properties, 178
  ActiveX controls, 149-150, 168-169
  image control, 262-263

Protocol, 355
public keyword, VBScript 2, 400

R

Radio buttons, 247, 276
Real-number division, 58
Record-type data, 415-416
RedisplayOrderForm() procedure,
  373, 380-382
Regular division, 66-69
Relational operators, 58, 85
rem, 8, 19
Replace function, VBScript 2, 408
Replacewith parameter, 408
Round function, VBScript 2, 412

S

Scope, of variables and constants, 48-49
<script>, 6, 7
ScriptEngine function, VBScript 2, 412
ScriptEngineBuildVersion function,
  VBScript 2, 412
ScriptEngineMajorVersion function,
  VBScript 2, 412
ScriptEngineMinorVersion function,
  VBScript 2, 412
Scripting object model, 177-192
  object hierarchy, 178-181
<script language=> tag, 276
Script object, 179, 180
<script> tag, 18, 46, 180, 276, 400, 417
Script Wizard, 167-169, 173-175
Scrollbar, 256, 259
Scrollbar control, 256-259
select case statement, 88, 108-120,
  128, 341
Send() procedure, 370
Server-side data validation, 194-195,
  372-378
SetVariable sub, cookies, 389-390
Shopping
  cookies, 383-390
  order form, 197-200, 204, 222,
    233-235, 361-363, 373, 381-382
  shopping cart system, 383-385
Single-line comments, 18, 25
SlotNum variable, 56
SmallChange property, 259

Sound
    ActiveX controls, 271-273
    music, 271-273, 352
    Web page greeting, 277
Spin button control, 153-154, 155
Split function, VBScript 2, 409
sqr() function, 122
src attribute, 265, 272
Start parameter, 408
start property, 268-269
Statement, defined, 20
step option, 103
String, defined, 45
String1 parameter, 408
String2 parameter, 408
String-parsing code, 145
StrReverse function, VBScript 2, 409
Sub procedures, 31
    calling, 130-135
    declaring, 130, 131, 134, 135
    defined, 121
    MsgBox statement, 122
    VBScript, 19-20
    Web games, 318-346
Subroutine, described, 19-20
Subtraction operator, 60, 65

T

tabindex property, 150
Tautology, 74
Text box, adding, 23-24
Text box control, 150, 152, 163, 300
TextStream object, VBScript 2, 410
Text strings, Visual Basic features omitted from VBScript, 420
Time, Visual Basic features omitted, 419
TimeCount variable, 302, 351-352
Time-of-day greeting, 277
Timer control, 13, 29-30
    game page, 283, 300, 301-302, 303, 350
Toggle button control, 252-256
Toolbox, controls, 159, 170-173
Trivia, Forsooth (game), 91-102, 108, 113-120, 279
Truth table, 74, 75, 79, 80, 84
    eqv operator, 75, 84
    imp operator, 58, 59, 75, 84
    xor operator, 75, 84

Truth-values, 59
Type conversion, Visual Basic features omitted from, 418
type...end type construct, 52, 415, 418, 419
TypeName function, VBScript 2, 411

U

<ul> tag, 198, 371
until clause, 107
URL, CGI program, 356, 359, 360
UseParensForNegativeNumbers parameter, 405, 407

V

Value parameter, 407
value property, 150
    option button, 251-252
    toggle button control, 256
Values
    defined, 24
    message box buttons and, 128-130
Variable parameter, 411
Variables
    arrays, 49-56
    assigning values to, 25-26, 40-43
    declaring, 2, 24-25, 36, 37, 40, 45-46, 314-317
    games, 307-309, 314-317
    global, 54, 417
    implicit, 46, 47
    multiple, 40
    naming, 25, 48
    scope, 48-49
    using with message box, 26
    Web game, 314-317
Variant data type, 10, 37-40, 414-416
vbBinaryCompare parameter, 407-409
vbGeneralDate format, 405
vbLongDate format, 405
vbLongTime format, 405
VBScript, 399
    ActiveX controls with, 2, 12-13, 26-31, 64-65, 147-156
    case sensitivity, 25, 48
    control structures, 417-418
    database publishing, 392-398
    described, 2
    forms, 413-414

game code, 91-120, 299-352
HTML, use with, 3-12, 17
image control, 254-255, 264
JavaScript used with, 276
line continuation characters, 55
VBScript 2, 128, 263, 275
   array handling, 401
   control structures, 401, 417-418
   data, 411, 414
   dates, 401-403
   declaring identifiers, 400
   forms, 413-414
   general string handling, 406-409
   LoadPicture function, 277-278
   message box, 128-129
   more new functions, 412
   object handling, 409-411
   option explicit, 417
   record data, 415-416
   string formatting, 403-406
   system I/O handling, 409
   times, 401, 403
   Visual Basic and, 413-420
   Visual Basic features omitted from, 418-420
vbShortDate format, 405
vbShortTime format, 405
vbTextCompare parameter, 407-409
VBX controls, 27
Video, with ActiveX, 269-271
Visual Basic, 2, 275, 353-354
   arrays, 50
   books about, 3
   CGI program in, 357, 363-370
   database publishing, 392, 393
   dim statement, 10
   endif, 30-31
   forms, 3-5, 413-414
   line continuation character, 372
   type...end type construct, 52
   variable, 24
   variant data type, 37
   VBScript 2 for, 413-420
Visual Basic 3, 363
Visual Basic 4, 363
Visual Basic 5, writing CGI program, 363-370

W

Wallpaper, 264-266
WAV file
   HTML code to play, 271, 272
   playing, 277
Web browser
   CGI program and, 354-358
   HTML layout control, 158
Web games. *See* Games.
Web pages. *See also* HTML.
   authoring tools, 12
   client-side data validation, 192, 193-235
   cookies, 384-390
   event subs, 187
   HTML code to set up, 133-134, 139-140, 143-144
   HTML layout with ActiveX Control Pad, 158-166
   images, 261-267
   loading speed, 275-276
   playing greeting, 277
   Script Wizard to add code, 167-169, 173-175
   sound, 271-273
   VBScript and, 2
   video, 267-271
   wallpaper, 264-266
Web publishing, databases, 391-398
Web server, CGI program and, 354, 355-357
WebSite (O'Reilly & Associates), 357, 363
Web sites
   cookies, 390
   Microsoft, 11, 63, 156
Weekday function, VBScript 2, 403
while clause, 107
while...wend statement, 89
William of Ockham, 264
window.document, 276
window object, 179, 180, 184, 185-187, 277
writeln method, 188-192
WriteLine method, 410
write method, 189, 192

X

xor, logical operator, 74, 84

JAVA • VB • VC++ • DELPHI • SOFTWARE COMPONENTS • OCX, DLL

Give Yourself the Visual Edge

Don't Lose Your Competitve Edge Act Now!

1 Year $21.95
(6 issues)

2 Years $37.95
(12 issues)

($53.95 Canada; $73.95 Elsewhere)
Please allow 4-6 weeks for delivery
All disk orders must be pre-paid

The first magazine dedicated to the Visual Revolution

Join Jeff Duntemann and his crew of master authors for a tour of the visual software development universe. Peter Aitken, Al Williams, Ray Konopka, David Gerrold, Michael Covington, Tom Campbell, and all your favorites share their insights into rapid application design and programming, software component development, and content creation for the desktop, client/server, and online worlds. The whole visual world will be yours, six times per year: Windows 95 and NT, Multimedia, VRML, Java, HTML, Delphi, VC++, VB, and more. *Seeing is succeeding!*

1-800-410-0192

See *Visual Developer* on the Web! http://www.coriolis.com

14455 N. Hayden Rd. Suite 220 • Scottsdale, Arizona 85260

WEB • CGI • JAVA • VB • VC++ • DELPHI • SOFTWARE COMPONENTS